Banned in Kansas

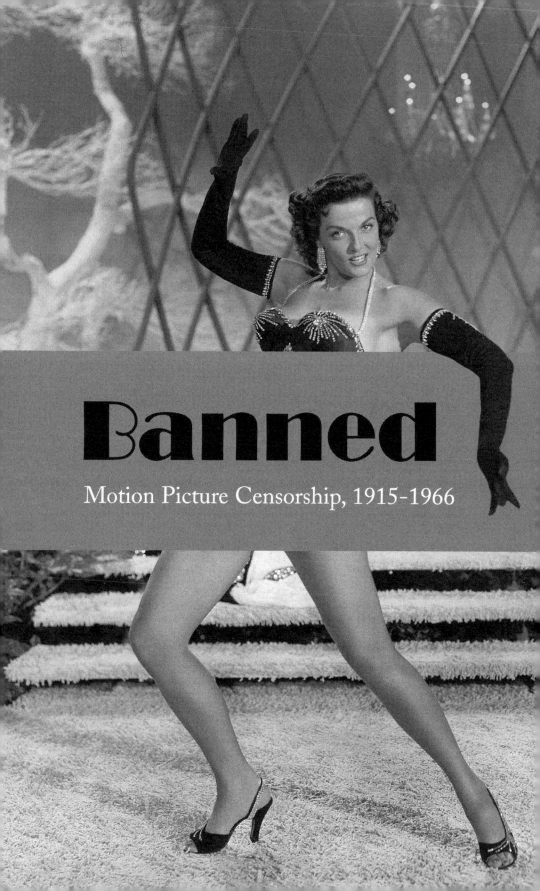

Banned

Motion Picture Censorship, 1915-1966

in Kansas

Gerald R. Butters, Jr.

Library of Congress Cataloging-in-Publication Data

Butters, Gerald R., 1961–
    Banned in Kansas : motion picture censorship, 1915–1966 / Gerald R.
Butters, Jr.
        p. cm.
    Summary: "This first book-length study of state film censorship examines
the unique political, social, and economic factors that led to its
implementation in Kansas, taking a look at why censorship legislation was
enacted, what the attitudes of Kansans were toward censorship, and why it
lasted for half a century"—Provided by publisher.
    Includes bibliographical references and index.
    ISBN: 978-0-8262-2110-0 (alk. paper)
    1. Motion pictures—Censorship—Kansas—History.   I. Title.
PN1995.63.K36B87   2007
363.3109781—dc22   2007009401

Designer: Kristie Lee
Typefaces: Adobe Caslon and Broadway Display
Cover photos courtesy of Photofest

For my mother

The Kansas spirit is the American spirit double distilled. It is a new grafted product of American individualism, American idealism, American intolerance. Kansas is America in microcosm.

—Carl Becker, "Kansas," in *Everyman His Own Historian: Essays on History and Politics*

Contents

Preface

When motion pictures were first introduced as a novelty to the American public, few realized the impact the medium would have on the culture and the social consciousness of the period. Motion pictures, first seen by social critics as a simple diversion for the working class, soon emerged as an important cultural and economic force in American society. Almost from the inception of film, the issue of control over the exhibition and content of this new entertainment medium became important politically and socially. As an increasingly large number of Americans flocked to see these new "photoplays," a powerful and forceful contingent of Americans attempted to control what the public saw.

This book is an examination of motion picture censorship in the state of Kansas. One of only a handful of states to establish a film censorship board in the United States, the Kansas State Board of Review of Motion Pictures was established in 1915 and functioned until 1966. Despite more than five decades of control over screen content, little is known about film censorship by either Kansans or those involved in film studies.

The implementation of motion picture censorship in Kansas was part of a larger nationwide scheme to enact film censorship in the early part of the twentieth century. In this study, the attempt to control screen content in Kansas will be placed in this nationwide context. Kansas, one of only seven states that ever enacted film censorship legislation, had a censorship apparatus that functioned longer than any other state's. This fact leads to a number of questions regarding the exceptionalism of Kansas: Why was censorship legislation enacted in this state? What unique political, cultural, or economic reasons might have caused Kansans to approve such a censorship program? Were most Kansans in favor of such censorship, or were there definite populations that supported or were opposed to such censorship? Why did censorship last in the state for more than a half century?

A series of contributing factors led to the implementation of motion picture censorship in the state. This nexus of factors included the reform movement of Progressivism, the support of the Kansas press and powerful state newspapermen, an unconscious fight against modernity, the dedication of Kansas citizens to the proper raising and education of children, an unequivocal concern over the maintenance of morality, and the prohibition of alcohol in the state.

Once the censorship apparatus was in place, state control over screen content became a divisive issue. Supporters of film censorship included progressive reformers, the educational establishment, and Governor Arthur Capper. Critics of censorship included motion picture fans and the state and national film industries. A contentious battle raged between these two forces from 1915 to 1917, until the Kansas legislature reworked the initial censorship bill, creating a process that was more amicable to industry members.

What is surprising about the Kansas State Board of Review is not that it was created but that it lasted as long as it did. During its lengthy existence (1915–1966), the board faced changing standards of public morality and decency, film industry self-censorship (and its decline), exploitation films designed to capitalize on shock value, and a judicial system that became increasingly hostile due to the court's expanding interpretation of the First Amendment. Like a Weberian bureaucracy, the Kansas State Board of Review appeared to survive changing economic, moral, political, and artistic climates. As early as the 1920s, the board had become part of the state's political patronage system, with jobs given for party loyalty and not necessarily for distinct qualifications. In the 1950s, once the board's critics began complaining that it was an anachronism of the past, it proved difficult to destroy. Despite judicial limitation of the board's powers, political attempts to shut it down, and complaints from the press, the board survived. The issue that supplied the fatal blow to the board in the mid-1960s was its inability to clearly define words such as *immoral, indecent,* or *obscene.*

An examination of classic and current literature related to movie censorship demonstrates that most film historians have ignored state censorship and have particularly neglected Kansas's effort to control screen content. Two classic sources—*Film Censors and the Law* by Neville March Hunnings and *Movies, Censorship, and the Law* by Ira Carmen—give brief, sketchy overviews of movie censorship in Kansas; neither is based on primary source material. *Banned Films: Movies, Censors, and the First Amendment* by Edward De Grazia and Robert K. Newman examines seven films banned in Kansas. The authors place primary emphasis on the films but have little to say about the internal workings of the censorship board itself. Film studies texts such as Garth Jowett's *Film: The Democratic Art* mention the establishment of a censorship

board in Kansas but provide readers with no further information on censorship in the state. Gerald Mast's *Short History of the Movies* gives an overview of
movie censorship but does not include Kansas in the discussion. Robert Sklar's
Movie-Made America includes a thorough account of film censorship but also
fails to include Kansas. Thus, while Kansas was one of the first states to enact
and enforce motion picture censorship, current film literature has little to say
about the role Kansas played in the history of film censorship in the United
States. The bulk of literature on motion picture censorship tends to deal with
industry self-censorship through the Production Code Administration or voluntary censorship by organizations such as the National Board of Review.
Film censorship on the local and state levels was an all too real economic concern for producers, distributors, and theater owners for more than fifty years,
but it has been a subject largely ignored by film historians. This book will
begin the process of helping us understand the complexities of societal control
over the motion picture screen.[1]

This book has been constructed using original primary source materials,
specifically, the records of the Kansas State Board of Review of Motion Pictures that are housed in the Kansas State Historical Society, Department of
Archives, in Topeka.[2] These records, utilized by few film historians, provide
an invaluable and detailed insight into the minds and attitudes of the censors.
They also aptly demonstrate the powerful forces of opposition to film censorship and the problems that the Board of Review faced in its day-to-day
operation. In addition to the records of the Kansas Board of Review, the
Kansas State Historical Society also houses the personal correspondence files
of Kansas governors. These files contain vital correspondence and shed light
on the attitudes of key Kansas politicians and the public toward movies and
censorship. The clipping files of the Kansas State Historical Society Archives
also contain important information on Kansas motion picture censorship and
help to create a chronological record of the board. Additional resources such

1. See Neville March Hunnings, *Film Censors and the Law;* Ira Carmen, *Movies, Censorship, and
the Law;* Edward de Grazia and Robert K. Newman, *Banned Films: Movies, Censorship, and the First
Amendment;* Garth Jowett, *Film: The Democratic Art;* Gerald Mast, *A Short History of the Movies;* and
Robert Sklar, *Movie-Made America.*
2. It is necessary to discuss the actual name of this censorship board. From 1915 to 1917, the title
of the board was very "loosely" applied. Most governmental documents and press reports referred to
it as the Kansas Board of Motion Picture Censorship or Censors; both names are used herein. After
new state legislation in 1917, the board was renamed the Kansas State Board of Review (hereafter
cited as KSBR). This mimicked the National Board of Censorship renaming itself the National
Board of Review (thus, in Kansas, de-emphasizing the actual act of censorship).

as *Variety,* the *Film Index,* the *Moving Picture World, Motion Picture News,* and other periodicals provide an important framework for the national scope on film censorship.

On a personal note, this project has been a detective story that has lasted for more than twenty years. My master's thesis, completed at the University of Missouri at Kansas City in 1988, concerned the Kansas Board of Review and Motion Picture Censorship from 1913 to 1924. Over the intervening period, as I completed my doctorate, wrote a dissertation and book on a completely different subject, and obtained my present professorial and administrative position, I could not forget these "ghost" censors who impacted the lives of generations of Kansans. They literally controlled what millions of Kansas movie fans could watch on film screens that ranged from rural nickelodeons to big-city picture palaces. These low-level Kansas bureaucrats had enormous influence over the popular culture of Kansas for more than fifty years. But this story, and their influence, has been largely forgotten. It has been my goal, through years of painstaking research, to attempt to reconstruct this story.

Acknowledgments

For a book that has been in the works for some twenty years, there are many people to thank. The genesis of the book was my course work under Greg Black at the University of Missouri at Kansas City. Greg demonstrated to me that you could make a career out of what you loved, in this case film history. He was tough and demanding with my writing, and that made all the difference.

William Tuttle, the director of my doctoral program at the University of Kansas, continued to encourage me to work in the field. Greg and Bill have been the finest of mentors.

I have an enormously supportive administration at Aurora University. Rebecca Sherrick, president; Andrew Manion, provost; and Lora de Lacey, dean of the College of Arts and Sciences, have been supportive of my research both financially and collegially. I also work with a wonderful faculty. Special thanks goes to Barabara Strassberg, Susan Palmer, Jim Galezewski, Dan Hipp, Donovan Gwinner, and my running buddies, Denise Hatcher and John Lloyd.

This book would have never come to fruition without the help of three individuals. My former editor Nancy Scott-Jackson first encouraged me to complete this manuscript. A chance meeting with editor Gary Kass led me to the University of Missouri Press. Gary's love for film and his professionalism and genuine friendliness made me confident that he was who I wanted to work with. Finally, Kansas historian and editor Virgil Dean literally molded this manuscript into what it is. Virgil always seemed to pop into the research room at the Kansas State Historical Society just as I was becoming discouraged. He has been a true friend in the way that he was exacting with my research and writing.

The unsung heroes of any manuscript are those librarians and research assistants at archives all across this country. I want to thank the library staff at the Margaret Herrick Library at the Academy of Motion Picture Arts and Sciences in Beverly Hills and the Motion Picture Division at the Library of Congress in Washington, D.C. A special thanks goes to the library staff and assistants at the Research Facility at the Kansas State Historical Society. For five years, this wonderful team answered many questions, literally lifted hundreds of boxes of primary source material over the counter so I could analyze them once again, and generally made me feel at home. The citizens of Kansas should feel lucky to have such a positive, warm staff to help those interested in Kansas history.

I feel very fortunate to have a wonderful group of friends who have encouraged my research and writing. A classmate at the University of Kansas, Rusty Monhollon, read the first draft of this manuscript and made some much needed suggestions. I also want to thank my partners-in-crime Lee James, Jim Kinzer, Aaron McKerry, James Kessler, Michael Meyer, Jeff Lodermeier, Joel Morton, Anson Christian, Canan Cullins, Charles Wilson, Enrique Nieto, Michael Kaufman, Aly Kassam-Remtulla, and Randy Jones.

Finally, I must thank Jarrett Neal. Without your love and support this book would not have been possible. You listened to the stories in this manuscript many times without protest. For that I am blessed.

Part of this manuscript has been previously published. "*The Birth of a Nation* and the Kansas Board of Review of Motion Pictures: A Censorship Struggle" was first published in *Kansas History: A Journal of the Central Plains* 14, no. 1 (Spring 1991): 2–14. I would like to thank editor Virgil Dean for permission to reproduce this material.

Banned in Kansas

One

Progressivism and the New Medium of Film

Motion pictures were an enormously influential medium of entertainment in the early twentieth century. In order to comprehend the national drive toward film censorship in this period, one must understand the nature of the early film industry. This chapter will examine the growth of the motion picture industry and the reaction of Americans, and specifically Kansans, to this new form of entertainment. The explosive popularity of motion pictures will be examined against the backdrop of Progressivism, the powerful and multifaceted social movement of the early twentieth century. Finally, the relationship between Progressives and motion picture censorship will be examined.

The first public exhibition of a projected motion picture before a paying audience in the United States took place at Koster and Bials Music Hall in New York City.[1] This "amazing Vitascope" (an early motion picture device) was one act of a vaudeville show. In 1896, the first motion pictures shown in Kansas toured the state under the management of C. H. Matthews. Matthews built his own moving picture projectors in order to avoid the expense of leasing a machine from Thomas Edison's company, which attempted to monopolize the

1. Joseph H. North, *The Early Development of the Motion Picture, 1887–1909,* 49.

1

manufacturing, distribution, and exhibition of early films. Matthews purchased a half-dozen films and began showing them. The earliest movies Kansans saw were extremely short in length—barely one to two minutes long. They were also far from exciting, at least by modern standards. The most thrilling on-screen event that happened in Matthews's compendium of films was a fisherman falling into a body of water. Like many early motion picture screenings, a narrator accompanied Matthews's program, explaining to the audience what they were viewing on the screen. Matthews's touring exhibition would stop in a town, city, or hamlet and run several programs a day under a tent or in another temporary structure. Admission to his selection of films ran from ten to thirty cents. Kansans seemed willing to pay the somewhat then hefty price to see this novelty.[2]

Matthews's touring exhibition was not a huge moneymaking success. His company consisted of an advance man who publicized the new entertainment to towns that were on the circuit, a pianist who accompanied the program, and an electrician. Matthews not only had to pay a salary to these three men but also had to cover their travel expenses and the purchase of new films. Since Matthews's projecting machine ran on electricity, he ran into all sorts of problems. First, most of Kansas was not yet electrified, so the exhibition of films in many localities was not possible. Second, several different types of electrical currents were in operation; standardization had not yet taken place. The city fathers of several localities would not allow him to use the motor on his film projectors out of fear that it would wreck the municipal power plant. Matthews eventually built a projector that was turned by hand, avoiding problems with electricity.[3]

Shortly after Matthews began his tour of the state, early film distributor Lyman Howe also began canvassing Kansas. Howe became an enormously successful traveling motion picture showman. His films were often sponsored by religious organizations in rural areas of Kansas, and Howe shared in the profits with the sponsoring group. His films were often accompanied by a phonograph that produced sounds suitable to the action on the screen. Later, he used actors behind the screen to add dialogue.[4]

By May 1897, only one year later, film historians estimate that several hundred projectors were in use across the country, including the state of Kansas.

---

2. John Lewis Felder, "Sunday Movies in Kansas," 10–11.
3. Ibid.
4. Charles Musser, *The Emergence of Cinema: The American Screen to 1907*, 178.

In 1898, film versions of historical events such as the Spanish-American War spurred the popularity of movies. The medium's "capacity as a visual newspaper" demonstrated that motion pictures could go beyond mere entertainment.[5] Filmmakers reenacted the Cuban crisis and the sinking of the *Maine* for a fascinated American public.

In 1902, businessmen John Schnack and R. T. Webb of Larned, Kansas, opened a franchise under the Edison Exhibitors Company. They toured the Great Plains states using the Edison kinetoscope machines. Other Kansas entrepreneurs jumped on the bandwagon, hoping to make easy money. Like many start-up businesses, early Kansas exhibitors had mixed financial results.

At the turn of the century, moving pictures were still a novelty. They were shown in arcades, parlors, dime museums, and vaudeville houses. Some vaudeville managers believed that "living pictures" were only a temporary sensation and eventually lost interest in their projection. Managers of photo parlors and arcades eagerly bought these projectors from vaudeville houses and pasted together photographs from their peep shows to make a reel that lasted from four to five minutes. The rear part of the arcade was then partitioned off and filled with chairs and a screen (or a sheet), and a theater was born.

The first semipermanent film exhibition center in Topeka was a tent called the Black Top. The film program began at eight o'clock each evening and lasted for an hour and a half. The admission fee was a quarter. The program included illustrated songs; a short, exciting film of the New York Fire Department making a run; and a western. But the Black Top was not a financial success. Like other touring film exhibitions, the owner of the Black Top had technical problems; the most significant was a flickering projector that made it almost impossible to watch the film.[6]

By 1905, patterns of film exhibition and spectatorship had begun to change in the United States, including the state of Kansas. Whereas motion pictures had previously been exhibited in a number of venues, the specialized storefront moving picture theater became the dominant site of film viewing in the period 1905–1907. These "nickelodeons" (so-named because of their typical five-cent admission) revolutionized the new screen entertainment. Film historians attribute this revolution to Harry Davis, a Pittsburgh, Pennsylvania, vaudeville magnate.[7] Beginning in the latter part of 1904, Davis

---

5. Ibid., 109.
6. Felder, "Sunday Movies in Kansas," 13.
7. Musser, *Emergence of Cinema*, 418.

began to open these small theaters in Pennsylvania, convinced that motion picture exhibition was a potentially lucrative business. His intuition proved correct, and within a matter of months Davis's "nicolet" was copied around the nation.[8] Nickelodeons changed the nature of spectatorship because audiences paid to see motion pictures exclusively and not other forms of "mixed" entertainment. Although sing-alongs or slides might accompany the moving pictures, films were the primary feature.

Historians have ignored the role of Kansas in this development and have largely focused on large urban areas in their studies. It is important, however, to understand how film culture also transformed the rural Midwest. The first moving picture theater in Kansas was the Patee Theater in Lawrence, one of the first permanent film theaters west of the Mississippi River. The Patee family first established the theater on the 700 block of Massachusetts Street in Lawrence and then permanently moved to 828 Massachusetts later in the decade. The Patee family, who had previously been involved in the vaudeville industry, believed in the possibility of exhibiting moving pictures as an exclusive attraction and not as a part of a vaudeville act. This made them pioneers in the film industry, though several difficulties had to be surmounted before the Patee Theater was operational. In 1903 Lawrence was not fully electrified, and the Patee family had to establish their own generating plant. It was also necessary for the family to send to New York for fixtures, a projector, and films. The theater did not have comfortable seats in the beginning. In many nickelodeons, patrons sat on kitchen chairs.[9] Like many early film exhibitors, the Patee family had limited capital to start their business. There was also a great deal of uncertainly whether the Kansas public would accept a night of entertainment that was based solely on watching short motion pictures. But the Patees were at the forefront of this revolution in cinema in their establishment of a permanent film theater. The vast majority of theaters that exhibited films in 1903 were still of a "mixed" variety, showing short films but also displaying numerous vaudeville acts. Therefore, contrary to most academic accounts, this was not just a phenomenon of the urban East Coast. Entrepreneurs like the Patees were experimenting with the exhibition of films in varied settings.

In 1904, Topeka obtained its first permanent movie house, established by the Stone brothers. The Star Theater exhibited three reels of pictures and had var-

8. Lewis Jacobs, *The Rise of the American Film*, 35.
9. "Lawrence, Today and Yesterday," supplement, *Lawrence Daily Journal World*, October 14, 1956, Kansas State Historical Society, Topeka (hereafter cited as KSHS).

ious vaudeville acts. Topeka obtained a new theater that showed films almost every year from 1905 through 1910, giving its citizens a wide choice of movie houses. The first film theater in Kansas City, Kansas, was the Electric Theater at Sixth and Minnesota. It was owned by businessman Arthur F. Baker.

The booming popularity of nickelodeons was preceded by a fundamental shift in filmic representation. In 1903, the U.S. film industry had begun to rapidly expand with the popularity of story-films such as *The Great Train Robbery*. This film, one of the best known and most commercially successful movies of the early silent era, was one of the first films to play in Davis's Pittsburgh nickelodeon, drawing in droves of audience members. The film was an absolute artistic and box-office success.[10] The Schnack and Webb company was one of the first to exhibit *The Great Train Robbery* in the state of Kansas. Therefore, the development of the story-film, combined with the enormous popularity of the nickelodeon, led to an explosive demand for film product. Motion picture production companies sprang up to meet this new demand. By the fall of 1905, nickelodeons had transformed and superseded other venues for film exhibition. They were simply the place to see motion pictures.

By 1909, eight to ten thousand nickelodeons covered the nation, and sixteen million Americans viewed motion pictures each week. Even in the economic recession of 1907, nickelodeon owners were doing booming business. These storefront theaters sprang up primarily in working-class neighborhoods. As Eileen Bowser points out in *The Transformation of Cinema, 1907–1915*, this does not mean that upper- and middle-class people did not see movies. "Respectable" individuals could see films at high-class vaudeville shows, museums of curiosities, legitimate theaters, or even churches.[11] By 1910, twenty-six million people, more than one-fourth of the American population, attended movies every week.[12]

In traditional accounts of film exhibition, historians mark the progression of films from being part of a vaudeville program (1896–1903), to the nickelodeon stage (1903–1911), to the building of permanent theaters for motion pictures (1912–1918). The rural nature of Kansas (accompanied by several large cities) did not necessarily fit this pattern. The Patee Theater in Lawrence predated most nickelodeons, and it appears that the theater exclusively exhibited

---

10. Ibid.

11. Eileen Bowser, *The Transformation of Cinema, 1907–1915*, 1.

12. John Whiteclay Chambers II, *The Tyranny of Change: America in the Progressive Era, 1890–1920*, 120.

motion pictures. The rural nature of the state made touring programs much more popular than they were in other parts of the United States. In rural areas, farmers and their families could travel to attend films only on the weekends, once their work was completed. It was difficult for permanent theaters in rural areas to stay financially afloat. In urban Kansas, conditions were more conducive to profit making. The Electric Theater in Kansas City was typical of the type that made the transition from nickelodeon to full-fledged theater. In 1906, the storefront had 144 kitchen chairs set before a screen. By 1910, the theater had 1,100 permanent seats. Baker, owner of the Electric, eventually became head of A. F. Baker Enterprises, which controlled a number of theaters throughout the state.[13] In the eastern part of Kansas, willing businessmen established theaters in many small towns. Earl Van Hyning owned theaters in Coffeyville, Independence, Ottawa, Parsons, and Iola. More isolated and sparsely populated parts of the state faced difficulty in getting the "pictures" to their communities. The town of Kincaid took matters into its own hands. The city government brought films to the citizens and charged them a five-cent admission. Cimarron and Syracuse, in extreme western Kansas, and Colony, in the eastern part of the state, did the same.

Between 1908 and 1913, motion pictures had grown enormously in popularity in the state. A discussion of the burgeoning influence of motion pictures in Kansas is necessary in order to understand the Progressive obsession with the entertainment. Prior to 1908, there was little newspaper advertising for films. Kansans found out what films were playing by the advertising that advance men promoted for traveling film shows or by running down to the local nickelodeon and seeing the list of current films posted on the ticket booth. In 1909, the *Topeka Daily Capital* contained entertainment advertisements but nothing related to motion pictures. It was not until the beginning of the new decade (1910–1911) that potential film patrons could find out what was playing at the nearby nickelodeon or theater by consulting their newspapers. In 1915, *Moving Picture World* claimed, "Five or even three or two years ago such a thing as a moving picture section in a daily paper was not even known. Today the moving picture sections are comparatively common."[14]

In the October 1, 1910, edition of the *Wichita Beacon*, the newspaper printed an advertisement for the Pastime Theater. The program included one hundred minutes of vaudeville and a new picture. Conforming to earlier

13. Felder, "Sunday Movies in Kansas," 13.
14. "Facts and Comments," *Moving Picture World*, December 4, 1915, 1799.

exhibition trends, at the Pastime, films were only one act of a multimedia bill. Other theaters in Wichita in 1910 catered exclusively to moving pictures. The Maple Theater ("Home of the Aluminum Screen") advertised there were "no tiresome waits or intermissions" and that their "pictures . . . do everything but talk." Due to increased competition, the price of admission to Kansas films dropped to a standard five cents, thus the name nickelodeon. The Colonial Theater, at 117 Market Street in Wichita, also charged a nickel for admission. Due to the short running time of most films in 1910, filmgoers were shown a "bill" of films. The Colonial claimed it showed "five big pictures and four of them comedies." In order to distinguish itself from theaters that catered to lower-class people, the Colonial claimed that its pictures were *Always First Class.*"[15]

For millions of Americans, the storefront theater was the place to find an affordable amusement that transfixed and mesmerized audiences. Most nickelodeon programs were only thirty minutes in length, so it was easy to fit a nickel's worth of entertainment into a workingman or -woman's (or child's) schedule. Davis opened up his Pittsburgh, Pennsylvania, theater at eight in the morning and was still turning away people at midnight.[16]

As movies grew in popularity, city officials and social reformers became concerned with the unrestricted growth of the nickelodeon. Any empty storefront room in which chairs, a screen, and a projector could fit could be transformed into a makeshift theater. Health concerns erupted because many of the nickelodeons were hastily constructed without regard to fire safety or sanitary conditions. In the early twentieth century, communicable diseases such as tuberculosis were still major health problems, so the concern was well founded. Health officials and social workers wanted to make sure these theaters were safe for everyone by having them abide by fire codes and have decent ventilation systems. *Moving Picture World,* one of the earliest trade publications of this dynamic new industry, described such conditions in 1911: "Some of the places are perfectly filthy, with an air so foul that you can almost cut it with a knife. The floor is generally covered with peanut shells . . . and everybody spits on the floor. . . . No wonder the societies and health authorities try to bar children from the moving picture show."[17]

---

15. Advertisements for Pastime and Maple Theaters, *Wichita Beacon,* October 1, 1910, 7; advertisement for the Colonial Theater, *Wichita Beacon,* October 3, 1910, 7.

16. Jacobs, *Rise of the American Film,* 35.

17. *Moving Picture World,* March 11, 1911, 539.

The beginnings of the American film industry coincided with the development of the golden age of burlesque theater. As early as 1900, American and European producers were making risqué, "bawdy" films that were meant to appeal to a lower class of theatergoers. Sexy and risqué material was introduced to film from almost the beginning of the medium.[18] One example was *What Happened on 23rd Street, New York City* (1901), in which wind blew up women's skirts, giving men in the audience a forbidden peek of female flesh. *What Demoralized the Barbershop* (1901) was a short film about even shorter skirts. A specific genre of early films was produced to appeal to young men, a significant component of the early moviegoing public. *The Corset Model, The Pajama Girl,* and *The Physical Culture Girl,* all produced in 1903, showed women in various stages of undress. Although these films were basically comic in tone, they attracted the ire of moralists and Progressive social workers who worried that such movies could warp young minds.[19]

The explosive growth of nickelodeons, coupled with the widespread popularity of films with somewhat risqué subject matter, caused some Americans to believe that films could be dangerous if not controlled. When motion pictures were first introduced to the American public, they were considered a mere diversion for the entertainment-hungry working class. As motion pictures began to draw in millions of Americans weekly, the creation of specific means to cope with this phenomenon was addressed by concerned citizens. At first, critical reaction to the new entertainment was mixed, and there was no agreement on what mechanisms should be established to ensure the most advantageous use of the medium's abilities to communicate and educate large numbers of people. Everyone from clergymen to lawyers and social workers offered advice on how to "improve the movies." As John Whiteclay Chambers II argues, "Americans quickly recognized movies as a powerful new medium capable of influencing masses of people and manipulating thought and behavior."[20]

The growing popularity of nickelodeons brought movies to the attention of middle-class men and women who served the institutions of social control—the churches, reform groups, and a segment of the popular press. As reformers began examining the content of motion pictures and the effect that the new entertainment was having on American society, many members of

18. Chambers, *Tyranny of Change,* 121.
19. Sklar, *Movie-Made America,* 23.
20. Chambers, *Tyranny of Change,* 122.

the middle class became concerned and alarmed about the medium's growing power. Reformers, educators, clergymen, social workers, and members of civic organizations became troubled that the new medium would be a negative force in American society. Perhaps the major concern was the impact that films were having on children. Vicious attacks were made on the industry, claiming that films were "demoralizing," "crude," and "vulgar."[21] In the early summer of 1908, the Kansas City Franklin Institute sent a settlement worker to investigate films being shown in nickelodeons. Charges were brought against one theater owner, and complaints were brought against several others.[22] Social workers claimed that "the influence of movies is now as important as that of newspapers and schools" and that "the question of the film's morals has become pertinent."[23] As children became exposed to newsreel and fictional accounts of crime, the police promptly blamed the supposed rise in juvenile delinquency on the movies.

In order to understand the community forces that concerned themselves with the persuasive powers of motion pictures, it is important to grasp the predominant political and social movement of the early twentieth century—Progressivism. Motion pictures often ran up against the multitudinous forces of the Progressives. Progressivism and its followers represented a group of remarkable scope and diversity. Progressives included educators such as John Dewey, social workers such as Jane Addams, and politicians such as Theodore Roosevelt. Many members of the growing middle class considered themselves Progressives. Scholars of the period recognized that the growing professional middle class "would form the bulwark of those men and women who dedicated themselves to replacing the decaying system of the nineteenth century."[24] Progressivism was a dynamic reform movement that was composed of many specific social movements.[25]

At the center of the Progressive movement was a campaign to reform politics and society. Progressives believed that urban and industrial growth could not occur as recklessly as it had in the late nineteenth century. Rapid industrialization had caused such problems as business monopolies, dishonest politics, crowded city slums, and poor working conditions in factories. Progressives held that order must be imposed by the government and social agencies to

21. E. J. McKeown, "Censoring the Movie Picture," 11.
22. Bowser, *Transformation of Cinema*, 38.
23. McKeown, "Censoring the Movie Picture," 9.
24. Bernard Bailyn et al., *The Great Republic*, 596.
25. Chambers, *Tyranny of Change*, 138.

reform the glaring injustices of modern industrial American society. Progressives feared that society was becoming too materialistic and devoid of "healthful" values. They believed it was necessary to uplift the quality of modern urban life.[26] The Progressive era was a time of general awakening of social thought, a reexamination of the institutions, attitudes, and culture of the American republic.

The Progressives placed a great deal of faith in science and the use of rational, scientific reasoning as an answer to many of the social problems of the day. This led to the growth of new fields such as psychology and sociology. A dedicated group of trained social workers infiltrated the urban landscape to eradicate visible social ills. Using the settlement house as a base of operations, these social workers also sought to diagnose and combat urban problems that were developing in modern American life. It was in the field of education that Progressivism placed its primary emphasis on scientific methodology. Education was at the mainstream of Progressive thought, and the public school was seen as a lever of social change and moral betterment.[27] Progressives believed that education could curb the irrationality in men and elevate them to a higher calling. They were committed to improving the quality and welfare of all levels of society.[28] Theodore Roosevelt said, "There are two gospels I always want to preach to reformers. The first is the gospel of morality, the next is the gospel of efficiency."[29]

It was natural that the movie house, an emerging, integral part of any city, would receive attention from Progressive social workers and educators. The vast ability of movies to entertain, influence, and inform the city's population became an increasingly important concern of these individuals. Social scientists began investigations into the emerging entertainment, and they discovered that movies were not as "innocent or innocuous as originally seemed."[30] As Progressives began adopting legislation to control the actual physical site of the motion picture theater, they found it difficult to control what was on the screen.

As the concern over motion picture content became more vocal, many concerned citizens began theoretically exploring the role that films could play in

26. See Suzanne Lebsock, "Women and American Politics, 1880–1920"; Arthur S. Link and Richard McCormick, *Progressivism;* and Daniel T. Rodger, "In Search of Progressivism."
27. Chambers, *Tyranny of Change,* 102.
28. Robert Fisher, "Film Censorship and Progressive Reform: The National Board of Censorship of Motion Pictures, 1901–1922," 143.
29. Chambers, *Tyranny of Change,* 140.
30. Jowett, *Film: The Democratic Art,* 76.

American society. Many dedicated Progressives believed that improvement and reform could be brought to many different industries and forums. Professor T. K. Starr of the University of Chicago argued that motion pictures were "a tremendous vital force of culture as well as amusement." Thomas Edison argued that the motion picture "will wipe out narrow-minded prejudices which are founded on ignorance, it will create a feeling of sympathy and a desire to help the down-trodden people of the earth, and it will give new ideals to be followed."[31] The social potential of moving pictures was a marvel to Progressive reformers; the medium's potential was both awe inspiring and frightening. Social reformer Carl Lathrope believed that the only way to make films a beneficial aid to society was "by some measure of social control."[32] The more enthusiastic reformers appealed to their political representatives to help prevent the misuse of the new medium.

Objections from reformers about moving pictures and their effect on society focused on the impact of motion pictures on children. There were frequent attacks on the motion picture industry, but no organized groups of any significance emerged to control what some called the "movie problem." Criticisms and condemnations came from many different sources, each with its own particular solution on how to deal with this "problem."

Reformers paid a great deal of attention to the supposed negative effects of motion pictures on the child. In the *Nation,* one author wrote, "The truth is that this new means for public amusement has brought with it great perils which we are only beginning to realize, for side by side with its educational possibilities are the dangers of unrestricted propaganda." Cranston Brenton, chairman of the National Board of Review of Motion Pictures, argued, "Hundreds of thousands of children daily are gaining their impressions of life, of education, of religion, of morality thru the easiest of all mediums—the things they see with entertainment and with little or no mental exertion." In the initial years of nickelodeons, moving pictures were assumed to be just a passing fad for working-class audiences. Once films increased in popularity, middle-class children began attending them in even larger numbers, symptomatic of the Progressive belief that parents had lost control over children's moral and social behavior.[33]

---

31. "The Moving Picture and the National Character," 317.
32. Jowett, *Film: The Democratic Art,* 82.
33. "The Regulation of Films," 487; Cranston Brenton, "Motion Pictures and Local Responsibility," 125; Garth Jowett, "A Capacity for Evil: The 1915 Supreme Court *Mutual* Decision," 64.

Progressives placed an immense importance on the role and responsibility of society to rear children properly. Garth Jowett, in *Film: The Democratic Art,* suggests that "the child symbolized all that the Progressives held sacred, for his innocence and freedom made him receptive to scientific, rational concepts of men like John Dewey, and he held the positive future of society in his development." Thus, much of Progressive social activism was directed toward the "proper" development of children. Those who were concerned about the negative effects of motion pictures believed that a child's development could be destroyed by the introduction of unacceptable or perverse acts through the cinema. In 1910, Mayor Joseph Seidel of Milwaukee announced that it was useless to provide recreational activities for the children of his city when "the nickelodeons attracted their baser passions." He remarked that one must then compete with the nickel theaters by having motion pictures in the schools.[34] Many Progressive educators and civic leaders agreed with Seidel and concurred that the purpose of films should be to teach rather than to simply entertain.

Jane Addams, a leading figure in Progressive social work, dedicated an entire chapter in her book *The Spirit of Youth and City Streets* to the possible negative influences of motion pictures on children. Her analysis, titled "The House of Dreams," explained that the movies were serving as recreation for children but were creating an unreal world for urban youth. She commented that the motion picture provided a "transition between the romantic conceptions which they vainly struggle to keep intact and life's cruelties and trivialities which they refuse to admit." Addams believed that immigrant youth had to acquire an accurate and clear picture of American life if they were to survive in the United States. She believed that movies had the potential to destroy a generation of children by "filling their impressionable minds with these absurdities which certainly will become the foundation for their working moral codes and the data from which they will judge the properties of life."[35]

Two of the major concerns regarding children and their relationship to film involved the depictions of sexuality and crime. Around 1900, American producers began to make films that pushed community standards of decency regarding dancing, costumes (or lack of them), and sexuality. Although the majority of theaters were reputed to maintain polite standards at all times, the smaller independent theaters and penny arcades were looking for a select audi-

34. Jowett, *Film: The Democratic Art,* 77; "The Socialist Mayor of Milwaukee on Moving Pictures," *Moving Picture World,* June 4, 1910, 928.
35. Jane Addams, *The Spirit of Youth and the City Streets,* 75–76.

ence. Citizens across the country became concerned that motion pictures and a "frank" use of sexuality (by early-twentieth-century standards) would have a disastrous effect on the sexual upbringing and morality of America's youth. Writing in the *Christian Century*, journalist Fred Eastman stated that "for girls, the harm lies in the love scenes which prematurely arouse their sex impulses." An author in *Outlook* wrote, "The story of the average screen drama plays upon the weakest, most illogical prejudices and sentimentalities of the less thinking classes far more than old-fashioned melodrama." He argued that "it is the psychology—or rather the absence of it—in the average moving-picture play that constitutes its greatest danger to the growing mind."[36] Despite a lack of supporting evidence, thousands of Americans read such claims.

The depiction of crime and its potential influence on children also created an uproar among social workers and educators. Those who were anxious to place the movies under more stringent control argued that children could be persuaded to engage in criminal activities by imitation of what they saw on the screen. As early as 1910, the *New York World* claimed that films were the cause for an increase in crime. The typical argument that films were the bane of Western civilization came from William A. McKeever, a professor at the Kansas State Agricultural College (now Kansas State University) in Manhattan. He stated that movies had come to replace the "cheap yellow paperback as a purveyor of cheap, trashy stories." He claimed, "The movies were ten times worse, more poisonous and hurtful to character, because they appealed to the senses in flesh-and-blood form." McKeever argued the movies frequently contained subject matter that was of a "criminal and degrading nature." Reports from around the nation came in about children who tried to imitate what they had seen on the screen. The *American Review of Reviews* noted that two Pittsburgh youths tried to hold up a streetcar after viewing a train robbery on a motion picture screen. The magazine also reported on a situation in which three Brooklyn boys had committed burglary to get the price of admission to unlimited western pictures.[37] Reformers claimed that such acts proved that there was a direct connection between motion pictures and crime, even though many other causes such as family instability and poverty were conveniently left out of the argument.

The physical setting in which films were shown was also a major concern of Progressive reformers. As previously mentioned, Progressives were worried

---

36. Fred Eastman, "Our Children and the Movies"; "Movies Morals and Manners," 695.
37. William A. McKeever, "The Moving Picture: A Primary School for Criminals"; "Moving Picture and National Character," 315–20.

about fire safety and health issues regarding these makeshift theaters. Progressives led the fight for protective social legislation to improve the physical conditions of public buildings. As they attempted to force cities to adopt sanitary, fire, and building codes to ensure the safety of their citizens, the nickelodeon became a subject of concern. Ordinances about ventilation, lighting, fire safety, and crowd control in public buildings also applied to nickelodeons. Enforcement of these regulations and the construction of actual movie theaters (as opposed to storefront theaters) vastly improved the standards of safety. But concerned citizens also watched in horror as crowds of people, unescorted women, and unsupervised children all crowded into the same theater with adult men. The Chicago Vice Commission found many cases in which young boys and girls were sexually abused in theaters, sometimes even in the middle of the afternoon.[38] William Healey, a pioneer in the study of juvenile delinquency, found that "under cover of dimness, evil communications readily pass and bad habits are taught. Moving picture theaters are favorite places for the teaching of homosexual practices." Some reformers also worried that young couples would pay more attention to each other than to the movies being shown on the screen. In 1919, Orrin G. Cocks stated what concerned parents had been warning about for years—that "seating accommodations promoted erotic congestion."[39]

Religious groups were actively involved in the discussion over motion pictures. When films were first introduced to the American public, many religious groups had hoped that films would become a medium of education and would teach youths proper morals and values. The Reverend James J. Durick of the Church of Our Lady of Good Counsel in Brooklyn claimed that films could be a source of moral uplift as well as instructive entertainment. To convince his parishioners, Father Durick invited them twice a week to see such films at the parish hall. In *Moving Picture World,* Father Durick claimed, "I had to fight the evils of moving pictures with its own weapons. At first, [films] were instructive, but suddenly there are pictures insidiously revealing vice and the suggestion of vile things."[40] Religious leaders such as Canon William Chase of the Christ Church of Brooklyn were some of the chief movers in the crusade to "clean up" the movies.

---

38. Jowett, *Film: The Democratic Art,* 82.

39. William Healey, *The Individual Delinquent,* 307; Orrin G. Cocks, "A Real Motion Picture Ogre," 20.

40. "How a Brooklyn Priest Deals with the Problem of Moving Pictures," *Moving Picture World,* October 29, 1910, 983.

In the field of education, motion pictures gained some early support, but many instructors were hesitant about readily accepting the new medium of expression. Faced with the fact that films were direct competition for the attention of young minds, some educators were convinced that it was better to ally themselves with the new medium. In a lecture to the teachers of Topeka, Kansas, Professor Milton Fairchild of Baltimore advocated the appointment of a "moral" instructor from the University of Kansas who would go about the state with a motion picture projector dispensing "visual education" on the effects of "wickedness and righteousness." On the other hand, Jane Eliott Snow, in *Moving Picture World*, declared that moving pictures were the "working man's college" because they gave him a broad and liberal education. Many educators claimed that industry-produced motion pictures failed to present proper moral instruction. Both religious groups and educators wanted films to teach proper behavior rather than "immoral" sexual behavior and criminal activity. These individuals were simply disappointed and angry over the product that the motion picture industry was providing. Kansas professor William McKeever claimed that motion pictures were causing children to "unlearn all the moral lessons of the schools."[41]

Educators, clergymen, women's clubs, and politicians all attacked the same issue: they claimed that movies taught antisocial behavior. While Progressive reformers were calling for an increased role of the government in curing the social ills of American society, they also looked to the government to control the "poison of the mind" that they claimed the industry spewed. As one reader in *Outlook* expressed, "Unless the law steps in and does for moving picture shows what it has done for meat inspection and pure food, the cinematograph will continue to inject into our social order an element of degrading principles."[42]

When reformers were calling for social control, they were talking about censorship. Censorship was a form of cultural intervention in which reformers could remove "offensive" material. The first recorded protest against a movie was with the film *Dolorita in the Passion Dance* (1897). This brief film showed a young woman in various stages of undress (but never completely nude). The film was a hit in the peep-show parlors of Atlantic City until it was ordered shut down by a judge in 1897 because of its "possible moral harm."[43]

41. McKeever, "Moving Picture," 184–86; Jane Eliott Snow, "The Working Man's College," *Moving Picture World,* March 19, 1915, 432; McKeever, "Moving Picture," 185.
42. Darrell O. Hibbard, "Moving Picture—the Good and Bad of It," 598–99.
43. Sklar, *Movie-Made America,* 30.

Between 1897 and 1907, judges throughout the nation made numerous decisions in which films were either banned or exorcised because of their possible "moral abuse." The first actual censorship legislation was passed and approved in Chicago. In 1907, Chicago had more than 150 theaters that showed motion pictures.[44] These establishments enjoyed a daily attendance that was estimated at one hundred thousand patrons. In a scathing editorial, the *Chicago Tribune* kicked off a censorship campaign, declaring that movies were "without a redeeming feature to warrant their existence. They appeal to the lowest passions of childhood and it is proper to suppress them at once. [There] should be a law absolutely forbidding entrance of any boy or girl under eighteen. The impact of these movies' influence is wholly vicious. There is no voice raised to defend the majority of five-cent theaters, because they can not be defended. They are hopelessly bad."[45]

On November 4, 1907, the City of Chicago passed an ordinance "prohibiting the exhibition of obscene and immoral pictures and regulating the exhibition of pictures of the classes and kinds commonly shown in mutoscopes, kinetoscopes, cinematographs and penny arcades." This ordinance effectively established the first governmental "societal control" over motion pictures. The legislation required that individuals who were involved in the business of exhibiting motion pictures secure a permit for their display from the chief of police. He was not to issue permits for films that he deemed "immoral" or "obscene."[46]

That same year, New York City became embroiled in a major controversy over motion picture censorship. In June, Mayor George B. McClellan received a condemnatory report from the city's police commissioner who recommended the cancellation of all licenses of nickelodeons and penny arcades. The police commissioner claimed that hastily built movie houses were dangerous for patrons and that in his opinion "questionable" material was being exhibited on the screen that might be harmful to New York citizens. The largest concentration of nickelodeons and film patrons in the country was found in New York City.

The issue of municipal control over motion pictures smoldered in New York City throughout 1907–1908. McClellan was under constant pressure

44. *Billboard,* March 17, 1907, 32.
45. Terry Ramsaye, *A Million and One Nights: A History of the Motion Pictures through 1925,* 474, 478.
46. Hunnings, *Film Censors and the Law,* 165.

from clergymen who were "protesting that [motion pictures] spread demoralization among the children . . . and keep children away from Sunday School."[47] Religious leaders of the Church of Christ and the Roman Catholic archdiocese were chief leaders in the movement to sanitize the movies.

On December 23, 1908, Mayor McClellan called for a public hearing to discuss the general condition of movie theaters. The *New York Times* described the meeting as "one of the biggest public hearings ever held in City Hall." The mayor listened to arguments against motion picture exhibition from almost every religious denomination in the city. Frank Moss, leader of the Society for the Suppression of Vice, a reform group, gave evidence and made an elaborate case against the movies. Moss brought various witnesses who claimed that they had seen unescorted children in nickelodeons and had witnessed the display of pictures that were "suggestive." Canon William Sheafe Chase of Christ Church of Brooklyn kicked off a thirty-year campaign against immoral movies when he testified that the industry had "no moral scruples whatever. They are simply in the business for the money there is in it."[48]

Theater owners and film manufacturers flocked to city hall to defend their livelihood and protested against any form of social control. The major defense for the industry was offered by Charles Sprague Smith of the People's Institute, a New York reform group. He argued that there were more pressing issues facing New York City than movies. J. Stuart Blackton of the Vitagraph Company, a major film producer, said that the film companies had agreed not to manufacture any more questionable films and promised to keep out the importation of such films from Europe. French films in particular had a reputation for being more adult than most American pictures in regard to marital infidelity and displays of sexuality. Theater owners feared an extension of censorship as practiced in Chicago and promised the mayor that they would not display any obscene motion pictures.[49]

After more than five hours of deliberation, McClellan decided to close all movie houses in the city of New York on December 24, 1908. The mayor revoked the licenses of all of the picture houses. The decision was dramatic and newsworthy enough to make the front page of the Christmas edition of the *New York Times*. The mayor claimed that his major concern was over the safety of the motion picture houses and that in order to gain the licenses back,

47. Ramsaye, *Million and One Nights*, 475.
48. "Says Picture Shows Corrupt Children," *New York Times*, December 24, 1908, 4.
49. Ibid.

the establishments would have to be checked by the chief of the fire department. The mayor also stated that he would again revoke the license of any theater that "tended to degrade or injure the morals of the community."[50]

The closing of nickelodeons and theaters threw the movie industry, then centered in New York City, into a state of chaos.[51] No theater owner, distributor, or film manufacturer knew what action would take place next. Theater owners and film producers quickly assembled to discuss the situation. William Fox, a leading film producer and owner of the Fox Film Corporation, told the group that the industry's very existence was threatened if McClellan's actions were followed by other governmental leaders. The first step was to obtain an injunction restraining the mayor from taking any further action against picture theaters. The injunction to reopen the nickelodeons was obtained from Judge William Gaynor, a candidate for mayor and a friend of the film industry.[52] On January 9, 1909, the municipal government countered by passing an ordinance banning children under the age of sixteen from theaters unless accompanied by an adult. This adult-escort clause would be economically devastating to the industry that depended on hundreds of thousands of children who attended New York City theaters alone each week. Theater owners responded by employing "surrogate parents" to accompany them into the theaters. Film-industry businessmen were not willing to submit to censorship action.[53]

From 1909 on, the film industry found itself under complete attack. While reformers across the United States were criticizing the motion picture industry and advocating governmental control, supporters rallied to the industry's defense. Film manufacturers, exhibitors, and distributors fought censorship on the grounds that it was un-American and abridged the constitutional guarantees of freedom of speech and of the press. *Moving Picture World*, for example, placed the responsibility of acceptable filmmaking on the individual

50. "Picture Show Men Organize to Fight," *New York Times*, December 25, 1908, 2.
51. It is necessary to define "industry" here. In early 1908, negotiations began among the various film producers to attempt to bring an end to years of fighting over patent rights on cameras, projectors, and other equipment used to make and display films. These discussions culminated in the incorporation of the Motion Picture Patents Company in September 1908. This company consisted of ten of the largest producers of motion pictures. There were independent companies outside of the system, but it can be said that the Motion Picture Patents Company represented industrial sentiments (Nancy Rosenbloom, "Progressive Reform, Censorship, and the Motion Picture Industry, 1909–1917," 44–45).
52. Bowser, *Transformation of Cinema*, 38. Gaynor was elected mayor of New York City in 1910.
53. Jowett, *Film: The Democratic Art*, 113.

manufacturer rather than accepting the reformers' remedy of censoring the entire industry. The publication claimed, "Censorship is an instrument of bigotry and oppression. If the censor is a fanatic, his likes and dislikes are obvious. If he is a politician, it may be possible to bribe him. . . . Exhibitors should fight censorship legislation."[54] Even some religious and educational leaders who questioned the morality of motion pictures opposed governmental censorship.

Opponents to governmental censorship of motion pictures further claimed that many of the criticisms of the outcomes of film viewing were simply not true. Following the conflict over censorship in New York City, an investigation of screen content was conducted by the police commissioner. In *American City*, Cranston Brenton reported, "The independent reports . . . demonstrated that by far the majority of films were wholesome and that adverse impact of the 'movies' had been guilty of great exaggeration."[55]

Nor did everyone believe that viewing a crime film would make individuals into criminals. A writer in *Moving Picture World* commented that "it is only a well-developed insanity that is affected by the suggestions gained from pictures. Newspapers might also be said to incite crime, but nothing is done about that. Children are not excluded from all Punch and Judy shows which are really brutal and often end in a hanging."[56]

Representatives of the film industry and advocates of constitutional freedom for the movies felt that it was better to let the public make up its own mind regarding films, rather than have some type of governmental interference. In *New Jersey Municipalities*, Progressive Orrin Cocks stated, "Americans choose the good in movies whenever they get a chance. . . . [I]nstead of berating the producers, a few people are telling the motion picture industry in straight, wise, sympathetic language that they want something good. The industry has responded to this friendly treatment." A writer in *Harper's Weekly* agreed: "The moral problems are better left to the public because they are bungled by politicians."[57]

By the end of the first decade of the twentieth century, Americans had begun to divide over the question of whether the government should control motion pictures. While the motion picture was becoming established as the

54. Stephen Bush, "The Previous Restraint," *Moving Picture World*, January 3, 1914, 25.
55. Brenton, "Motion Pictures and Local Responsibility," 126.
56. "Exclude the Criminal: Or Some Further Limitations of the Picture," *Moving Picture World*, August 27, 1910, 456.
57. Orrin C. Cocks, "Good Movies Go Strong," 147–50; "Morals and Movies," 577.

most popular form of entertainment in the early part of the century, the fledg-
ling industry became embroiled in fighting the threat of censorship. Several
strategies to fight this censorship were under way. First, the industry increasingly began to base films on acknowledged cultural masterpieces, demonstrating that motion pictures could be uplifting and educational. Cinematic
versions of *Julius Caesar, Romeo and Juliet, A Doll's House, Faust,* and *A Christmas Carol* were all produced between 1908 and 1910. Second, trade publications became involved in the dispute, encouraging producers to stay away from
certain subject matter.[58] On January 2, 1909, for example, *Moving Picture World*
recommended that the following items be banned from the screen: religiously
offensive material; contemporary sensational crime; shots of prisons, convicts,
and police stations; and scenes of morbidity.[59]

What became increasingly apparent was that if the industry was going to
continue to grow, some type of regulating agency that would satisfy both the
industry and the demands of reform and religious groups needed to be established. The People's Institute of New York attempted to negotiate a truce. The
People's Institute was a reform group whose members included personnel of
the Society for Prevention of Crime and the board of education and members
of various church societies. The institute's leaders included John Collier, a
motion picture and theater critic, and Charles Sprague Smith, a Progressive
reformer. The People's Institute was the embodiment of the Progressive spirit,
a dedicated group of reformers with genuine concern for the city of New York.

In 1909, the institute brought together ten New York civic organizations,
under the title of the National Board of Censorship, to sponsor a nongovernmental motion picture censorship board. Movie producers approved of a plan
that called for them to submit all films to the board for previewing. All films
were reviewed by small subcommittees that consisted of four to ten members.
A majority would then rule if the film would be classified as "Passed," "Passed
with Changes as Specified," or "Condemned." The industry agreed to cut out
any footage that the board recommended.[60] The decisions of the board were
then mailed out in a weekly bulletin delivered to more than four hundred
social and civic organizations. The industry even gave the Board of Censorship some financial support, but this later had to be withdrawn out of fear of
a conflict of interest. Collier, secretary and public spokesman of the National

---

58. Bowser, *Transformation of Cinema,* 42–43.
59. *Moving Picture World,* January 2, 1909, 200.
60. Jowett, *Film: The Democratic Art,* 112.

Board of Censorship, realized the growing importance of the motion picture in American life. He emphasized the positive aspects of the beleaguered medium. He stated that "the motion picture show is one of the silent, unregarded and largely misunderstood agencies which are making history. . . . The motion picture is the foremost art influence among wage-earners of our country." Collier believed that the public, through the National Board of Censorship, should censor its own amusements and not leave it up to a governmental body. The National Board of Censorship and the industry realized that the goal should be uplift. Many leaders of the People's Institute and the National Board of Censorship feared what might happen if a small group of people (censors) gained control over the screen. One of these leaders, W. Stephen Bush, warned in 1914 that "this constant talk about censorship has stimulated the army of cranks into unwholesome activity. The very words of censor and censorship are odious and remind us of the times when the public hangman was wont to burn books which were disapproved by the authorities only to be afterwards enthroned in the esteem and the affections of mankind. The censor is nothing more and nothing less than an inquisitor, whose office has been held in abhorrence through the centuries."[61] Progressives were divided over governmental interference in motion picture content. Some Progressives, like Collier and Bush, believed in endorsing films of merit and championing the "art of the people" that was transforming American cultural life.[62] Others believed that the motion picture was harmful enough to children that the government needed to step in and regulate it.

In reality, the National Board of Censorship was not a censorship apparatus but a promoter of good films. A title "Approved by the National Board of Censorship" could be attached to a film with the specific purpose of avoiding local censorship. The board made an adamant effort to dissociate itself from being an actual censorship board. The motto of the board was Selection Not Censorship, and it devoted much of its energy to combating both federal and state censorship proposals. The board's operations were called "voluntary," and its power was said to be "only through the positive and continuing wish of the movie community."[63] This attitude was reflected in 1915 when the

61. Bowser, *Transformation of Cinema*, 44.

62. Collier quoted in Jowett, *Film: The Democratic Art*, 112; W. Stephen Bush, "No Distinction of Censorship," *Moving Picture World*, January 17, 1914; history of the National Board of Review, National Board of Review Web site, http://www.nbrmp.org/about/history.cfm.

63. Richard S. Randall, *Censorship of the Movies: The Social and Political Control of a Mass Medium*, 12.

agency changed its name from the National Board of Censorship to the National Board of Review. The industry enthusiastically supported the national board, fearing it might be a last chance against social reformers and would-be censors.

Advocates of censorship, such as William Chase, considered the National Board of Censorship inadequate because it reached only those film manufacturing companies that were willing to submit their products to it. These advocates claimed there were ways for willing companies to get around the board. Before a film had passed the scrutiny of the board, copies of it could be sold to distributing agents with the sole agreement that it would not be released before a certain date. The distributors, as the owners of the film, could do anything they wanted with it. The film passed out of the hands of the National Board of Censorship. Chase represented the religious community who believed that governmental film censorship was necessary.

The National Board of Censorship received widespread journalistic coverage, and in many ways John Collier became the spokesman for the anticensorship movement. Collier wrote in *Survey* that "censorship is impractical and dangerous because the means involved are too crude for the ends sought and are largely unrelated to the ends sought." Critics claimed that the board was simply a tool of the industry, a smoke-screen board that would approve all films submitted. Collier admitted that the origins of the board could be traced to the relationships among producers, distributors, and the public but defended the right of the people to choose their own forms of entertainment.[64]

The National Board of Censorship considered itself a success in its early years of operation. By 1914, it was estimated that 95 percent of all films shown across the nation were reviewed by the National Board of Censorship.[65] Many religious leaders and moralists became unhappy over the failure of the National Board of Censorship to censor films more vigorously. State and municipal governments, therefore, began taking "the movie problem" into their own hands. The film industry began spending enormous amounts of time, effort, and money lobbying against governmental censorship. Motion picture companies hired lawyers and political consultants to persuade local, state, and federal officials not to enact censorship legislation or ordinances. If each city and state would adopt separate censorship boards, with their own standards, the result could be chaos for the industry. A writer in *Moving Pic-*

64. John Collier, "Censorship and the National Board."
65. Fisher, "Film Censorship and Progressive Reform," 149.

ture News argued, "One of the most difficult problems confronting the industry to-day is that of the film censor. State censorship, unless every State adopted the same legislation, would be very chaotic."[66] Many reform groups and members of the clergy were dissatisfied with the industry's attempt to avoid what they considered the real issue: the removal of all "offensive" features from motion pictures.

In 1911, Pennsylvania became the first state to establish a censorship board. Reform groups, women's clubs, and religious leaders organized a campaign for state censorship of motion pictures. The reactionary views of those in Pennsylvania who supported state censorship can be summed up in the words of the Reverend Edward G. Garesche: "Seventy five percent of all films are slapstick comedies, rough and vulgar entertainment. Only five percent are educational. . . . [A] sure remedy is censorship." A writer in *Literary Digest* reiterated this sentiment: "The movies are of immense importance. They are making the taste of millions. They are making it bad, execrable taste—bad and execrable, because it is based on sensation, and is to that extent wholly animalistic." In Pennsylvania, a board of three censors was authorized to review all films in the state and given power to issue permits for those that were "moral and proper" and withhold those that were "sacrilegious, obscene, indecent or such as in the judgment of the board to debase or corrupt morals." The legislation clearly identified items that would be banned from Pennsylvania screens. They included nudity, sexual liaisons, infidelity, and violence.[67]

By 1913, the state legislatures of Ohio and Kansas were willing to follow the example set by Pennsylvania. The attempt to create motion picture censorship commissions in these two states would lead to a major Supreme Court case that would determine the constitutionality of governmental motion picture censorship in the nation. It would be a landmark case that would impact freedom of the screen for more than thirty-five years—and Kansas was at the heart of it.

---

66. "The Censoring of Film," *Motion Picture News*, March 15, 1913, 7.
67. Edward F. Garesche, "Pastors and the Censorship of the Movies," 256–66; "Movies Crimes against Good Taste," 592; Hunnings, *Film Censors and the Law*, 186.

Two

Kansas and the Fight over Motion Picture Censorship

The phenomenon of film censorship in Kansas involved the complex intersection of moral, political, and social forces in the state. As in Pennsylvania, a coalition of political and religious groups, Progressive reformers, and concerned citizens demanded the passage of film censorship legislation in Kansas. Although the citizens who actively backed film censorship in the state constituted only a small minority of the population, the fact that they held important social and political influence enabled them to force censorship legislation through the state government.[1] In a letter to Governor Arthur Capper, Mary Hamphill, president of the Olathe Progress Club, expressed the views of those individuals who supported motion picture censorship: "We must call your attention to the unfit character of many of the motion pictures being shown in our local theater. As careful mothers and good citizens we must protect against pictures of this nature being provided for our children and our neighbor's [*sic*] children. This would suggest a more careful selection of films, a stricter censorship and the desirability of a larger

---

1. As Chambers argues, "The progressive leadership came primarily from the urban and small-town middle and upper classes, particularly well-educated and socially secure white Anglo-Saxon Protestants" (*Tyranny of Change*, 138). This group was the political leadership of Kansas.

percentage of pictures that are instructive and elevating as well as merely entertaining."[2]

Although there were supporters of film censorship in almost every state in the Union, Kansas was one of only seven states to ever enact film censorship legislation. The question is, why Kansas? A combination of factors created the political and social climate for motion picture censorship to be enacted.

In Kansas, the political and social forces that created the state censorship board grew out of a long reform tradition. In the late 1800s, the Populist Party had gained control of the state government in Kansas and brought with it reforms that included an irrigation bill, a concerted attempt to enforce prohibition in the cities, the "busting" of railroad monopolies, and a graduated income tax.[3] Kansas was at the center of the Populist movement in the 1890s and had elected a Populist U.S. senator, two governors, several congressmen, numerous judges, and a significant part of both houses of the state legislature.[4] The Populist Party had declined by the early 1900s, but Progressive Republicans carried on the reform tradition, and Kansas was a bastion of Progressive thought. Populism had made a significant impact on Kansas public opinion, and this need for public reform was adopted by the Progressives. Progressivism was important both politically and socially to the state. Social workers, newspaper editors, and politicians all contributed to the reform spirit. Laws outlawing child labor, establishing primary elections, developing juvenile courts, and giving women the right to vote were all issues that these Progressives supported.[5]

Progressivism in Kansas operated on both the local and the state level. Local Progressives in Emporia demanded improvements in public services and were concerned over the physical improvement of the city. Petitions flooded the Emporia City Council as demands were made for new streetlights, sidewalks, gutters, and sewers. Sally Foreman Griffith argues that this demand for an expansion of local public services was consistent with nineteenth-century boosterism. This boosterism eventually became Progressivism; in fact, she claims that the two words were synonymous in the first decade of the twentieth century.[6]

---

2. Mary Hamphill to Governor Arthur Capper, December 4, 1916, Box 37, File 29, Capper Papers, KSHS.

3. Craig Miner, *Kansas: The History of the Sunflower State, 1854–2000*, 182.

4. Leo E. Oliva, "Kansas: A Hard Land in the Heartland," 261.

5. Jowett, *Film: The Democratic Art*, 190.

6. Sally Foreman Griffith, *Hometown News: William Allen White and the Emporia Gazette*, 131–32.

The Republican Party in Kansas was not enthusiastically united behind the principles of Progressivism. In the first few years of the new century, a significant power struggle took place between traditional Republicans and the new reform faction of the party. Progressive Republicans won their first significant victory in 1904 when Edward Hoch was elected governor.

These were years in which the journalistic practice of muckraking was making a significant impact on the American conscience. This form of exposé journalism explored the corporate and governmental abuses in American society and the social injustices that the American people faced. The abuses of big business were exposed in periodicals such as *McClure's*, in which Ida Tarbell detailed the abuses of John D. Rockefeller in her "History of the Standard Oil Company." This form of muckraking journalism was attractive to a segment of the Kansas population who believed that the business of the state was becoming dominated by "foreign" corporations.[7]

In the period 1900–1915, Kansas witnessed a significant transformation both economically and socially. Confronted with the explosion of modern urban society and technology, Kansas Progressives took a scientific, rational approach to solving the problems that the state faced. Kansas Progressive legislators had no problem passing legislation meant to deal with such issues. In *Kansas: The History of the Sunflower State, 1854–2000,* Craig Miner lists a voluminous number of laws that Progressive legislators passed during this era. They included bills on

> primary elections, football regulation, the public utilities commission, city commissions and city managers, consolidating state agencies, the state board of administration, anticigarette moves, initiative/referendum/recall, the civil service merit system, insurance regulation, workmen's compensation, blue-sky securities regulation, woman suffrage, the state art board, capital punishment, the pure shoe law, child hygiene, interracial marriages, displaying radical flags, mine and factory inspection, the juvenile court, eugenic matrimony, the bank guaranty law, the public defender, movie censorship, the eight-hour day, and the state printing plant.[8]

One contemporary argued, "[Kansas] is a state of ideas, . . . a gushing fountain of ideas, a swarming hive, an avalanche, a cyclone of ideas." In 1912, a social scientist of the period agreed: "It would be hard to find a state with

7. Ibid.
8. Miner, *Kansas,* 202–4.

more progressive measures than Kansas."[9] Much of this legislation was not always well thought out, though. In fact, this experimental, or trial-and-error, form of legislation became a hallmark of Kansas politics in this era. This will be aptly demonstrated as we review the continuous revision of legislation concerning motion picture censorship in the state. Bills were passed in 1913, 1915, 1917, and 1919. Successive pieces of legislation either corrected inadequacies or clarified issues in previously passed bills.

In 1910, University of Kansas historian Carl Becker wrote an influential essay titled "Kansas" in which he attempted to explain the mentality of the people of the state. This essay proves to be invaluable in helping to understand the mind-set of Kansans in the early part of the twentieth century. Becker argues that "Kansas is no mere geographic expression but a state of mind." According to Becker, within this Kansas mind-set was a strand of puritanism. "Like St. Augustine, [Kansans] have their City of God, the idealized Kansas of some day; it is only necessary to have faith in order to possess it."[10] This idea of creating a more perfect society by eradicating the social ills of the state was the bedrock of the Progressive mentality.

Kansas was a bastion of Progressive thought in the early twentieth century. Special-interest groups in the state were behind efforts to harness the government to combat what they believed were social abuses, inequities, or immoral activities. Historian Robert Sherman La Forte explains that Kansas Progressives were "conservative in outlook, somewhat simplistic, and certainly not revolutionary."[11]

Behind this bedrock of Progressivism, though, were five additional rationales that help to explain why Kansas was one of the few states in the Union to adopt motion picture censorship. The first rationale was the support of a great deal of the Kansas press and the influential Kansas newspapermen behind these powerful state newspapers. They included William Allen White, Arthur Capper, and Edward Hoch. All three men were not only significant members of the press but also active politically. William Allen White was the editor of the *Emporia Gazette* and a prizewinning journalist who received national attention for his editorials.[12] A Progressive Republican, White enlightened

9. Robert Smith Bader, *Hayseeds, Moralizers, and Methodists: The Twentieth-Century Image of Kansas*, 18, 13.

10. Carl Becker, "Kansas," in *Everyman His Own Historian: Essays on History and Politics*, 2.

11. Robert Sherman La Forte, *Leaders of Reform: Progressive Republicans in Kansas, 1900–1916*, 6.

12. For more information on William Allen White, see Griffith, *Hometown News;* and Walter Johnson, *William Allen White's America.*

many Kansans on the problems of economic growth and partisan politics. White was the personification of early-twentieth-century Kansas and, as Robert Smith Bader argues, "spoke and wrote in the majority view, at least as he perceived it." Although he did not specifically endorse film censorship, White strongly believed in prohibiting films such as *The Birth of a Nation* that stirred up violence and anger. White's notion of the idealized local community did not fit with motion pictures that corrupted morals and provided feelings of hostility. White commented, "The trouble with the moving-picture business is chiefly the lack of standards."[13] Arthur Capper was the editor of the *Topeka Daily Capital,* a two-term governor of Kansas, and a U.S. senator.[14] Capper was enormously influential in state politics and Kansas journalism. Without his support, film censorship may not have occurred in the state. He promoted the idea of film censorship in his newspaper and strongly backed the Kansas Board of Censorship despite the political problems the board often caused him. Edward Hoch was editor of the *Marion Record* and a two-term governor of Kansas. A strong Prohibitionist, he believed that saloons, bars, alcohol, and drunkenness should never be shown on Kansas motion picture screens. These three men were influential nationally as well. They were responsible for the fact that politics and journalism were invariably intertwined in Kansas from 1900 to 1920. Their ideas, as both Progressive reformers and media indoctrinators, were extremely critical for Kansas minds. They helped create an environment conducive to the acceptance of motion picture censorship.

The second rationale in explaining the acceptance of motion picture censorship by some citizens in the state was an unconscious fight against modernity. This was an attempt to preserve the "traditional" Kansas way of life. A common sentiment in prewar Kansas was that modern life was simply moving too fast. Sudden, dramatic changes in American society, particularly in regard to technology, were taking place. By World War I, the automobile was beginning to have a significant impact on the state. In 1913 and 1914, automobile owners registered more than ninety thousand cars in Kansas.[15] Automobiles were transforming work patterns and connecting rural residents with

---

13. Bader, *Hayseeds, Moralizers, and Methodists,* 6; William Allen White, "Chewing Gum Relaxation," in *The Movies on Trial: The Views and Opinions of Outstanding Personalities against Screen Entertainment Past and Present,* ed. William J. Perlman, 4.

14. For more information on Capper, see Byron Monroe Crowley, "The Public Career of Arthur Capper prior to His Senatorial Service"; and Homer E. Socolofsky, *Arthur Capper: Publisher, Politician, and Philanthropist.*

15. Miner, *Kansas,* 182.

urban areas in a way deemed unimaginable fifteen years earlier. The popularity and sheer novelty of the airplane, phonograph, and telephone were connecting Kansans to the larger American community in more direct, physical ways. Moving pictures were a modern threat to this sense of rural continuity and agrarian sensibility. By 1910, motion pictures were no longer a mere novelty; they were becoming a staple of entertainment in big and small Kansas cities and had indeed infiltrated every town, village, and hamlet in the state. Moving picture theaters, nickelodeons, and tent theaters dotted the Kansas landscape. Many Kansans questioned motion pictures: Were they a sign of progress or a symbol of the corrupting influences of modernity? Would motion pictures be a medium that would uplift and engage Kansas minds, or would they be a form of entertainment that would debase and corrupt?

Modernity and its technological inventions and achievements were looked upon in a positive fashion by many Kansans, but they were also permanent demonstrations that a "traditional" agricultural way of life, with its own sense of community, harmony, and insular patterns, was soon disappearing. This was a frightening and unsettling notion for many adult Kansans. Film historian Garth Jowett explains that the fight over censorship was more than a struggle between reformers and filmmakers: "For the long dominant Protestant segment, the new entertainment medium was, in reality, a dramatic and highly visible symbol of those social and political changes in turn-of-the-century America which they seemed powerless to prevent and which threatened to inexorably alter the face of the nation they had striven to build."[16]

This sentiment is quite apparent in the speeches and correspondence of Arthur Capper. Capper ran for governor based on sentiments that reflected that rural Kansas was losing its grip on its young. In a speech at the Idau Farmers' Picnic on June 11, 1914, he claimed that "aside from the luring opportunities for making money, the 'call of the city' is perhaps a wholesome craving, born as it is of the desire for fellowship, for amusement and culture." Capper was well aware of the attractions of big-city life. He maintained, though, that "the *cost* of gratifying this desire in the city is *very great*, involving loss of neighborliness, curtailment of freedom, sacrifice of identity." To reel in his rural audience who had been warned about urban life, he argued, "We read in the newspapers day after day the stories telling of separations and divorces and fights in the cities, of arrests for drunkenness and murders resulting from drink. We read of the poverty in the slums where children

16. Jowett, "Capacity for Evil," 60.

swarm, and of the vulgar display and extravagant follies of the rich." In order
to reflect the current obsession with "white slavery," he preached, "we see the
foolish girls, both in country and town, who caught by the glitter of the city,
flock on its streets, often to fall a prey to the lust of men who glory in their
shame." Then, in order to contrast the wholesome country life with the
immoral squalor of the city, Capper continued, "When we think of all this in
the great cities, can we doubt for a moment, my friends, that the clean, wholesome life of the Kansas country folk, as we find it typified in a quiet, decent,
law-respecting community like Clay county, is far and away the happiest, the
most *useful life*. We must, therefore, both from an economic and a moral
motive, do everything possible to keep our people who live in the country and
the small towns from rushing in to the already overcrowded cities."[17]

Capper's campaign speech was emblematic of a larger social phenomenon
impacting rural Kansas—the Country Life Movement. The rapid decrease of
the farm population and the diminished importance of rural society were
troubling to many Kansans.[18] One of the goals of the movement was to keep
rural youths from fleeing to the cities. Thus, comparisons were often made
between the "wholesome life" of agrarian America and the sinfulness and
moral laxity of urban areas. Motion pictures were a living, moving example of
the squalor and pestilence that Capper and rural Kansans were trying to
guard themselves against. Capper made similar speeches all over the state and
obviously touched a nerve; in November he won the governorship.

A third rationale for motion picture censorship was the priority that
Kansas Progressives gave to the proper raising and care of children. Kansans
were dedicated to providing a good public education for their youngsters.
During this era of scientific management and the cult of efficiency, money
and manpower were directed toward the effective management of educational resources in the state.[19] This also meant efficiently eliminating what
they deemed to be noxious forms of detrimental influence—"obscene," "indecent," or "corrupting" motion pictures.

This sentiment was closely correlated with the fourth reason: an unequivocal Kansan concern over maintaining morality. When William Allen White
contemplated "spiritual growth in the hearts of the American people,"

17. Capper, speech to Idana Farmers' Picnic, June 11, 1914, Box 46, "Speeches, 1911–1914," Capper Papers, KSHS.
18. William L. Bowers, *The Country Life Movement in America, 1900–1920*, 15.
19. Miner, *Kansas*, 205.

Kansans could leap to the conclusion that debasing forms of popular entertainment must be controlled and kept from the eyes of young people.
Kansans viewed themselves as morally superior to the corrupting influences
of the East. Henry May argues, "In the Midwest, morality was linked to
progress even more closely than elsewhere." Kansans considered their state to
be puritan and moral. The nineteenth-century attitude toward sexuality and
social mores was sacred to the overwhelming majority of Kansan citizens. In
a 1914 speech, Arthur Capper argued, "We are at last beginning to understand that as much expert knowledge is required for cleansing the morals of a
city as from cleaning of its streets or disposing of its sewage."[20] Therefore,
why not promote a board of motion picture experts—would-be censors—
who could clearly identify scenes, shots, titles, or stills in films that might be
offensive to Kansans and properly remove them?

This crusading sense of cleaning up the streets was not geared exclusively to
motion picture exhibition. Both Wichita and Emporia launched vice crusades
in the 1910s to eradicate prostitution, drug abuse, and female cigarette smoking from their communities. In late 1913, an Emporia movie house, the Star
Theater, was prevented from continuing vaudeville performances due to an
injunction by the county attorney. Congregational and Presbyterian ministers,
educators, and the City Federation of Women's Clubs had gotten on the bandwagon and petitioned municipal authorities to investigate the show. The city
superintendent of education agreed that the production would "corrupt the
morals of young people, who composed 90 percent of the audience. The whole
performance was abnormal in the life of Emporia. It might pass in Chicago,
but not in Emporia." This educator's remarks crystallized the sentiments that
would lead to acceptance of motion picture censorship. First, entertainment
could be morally corrupting. Second, motion pictures must be controlled since
children often made up the majority of the audience. Third, standards that
might prevail in the East or in big cities were often not acceptable in the "pure"
state of Kansas. Carl Becker quotes E. H. Abbott in his "Kansas" essay: "It is
the quality of piety in Kansas, to thank God that you are not as other men are,
beer-drinkers, shiftless, habitual lynchers or even as those Missourians."[21]

This interference on the part of state or city government in determining
what was "moral" or "immoral" for Kansans was readily accepted by many

---

20. Henry Farnham May, *The End of American Innocence*, 92; Capper, speech at National Purity
Conference, November 8, 1914, Box 46, Capper Papers, KSHS.
21. Griffith, *Hometown News*, 197; Becker, "Kansas," in *Everyman His Own Historian*, 25.

Progressive reformers. Arthur Capper believed that the state government must be proactive in protecting the physical and moral health of its citizens. In 1915, Capper argued, "It is the part of the good citizen not only to protect his own health, but to do everything possible to protect the health of his community. And it is the business of the state to see that the individual does this. . . . It is the idea of society protecting against the ignorance, the carelessness, the indifference of the individual."[22]

The final impetus behind film censorship in the state was another Kansas phenomenon: the prohibition of alcohol. Kansas was synonymous with the temperance movement. It was the first state in the Union to add a prohibition amendment to its constitution. Theoretically, Kansas was a dry state in the late nineteenth century, but enforcement problems kept the state "wet" in many communities. Carrie Nation's smashing of bars at the turn of the century highlighted this gaping hole. Prohibition was one of the unique features of the early-twentieth-century reform movement that divided Progressives nationally. Some saw the consumption of alcohol as an individual choice, while others saw it as a slippery slope toward hell. Kansas Progressives largely supported the temperance and prohibition movements and strongly believed in using state, municipal, and law enforcement authorities in eliminating the evil drink from the state. By 1910, Progressives had been successful in getting law enforcement to crack down on alcohol production and consumption, even in urban areas such as Kansas City and Wichita that were reluctant to give up the drink.

The support for prohibition in the state was threatened by the growing popularity of the motion picture. Many early silent films took place in saloons, bars, and cabarets. Many of the individuals who consumed alcohol in films were sophisticated, witty, beautiful, handsome, heroic, or cunning. These were attractive qualities that temperance supporters were afraid youngsters would associate with the consumption of alcohol. If children, let alone adults, were not able to go into a bar or saloon in Kansas, why should they be allowed to view such despicable locations in the movies? Drunkenness was also a common device used in slapstick and other forms of early comedic films. It was not linked to alcoholism and the many social problems that were created when one member of the family became addicted to the "devil's drink." Therefore, this association of drunkenness with humor was offensive in the minds of many prohibition supporters, and they believed it must be stricken from films that were exhibited in the state.

22. Capper, speech at Sanitation Day, Fredonia, October 3, 1914, Box 47, Capper Papers, KSHS.

Motion picture censorship was not the initial issue that drew the attention of Kansas politicians to the new phenomenon of motion pictures in the state, though. The enforcement of blue laws, which closed businesses including film theaters, was. Blue laws, which forced most businesses in the state to close on Sundays, were first passed while Kansas was still a territory. The enforcement of such provisions, which operated on both a municipal and a state level, was sporadic. It often depended on the moral constitution of politicians in office. In 1908, Topeka experienced the first citywide crackdown on all Sunday business activity. The only enterprises not closed were the city's theaters and shoe-shine stands. The mayor, acting through the city attorney, did not close theaters because a case was pending before the Shawnee County District Court considering the matter. The case made its way to the Kansas Supreme Court, which declared that the closing of film theaters was binding under present state blue laws. Most cities in Kansas ignored this judicial decision, though, and passed ordinances allowing nickelodeons to stay open on Sundays. The two outstanding exceptions were the cities of Wichita and Topeka.[23]

On April 28, 1911, Mayor J. B. Billard of Topeka proposed a revision to the Sunday blue laws. He asked the city council to allow all "decent" places of amusement to open on Sundays. Billard's decision had a social and economic rationale. He believed that this would give working people entertainment on their day off. Billard argued, "Sunday is the only chance to take their families to the theaters and the harmless places of amusement. People who can afford carriages and motor cars are not tied down in this matter." He also believed it would encourage travelers and Kansans in nearby communities to come to the city on Sundays and spend money.[24] On May 1 the mayor and two other commissioners, H. P. Miller and E. B. Stotts, combined their votes to pass the ordinance by a vote of three to two. Commissioner Stotts claimed that at least 80 percent of his supporters wanted the theaters to be open on Sundays. Stotts and Billard's critics claimed that theater owners had supported them in their campaigns financially and now the politicians were paying off their supporters. Members of the Woman's Christian Temperance Union (WCTU) came to the May 1 meeting of the city council only to discover the vote had already taken place. They were angry that they were not able to express their views in maintaining strict blue-law standards. The new ordinance said that

23. Felder, "Sunday Movies in Kansas," 15, 21, 20.
24. "To Open Theaters," *Topeka State Journal,* April 28, 1911, 1.

blue laws did not "apply to people managing, supervising or selling tickets or employed with theatrical houses or companies, moving picture shows, baseball games and other innocent amusements."[25]

On April 29, 1912, Attorney General John Shaw Dawson, acting on the part of the state, said that theaters in Topeka would not open, ordinance or no ordinance. Mayor Billard, in a heated response, asked why Dawson did not want to shut down Sunday ball games. Dawson replied on May 1 that according to a 1908 Kansas Supreme Court decision, the operation of Sunday theaters was illegal but the playing of baseball games was not. Billard questioned this logic and asked why it was legal to sell tickets to Sunday baseball games and not to film shows if the morality of the legislation was truly about not performing "labor" on Sundays.[26]

The talk of opening film theaters in Topeka on Sundays quickly ended when, on May 4, the attorney general sent a telegram to the county attorneys and sheriffs of Wyandotte, Leavenworth, Atchison, Crawford, Cherokee, and Montgomery Counties explaining that they were to "notify all theater owners and managers in your county to close on Sunday and remain closed on account of the violations of the Sunday labor law. If managers offer to fight, make the arrests at the proper time. Theaters will be closed on Sunday."[27]

The attorney general realized the uncertain danger of city ordinances that overrode state laws and judicial review. He asked, "Supposing the city commissioners should repeal the ordinance regarding the sale of liquor. Would that give the jointists and bootleggers the right to begin doing business in Topeka? Not for a minute. Neither does the repeal of the theater ordinance give the theatrical men any rights they did not have."[28] What had begun as a local matter in Topeka now impacted the rest of the state. The attorney general could not close theaters in the state capital on Sundays and allow them to continue to operate in Leavenworth, Atchison, and Kansas City. Theater owners who lived close to the Missouri border argued that they may have to close up because they would lose so much business to their eastern neighbors in Missouri who could stay open on Sundays.

Several theater owners decided to test the attorney general's decision. The first case to go to court involved Frank E. Feist, Hattie Feist, and Minerva

25. Felder, "Sunday Movies in Kansas," 23.

26. "State Says No," *Topeka State Journal*, April 29, 1911, 1; "Dawson to Billard," *Topeka State Journal*, May 1, 1911, 1; "Mayor to Dawson," *Topeka State Journal*, May 2, 1911, 1.

27. Felder, "Sunday Movies in Kansas," 24.

28. "Dawson Won't Allow Theaters on Sunday," *Topeka Daily Capital*, April 30, 1911, 19.

Chatburn. They were accused of operating the Electric Theater in Atchison on a Sunday. Atchison theaters took huge losses with the enforcement of the blue laws because Sunday-evening shows brought in more money than any other evening. Being directly across the Missouri border, avid moviegoers could simply cross the state line to see their favorite film stars. The three defendants were found not guilty by a jury in June 1911. One of the jurors said he based his decision on the fact that moving picture shows had become a necessity and, therefore, were permissible. The juror claimed, "People demand amusement and recreation."[29] Obviously, the average Atchisonian considered access to motion pictures on Sunday a right.

Another test case took place in Pittsburg. Violence erupted in the city when theaters were closed on Sunday. Frank H. Bailey opened his motion picture theater on June 7, 1911, to test the attorney general's decision. He was arrested, and other theater owners and filmgoers collected funds for his defense. After a two-hour hearing, a twelve-man jury found him not guilty, and the courtroom burst into applause and cheering that lasted for ten minutes. The next Sunday, all film theaters in Pittsburg were open and operating.[30]

Over the next few years, the enormous popularity of movies in Kansas and the failure of law-enforcement officers to enforce the state blue laws made the attorney general's decision almost meaningless. Historian Robert Sherman La Forte claims that "only the popularity of baseball and other entertainment saved Kansans from stringent blue laws."[31] By 1913, the only town or city in Kansas that was not screening Sunday movies was Topeka.

By 1913, the year that the Kansas legislature passed the initial censorship legislation, motion pictures had become big business and permeated the social fabric of the state. In Topeka, one could watch *Bronco Billy and the Rustler's Child* at the Aurora Theater or see a number of Civil War–related films. The fiftieth anniversary of the war made it a significant and popular genre of film in the era 1913–1915. One could watch *The Sinews of War,* a two-reeler about the siege and fall of Richmond at the Best Theater, or *The Battle of Bloody Ford* at the Aurora.

Civil War films were also popular in small towns like Clifton. The March 28, 1913, *Clifton News* ran the following advertisement for the Electric Theater:

29. Felder, "Sunday Movies in Kansas," 20.
30. *Topeka Daily Capital,* June 21, 1911, 5.
31. La Forte, *Leaders of Reform,* 202.

To-Night
March 27th

on our program we have one of the best lessons for boys and young men
ever written either in words or pictures. See the price Harry Meyers paid
for his re-formation. We want every boy to see this. He learned his lesson but what a price. This picture has been featured all over the country
in Sunday lessons for boys and young men.

Program
The Derelicts Return
(synopsis above)

The Soldier Brothers of Susannah
(A Civil War drama full of interesting situations)

An Aeroplane Love Affair
(Good comedy. Geo. Beatty's aeroplane is used and makes some interesting flights).

Remember we are running every night now with Three new pictures
each night. Our Matinee at 2:30 each Saturday is a feature for the farmers and others who can't attend our night shows. We give you the best
programs we can get. Come once and you will keep coming.[32]

Morality tales, Civil War adventures, and airplane dramas were not all that
Kansans were seeing on the screen. The *Topeka Daily Capital*, in its March 5,
1913, edition, advertised a lecture by Captain Roald Amundsen, South Pole
explorer. Moving pictures and colored slides accompanied the famed adven-
turer's program.[33] It is estimated that, by 1913, more than five hundred movie
theaters or nickelodeons existed in Kansas. Motion pictures had become
enormously influential in the state socially, economically, and culturally.
Many reformers believed the unrestrained influence of this medium had to be
controlled.

By 1912–1913, Progressive reformers had organized their forces and persuaded the Kansas legislature to establish official motion picture censorship
in the state. In 1912, George H. Hodges narrowly beat Arthur Capper for
governor of Kansas. The Democrat, riding the coattails of Woodrow Wilson
to victory, was aided by the fact that his party gained a majority in both the

32. Advertisement for Electric Theater, *Clifton News*, March 28, 1913.
33. *Topeka Daily Capital*, March 5, 1913, 12.

state senate and the state house of representatives. The election of Hodges was not an end to Progressivism in the state. Progressive Democrats combined with Progressive Republicans to continue the reform tradition in Kansas, and significant changes were made in the operation and administration of the state government. In the 1912 election, Kansans gave women the right to vote. Hodges, in his term as governor, asked for and received a better child labor law, legislation for better schools, stronger business regulation, and judicial reform. The Progressive legacy continued.

Near the end of the legislative term in March 1913, Senate Bill 367 was considered by the legislature. This bill, if passed, would create a board of motion picture censorship in the state. Frustrated film exhibitors began sending letters and telegrams to Hodges, asking him to veto the measure. Several members of the Wichita Business Association telegrammed Hodges, "We join the Kansas Branch of the Motion Picture Exhibitors League of America in protesting Senate Bill three hundred sixty seven." J. N. Keith of Coffeyville telegrammed the governor, "[The proposal] is unjust and indefensible. Do not think it right in any event—the motion picture is the poor man's show and should be displayed without conclusive reason."[34]

A great deal of protest against the proposed bill was due to the exhibitors' misunderstanding of the censorship fee arrangement. Many theater owners read the pending bill to mean that every single exhibitor would have to pay two dollars for each reel that they showed in their theaters. This would be so economically devastating to exhibitors that censoring fees would often be higher than their gross take. C. H. Jones, the mayor of Galena and head of the Galena Commercial Club, telegrammed Hodges that if the bill passed, his theater would have to close. E. Wayne Martin, owner of the Pearl and Elite Theaters in Hutchinson, called the proposal "drastic action." W. B. Moore, manager of the Midway Theater in Galena, explained that it would cause exhibitors in small towns to go out of business. Hodges's secretary did have the time to write one concerned theater owner. He explained to Mr. I. C. Rush of Clifton on April 6, 1913, "My dear sir—will say that I think you have a mistaken idea in regard to the film tax. My understanding is that the tax is placed upon the film and then when it is passed the makers are privileged to make as many reels as they desire, so if the same picture is shown in hundreds of theaters in the state,

---

34. Telegram from Hadley, Cooper, Neal, and Wilson to Governor George Hodges, March 8, 1913; telegram from J. N. Keith to Hodges, March 11, 1913, both in Box 11, File 3, "Movies," Hodges Papers, 1913–1915, KSHS.

there is but one tax paid and not a tax for each picture." The threat of censorship was a primary motivating force for significant organizational efforts by the industry in the state. A preliminary meeting of Kansas motion picture exhibitors was held in Kansas City, Missouri, on November 7, 1912. A representative gathering of exhibitors assembled at the Electric Theater in Kansas City, Kansas, the next day to form the Kansas Exhibitors State League.[35]

Kansas legislators seemed unconcerned that they (along with Pennsylvania legislators) were setting national precedent with a state motion picture censorship bill. Carl Becker quotes a state legislator in his "Kansas" essay: "In Kansas, we don't care much what other states are doing. Kansas always leads, but never follows." Becker then claims that this "disregard of precedent" was an "article of faith." The historian theorizes that Kansans had a high regard for their ability to endure on the frontier, and after conquering nature, they were ready to harness human nature. He argues, "Kansans set their own standards, and the state becomes, as it were, an experiment station in the field of social science."[36] The Kansas legislature was willing, therefore, to use science, efficiency, and "superior" Kansas morality to control the new medium of motion pictures.

On March 13, 1913, the last day of the legislative session, Senate Bill 367 was passed and signed by the governor. A detailed analysis of this legislation is necessary in order to understand the motivations behind the procensorship forces and the strategies they sought to employ to battle the negative influence of motion pictures.

The bill was to take effect on April 1, 1913, only a few weeks after it passed. The rush to censorship implies two critical factors in this movement. First, the problem was considered serious enough that it was believed the state should take immediate action. Second, the implication was that this task would be easy, when in reality, many parts of it had not been well thought out. This rush to legislate, without considering the economic or social implications of motion picture censorship, would prove to be a consistent theme throughout the 1910s.

Control over the censorship process was given to the state superintendent of public instruction. This correlates with the Progressive obsession over the

---

35. Telegram from C. H. Jones to Hodges, March 11, 1913; telegram from E. Wayne Martin to Hodges, March 11, 1913; telegram from W. B. Moore to Hodges, March 11, 1913; letter to I. C. Rush from the personal secretary of Hodges, April 6, 1913, all in ibid.; "Kansas Exhibitors State League," *Moving Picture World*, July 12, 1913.

36. Becker, "Kansas," in *Everyman His Own Historian*, 27.

educational and moral development of children; it only made sense to delegate this responsibility to the top educator in the state. This delegation of authority contrasted with the system in Pennsylvania, the only other state to have a censorship board at the time. Pennsylvania's censorship board was independent and had no relationship with the state's education department. The legislation in Kansas deemed that it "shall be [the state superintendent of public instruction's] duty to examine all moving picture films or reels intended for exhibition in this state, and approve such as he shall find to be moral and instructive, and to withhold his approval from such as tend to debase or corrupt the morals."[37] This gave an enormous amount of power to the superintendent of education. He was given the sole prerogative to determine what was "moral," "instructive," "debasing," or "corrupt." It also created an entirely unrealistic workload for the superintendent. How was he supposed to carry out all of his normal duties—which were enormous in this period due to the expansion of secondary and higher education—and examine each and every motion picture film and reel that was to be exhibited in the state? Although there was a provision in the legislation that allowed him to hire "one or more additional clerks in his office as may be necessary," this was to be done only "for good and sufficient reasons" and only if it could be proved to the governor that he needed the help. This was an example of the phenomenon of rushing to legislate without really considering the implications. Kansas Progressives often suffered from this fate. If the superintendent was going to hire clerks, the legislation was not clear as to exactly what their responsibilities would be. Would they simply publish the findings of the superintendent? Or would they possibly do some of the censoring? What would be the implications of having a low-level, perhaps semieducated clerk determine the morality of entertainment for more than one million Kansans? These were questions that were not answered by the details of the bill.

After the superintendent examined and approved each film, there was to be a stamped, written certification by him demonstrating that the film had been approved. The date of the examination and approval was to be written on this document. The superintendent was to keep an accurate and thorough list of each film approved and disapproved. For those reels not approved, he was responsible for briefly stating the reasons the film was not allowed in the state.[38]

---

37. Senate Bill 367 found in *Kansas State Boards and Institutions*, chap. 294, p. 504.
38. Ibid.

Motion picture censorship was also a moneymaking scheme on the part of the state government. It may not have been deliberately designed to serve this function, but in the first year of censorship, that would prove to be the outcome. All distribution companies were responsible for paying two dollars for each moving picture film or reel examined by the superintendent. This wording alone demonstrates the legislators' unfamiliarity with the exhibition process. In the early years of cinema, 1897–1903, most films were one reel in length. This was not the case in 1913, as story-films had taken over the market. The question became, was this two dollars per film or two dollars per reel that was to be paid to the state superintendent? Two dollars per reel was not an insignificant amount of money for film distributors, and this was thought to be deliberately punitive by the industry. The legislation clearly stated, "No picture, film or reel shall be examined until such fee shall have been paid to [the superintendent of instruction]."[39] Therefore, it became illegal to exhibit any motion picture that had not been approved by the superintendent of instruction or if the fee for such an examination had not been paid to the state. If a theater owner was found guilty of exhibiting an unapproved film, he was guilty of a misdemeanor and fined between twenty-five and one hundred dollars. He could be charged this amount for each unapproved reel or film, meaning that an exhibitor who decided to avoid the censorship process could literally be fined out of business. Each unapproved moving picture reel or film was considered a separate offense. Each day the unapproved film was exhibited was also considered a separate offense. The reformers were dead serious about cracking down on theater owners who exhibited offensive material. They were ready to hit them where it counted—in the wallet.

Submitting all films for inspection and paying censorship fees were not the only responsibilities of the industry. Every moving picture distributor and producer was required to provide a description of the film or reel that they wanted exhibited in the state to the state superintendent of instruction. Within this description they were to "describe the scenes and purposes of any film or reel." In this period of film history, it was common for the major film distributors to publish catalogs of all films they had readily available for distribution. Copies of this material were to be turned over to the superintendent. This, perhaps, would have been an easy way to spot those films (scandalous dances, violent slapstick, executions, salacious nudity) that were advertised with more prurient interests in mind.

39. Ibid.

Section 5 of the legislation gave the superintendent the general power and authority to supervise and regulate the exhibition of moving pictures in all places of amusement in the state. By 1913, motion picture theaters were replacing storefront theaters or nickelodeons in major urban areas such as Kansas City, Topeka, and Wichita, although films were still shown in various types of venues throughout the state. Therefore, for the superintendent to be thorough in his job, it was necessary for him to be able to "investigate" all locations where films were displayed.

Section 5 also attempted to give the superintendent hazy guidelines on what to censor out of films. The legislation, taken almost verbatim from Pennsylvania's censorship law passed in 1911, states that the superintendent should "disapprove such moving-picture films or reels as are sacrilegious, obscene, indecent or immoral, or such as tend to corrupt the morals." The wording of this legislation would give him the power to censor images, words, and scenarios.

The superintendent was not the final authority, though. Section 5 included an appeal process. It set up a "commission" consisting of the governor, attorney, and secretary of state. Any moving picture or film corporation that wanted to challenge a decision by the superintendent could bring the case to this board. If a majority on this commission ruled in favor of the film, then the superintendent would have to accept the findings.

The passage of this 1913 legislation would seem to begin the censorship process in the state. But this was not to be the case. Motion picture censorship was not given financial support at the time, making the inspection of films in the state virtually impossible. The rationale behind this is not exactly clear. It could have been resistance to the board by some members of the legislature, or, more likely, the board was not activated until a crucial Supreme Court decision regarding the constitutionality of motion picture censorship in the nation, be it municipal, state, or federal. From April 1913 until April 1915, no film censorship occurred in the state of Kansas.

The motion picture industry began a long, arduous campaign against film censorship throughout the nation in this two-year interval. The goal was to ensure that the United States Supreme Court would rule against the constitutionality of it. The industry objected to censorship on a number of grounds. First, representatives claimed that film censorship violated the First Amendment of the Constitution that guaranteed freedom of speech. Writers and authors across the land saw the threat of movie censorship and believed that it might lead to further censorship in other artistic media. They maintained that obscenity laws on the books already covered any necessary censorship. Second, industrial leaders argued that no prior censorship standards had been established. This would lead to an inconsistency in determining what content was considered to be unfit in films. Journalist W. P. Lawson argued that "producers will learn nothing from the moral judgments of the censors, nor will they be able to accommodate their future plans to those judgments. But it is admitted that film censorship cannot be reduced to detailed and unchangeable prohibitions. It encounters many problems which are still obscure and incapable of exact definition and regulation."[40] This form of argument began in the mid-1910s when motion picture censorship was just getting off the ground. Studio executives insisted that they could police themselves. Third, the industry maintained that censorship was a costly process. Censorship fees had to be paid to individual state boards. If scenes or even an entire film was condemned by a state, thousands of dollars of production costs would be wasted. Censorship would lead to higher admission costs for fans and less profit for the film companies.

On February 23, 1915, a critical Supreme Court decision had a far-reaching impact on the moving picture industry and film censorship in Kansas. Three separate cases, combined into one case, sustained statutes in Ohio and Kansas that had legalized governmental censorship of motion pictures prior to their exhibition. These cases were *Mutual Film Corporation v. Industrial Commission of Ohio, Mutual Film Corporation v. Industrial Commission of Ohio*, and *Mutual Film Corporation of Missouri v. Hodges, Governor of the State of Kansas*.[41] Collectively, these cases became known as the *Mutual Film* decision.

The case began when the Mutual Film Corporation, a major film distribution company, filed suit against the States of Ohio and Kansas, claiming that prior censorship of films was unconstitutional. Mutual Film based its case against the Kansas statute on three grounds: moving picture censorship imposed an unnecessary economic burden on interstate commerce; the statute was an invalid delegation of legislative power to the Board of Censorship because it failed to set up exact standards by which films were to be approved or rejected, and, therefore, the censor's personal tastes would become the law; and the statutes violated the free-speech guarantees in the federal and state constitutions by censoring films prior to their exhibition.[42]

---

40. W. P. Lawson, "Standards of Censorship," 63.
41. Gilbert H. Montague, "Censorship of Motion Pictures before the Supreme Court," 82–83.
42. Randall, *Censorship of the Movies*, 21.

In a monumental decision, the Supreme Court ruled unanimously against the Mutual Film Corporation. Justice Joseph McKenna, who wrote the majority decision for the Court, contended that the company's complaints about interstate commerce and the delegation of legislative power were invalid. The Court determined that motion pictures were not protected under the First Amendment's guarantee of free speech. McKenna explained: "The exhibition of motion pictures is a business, pure and simple, originated and conducted for profit . . . not to be regarded nor intended to be regarded by the Constitution, we think, as part of the press of this country or as organs of public opinions. They are mere representations of events, of ideas and sentiments, published or known—vivid, unusual and entertainment no doubt, but capable of evil, having power for it, the greater because of their attractiveness and matter of exhibition." With the *Mutual Film* decision, the Supreme Court declared that film censorship was constitutional.

The Supreme Court's suppositions about films had several far-reaching consequences. First, the Court held that movies were a "business, pure and simple," conducted solely for the financial gain of the industry. Since the motion picture industry was a business, it could be regulated, as had the railroad, meatpacking, and other industries. Another important supposition of the Court was that movies were powerful instruments in shaping opinion, and if controlled by evil, unscrupulous, money-hungry individuals, great damage could occur to society. McKenna commented, "Other states have considered it to be in the interest of the public morals and welfare to supervise moving picture exhibitions. We would have to shut our eyes to the facts of the world to regard the precaution unreasonable as the legislation to effect it a mere wanton interference with personal liberty."

This "capacity for evil" of the burgeoning motion picture industry seemed to have had a powerful influence on the rationale behind the Court's decision. As the Court saw it, the movies' power for evil outweighed all other considerations. The Court did not view the motion picture in the same realm as the spoken or written word. Instead, the Court compared films to the "theater, the circus, and all other shows and spectacles." Thus, the Court did not feel that the makers of motion pictures had the same First Amendment rights as had authors of books or speeches.

The *Mutual Film* decision's immediate effect was the firm establishment of film censorship in the states of Ohio, Pennsylvania, and Kansas. These states now had the approval of the highest court in the land. The moving picture industry now had no choice but to fight state and local censorship. The industry paper *Motion Picture News* warned, "The time has come for immediate action against the legalized censorship of motion pictures. The necessity for such action has long been evident, but the crisis is now here! . . . [N]ew bills are pending in eight states, and unless their passage is adequately controlled they will almost certainly become laws within three weeks."[43]

There were major consequences that came out of the *Mutual Film* decision. The judgments in these three cases settled any questions about moving picture censorship in the United States for the next thirty-seven years. During this time, it was accepted by all lower courts that film censorship was constitutional. Not until another Supreme Court decision, *Joseph Burstyn, Inc. v. Wilson, Commissioner of Education of New York, et al.* (1952), did the constitutionality of film censorship begin to erode.

There was a widespread national reaction to the *Mutual Film* decision. Those individuals who applauded the Supreme Court decision were Progressive reformers and conservative citizens who supported motion picture censorship. These individuals believed that the industry was becoming too powerful, too unwieldy and influential, and should be controlled. Advocates of censorship believed that previous pledges of reform by the film industry had not been honored and that a legal authority to eliminate harmful features was absolutely necessary. A columnist in the *Nation* wrote, "The truth is that this new means for public amusement and education has brought with it grave perils which we are not only just beginning to realize." Many Progressive reformers believed that motion pictures were like a cancer on society and that film censorship would help cure the disease. In *Drama* magazine, Thomas Dickinson announced, "Censorship under a democracy is an aid to education and prepares the young for citizenship."[44] Censorship was seen not as an infringement on First Amendment rights but as a safeguard for society from undesirable thoughts or actions.

Those who opposed the *Mutual Film* decision included members of the industry, citizens who believed the right of freedom of speech contained in the First Amendment was being obstructed, and ordinary people who did not want their movies tampered with. An editorial in the journal the *Independent* noted: "The motion picture is both journalism and drama, already the most popular form of the latter and likely to become of equal importance in the former field. To hamper this art in its infancy by shackles from which the older

43. "Three Weeks Left for Action," *Motion Picture News*, March 6, 1915, 29.
44. "The Regulation of Films," 487; "The Theory and Practice of Censorship," 248–61.

arts of representation have with difficulty, freed themselves, is to do untold harm to its future development." Prior to the *Mutual Film* decision, John Collier, one of the founders of the National Board of Censorship, argued in *Survey* that "the continuance and future extensions of censorship in the United States depend upon the American public. Manifold influences are at work for these extensions. They have concentrated on motion pictures for the moment because they are ubiquitous, disturbingly potent and new."[45] The *Mutual Film* decision was of great interest to individuals working in journalism and in artistic fields who worried that their own forms of expression might be more firmly censored. Early film critics and intellectuals realized the potential of the cinematic medium and realized that with this Supreme Court decision, the artistic progress of the motion picture might be brought to a halt.

John Collier realized the potential dangers of the *Mutual Film* decision. In *Survey,* he observed, "In sustaining the Ohio and Kansas laws, the Supreme Court broadly denied to motion pictures and by favorable if not absolute implication to theaters in general, the constitutional protection [of freedom of speech and of the written word]. The decision is unequivocal, far reaching. It may prove to have opened the way for extensions of censorship broader even than of the field of the theater."[46]

The motion picture press roundly denounced the Supreme Court decision. In Chicago, the *Exhibitor's Herald* proclaimed that "the public does not want censorship." *Motion Picture News* quoted anticensorship editorials from seventeen states. Among these were the *Exhibitor's Trade Review* that called on exhibitors to "influence public opinion through the screen and in every possible way for the overthrow of censorship." Even the nonindustry press joined in the fight against censorship. The *New York Evening Mail* pointed out that "the man who exhibits an immoral picture can be hauled before the judge and punished." "What," the author asked, "would censorship accomplish that can not be accomplished now?" The *New York Morning Telegraph* claimed that the establishment of motion picture censorship impeached the good faith of producers who "have pledged themselves to cooperate with the authorities in driving out undesirables."[47]

The *Mutual Film* decision was a signal for municipalities and states to implement motion picture censorship in their own jurisdictions. The Supreme

45. "No Censorship," 432; John Collier, "The Learned Judges and the Films."
46. Collier, "Learned Judges and Films."
47. "The Nationwide Battle over Movie Purification," 32–33. This article summarizes industrial response to the *Mutual Film* decision.

Court's decision was consistent with the view that local communities had the right to control live stage performances and vaudeville shows. In a letter to Emporia, Kansas, resident Juliet King, newly elected governor Arthur Capper expressed the belief that "a picture that is so common-place in New York as to cause no comment, nor to be questioned by the national board of censors, may cause indignation in Kansas, where we live in a different environment."[48] This remark by Capper demonstrates the eventual failure of the National Board of Censorship (which in 1915 changed its name to the National Board of Review) to stem the tide of objectionable films. In Capper's view, different standards of morality existed in the heartland and the big city.

Governor Arthur Capper played a prominent, if not the most important, role in the development of motion picture censorship in the state. Capper came to prominence in the state as a newspaperman. In 1901, he gained majority ownership of the *Topeka Daily Capital,* one of the most important dailies in Kansas. By 1910, he had created a multistate farm-paper syndicate, greatly enhancing his wealth and influence. Without the background of years of elective service, Capper was nominated for governor in the Republican Party primary in 1912. He gained 70 percent of the vote against his opponent, demonstrating his popularity. In November, he lost in the general election to Democratic candidate George Hodges in the closest gubernatorial contest in Kansas history. His loss was partially attributable to the split between the regular Republicans, headed by President William Howard Taft, and the Bull Moose Republicans, led by Theodore Roosevelt. In 1914, Hodges and Capper squared off again, but in this election, women were allowed to vote for the first time in Kansas history. Capper said he had the "honor of being the first native elected governor and the first elected at the time when intelligent women had something to say about who would be governor."[49] He began his first term of office with the unusual distinction of having the state senate in the hands of the Democratic Party. He served as governor during the censorship board's first four years of operation, and he continued to exert political influence on motion picture censorship when he was elected to the U.S. Senate in 1918.

When Capper was inaugurated in January 1915, he pushed for reforms that showed the "Progressive forward looking spirit of the Kansas people." Typical of early-twentieth-century Progressives, Capper believed in using

48. Capper to Juliet King, August 4, 1916, Box 8, File 176, Capper Papers, KSHS.
49. Socolofsky, *Arthur Capper,* 86.

government to help protect the general public. In his inaugural address, he prophesied that the next two years (1915–1916) would show Kansas making a "slow but sure advance in human progress, for loftier ideals, for a wider and deeper justice, for a quickened sense of public honor and public duty, towards making our beloved state a little more decent, happier and a more God-like place to live." During his first year of office, he sponsored important reforms such as the creation of a state civil service commission, pensions for widows with dependent children, and an improved educational system. He also pushed for radical changes in the administrative affairs of the state. In a speech to the Lyons Republicans in the summer of 1914, while he was campaigning for office, Capper stated, "I am proud to support the present-day program which places humanity above the dollar, which inaugurates those *vitally constructive* measures, social, moral, educational and economic; that are destined to lift all humanity to a higher level."[50]

Capper believed that movies needed regulation by the state. Like other Progressives, his principal concern was Kansas children. In 1914, he stated, "The boys and girls on the farm, need so badly, the wholesome kind of social life." He was determined to enforce motion picture censorship in the state. He claimed, "As long as certain classes of moving picture houses, disreputable poolrooms and other amusement enterprises cater to depraved taste, as long as immoral books and suggestive songs are within the reach of our high school pupils," the state would obviously be corruptible.[51]

Capper used his ownership of the *Topeka Daily Capital,* one of the most influential newspapers in the state, to push for movie censorship. The other leading paper in Topeka was the *Topeka State Journal.* The *Journal,* which was also widely circulated across the state, took a more negative view of film censorship. On February 24, 1915, both papers reported on the *Mutual Film* decision. The *Daily Capital* ran the headline "Holds Kansas Law Censoring Movies Is Constitutional." The newspaper reported to its readers that the Ohio and Kansas moving picture censorship laws were held up as constitutional by the Supreme Court. The Kansas and Ohio laws were practically identical except for matters of overall authority. The Kansas statute conferred this authority upon the state superintendent of education, whereas

50. Capper, first inaugural address, January 11, 1915, Box 47, "Speeches, 1914–1916," Capper Papers, KSHS; Capper, speech to the Lyons Republicans, June 6, 1914, Box 46, "Speeches, 1911–1914," p. 23, Capper Papers, KSHS.

51. Capper, speech to the Idana Farmers' Picnic, p. 5; Capper, speech to the Colored ME Church, Lawrence, June 14, 1914, Box 46, "Speeches, 1911–1914," p. 7, Capper Papers, KSHS.

the Ohio law had a board of censors that acted under the Industrial Commission of the state.[52]

John Dawson, justice of the supreme court of Kansas, promptly sent a letter to Charles Sessions, secretary to Governor Capper. This letter was a direct response to the *Mutual Film* decision. Dawson wrote, "I think it only proper that I should remind you and the Governor that this will call for a specific appropriation of the inspection fees to carry into effect the purposes of the act." The 1913 legislation had not addressed how the Kansas Board of Censorship would be funded. Dawson explained that the problem with the previous legislation was that the inspection fees were to be paid out of the general revenue fund, and no appropriation, except a nominal one of one thousand dollars in the miscellaneous appropriations act, was made to administer the law.[53] This was problematic because Dawson realized that the superintendent of public instruction was responsible for the Board of Censorship and would obviously have to hire a staff to help him. This issue was not addressed. Dawson was particularly worried since the legislative session was coming to a close, and he realized that unless the Ways and Means Committee of the state legislature promptly acted, the bill might be delayed for a year.

Throughout the month of February, even before the *Mutual Film* decision, the legislature dealt with the issue of how to pay for the Board of Censorship. There was considerable discussion on how to fund the censorship process. One suggestion would impose a tax of three hundred dollars a year on every moving picture establishment. *Moving Picture World* reported that this tax would wipe out 90 percent of the movie houses in the state. A letter from H. P. Troth of Valley Falls, Kansas, to Governor Capper illustrated motion picture theater owners' fear that film censorship might put them out of business. I have chosen to run this letter in its entirety because it illustrates the fact that ordinary Kansans, not just wealthy New York film distributors, were impacted by this impending censorship.

> Sir—
> A bill has been introduced in the legislature levying a County tax of $300 on every picture show—which will if passed, put every show in small towns out of business—shutting out the entertainment the people demand—and causing a loss of a good many Thousand dollars.

52. "Holds Kansas Law Censoring Movies Is Constitutional," *Topeka Daily Capital,* February 24, 1915.

53. John Dawson to Charles Sessions, 1915, Box 3, File 236, Capper Papers, KSHS.

Surely the man that framed the bill—don't know that there is very little more than a living in the business in the small towns—once that there are times a man has to get out and do other work to keep up.

Let me tell you a little about myself.

I started this show 6 years ago took the outfit on a debt.

I found the people wanted the entertainment. So I started in to improve it at that time—the film service wasn't very good once We had to run our program throw and cut out any thing that was suggestive in it. But now it is different. The film co's are making better class of pictures and the exhibitor don't have to show anything that is the least bit out of the way—last 2 year I only had two films that I had to censor—the worst thing we have now is the vaudeville acts.

Last year I bought an old building on the installment plan. Paying by the month and by doing odd jobs, have been able to remodel it. But winter comes on and I didn't get it finished inside. I built this building over the old one—tore out the old one and never stoped the show—don't the work myself with a man to help now and then. I haven't made anything this winter—more than keeping up my payments and a living.

If this bill is passed it not only cleans me out everybody else interested in my deal. And the other exhibitors that are in the same fix.

I don't know where you stand on this bill—But believe you are a man with good sound sence and that you will do all you can to put this bill in the waste basket.

We favored you.

Favor us.

Yours.[54]

Capper had his secretary Charles Sessions write the theater owner back that week. He explained that he "does not believe he wants to see the motion picture business ruined by excessive tax" but warned Mr. Troth that since the bill was pending in the legislature, he and other theater owners should write their congressmen, protesting against such a bill.[55]

The film industry in Kansas organized in an attempt to try to defeat any censorship bill. W. B. Moore, president of the Kansas branch of the Motion Picture Exhibitor's League of America, got busy. He wired many exhibitors

54. "Kansas Legislation," *Moving Picture World,* March 20, 1915, 1792; H. P. Troth to Capper, February 15, 1915, Box 8, File 176, Capper Papers, KSHS. I purposefully did not correct any of the misspellings.
55. Sessions to Troth, February 19, 1915, Box 8, File 176, Capper Papers, KSHS.

and sent special-delivery letters to every theater owner in the state, urging them to get in touch with their representatives. He outlined a campaign to try to defeat the bill.[56]

The industry was not successful, though, because the Kansas legislature promptly passed a new bill that provided the necessary funding to implement film censorship. The bill that ended up being passed was almost identical to the 1913 piece of legislation with the exception of an important provision that provided funding for the board. The legislature decided to charge companies two dollars a reel for inspection of their films. This inspection fee would then make the Board of Censorship economically self-sufficient.

In 1913, shortly after the initial censorship legislation was passed, I. C. Rush, owner of a film theater in Clifton, wrote Governor Hodges regarding his concerns about the new legislation. Rush anticipated a number of the problems that the new censorship board would face, and he expressed the concerns of the theater operators:

> My attention has been forcibly called to the new Censorship law governing Moving Pictures as I am unfortunate enough to own the Theatre in Clifton. You can no doubt see at a glance the injustice of this law which if enforced will close every theatre in the small towns of Kansas. I know that there are some Films being shown which ought not to be but this law puts the good pictures out of business as well as the bad. I have several times turned down chances to run such subjects as "The James Boys in Missouri" and would like to see them prohibited but the new law eliminates both good and bad together.
>
> The fact that the law imposes an impossible duty on the Superintendent of Public Instruction when it presumes that he can censor 400 films per week, but goes to show that the subject was not thoroughly considered by those who passed it. It occurs to me that if we want to put those bad pictures away the law should have provided that any picture reported to the State Superintendent as being immoral or indecent should be censored and if passed by him then all right but if condemned then it should not be run again.
>
> I have run about 14,000 films since I started and I have but three that were at all out of the way. I trust some way will be found so that Moving Pictures can continue to be the poor man's entertainment as I am sure they are filling a large place in the lives of the people of the small towns

---

56. "Kansas Legislation," 1792.

where we don't have the chance of seeing first class shows. I feel that newspapers and magazines and also cheap road shows need censorship just as bad or even more so then [*sic*] the movies.[57]

Motion picture censorship may have been passed by the elected officials of the state, but they did not anticipate the multitude of problems and difficulties such an endeavor would cause. Passing censorship legislation did not make for effective censorship. The first several years of the Kansas Board of Censorship would be a period of turmoil for both supporters and enemies of the process.

57. Rush to Hodges, April 4, 1913, Correspondence File, Box 18.11, File 3, Hodges Papers, KSHS.

Three

"We Can Hardly Make Any Definite Rules"

The Difficulty of Censorship as Practice, 1915

In March 1915, the administration of Arthur Capper began making plans to make the Kansas Board of Censorship operational.[1] Wilbert Davidson Ross, superintendent of instruction from 1913 to 1919, was in charge of the management of the Kansas state censors. The Reverend Festus Foster, a Congregational pastor from Topeka, and Miss Carrie Simpson, a Paola schoolteacher, were chosen to assist Ross as the actual censors. There were no specific requirements for being a film censor in the state. One can speculate that Foster was chosen for his religious affiliation, Simpson for her educational background, and that they were both considered to be of high moral character and politically connected in some way.

By April 1915 the board was up and running. The press began to actively report on the board's activities and inform citizens of the possible repercussions of its actions. In the April 1, 1915, edition of the *Topeka Daily Capital*, Ross explained that state inspection of moving pictures would start within the next few weeks. He explained that the only problem was that the board had no

---

1. The name of the board in this period was quite fluid. In a great deal of correspondence, it is referred to as the "Kansas Board of Censors." The first official published documents call the apparatus the "Kansas State Censors."

dark room where the actual process of inspection could take place. Representatives of the film corporations spent the morning of April 2 in conference with Ross, learning about the logistics of the censorship process. The *Daily Capital* announced that the film-inspection process would begin on April 12.[2]

Several days before censorship actually began, Ross gave an interview to the *Kansas City Star*. His comments anticipated problems the board would face in its first few months of existence. Reporting that "we are pioneering on this proposition right from the start," Ross explained, "We can hardly make any definite rules as to what will be permitted and what should be removed from the moving picture." This lack of a set of definite standards on what would be prohibited and what would be allowed on Kansas motion picture screens created a twofold problem. First, motion picture companies could not anticipate what Kansas censors would remove from the screen. Second, this lack of a doctrine of established standards would make the censorship process highly arbitrary and based on personal standards. Ross explained that he would "direct [Foster and Simpson] to prohibit scenes of debauchery, actual murders, robberies or other crimes at the start." Ross also demonstrated to temperance and prohibition advocates that he was supportive of their movement. He said, "Kansas is a Prohibition state and few of her children ever see a drunken man and few ever see the inside of a barroom, even outside of the state." Ever protective of children, like all good Progressives, he explained, "It doesn't seem proper to me that children should be allowed to see scenes of debauchery in the movies that they could not see with their own eyes in Kansas." Ross's explanation that the censors would "develop a set of rules later" so that film distributors "can tell what films cannot be shown in Kansas" would indeed prove to be problematic and frustrating for film producers and exchanges (film distribution companies).[3]

When the Board of Censorship began its work on April 12, 1915, it was not given any office space. The first eight months of its existence were spent at nearby Topeka theaters. On April 12, Foster and Simpson conducted their state inspection of films at the Orpheum and Best Theaters. It was agreed that the censors would operate in this fashion until proper facilities could be found by the state. They spent their mornings viewing films and their afternoons filing reports on the films they had inspected.

2. "Ross Plans for Movie Inspection," *Topeka Daily Capital*, April 1, 1915, Clipping File, KSBR, KSHS; "Minister and Woman the Film Inspectors," *Topeka Daily Capital*, April 3, 1915.
3. "Even Movies Must Be Dry," *Kansas City Star*, April 9, 1915, Clipping File, KSBR, KSHS.

Film distributors estimated that the state received about 125 new films a week.[4] This would not have been a difficulty in 1905 when moving pictures were one to two reels in length, but by 1915 the feature film, with a two-hour running time or longer, was starting to make its mark. Ross explained that films would be reviewed by actual inspection or from printed description. Almost all films ended up being physically inspected by the censors by viewing the movies themselves, not trusting the descriptions the exchanges gave them.

On April 12, 1915, the censors began their work after being sworn in by Governor Capper. Both censors began viewing films at local movie houses. Foster spent his morning at the Best Theater watching ten films that had been sent by the Universal Company, which had an exchange based in Kansas City. These films included *Saved by a Dream, A Mixed-Up Elopement, The Streets of Make Believe, Skipper Simpson's Daughter, A Wild Irish Rose, The Old Tutor's Dream,* and *The Black Box.* After viewing the films, Foster commented, "There was not anything that was questionable in the pictures I saw."[5]

In examining motion pictures, censors had three options to choose from when deciding upon the appropriateness of a particular film. First, the film could be accepted as it was. Second, the film could be accepted after the removal of certain scenes or titles (approximately 5 percent to 10 percent of all films in Kansas were dealt with this way). Third, the film could be rejected in its entirety and banned from distribution and exhibition in the state of Kansas. Distributors who had their films rejected often questioned the censors regarding what was considered objectionable or what features were so undesirable for the film to be rejected in toto. Based on these comments, distributors would often edit out and "rebuild" such pictures, hoping to get approval the second time they were submitted to the board in a cleaned-up, sanitized version.

It was made very clear that "national censorship" would not be accepted by the state. This was a clear reference to the National Board of Censorship. By 1915, widespread dissatisfaction had developed in regard to the National Board. In the first few years of the National Board's existence, it was looked upon favorably by the popular press and leaders of reform.[6] Progressives believed that the board would be able to control the industry without resorting to outright censorship. Despite its name, the National Board of Censor-

---

4. "Censor of Movies," *Topeka State Journal,* April 12, 1915, in ibid.
5. Ibid.
6. Jowett, *Film: The Democratic Art,* 90.

ship was never actually a censoring board; it had no actual powers over the exhibition of films. A film condemned by the National Board of Censorship could still play almost anywhere in the nation; the organization had no legal or judicial power over the exhibition of films. As a result, in 1915 the board changed its name to the National Board of Review, which more clearly reflected its responsibilities. Many social conservatives were unhappy with the National Board of Censorship/Review by 1915; they believed that the board had done little to stem the tide of "objectionable" films that had supposedly flooded the screen. Kansas, therefore, decided to take matters into its own hands. Confusion soon developed regarding the relationship between the Kansas Board of Censorship and the National Board. Lew Nathanson, manager of the Best and Cozy Theaters (where Miss Simpson was viewing her films), commented, "The whole bunch of films already had been censored by the national board and the Kansas City (Missouri) board. It was a safe bet they would get by."[7] Of course, for Ross, Simpson, and Foster, there was no safe bet.

Later in the afternoon of April 12, Simpson and Foster viewed a film of a more provocative nature. *When We Were Twenty-one* (1915) was a Famous Players release, distributed by Paramount, thus a major studio release. The film was a dramatization of a Broadway play by Henry V. Esmond. Set in a London supper club, *When We Were Twenty-one* was both a comedy and a morality play about a wayward boy and a stripper who fall in love. The *New York Times* described the club as a "place where you did not bring the wife or children" and noted that the stripper's skill "was a new feather in the act of disrobing."[8] The film included subject matter that infuriated social conservatives, including scenes of drinking, gambling, "provocative" dancing, and sexuality. Although *When We Were Twenty-one* may have been acceptable in New York City, the film was going to cause some real problems in the Sunflower State.

While the film was currently playing at the Iris Theater in Topeka, the Congregational minister and the schoolteacher sat down to view it. The first crisis in Kansas film censorship then erupted. Storming out of the theater, the censors immediately informed the manager, Grady Montgomery, that the film could no longer be shown. The censors objected to scenes of drinking, gambling, and a "strip act" by the female lead, "Firefly."[9]

7. "Censors Anger City Movie Fans," *Topeka State Journal,* April 13, 1915, Clipping File, KSBR, KSHS.
8. Review of *When We Were Twenty-one, New York Times,* February 11, 1915, 26.
9. "Censors Anger City Movie Fans."

A shouting match developed in the theater lobby between the indignant censors and Montgomery. According to the *Topeka State Journal,* "Words of scorn . . . were openly expressed." Montgomery begged the censors to allow him to screen the film one more time that night; he had already advertised and promoted the film and did not have an alternate picture to screen. The censors capitulated, and Montgomery began a defensive move against the censors. At the evening performance of *When We Were Twenty-one,* the ushers gave each patron a printed card in which they were to answer the following question: "Should this picture be condemned or not?" Twenty-eight filmgoers answered in the affirmative, whereas an overwhelming 504 patrons argued that the film should not be censored. That next morning, Montgomery was forced to ship the film back to the Universal Exchange in Kansas City. The *Atchison Globe* reported that there was a "near riot" in Topeka when news circulated around the city that *When We Were Twenty-one* had been ordered out of the state.[10]

The controversy over *When We Were Twenty-one* created an emotional and often hostile reaction in Topeka. The press eagerly reacted to the controversy. Governor Capper's *Topeka Daily Capital* tried to downplay the quarrel. Superintendent Ross commented, "This department is not starting out on any wholesale banning of films at all." The partisan press actively encouraged the debate. The *Topeka State Journal,* Capper's competitor in the state's capital, took an oppositional stance to the Board of Censorship's actions. Calling the film "a pleasing picture," the paper began its account, "Topeka motion picture patrons today are mad and not the slightest feeling of love and affection is displayed between them and the censorship board." With hostile bylines such as "Local Houses Cannot Show Films of Real Merit" and, sarcastically, "Travelogues and Scenes from Siam Soon Favorites," the paper angrily attacked the censor board and, indirectly, the administration of Arthur Capper. The *Journal* sent several reporters to view the "offensive" film. They argued that they were not morally outraged. In their perspective, *When We Were Twenty-one* "showed several well dressed men and a few women in a finely furnished club room." One, probably two, was "drinking some liquid, probably water or coca cola." As for the so-called strip, the *Journal* told the readers that Firefly "rendered a graceful and not obscene dance." Somewhere between the puritanical views of the censors and the politically hostile perspective of the *Topeka State Journal* was the truth. By 1915 standards, *When We Were Twenty-one* pushed the enve-

10. Ibid.; "A Censor Board That Is Proving Its Own Undoing," *Motion Picture News,* May 15, 1915, 32.

lope in its depictions of sexuality, "appropriate" behavior, and, for Kansas tastes, the consumption of alcohol. But the *Topeka State Journal* warned that "taking the condemnation of *When We Were Twenty-one* as an example, the following pictures which were taken from recognized and standard works of literature would be banned from the state—*The Sea Wolf, The Tale of Two Cities, Les Miserables, The Prisoner of Zenda, The Iliad, Quo Vadis, Cabiria, Dubarry,* and *Macbeth*." Placing *When We Were Twenty-one* in the same league with classics by Hugo, Homer, and Shakespeare is a stretch. The *Topeka State Journal* warned that the "outlook seems indeed gloomy for movie fans." The newspaper then sarcastically suggested that future city screens would be relegated to "little travelogues, little tea party films, kid comedies, fairy tales, providing that the wearing apparel of the fairies is not too scanty, [and] studies of the life of birds, plants and insects."[11]

When We Were Twenty-one was not the only film banned from Kansas on April 12.[12] A sparring match between heavyweight boxer Jess Willard and his partner was also condemned. Boxing matches were an enormously popular subject for early filmmakers. Boxers like Jack Johnson and Jess Willard were film personalities in their own right, starring in filmed matches that attracted millions. Willard had special significance for the people from Kansas because he was a statewide hero. The "Pottawatomie Giant" was the first heavyweight boxing champion from Kansas. Willard was also a "racial hero" for defeating African American boxer Jack Johnson, establishing him as the "Great White Hope." But the brutality of boxing and its association with an exclusively male domain (the boxing arena) were disturbing for Progressives who realized that these films would also be viewed by women and children. The censors were kind enough to allow the Orpheum Theater in Topeka to show the film one last time that night. W. A. Andlauer, the manager of the Orpheum, defended his reputation: "If I showed repulsive films, then people would stop attending the theater. Business would fall off."[13]

Capper and Ross quickly had to defend the actions of their board due to the press attention. That week, Ross attempted to calm fears by arguing there was "no occasion for excitement over the inspection of movies." Obviously referring to the *Topeka State Journal* hysteria, he claimed, "A number of perfectly

11. "Film Censorship to Be Sound," *Topeka Daily Capital,* April 13, 1915, 1; "Censors Anger City Movie Fans."

12. The Appeal Board eventually overruled the Board of Censors, and the film was allowed to be exhibited in the state.

13. "Censors Anger City Movie Fans."

well meaning persons are working up a great deal of unnecessary excitement about movie censorship." Ross argued that the censorship process was beneficial for the state because it would eliminate bad films, allowing parents to feel safe about sending their children to the picture show. He went so far as to argue that motion picture censorship would actually increase attendance at Kansas theaters. Ross also began to backpedal regarding the previous doctrine that all depictions of alcohol and bars would be stricken from films in Kansas. In the *Topeka State Journal,* Ross stated, "The idea that such pictures as *Ten Nights in a Bar Room* [a popular temperance drama] and other similar pictures cannot be shown is a gross manipulation of my statement. In fact, I never said that no drinking scenes should be shown. Judgment will be used in all matters of the kind."[14]

The editors of the *Topeka State Journal* warned local citizens that Kansas would continue its reputation as a "rube" state and would lose the quality, sophisticated films that the studios had to offer. Ed Howe, in the *Atchison Globe,* claimed that "Atchison and the whole State is howling over another fool law passed by our legislature, and Kansas throughout the country is receiving a lot more of rube publicity." The *Topeka State Journal* quoted an unnamed film distributor: "We certainly don't care. . . . If Kansas wants to be foolish and silly, that's her business. We have high grade pictures for sale but if a censor or inspector wants to be technical, it's all right with us. We have a fine collection of travelogues and pictures about nothing much at all. If Kansas is being offended by the offering of real talent and the best pictures of the year, we have a big collection of junk that won't offend anyone."[15]

The Kansas Board of Censorship was not the final word in what could be shown on Kansas motion picture screens. The 1915 legislation that established the board included a provision for an Appeal Board that consisted of the governor, the attorney general, and the secretary of state. Any film that was condemned by the Board of Censorship could be taken to the Appeal Board. If two out of three members of the Appeal Board did not find the film objectionable, the majority decision of the board would override the Board of Censorship, and the film could be exhibited. The first film taken to the Appeal Board was the Jess Willard sparring match.[16]

14. "Film Censorship to Be Sound"; "They Don't Care," *Topeka State Journal,* April 15, 1915, Clipping File, KSBR, KSHS.
15. "A Censor Board That Is Proving Its Own Undoing," 32; "They Don't Care."
16. Despite a great deal of research, I did not discover the Appeal Board's decision on this match.

The first few months of the existence of the Board of Censorship were a hectic time for Simpson and Foster. Ross, because of his enormous responsibility as superintendent of instruction, tended to serve primarily as "spokesman" for the group and was not involved in the day-to-day process of viewing films. Simpson and Foster had to review every new film brought into the state, but to add to their duties they also had to view every film that already existed in the state. Simply put, they had to play catch-up. The *Topeka State Journal* reported in June that the state received 5,564 new films every year, more than ten million feet of new film reels. In the first six weeks that the censors were on the job, 642 films had been sent to the state for approval, an average of 107 new films every week. Although many were short subjects of one reel (eight to ten minutes in length), some films were now averaging from four to six reels, and several newly imported Italian films, including *Quo Vadis?* (1913) and *Cabiria* (1914), were ten reels in length.[17] Film producers in Italy had begun making spectacle films as early as 1910. These films were much longer than typical American films; more lavish in regard to sets, costumes, and extras; and an impetus to feature-film production in the United States.

The censors constantly found themselves on the defensive. Despite the fact that they had rejected less than 1 percent of all films submitted to the state, they underwent frequent criticism and sarcastic commentary from the press. *Motion Picture News* argued that "the state censor board of Kansas was probably created to be a public protector, but—if the editorials in the newspapers are to be believed—it has already become a public nuisance." The difficulty came when its members made comments such as "We are not adhering strictly to any set rule in our decision," which Simpson made in June. She explained that the films most heavily censored were cheap, melodramatic productions and not big studio releases. A critic of the board claimed that "unless their rulings are modified, politicians believe the censor board will be an issue in Kansas politics next year. More editorials are carried in Kansas newspapers on the movie censor board than on the war, the doings of the last legislature and the Kansas rate hearing combined."[18]

What many individuals feared was that entertainment-starved rural Kansans would lose one of their primary sources of enjoyment. One editorial writer argued, "Deprived of many of the means of enjoyment open to city

17. "Ten Million Feet," *Topeka State Journal,* June 2, 1915, Clipping File, KSBR, KSHS.
18. "A Censor Board That Is Proving Its Own Undoing," 32; "Ten Million Feet"; "A Censor Board That Is Proving Its Own Undoing," 32.

people, the rural inhabitants of Kansas turn logically to motion pictures. They find in these pictures an inexpensive and entirely satisfactory source of recreation. The people of Kansas are not children that they need to have chosen overseers to dictate to them the kind of fun they shall enjoy."[19]

Not all parties were opposed to the actions of the censorship board. Women's clubs throughout the state were enthusiastic about the control over screen content. As early as 1913, the Woman's Christian Temperance Union, the most influential women's club in the state, proclaimed in its publication, *Our Messenger,* "We are glad of following laws which were passed [concerning state censorship of films] and also glad we could have the privilege of working for them." Women's organizations did not want to shut down film theaters. They took a pragmatic approach to the usefulness of the medium. One contemporary author wrote, "The fact that the cheap show has come to stay is generally recognized and the aim of the women is to make it of the greatest possible value to the community."[20]

In the summer of 1915, the Kansas state censors turned their attention from the censorship process to its enforcement. It was a difficult, cumbersome, and expensive process for individual theaters and exchanges to send all old and contemporary films to Topeka to be censored. Films that had not been approved by the censorship board were still being exhibited in the state. By July, the board planned an airtight enforcement of the law. Superintendent Ross sent out a memo to all movie theaters and exchanges in the state that read, "It has come to the attention of the censors that moving pictures are still being shown in the state which have not been submitted for inspection and approved. This is a clear violation of the law and subjects the exhibitor to a fine of from twenty-five dollars and one hundred dollars for the first offense and not less than one hundred dollars for each subsequent offense. If care is not taken to see that only censored films are exhibited, the Attorney General will be asked to begin prosecution of all offenders."[21] Ross gave all parties in the industry until August 15, 1915, to get their business in order and submit all films to the Board of Censorship. After August 15, county attorneys were instructed to bring action on the first violation of the law in their jurisdictions. Ross went so far as to suggest that theaters that exhibited films that did

19. "Anti-Censor Arguments on Slides Aid Kansas Fight," *Motion Picture News,* August 14, 1915, 29.

20. *Our Messenger,* April 1913, 2, KSHS; Frederic J. Haskin, "Women's Club Work IV—in Civic Activities," Clipping File, Women's Clubs, KSHS.

21. "Bars Uncensored Films," *Topeka Daily Capital,* July 9, 1915, Clipping File, KSBR, KSHS.

not have the stamp of state approval would be closed under order of the attorney general.

As the August 15 deadline approached, film theater managers in Kansas complained that they could not obtain censored films quickly enough to offer their patrons new products. They blamed the censorship board. Ross, in turn, blamed the film-exchange companies, which were largely based in Kansas City, Missouri. Theater managers believed they could not get new films because the censorship board was not working fast enough, but Ross claimed, "The film exchanges are using this excuse to put out some old uncensored films they know will not get by the Board. They want to clean up on these instead of sending new and better films into the state."[22]

In September, Ross put the Reverend Foster on the road as a traveling censor and inspector. His goal was to investigate whether theaters were exhibiting films without the stamp of approval of the Board of Censorship. He left Topeka on September 21, not letting the press know which direction he was headed so that theater managers would not be tipped off. Besides looking for films that had not been approved, he was also on the lookout for inspected films that were supposed to have scenes deleted but instead were exhibited intact.[23]

The summer of 1915 was also the period in which the film industry in Kansas began to organize to protect itself economically from the new reality of film censorship. Arguably, the advent of motion picture censorship in the state was the most crucial factor in causing film theater owners and distributors to organize in a professional and powerful manner. It was estimated that in the summer of 1915, there were approximately five hundred theaters in Kansas that exhibited films. The vast majority of these theaters received their films from the major exchanges located in Kansas City, Missouri. The few exceptions were those theaters in far-western Kansas, where films were received from Colorado. The market in western Kansas was so sparse that enforcement of the censorship law in that region of the state was lax. The expense of censorship was paid by the film exchanges but then filtered down to the Kansas theaters. There were three major expenses related to film censorship. First, the exchanges had to pay two dollars a reel for the censorship fee. Films had to be inspected only once, and when approved they could be distributed throughout the state. Second, the exchanges were compelled to

22. "Ross Knocks Out Plan to Show Bad Pictures," *Topeka Daily Capital,* August 3, 1915, in ibid.
23. "Foster Will See Films Shown in Other Towns," *Topeka Daily Capital,* September 22, 1915, in ibid.

pay for shipping to and from Topeka so the film could be inspected. Third, the exchanges were forced to hire a theater in the state capital so the censors would have a place to view the film. This entire process meant that each reel had an additional expense of four dollars added to it due to the advent of censorship. It was estimated that in 1915, film manufacturers and distributors would be spending eighteen to twenty thousand dollars for the censorship process in Kansas, a huge sum of money that significantly ate into industry profits.[24]

Exhibitors in the state had costs passed down to them that averaged fifty to three hundred dollars a year, based on their attendance and gross receipts. This became a matter of tremendous concern for the film companies in 1915 because censorship legislation was being considered in a number of different states. In addition to Kansas, Ohio and Pennsylvania already had motion picture censorship. If each state had a separate censorship fee and different standards for what material was acceptable in the state, censorship could be a logistical and economic nightmare for the industry. Film manufacturers, distributors, and theater owners realized that they had to organize in order to protect themselves financially.

For those in the film industry, the economic consequences of film censorship in Kansas became particularly galling when it was revealed that the state was making a nice profit off the system. The Board of Censorship was clearing one thousand dollars a month in net profit by the summer of 1915, making the board look much more like a revenue-producing agency than one that was attempting to protect morality in Kansas.[25] The grumbling of those in the industry convinced many members that they should fight the law by having it repealed through a referendum or at least have it seriously amended.

In August, the Film Exchange Men's Association of Kansas City began organizing to fight film censorship in the state. Kansas did not allow referenda in 1915, so the legislation could not be recalled. But the organization believed that there was a way to amend the law so that neither the exhibitor nor the exchange would feel the economic pinch of censorship. One of the suggestions made at the association's meeting in August was that if at least five citizens in the state objected to a particular film in written form to the superintendent of public instruction, then that movie should be censored and the cost of the censorship thrown on the shoulders of the owners of the film.

24. "Pass Fees Along," *Topeka Journal,* July 17, 1915, in ibid.
25. Ibid.

Therefore, not every film would be censored, only those that were considered controversial by the citizenry.[26]

The Film Exchange Men's Association decided to take its case to the public. In the summer of 1915, the organization produced a series of slides that they placed in a newsweekly to be shown to theater patrons across the state. The slides read, "This theatre pays its share of an unjust two dollars per reel tax, to the State of Kansas, because our august legislature thought you didn't know any better than to pay us your money to see something that would injure you. Next thing you know, they will be appointing an inspector to charge you two dollars each morning for an inspection of your person to see that you are properly clothed and that you have no concealed weapons." Being part of a newsreel, the organization was forced to submit the film to the Board of Censorship. Carrie Simpson, upon inspecting it, demanded that the slides be cut out. The Exhibitor's League and the motion picture industry in Kansas went wild. *Motion Picture News* screamed, "The censors are of the opinion that no criticism of the law should be flashed on the screens of the state so that the citizens may see how unjust the law is. The charge of the film men is that this strikes at the very roots of free speech and a free press."[27] Simpson's actions also forced everyone concerned to question whether the board technically had jurisdiction over slides. Film-industry members obviously had a point: there was no question of immorality in the slides of the Exhibitor's League; it simply looked like an arbitrary method of suppressing free speech or criticism. Simpson's censoring did not stop the actions of the league. In fact, it seemed to goad them into preparing new slides to fight censorship in the state.[28]

The frustration over censorship in the state culminated with a meeting of the Kansas branch of the Moving Picture Exhibitor's League of America in Pittsburg, Kansas, on October 18–19, 1915. The *Pittsburg Daily Headlight* said that every man at the convention was a "natural orator" on the subject since it affected everyone in attendance. The organization decided to design both a political and an organizational battle plan to curb or defeat the censorship legislation. Anticipating the upcoming elections, P. J. Concannon, secretary of the state organization, suggested having theater operators grill prospective

26. "Kansas Exhibitors Face Burden of Censor Tax," *Motion Picture News*, August 7, 1915, 43.
27. "Kansas Board Shields Censor Law from Criticism," *Motion Picture News*, August 18, 1915, 45.
28. "Kansas Dailies after Scrap Officious Censor Board," *Motion Picture News*, September 25, 1915, 52.

political candidates on their views on motion picture censorship. He believed that candidates should be forced to take a definite stance on the issue. For those candidates who believed in repealing, or at least modifying, the legislation, Concannon suggested that theater owners "make [their] screens a campaign orator" and that such owners actively campaign for such candidates.[29]

In a revealing set of comments, Concannon, an insider, attempted to explain the difficult position the industry was in. In clarifying why censorship should be debated in the state, he argued, "Frankly, the first picture shows were carelessly run. . . . [F]ilms were quite generally shown that would not be tolerated now by the producer, exhibitor or the public. This gave the moving picture business a black eye and this comes from unjust opposition from which the exhibitors have had to deal today." Concannon claimed that the demand for reform was coming out of either ignorance or corruption. He stated that "the demand for strict censorship, the denunciation of film drama or entertainment comes from people who are familiar with the show not as it is today but as it was in its infancy." Angry that "the demand for censorship comes from well meaning but uninformed people," he asserted that "reform is now being capitalized by the political grafter." Concannon's theories on the immorality of early cinema are hard to accept; by 1915, film studios were dealing in much more adult matter (as demonstrated by the supposed "rape" scene in *The Birth of a Nation*, discussed in the next chapter). But he did succinctly explain one of the fundamental problems with censorship: "The theory of censorship in the mind of the man who would force it into use is 'you are not capable of judging what pictures are good for you to see and I must have two or three people select them for you.'" Concannon suggested that the state accept the direction of the National Board of Censorship, but that option was less viable in Kansas by that time.[30]

The first day's meeting of the Kansas branch of the Motion Picture Exhibitor's League of America was a long series of denunciations of film censorship and, specifically, the censors. Into the lion's den walked the Reverend Festus Foster, one of the principal objects of scorn. Foster attempted a conciliatory message to the unsympathetic crowd. He vigorously defended the actions of the censors, castigated the movie men, and "suggested that they could accomplish more by cooperation toward getting changes made in the law than they could by denunciation."[31] Foster's contention that the law

29. "Wage a Bitter War against Censorship," *Pittsburg Daily Headlight*, October 18, 1915, 1.
30. Ibid.
31. "Said Censor to Be Censored," *Kansas City Times*, October 20, 1915, Clipping File, KSBR, KSHS.

could be changed was an admission that there was something fundamentally flawed about the process, specifically, the economic burden it was placing on the industry. He suggested that the film people take up the matter with the governor and state superintendent of instruction and recommend concrete changes in the law.[32]

The organization passed a number of resolutions and principles at the October meeting that directly dealt with the censorship issue. The major resolution adopted stated:

> Whereas the enactment and enforcement of hostile burdensome, un-American and intolerable censorship laws as relating to the exhibition of moving pictures in the state of Kansas has brought about a condition which threatens the stability and prosperity of the industry, and—Whereas in the administration of the laws the exhibitors have met with what to them seems an nonreasonably [sic] strict prejudicial interpretation therefore, be it
>
> Resolved, That the members of the Moving Picture Exhibitors League, Kansas Branch, in convention assembled on this 18th day of October 1915 in Pittsburg, Kansas, in recognition of the paramount importance of securing an abatement of these conditions do hereby pledge its membership to the support of an organization to be known as the "Amusement Association of Kansas."[33]

This new organization was created at the October meeting so that film exchanges and theater owners could come together to fight the process of censorship. These two groups had a history of contention; theater owners believed that they were being exploited by film exchanges, and the exchanges were often frustrated by the lack of business acumen of the theater owners. In August, the Film Exchange Men's Association of Kansas City had made the decision to pass the cost of censorship on to the theater owners, which furthered animosity between the two groups. Censorship was economically threatening enough to both groups to force them to work together. The goal of the new organization was to "take the active work from the shoulders of the league and the exchange men's association in their fight against unfair censorship that is now being enforced." The movie men in the state were criticized by those in the national industry for not organizing and fighting

32. "State Censor Faced Movie Convention," *Pittsburg Daily Headlight*, October 19, 1915, 1.
33. Ibid.

against censorship at an earlier date. This time, though, Kansas theater managers and exchange men turned out in force to "combine in their efforts to
secure a saner censorship in the state."[34]

The Amusement Association of Kansas adopted two major principles. First,
the association pronounced, "We favor in every branch and department of the
business of public amusement, a policy of clean, honorable, honest and ethical
business practices and in fair dealing with all relations with the public and each
other." Second, the organization affirmed, "We utterly condemn the exhibition
at any time or place any lewd, indecent, suggestive or immoral play, act, performance of moving picture film and pledge this association and its membership to the active and energetic suppression of any such play, act, performance
or moving picture film."[35] This concept of industry self-censorship was a stance
that would be adopted and pledged many times in the next twenty years.

The industry attempted to shore up its resources but also have a good time.
On the final night of the convention, after industry members took a puritanical pledge of film decency, exhibitors, film-exchange representatives, and
members of the Pittsburg Board of Public Welfare attended a presentation of
the Fox film *Sin* at the Grand Theater. It is fascinating to consider why this
film was shown. *Sin* starred Theda Bara, the "bad" woman of cinema in the
mid-1910s. The film was a brand-new release from the Fox Film Corporation. In the film, Bara plays Rosa, an Italian peasant girl who dumps her
sweetheart, Luigi, for the Americanized Italian Pietro, head of the Camorra,
a New York crime syndicate. Luigi, desperately in love with Rosa, follows her
to New York. In order to prove his love to her, Pietro says he will steal the
jewels of the Madonna statue in the neighborhood Catholic church. Impressed
by this devotion, Rosa brags to Luigi of Pietro's plans. Not to be outdone,
Pietro decides to steal the jewels himself. The film ends with a double suicide.
Rosa "becomes insane at the enormity of the crime, alternately laughing and
crying" while Luigi shoots himself on the church steps.[36]

Apparently, a pledge by the Amusement Association of Kansas was one
thing and a good time was another. How this film was allowed to be displayed
is questionable since it was a production condemned by the Kansas Board of
Censorship. Perhaps this was a deliberate ploy to shock the guardians of
reform. The film included religious sacrilege, a double suicide, a love triangle,

34. "Kansas Will Present Solid Front against Censorship," *Motion Picture News*, October 6, 1915, 43.
35. Ibid.
36. *Chicago Daily News* quoted in Ronald Genini, *Theda Bara: A Biography of the Silent Screen Vamp*, 30.

and a lusty woman. The Pittsburg Board of Public Welfare was apparently appalled by *Sin*, claiming, "We as a board wish to commend our state legislators who made it possible for Kansas to have a state censorship and we also wish to commend the state censor board for its good work which has raised the standard of films being shown throughout the state."[37] But what about *Sin*?

One of the major problems that film exchanges and theater managers had with the Board of Censorship was the confusion over whether a film had actually been passed by the board or not. In July 1915, a controversy broke over the film *Ghosts* (1915), based on the famous Henrik Ibsen play. In the film, Helen is in love with a poor pastor but is induced to marry Captain Arling, a notorious womanizer, for his money, even though the family doctor warns that he may pass on his venereal disease to any potential children. Arling has an affair with a neighbor's wife, and they have an illegitimate child, Regina. The parentage of the child is kept secret. Meanwhile, Helen and Arling have a son, Oswald. When Oswald is a young man, studying art in Paris, he begins to suffer from fits of insanity. His mother introduces him to Regina, whom she considers of upstanding character. They eventually fall in love and plan to marry. Shortly before the marriage ceremony is complete, the doctor reveals that they really are brother and sister. Oswald, embittered, begins to lose his mind. His mother eventually finds him in the study playing with sunbeams. Incest, insanity, illegitimacy, and alcoholism were heavy themes for early-twentieth-century audiences. *Variety* argued that "in certain sections of this country this picture is going to have some of the censors burning the midnight oil in sizing up each angle with some perhaps pronouncing it unfit for the public. Other censors will aver that it has a powerful moral and teaches a lesson from which the younger generation can reap a lasting benefit." The trade publication absolutely predicted what happened in the state of Kansas. One of the censors saw *Ghosts* in the morning and, after ordering several cuts, officially passed it. Later that afternoon, the other censor screened the film at the Novelty Theater and suggested several more cuts. The next day, Simpson and Foster decided it was easier just to eliminate the picture in its entirety. They must have agreed with *Variety*, which believed it was "a very morbid, grewsome [*sic*] subject. It is not the type that the average movie fan relishes." The Majestic Motion Picture Company, producer of the film, decided to fight, since the film had "officially" passed in the morning. Film exhibitors said they would "buck the board" and test the ruling by showing

37. Ibid.

the film in their theaters.[38] It is unknown whether the company followed through with its threat.

The Fox Film Corporation faced a similar battle with its film *The Devil's Daughter*. The film was passed by the board and commercially shown at the Iris Theater in Topeka. The film was later "recalled" by the board in order for it to be reexamined. Apparently, complaints from some audience members caused this action to take place. The Fox Film Corporation responded by threatening a ten thousand–dollar lawsuit if the film could not be exhibited since it had initially passed the board.

The board attempted to alleviate the problem of owners determining which films had passed and which had been rejected by publishing lists and making them available to county attorneys. Beginning in October, weekly lists of approved and rejected films were made available to them. Quarterly compendiums of such information were published by the State Printer for public use.

As Ross and the attorney general began their crackdown on violations of the censorship law, they instructed county attorneys to keep close tabs on movie houses in their regions and prosecute all cases of violation of the law. Attorney General Sardius Brewster mailed the following letter to county attorneys:

> Some of the picture companies are not only showing pictures that have been rejected, but are attaching to rejected pictures the certificate of the state superintendent that the pictures have been examined, passed and approved. This conduct on the part of the proprietors of moving picture houses or the owners of the films has made it necessary for Mr. Ross to take action and it is the desire of this office that the county attorneys cooperate with Mr. Ross in every way in the enforcement of this law. This act has been before the Supreme Court of the United States and its constitutionality upheld.[39]

The first arrest in the state for violation of exhibiting uncensored films was that of Herbert Welsh, the manager of a theater in Atchison. The Reverend Foster had been traveling across the state for several months gathering evidence against those who violated the law. Welsh displayed a film titled *Emmy of Stork's Nest* (1915), and Foster proceeded to the justice of the peace to get a

38. Review of *Ghosts, Variety,* June 11, 1915, 19; "Will Sue State," *Topeka State Journal,* July 21, 1915, Clipping File, KSBR, KSHS.
39. "Must Be Censored," *Topeka State Journal,* October 9, 1915, Clipping File, KSBR, KSHS.

warrant. Welsh testified that he was unaware that the picture had not been approved but pleaded guilty and paid a twenty-five-dollar fine.[40] Later that month, sixteen exhibitors in Kansas City, Kansas, were ordered to appear before the county attorney for showing uncensored films and films that had not been edited when the board deemed that scenes had to be eliminated in order to be exhibited.[41]

Exactly what were the Kansas censors finding objectionable in motion pictures in the first six months on the job? In the summer of 1915, they were watching an average of twenty-three films a day. Only 2 percent were outright condemned by the board. A much more significant number of films had scenes eliminated from them because the censors deemed "they were not fit for the eyes of children."[42]

By far, the major concerns of the censors were scenes of alcohol consumption or the display of settings in which alcohol was imbibed, such as cabarets or bars. If adults were not allowed to drink in such establishments in Kansas, why should children be allowed to see such locations? Sixty-seven pictures had drinking scenes eliminated in the period April–October 1915. *The Yankee from the West* (1915), a Majestic western-adventure, had five bar scenes eliminated, whereas the feature film *Winning the Futurity* (1915) had two bar scenes and one drinking scene removed.[43] If motion picture distributors did not remove such scenes, technically the film could not be legally displayed in the state. Depictions of women smoking (still considered unladylike behavior in 1915) and sexually suggestive material (including nude scenes and bathing) were the next-largest categories of material that the censors eliminated. Each category had twenty films that had such depictions censored out. Other subjects that the censors found taboo included scenes of violence (six films), death scenes (six films), provocative dancing (two films), and gambling (nine films). Ross claimed, "We will not permit any murder or robbery or any other crime to be actually shown on the film. If such a section cannot be removed, the entire film must be thrown out. Our rule to start is that no crime or debauchery shall be displayed."[44]

40. "First Fine Is Paid," *Topeka State Journal,* November 26, 1915, in ibid.

41. "Neither Judge or Jury Needed while Foster Is Censor," *Motion Picture News,* October 23, 1915, 65.

42. "Job of Real Fun," *Topeka State Journal,* July 24, 1915, Clipping File, KSBR, KSHS.

43. "Complete List of Motion Picture Films Presented to the Kansas State Censors for Action from April 10, 1915, to October 1, 1915, Inclusive" (Topeka: Kansas State Printing Plant, 1915), KSHS.

44. "Kansas Censorship Now in Force," *Motion Picture News,* May 1, 1915, 57.

In the period October 2, 1915, to January 1, 1916, the censors became much more explicit in their description of what they argued must be eliminated. The following table includes the subject matter that the censors found offensive and the number of films that were exorcised for including such subject matter:

Cruelty—1
Smoking by Women—18
Gambling—8
Drinking—30
Sexual Suggestiveness—32
Language—9
Location (cabaret, underworld, bedroom, café)—14
Provocative dancing—5
Violence—15
Narcotics—2
Death Scenes—8[45]

The Janitor's Wife's Temptation (1915), a Keystone production, is a good example of the censors' work in this period. The censors gave the following directions to the distributors: "Reel One—eliminate scene where girl sits on janitor's lap; eliminate scene of nude model; eliminate ballet scene at end of reel two. Eliminate all wineroom scenes of old men and young girls, reduce all suggestive scenes to a flash, eliminate kooche dance by girl on table, eliminate scene where girl kicks janitor on the neck."[46]

The members of the board got wise to what the exchange companies and theater owners were doing with censored films. Exchanges that had movies with edited scenes were often allowed to keep the pieces of film with the material that had been rejected by the censors. Beginning in October, the board decided that they would keep the deleted scenes. This would keep the exchanges from the temptation of reinserting questionable material before screening such pictures.[47]

Forcing motion picture exchanges to delete certain scenes or titles was tricky, cumbersome, and economically challenging to the film interests. But condemning a motion picture in its entirety meant that the production com-

45. "Complete List of Motion Picture Films Presented to the Kansas State Censors for Action from October 2, 1915–January 1, 1916: List of Films Reviewed" (Topeka: Kansas State Printing Plant, 1916), Box 58-5-4-5, KSHS.
46. Ibid.
47. "Kansas Keeps the Pieces," *Moving Picture World,* October 30, 1915, 831.

pany had no chance to recoup their costs; no censoring or editing would allow the film to be exhibited in the state. The loss of the Kansas market may not have been a tremendous concern to motion picture production companies in 1915, but what the state represented was extremely serious. Numerous states and municipalities across the nation were considering censorship that year. Ohio, Pennsylvania, and Kansas now had censor boards; what was to keep other governmental bodies from adopting prior restraint?[48] If Kansas could successfully keep offensive, immoral, or harmful films outside its borders, other jurisdictions might follow its example. "Successful" motion picture censorship in Kansas, therefore, had enormous national ramifications.

Between April 12 and October 1, 1915, the Kansas Board of Censorship rejected fourteen films in their entirety. A number of these films were shorts, one to two reels in length, minimizing the economic damage to the production companies. But a number of the films were feature films from major studios. An examination of several of these films is necessary in order to have an understanding of the motivations of Foster and Simpson. *The Woman* (1915), an Essanay feature, involves two politicians (father and son-in-law) trying to ruin a senator by revealing that he had a one-night stand with a woman from a good family. The two corrupt politicians use bribery and scandal mongering to figure out that the young woman is actually their own daughter and wife! Although this film stretched the limits of believability, its narrative centered on a dangerous nocturnal sexual liaison that made the censors nervous, and they decided to ban the feature.[49]

Up from the Depths (1915), a Reliance picture, involves a traveling revivalist preacher, Judson Davids. He persuades Daire Vincent, a small-town girl, to run off with him. Within a year, he deserts her without marrying her and travels to New York City, where he perceives ample opportunities for graft. While leading a crusade movement in the city, he finds numerous possibilities to steal from various charities. Daire gives birth to Davids's illegitimate child, and because she is deserted, she is forced to become a dance-hall girl in order to take care of the baby. Daire rises in the ranks of the dance-hall circuit, eventually landing a job at the infamous Mozart Dance Hall. Davids, over time, has married a sickly, childless woman. He decides to raid the Mozart Dance Hall for publicity purposes. He discovers there that he has a child with Daire, but

48. Laura Wittern-Keller, "Freedom of the Screen: The Legal Challenges to State Film Censorship, 1915–1981," 52–53.

49. Patricia King Hansen, ed., *American Film Institute Catalog of Motion Pictures Produced in the United States, Feature Films, 1911–1920*, 1053.

although it pleases him, it eventually kills his wife. During the raid, Davids is wounded. He wants to marry Daire, and a local priest convinces her to do so since it will legitimate their son.[50] *Up from the Depths* obviously disturbed the censors for several reasons. In the 1910s, censors were often nervous about motion pictures that depicted ministers, priests, or rabbis in a negative light, particularly a religious man as corrupt as Davids. The dance-hall location, with its opportunity to show a lot of shapely legs, was also considered danger- ous. Finally, the sexual relationship outside of marriage and the illegitimate child that it created were too much for the censors to bear. As a result, they condemned the film in its entirety.[51]

The advent of World War I added political concerns to the growing list of taboo subjects on the screen. *In the Name of the Prince of Peace* (1915) con- cerned a father-daughter relationship. Helena, the daughter, is sent to a con- vent due to a harmful childhood prank. Her father, a baron, joins the German military when the war begins. After the French lay violent siege to the convent in which Helena is living, the Germans battle to recapture it. The baron exchanges uniforms with a captured French spy and enters the convent to obtain important information and rescue his daughter. After a French soldier sees Helena address her father, he realizes that the baron is a German. Helena, who was forced to take an oath of truthfulness on the cross, reluctantly reveals that her father is German. The baron is ruthlessly executed on the steps of the convent altar. Helena rushes to him and is also shot. The film ends when "their spirits and those of other dead soldiers rise and appeal to the Prince of Peace to end the war."[52] The film was not provocative in terms of sexual morality or "immoral" behavior. Scenes might have been considered violent due to the fact that it was taking place during wartime. But perhaps what might have con- vinced the censors to condemn the film was its strong pacifistic tone. *Variety* noted that the film did "nothing more than appeal to the nations of the coun- try to stop the war." But even this was not unusual in a nation that was funda- mentally divided over American preparation and possible participation in the war. Governor Arthur Capper was strongly and publicly against U.S. involve- ment in the war, a sentiment shared by many of the people of the state. Per-

---

50. Ibid., 976.
51. "Complete List of Motion Pictures, October 2, 1915–January 1, 1916," Box 58-5-4-5, KSBR, KSHS.
52. Hansen, *American Film Institute Catalog, 1911–1920,* 450.

haps it was the depiction of the "real devilish" French troops, future allies of the United States, that made the censors so nervous.[53]

During the first four-and-a-half-month period, two films were rejected by the Board of Censorship but overruled by the Appeal Board consisting of Governor Arthur Capper, Attorney General Sardius Brewster, and Secretary of State John Botkin. These films were *Father Takes a Hand* (1915, Reliance) and *When We Were Twenty-one* (1915, Paramount).

Perhaps the most disturbing rejection by the Board of Censorship was a Pathe newsreel of the Leo Frank case. Frank was arrested for the murder of thirteen-year-old Mary Phagan in April 1913. Phagan had been an employee of the Atlanta pencil factory where Frank was the manager. Frank, a Jew, was immediately suspected in the case despite the lack of any conclusive evidence of his guilt. After two years of trials, accompanied by sensational newspaper coverage, blatant anti-Semitism, and public hysteria, Frank was sentenced to death. The governor of Georgia eventually commuted his sentence, but Frank was kidnapped and lynched by a mob near his hometown. The case was confirmation of anti-Semitism at its ugliest, and the censor board's decision not to allow the coverage on the screen is highly questionable. Was the avoidance of the scandal a perpetuation of anti-Semitism? Or was it a misguided attempt to "protect" Kansas children from the harsh realities of the world? The censoring of the Pathe newsreel demonstrated that film censorship in the state could also be used for political purposes.[54] The censor board edited other Pathe newsreels. Pathe News no. 9 had scenes edited that displayed a parade of "wets" protesting a major decision to close saloons on Sunday.

In the last three months of 1915, a noticeable split occurred between the Board of Censorship and the Appeal Board in terms of what was considered "appropriate" content for the cinema. Within a three-month period, twelve films that the censors rejected were passed by the Appeal Board. The very existence of the Appeal Board created real problems for the governor, attorney general, and secretary of state. Moving picture exchange men realized that raising a vigorous protest every time a film was heavily edited or barred could create real problems for these three men. The appeal became a tool by

---

53. Review of *In the Name of the Prince of Peace, Variety,* April 30, 1915, 18.
54. "Complete List of Motion Pictures, October 2, 1915–January 1, 1916," Box 58-5-4-5, KSBR, KSHS. The reaction of the Appeal Board to the censoring of the Leo Frank case is unknown; no documentation exists that proves their decision either way.

which the industry could obstruct censorship, and, as the *Topeka Daily Capital* reported on October 30, 1915, "in the last few weeks they have been doing it with a vengeance." The way that the legislation was written, the governor, attorney general, and secretary of state were expected to drop everything anytime a film was appealed. This made film viewing a new priority for the executive staff, and it infuriated Governor Capper. Since there was no projector or screening equipment nearby, this meant that the three men had to travel to a local Topeka theater to view the film being appealed. As the *Daily Capital* reported, "It is now the plan to wear the state officials out."[55] Capper began making suggestions around the statehouse that the legislature rewrite the censorship bill and drop the Appeal Board at the next session.

By the end of the year, the governor took steps to make the appeal process easier on him and the other two government officials. He announced that the Appeal Board would view films only twice a month and that preparations were being made to equip a room in the statehouse where the censors and members of the Appeal Board could do their work without leaving the building. Charles Sessions, private secretary to the governor, explained, "A systematic campaign was waged to make the members of the Appeal Board sick of their jobs—the idea that these three men will have to drop all other business and look at rejected movies has been overlooked."[56]

Why were so many films being rejected? And why was the Appeal Board overruling the Board of Censorship in so many cases? Often, it simply seemed to be a question of standards. The Board of Censorship, made up of Foster and Simpson, was much stricter in regard to matters of sexual morality and modern behavior. One clear example was the controversy over the film *Carmen* (1915). The film was one of the most respected productions of the year, starring the internationally known opera diva Geraldine Farrar and up-and-coming star Wallace Reid. Based on the famous story by Prosper Mérimée, the film centered on Farrar in the title role as a tempestuous gypsy who infatuates and seduces men and manipulates everyone to her own advantage. Farrar was dynamic in the role, and the film was given cachet as a class act due to Farrar's operatic reputation and the fact that it was based on a classic story. When the film was rejected by the Board of Censorship, the press had a field day. The *Kansas City Times* exclaimed, "Kansas has its own idea of art. Any time Kansas

55. "Legislature May Cut Out Censor's Appeal Board," *Topeka Daily Capital*, October 30, 1915, Clipping File, KSBR, KSHS.
56. "Another Jolt for Movie Men," *Topeka Daily Capital*, December 28, 1915, in ibid.

hasn't its own ideas, it isn't Kansas." A. Malmstrom, chief scale inspector of the AT&SF Railroad in Topeka, wrote a scathing letter to the governor. He and his wife saw the film at the Iris Theater in Houston, Texas, before a packed house. He reported that "the picture [was] greatly admired by everyone and how anyone could be so prejudicial as to try to stop the views of the people of a whole State, a grand production like this is beyond my comprehension." Malmstrom could not understand what the censors were thinking or why Kansans should be denied this great piece of art. He argued, "The title role in the picture is played by one of the greatest living actresses, Geraldine Farrar, and this lady would surely not loan herself to any indecency." Even though he recognized that the Appeal Board later overturned the Board of Censorship's decision on *Carmen,* Malmstrom called Ross "hypocritical" and said that he was "using his office for personal grudge."[57] Obviously, the critical issue between the Appeal Board and the Board of Censorship was differing standards of what was considered "decent" and "moral" on the screen.

Capper did not usually respond to personal complaints about individual motion pictures, but this time he made an exception. It may have been Malmstrom's influential railroad position or the controversy about the banning of the film, but nonetheless Capper wrote Malmstrom. "I agree with you in regard to this picture. It is a beautiful thing and I believe the people of Kansas ought not to be deprived of the privilege of seeing it and so I voted when the matter was presented to the appeal board." Capper then defended his board, arguing that they wanted only elimination of harmful scenes and not a wholesale rejection of entire films and pointed out that the Ohio Censor Board had banned the film outright. So did Kansas—Capper simply got his facts wrong. Then Capper, in a revealing moment, expressed his displeasure with how the censorship process was proceeding: "Possibly Mr. Ross has gone a little too far in a few instances, but I think that in the main his work has been along the right lines, it would be strange if they did not make a mistake occasionally. . . . I am not a crank on these matters. I want to see all interests have fair consideration."[58] Capper did indeed have a public reputation as a fair man. But motion picture censorship, which he advocated, was becoming troublesome for him in his daily work life, and it was becoming politically dangerous.

57. "Kansas and the Movies," *Kansas City Times,* October 28, 1915, in ibid.; A. Malmstrom to Capper, October 26, 1915, Box 3, File 236, General Correspondence, 1915, Capper Papers, KSHS.
58. Capper to Malmstrom, October 28, 1915, Box 3, File 236, General Correspondence, 1915, Capper Papers, KSHS.

Examples of when Ross and the Board of Censorship "went too far" and banned films in their entirety include *The Lily and the Rose* (1915, Fine Arts Film Company), a Lillian Gish production about infidelity, suicide, and exotic dancers (not Gish!); *On Her Wedding Night* (1915, Vitagraph), a potboiler involving murder, illegitimacy, and the malicious use of acid to disfigure a character's face; and *The Ring of the Borgias* (1915, Thomas Edison), involving seduction, murder, and a ring that contains poisonous cobra venom.[59] Perhaps the most intriguing of the bunch in which the Appeal Board overruled the Board of Censorship is the American Film feature *The Miracle of Life* (1915). The film concerns a young society woman who finds herself pregnant and goes to a family friend to find the swiftest means of abortion. The friend gives her a potent drug. As she lies in her bed that night, she brings the abortion pill to her lips, falls asleep, and begins to dream. In her dream, her husband finds out about the abortion and divorces her. She ends up an old woman, alone. She is visited by an apparition—the ghost of the "child that might have been." The ghost takes her on a journey where she sees her happily remarried husband with a family of his own. They go to Babyland, where hundreds of smiling infants wait for her. Then the film shows her damned, decrepit, and alone. When she wakes up, she finds out that she never took the poison and rushes to tell her husband the good news that she is pregnant.[60]

The Miracle of Life is an excellent example of the fundamental distinctions the Board of Censorship and the Appeal Board made when considering the acceptability of films. The Board of Censorship either banned or forced elim-inations on all controversial subject matter, regardless of the moral outcome of the story. Virtually all of the films overruled by the Appeal Board ended in typical melodramatic fashion, with a happy heterosexual coupling/romance/ marriage or a unified family. For the Board of Censorship, though, the end did not justify the means. Suicide, murder, abortion, exotic dancing—these were simply not appropriate subjects for Kansas audiences to view no matter what the outcome of the film. The Appeal Board, perhaps a littler wiser and worldlier, seemed more preoccupied with the happy ending than with the questionable subject matter that led to it.

Even *Variety*, the somewhat cynical trade paper, argued that *The Miracle of Life* was "a picture that will undoubtedly pull money, but it should be shown with discretion, for it is not a picture for children to see." The publication

59. Hansen, *American Film Institute Catalog, 1911–1920*, 624–25.
60. Review of *The Miracle of Life*, *Variety*, October 8, 1915, 21.

even questioned the morality of the film's philosophy, stating, "The scenario's story is supposed to carry a moral that it 'is better to have children than to spend one's old age in solitude' and as a matter of fact the picture shows that no matter how these children are obtained, whether it be in the bonds of wedlock or not, the children should be born."[61]

By the end of 1915, the state of Kansas had a censorship apparatus that made few people happy. Foster, Simpson, and Ross, the Board of Censorship, found themselves under constant attack and ridicule. Capper, Brewster, and Botkin, the Appeal Board, found themselves bogged down in an appeal process that seemed ridiculous, taking far more time and energy than they could have dreamed of. Many Kansas citizens were also not happy with the fact that they could not see high-quality films such as *Carmen*. But the most frustrated seemed to be those individuals in the motion picture business— theater owners and managers, exchange men, and producers. They were being hit hard financially, and many questioned the motivation and aptitude of the decision makers on the censorship board.

For Governor Arthur Capper, however, the problem was also political. In Malmstrom's angry letter regarding *Carmen*, he wrote, "If it is continued the people will raise up their wrath, and although the peaceful people of our State and Nation are not inclined to use force, they have got a greater weapon than any nation on Earth, namely their Vote, and the day of reckoning surely will come through that resource."[62] Governor Capper realized that the motion picture censorship process must be fixed. But little did he realize how politically explosive motion pictures could be until the release of *The Birth of a Nation*.

61. Ibid.
62. Malmstrom to Capper, October 26, 1915, Capper Papers, KSHS.

Four

The Birth of a Nation and Kansas

Challenged more than one hundred times in and out of courts throughout the United States, D. W. Griffith's controversial film *The Birth of a Nation* clearly illustrated the difficulties many Kansans had in dealing with the powerful new medium of motion pictures. When President Woodrow Wilson saw the film, he called it "history written with lightning."[1] Members of the U.S. Supreme Court concurred that the film was an accurate account of the Civil War and Reconstruction. Yet Griffith's controversial portrayal of this turbulent period in American history has been banned more than any other film in American history. *The Birth of a Nation* truly tested the Kansas Board of Censorship. For nine years and through the terms of three governors, the film haunted everyone connected with the censorship board. The film took the Board of Censorship and made it into a political tool of the governor of the moment.

The Birth of a Nation, released in 1915, was also a milestone in the history of cinema. The film clearly illustrated the pervasive power that the film medium could have on the American social conscience. The film became a cause célèbre, a topic on the tongue of every politician, moviegoer, and social

1. Eileen Landay, *Black Film Stars: A Picture Album,* 26.

worker in the United States. *The Birth of a Nation* rewrote American history and made its citizenry dwell on the role of African Americans in society and the sectional differences that still divided the nation more than a half century after the end of the Civil War. The initial reaction to the film could be described as "varied hysterics." Millions laughed, cried, cheered, and cared about the people on the screen. Countless others saw the film's harsh images and were horrified by them. When *The Birth of a Nation* was first exhibited in Boston, three thousand people marched in protest and demanded that the film be stopped because of its overt racism. Similar protests erupted in New York City, Chicago, and Cleveland. Jane Addams said that she was "painfully exercised over the exhibition." Harvard president Charles E. Eliot charged that the film was a "tendency to perversion of white ideals."[2]

From its very beginnings, the Kansas Board of Censorship fought a number of problems that placed it in a precarious situation. One of these was *The Birth of a Nation*. The film touched the emotions of thousands of Kansas citizens, as the state had a long and proud tradition of antislavery sentiment. In "Bleeding Kansas," proslavery and antislavery forces fought a national prelude to the Civil War. Kansas's entry into the Union in 1861 as a free state was a major victory for the antislavery forces. Their sacrifices were honored by Kansans who believed in a traditional Northern interpretation of the Civil War and Reconstruction. *The Birth of a Nation* and its pro-Southern historical interpretation of the Civil War and Reconstruction ran counter to many Kansans' views of this turbulent period of American history. The harsh racial image of African Americans in the film also disturbed the ancestors of those citizens who helped to free the slaves.

Although *The Birth of a Nation* was and still is a controversial film, it was also a triumph in terms of film technique. Many of the film techniques used today such as night photography, moving camera shots, soft-focus photography, split screens, and acute camera angles were popularized in the movie. The film established Griffith as one of the premier cinematic figures in the early twentieth century.

The genesis of the film was from two of Thomas W. Dixon's books, *The Leopard's Spots* (1902) and *The Clansman* (1905). Born in 1864 in a farmhouse near Shelby, North Carolina, Dixon was eight years old when he allegedly accompanied his uncle to the state legislature in South Carolina where he saw in the body "ninety-four Negroes, seven native scalawags [white

---

2. Jowett, *Film: The Democratic Art,* 102.

South Carolina Republicans] and twenty-three white men [presumably carpetbaggers from the North]."[3] The scene made an impression on young
Dixon. The sight of "Negroes and undesirable whites" running the legislature
profoundly shaped his future career. Dixon was raised in an environment of
racism where African Americans were seen as inferior to whites, immigrants
were not to be trusted, and Southern white "trash" was not to be associated
with. Dixon learned the class patterns of the South before the Civil War and
how important it was that its citizens return to "traditional" roles.

As a young man, Dixon appears to have been both restless and talented. He
was at various times an actor, clergyman, essayist, and lecturer. After hearing
Justin D. Fulton speak in Boston on "the Southern problem" (the inability of
the South to run its own government), Dixon found his lifework. Outraged
at Fulton's derogatory remarks against the South, he interrupted the minister
halfway through the lecture to denounce his remarks as "false and biased."[4]
Dixon's main purpose in life became the desire to "set the record straight"
regarding Reconstruction.

Dixon consequently turned to fiction to tell his story. His first novel, *The
Leopard's Spots: A Romance of the White Man's Burden,* was a conscious attempt
to answer Harriet Beecher Stowe's classic abolitionist novel, *Uncle Tom's
Cabin.*[5] Whereas Stowe's novel attempted to show the nation the cruelties of
slavery, Dixon attempted to show the horrible anguish the Southern white
man suffered in the Reconstruction era. Stowe used her villain, Simon Legree,
to illustrate the exploitation of blacks in a physical sense. Dixon countered by
demonstrating how carpetbaggers misused blacks politically. Dixon took a
character from Stowe's novel, a freed black slave, and transformed him into a
graduate of Harvard, a poet and scholar who overreaches his societal boundaries when he asks to marry the daughter of a white defender of the Negro
cause. Dixon's novel was an instantaneous success, selling more than one hundred thousand copies in its first three months of publication.

The Leopard's Spots established Dixon in the public eye as an "expert" on
Southern life and Reconstruction. He believed that there was an evolutionary
gap between the black and white races and that racial peace could occur only
with the complete separation of the races. Dixon's "nightmare" in life was that
of miscegenation, which he believed would lead to the mongrelization of the

3. John Hope Franklin, "*Birth of a Nation*—Propaganda as History," 12.
4. Richard Schickel, *D. W. Griffith: An American Life,* 78.
5. Ibid.

white race. He suggested that all freed slaves be returned to a new homeland in Africa. Although the "Back-to-Africa" movement was to become popularized by black leaders such as Marcus Garvey and others some twenty years later, Dixon believed that a complete exodus of African Americans out of the United States was the only way that the country could be "saved." Dixon also despised the treatment that the North supposedly gave the South during the Reconstruction period and the dwindling power of states' rights.

The success of *The Leopard's Spots* led to a constant demand for Dixon as a lecturer and writer. Tall and commanding, he preached his diatribe on race, Reconstruction, and the Southern way of life across America. Before the public, Dixon tried to tone down his aversion toward Northerners and immigrants, stressing instead his fears of free, political black men. Dixon told audiences, "My object is to teach the north, the young north, what it has never known—the awful suffering of the white man during the dreadful reconstruction period. I believe that Almighty God anointed the white men of the south by their suffering during that time . . . to demonstrate to the world that the white man must and shall be supreme."[6]

Within a few years, Dixon completed his second and most famous novel, *The Clansman: A Historical Romance of the Ku Klux Klan*. *The Clansman* was a reworking and expansion of *The Leopard's Spots* with a heavier stress on the heroism of the Ku Klux Klan and a vicious attack on Dixon's bête noire, Thaddeus Stevens, the Pennsylvania leader of the Radical Republicans. Taking great liberty with Stevens's biography, Dixon portrayed him in *The Clansman* as a despicable individual who lived with a mulatto mistress. Dixon dwelled on the immense injustices that he claimed white people suffered during Reconstruction, and he cast the Ku Klux Klan in the heroic role of returning the Negro to his place of inferiority. *The Clansman* was even more successful than *The Leopard's Spots*, which led Dixon to consider its possibilities as a drama. In 1906, *The Clansman* was converted into a play and successfully toured the Midwest and the South.

That same year, a little-known southern actor, David Wark Griffith, starred in another of Dixon's plays, titled *One Woman*. Griffith learned his trade under the guidance of Edwin S. Porter, who directed *The Great Train Robbery*.[7] Griffith made hundreds of one-reel films from 1908 until 1912. He was an innovator and popularized such film techniques as the pan shot and

6. Thomas Cripps, *Slow Fade to Black: The Negro in American Film, 1900–1942*, 44.
7. Schickel, *D. W. Griffith*, 91–92.

the traveling shot, cross-cut editing, artificial lighting, and the use of ensemble acting. Griffith developed the use of the narrative film, which told long and complex stories with performers who acted realistically and emotionally. Inspired by the Italian spectacles, he helped conceive the idea of the feature film in the United States.

For his first independent project in 1914, Griffith chose Dixon's novel *The Clansman*. Dixon had for some time tried to persuade film producers throughout the United States to put his novel to film, but they insisted that *The Clansman* was too long, too serious, and too controversial. Griffith decided to film the novel on his own for several reasons. First, the novel appealed to him because it was an epic story, one that covered the age before the Civil War, the war itself, and the turbulent postwar era. In that sense, the novel was an excellent source for a full-length feature film. There were superb opportunities for thrilling drama, with grand armies, sweeping war scenes, and intense emotional impact. Second, Griffith was attracted to the novel because of its message. He was a southerner, and his father had served in the Confederate Army. Griffith's knowledge of history was limited, but he was moved by Dixon's political views on African Americans. When he portrayed African Americans on film, they were either "good" or "bad" and always shown in a condescending manner. Griffith shared Dixon's views on Reconstruction and the South, but his views were more sentimental in nature in contrast to Dixon's violent racial ideology. Griffith once commented on his heritage and its effect on the film: "I used to get under the table and listened to my father and his friends talk about the battles and what they'd been through and their struggles. Those things impress you deeply—and I suppose that got into *The Birth*."[8]

Griffith and Dixon arranged to collaborate on the film in 1914, and throughout that year the pair tried to raise the capital to film the picture. The actual scenario of the film was written by Griffith and Frank Woods, based on both of Dixon's plays, *The Clansman* and *The Leopard's Spots*. Griffith's own company, Epoch, produced the film. *The Birth of a Nation* was rehearsed for six weeks and filmed in nine weeks, and final editing took another three months. The leading actors in the film were Lillian Gish, Mae Marsh, Henry B. Walthall, and Miriam Cooper.

The film focuses on the relationship between a good, "decent" family of the South, the Camerons, and their Pennsylvania friends, the Stonemans. The movie opens with a prologue, which includes a scene showing blacks being

8. Ibid., 77, 236–37.

sold into slavery at auction. The title introducing it indicates one of Griffith's main themes: "The bringing of the African to America planted the first seeds of disunion." The film argues again and again that the black presence in the United States brought disruption and then disunion to the nation.

Before the Civil War, the Cameron family is portrayed as living in a "quaintly way that is no more." Dr. Cameron and his sons are sturdy, benevolent fathers to their childlike servants—the slaves, who appear happy and content. In the fields, the slaves cheerfully pick cotton. In the living quarters, they dance and sing for the white man. Big Mammy contentedly does her chores. The Stonemans come to visit their southern friends, having a good time until the impending war puts a stop to their visit.

The movie then shifts to Washington, D.C., where Arthur Stoneman, patriarch, hurries to business. Stoneman is closely patterned after Thaddeus Stevens, the antislavery Republican congressional leader. Stoneman, an ardent advocate of black rights, keeps a mulatto mistress in Washington, D.C. This interracial relationship is described in a title as "a weakness that is to blight a nation."

During the Civil War, the years take their toll. In Piedmont, where the Camerons have their home, black raiders terrorize the poor white family, and the South is left in devastation. "Ruin, rapine, and pillage" are all that is left of the South. Two of the Cameron boys and one of the Stonemans are killed in battle. The first half of the film ends with the assassination of Lincoln, leaving the Camerons to ask gloomily, "What is to happen to us now?"

The answer is Reconstruction. White carpetbaggers and "uppity" blacks from the North come south to exploit and corrupt freed slaves. In the film, these forces turn congenial Negroes into renegades who seek revenge against their former masters. One card in the film reads, "Lawlessness runs riot." The entire South is then pictured as being overrun by blacks. African Americans don't work; they just dance, sing, and drink. African Americans pictured in the movie take over all aspects of life. In the legislatures of the South, black lawmakers are pictured as stupid, arrogant, and lustful. In the state senate halls, they eat chicken, drink whisky, and take their shoes off. The movie climaxes when a renegade black named Gus attempts to romantically pursue the younger Cameron daughter.[9] Rather than face such a horrible fate, the

---

9. This is often described as the "rape" scene by many commentators in the field. I wholeheartedly agree with Thomas Cripps who, in *Slow Fade to Black*, questions if the intention of this scene is perhaps not that of rape.

girl commits suicide. Arthur Stoneman is faced with a terrible dilemma when a mulatto, Silas Lynch, approaches him and asks permission to marry his daughter, Elsie. At this time, Stoneman realizes that he no longer believes in racial equality and attempts to save his daughter from such a fate.

All things look incredibly bleak in the movie when the heroes come forward—the Ku Klux Klan. These protectors of white morality battle the blacks and carpetbaggers in direct confrontation. Defenders of white womanhood and white justice, they attempt to restore the South to everything it had been before the war. Bound and gagged, Elsie is taken to a cabin where Lynch is determined to marry her. Then the Klan rides into town, frees Elsie, and rescues the town from violence. The next scene is that of African Americans throwing down their weapons and scurrying away. The film comes to a close with an allegorical future of Mars that dissolves into the "Prince of Peace." The film suggests that life in the United States would be much better, and the world would be filled with "the halls of brotherly love," if blacks would go back to Africa.[10]

On February 8, 1915, the film opened at J. R. Clune's Auditorium in Los Angeles under the title *The Clansman*. On March 3, 1915, Griffith changed the film's name to *The Birth of a Nation* and rereleased it at the Liberty Theater in New York. The film was an enormous financial and critical success. George D. Proctor in *Motion Picture News* declared that the film was "the greatest picture ever produced." He wrote, "*The Birth of a Nation* is a most happy and strong combination of spectacle and story. To do the spectacle justice is practically impossible." The Reverend Thomas B. Gregory wrote in the *New York American*, "As an educator, its value is well-nigh inconceivable and its chief value in this direction lies in its truthfulness." Hector Turnbull of the *New York Tribune* called it a "spectacular drama" with "thrills piled upon thrills."[11]

Yet despite this praise, *The Birth of a Nation* quickly became embroiled in a morass of controversy. Even before the film reached New York, the National Association for the Advancement of Colored People (NAACP) had begun action against the film. Thousands of pamphlets were mailed asking citizens to demand that the film be barred from their region. The NAACP knew that it was in for a horrible struggle. The film, in its technique and vast scenes, was a masterpiece, yet in the view of the organization, it contained a brutally

10. Daniel J. Leab, *From Sambo to Superspade: The Black Experience in Motion Pictures*, 32.
11. George D. Proctor, "Review of *The Birth of a Nation*," *Motion Picture News*, March 13, 1915, 49–50; Thomas B. Gregory, "Review of *The Birth of a Nation*," *New York American*, April 2, 1915, 23; advertisement for *The Birth of a Nation*, *New York Tribune*, March 7, 1915, sec. 3, p. 6.

racist message. The West Coast secretary of the NAACP admitted, however, that "from an artistic point of view [the film is] the finest thing of its kind I have ever witnessed."[12]

Many well-known figures spoke out against the film. They included Harvard University president Charles Eliot, black leader Booker T. Washington, Rabbi Stephen Wise, and *New York Evening Post* publisher Oswald Garrison Villard. Over the next year, the film was banned in the state of Ohio and the cities of Denver, Boston, St. Louis, Chicago, and Pittsburgh. Despite widespread banning, more than twenty-five million people had seen the film by 1916.[13] In New York City, it was estimated that 825,000 people had seen the film.

The Epoch Producing Company, distributor of the film, was aware of the hard-line conservative stance that the Kansas Board of Censorship had displayed during its first eight months of operation when it had banned many films. Epoch was afraid that *Birth* would suffer the same fate. In addition, Kansas had a long tradition of pro-Union sentiment, and the film was bound to cause a controversy. In November 1915, the distributors decided not to present the film to the board because they did not want to risk the probable denial of the film in the state. They argued that they heard that the film had been condemned in advance.[14]

The Birth of a Nation did open in Kansas City, Missouri, on October 24, 1915. The State of Missouri did not have a censorship board at this time, but the City of Kansas City, Missouri, did. The picture passed the censorship board and played to the public with little conflict. It was an immense hit in Kansas City, and many who lived in the eastern part of Kansas crossed the state border to see the controversial film.

The immense popularity of the film and the public demand from many Kansans to view *The Birth of a Nation* eventually influenced the film company to submit the movie to the Board of Censorship in December 1915. The board members viewed the film and ruled that it could not be exhibited in Kansas. Superintendent of instruction Ross issued a statement that denied exhibition of the film because: (1) *The Birth of a Nation* was historically inaccurate. The board believed that Griffith had taken license with his depiction of certain facets of history in order to appeal to emotions. Examples included the similarity between Stoneman and Thaddeus Stevens and the portrayal of

---

12. Cripps, *Slow Fade to Black*, 53.
13. Landay, *Black Film Stars*, 26.
14. "Kansas Cut Out," *Topeka State Journal*, 23 November 1915, Clipping File, KSBR, KSHS.

the heroism of the Ku Klux Klan. (2) The board believed that the film was full of racial hatred, promoting the idea that black Americans were the root of many social problems in the United States. In the board's view, African Americans were continuously portrayed in a negative light. (3) The film was immoral and sexually suggestive because of the implication of rape and miscegenational situations that the board judged to be inappropriate. And (4) *The Birth of a Nation* could inspire sectional bitterness between the North and the South.[15]

The Epoch Producing Company appealed the decision, and on January 24, 1916, the film was presented to the state Appeal Board. Sardius Brewster, the attorney general, and John Botkin, the secretary of state, were present, but Governor Arthur Capper did not view the film himself. He gave the task to his private secretary, Charles Sessions. Capper initially appeared not to take sides over the *Birth of a Nation* ruling, perhaps waiting to see the popular reaction to the film's ban.

H. A. Sherman, manager of the Epoch Producing Company, pleaded his case before the Appeal Board on January 24. He stated that the film was elevating, a true historical representation that promoted peace between the black man and the white man. Brewster, a foe of the film, grilled Sherman on the accuracy and historical representation of the movie, and he called attention to the misrepresentation of Thaddeus Stevens and several other "distortions" of history. Sherman replied that Brewster was the first "living" man to ever question the film's historical accuracy. Additionally, to appease concerns over the portrayal of African Americans, an extra hundred feet of film had been produced, portraying the "wonderful" advances that African Americans had made since the war; he promised that this footage would gladly be added to *The Birth of a Nation* when it was displayed in Kansas.[16] Brewster questioned the necessity of this extra film if the movie's basis was not prejudicial. Sherman then blatantly lied to the court to defend the film: "I even understand that Booker T. Washington himself has cordially endorsed *The Birth of a Nation*."[17] After hearing the arguments of Sherman, the decision was made to uphold the rejection and bar the film from the state.

---

15. "*Birth of a Nation* Rejected by State 'Movie' Censors," *Topeka Daily Capital*, January 25, 1916, in ibid.

16. Nikkie Fleener, "Answering Film with Film: The Hampton Epilogue, a Positive Alternative to the Negative Black Stereotypes Presented in *The Birth of a Nation*," 410–11.

17. "*Birth of a Nation* Rejected by State 'Movie' Censors." Washington never endorsed the film; in fact, when Washington's Tuskegee Institute was approached about helping to produce the additional footage tacked on to *The Birth of a Nation*, Washington refused.

Superintendent Wilbert Ross issued the following statement after the Appeal Board's decision: "The picture is rejected because it is not proper, is not instructive, and from its false title through its issue of misrepresentations of the north, the Negro and our country's history to the final culminating travesty which pictures peace on earth and good will to men as outcome of passion, of hate and murder it is vicious and immoral—immoral not alone in the parts that are sexually suggestive, but in its whole revelation of race prejudice and sectional bitterness."[18]

The decision to ban the film was influenced by a variety of factors. The state had a long tradition of antislavery activism. A large number of free African Americans had come to live in the Quindaro and Lawrence regions of Kansas to escape slavery. Kansas joined the Union on January 29, 1861, after several Southern states had seceded. The Civil War started within a few weeks, and Kansas became involved in the violence. In 1863, Confederate raiders under William C. Quantrill burned most of Lawrence and killed about 150 persons. During the war, Kansas sent more men to the Union army, in proportion to its population, than any other state. After the war ended in 1865, thousands of Union veterans and newly freed slaves moved into Kansas to claim land. These historical influences had a great impact on Kansas's acceptance of a film that was perceived to be blatantly racist and anti-Union.

The Board of Censorship faced a constituency of former Union soldiers and their families, who protested the gross displacement of history in *The Birth of a Nation*. The Grand Army of the Republic (GAR) led the fight against the film, objecting to what it considered the obvious Southern slant of the picture and the incorrect portrait of Northerners during Reconstruction. C. A. Meek, commander in chief of the Kansas GAR, met with the board in person on January 24, the day of the appeal decision, and said that he "protested, in the name of the old soldiers, against allowing the false name of the old soldiers, against allowing the false impression created by the picture to be spread over the state. . . . [I]t makes out that the North was all wrong and the South right in the Civil War. It holds up the Ku Klux Klan as knight errants protecting the helpless."[19]

Another political factor was Arthur Capper. If Capper and the Board of Censorship allowed the film to be shown, a large constituency of voters would

18. Ibid.
19. "G.A.R. Protest Declares Picture as Base Libel," *Topeka Daily Capital,* January 25, 1916, Clipping File, KSBR, KSHS.

be upset with the decision, which could have a definite impact on the governor's political future. Some voters were offended by what they considered gross inaccuracies that the film portrayed and felt as if their family honor and tradition were threatened by the depiction of these scenes. The decision of the Appeal Board, it was argued, protected African Americans by banning a film that had the potential of inciting violence. Additionally, the decision justified the actions of all Kansans who had fought in the Civil War to protect the Union. Capper wrote Iowa governor G. W. Clarke on January 13, 1916, eleven days before the Appeal Board decision, "I have not hesitated, however, to say, that if the proposed exhibition still carried the objectionable features, which I knew it had in eastern states, I shall do all in my power to bar it out of Kansas."[20]

Capper had strong personal views that were racially progressive for his time. While he was running for governor and then for reelection in 1917, he regularly addressed African American organizations. In an address at Webster University in Kansas City in 1916, Capper proclaimed, "Injustice and brutality are prolific breeders. Oppression and denial of the constitutional rights of men and citizens, as intelligence increases, are bound to bear fruit. There will come a time when desperate measures will intervene to end injustice." It was under this premise that Capper took the "desperate measure" to put political pressure on both the Board of Censorship and the Appeal Board to prevent *The Birth of a Nation* from being shown in the state. Capper argued, "For years we have at times mercilessly shot, hanged or burned at the stake the Negroes who committed or were suspected of committing offenses against white women. Without any show of 'due process of law' more than 3000 colored men have thus been ruled into eternity by lawless white mobs since 1885. Such conduct smirches any assertion we might make that ours is a higher civilization."[21] These were very strong words for a politician in 1916. But Capper, known as a moral man, knew that *The Birth of a Nation* would perpetuate the myth that African American men lusted after white women sexually and that lynching was justified.

The Epoch Producing Company could not compete with the various interest groups. Many individual citizens also wrote Governor Capper and asked him not to allow the film to be shown. This strong pro-Northern, pro-

---

20. Capper to G. W. Clarke, January 13, 1916, Box 48, File 1916, "Speeches, 1916–1925," Capper Papers, KSHS.
21. Capper, speech at Webster University, June 8, 1916, in ibid.

Union sentiment fought against the film's release in the state. But the strong reaction against the film by the African American population in the state and Arthur Capper's strong views against racism were the primary motivating forces. Capper wrote, "We have a large Negro Population in Kansas. As a rule they are good citizens who are attending strictly to their own business, and I am opposed to exhibitions of this kind which excite race prejudice."[22]

Democratic-based newspapers throughout Kansas argued that the *Birth* decision was a political maneuver by Republicans to appeal to the Negro vote. The *Topeka State Journal* noted: "Almost without exception the action of the state censors has been branded as a ploy for Negro votes." The *Independence Daily Reporter* claimed, "In rejecting *The Birth of a Nation* in Kansas the moving picture censor board has made a serious mistake. It has allowed the fear of a loss of Negro votes at the polls next fall to overshadow its duty."[23] Although African Americans composed less than 5 percent of the population in Kansas, Capper chose not to allow the film to dehumanize these citizens. He possibly could have lost two distinct voting groups if the appeal had over-turned the censors' decision—pro-Union sympathizers and the black vote.

Many newspapers in Kansas, particularly the Democratic press, directed their criticism toward W. D. Ross and the censorship process. To exclude Kansas citizens from the most highly praised and influential film of the era was beyond reproach in many editors' minds. One such example is the sentiment expressed by the editor of the *Concordia Blade*:

> The Birth of a Nation will not be allowed to be shown in Kansas. The high and mighty state movie censor, the Honorable W. D. Ross who never in his life had an original idea and who is of a high caliber that he would make a good ward healer in a country school district has set his mighty mind at variance with some of the greatest in this country and says that this conceded masterpiece of the movies will corrupt the morals of the people of Kansas. The refusal of the picture was based on the fact that it is not instructive and the people of Kansas must have their morals looked after by a thirty dollar a month country school teacher and a broken down preacher that can't hold a job in the pulpit but through some political will was given a position where he can shape the morality of the state through arbitrarily saying that "Thou Shall

22. Capper to Clarke, January 13, 1916, in ibid.

23. "Hammers Are Out," *Topeka State Journal*, February 7, 1916, Clipping File, KSBR, KSHS; *Independence Daily Reporter* as quoted in ibid.

Not." Some of the Concordia people who have seen the picture say that it is, without a doubt, one of the greatest productions that has ever been offered to the American people and makes those who claim to have a half way mind of their own, peeved to have . . . [t]his country school teacher deprive them of an opportunity to enjoy the privileges that people of other states have. All of the larger cities of this country have shown The Birth of a Nation but Kansas people are so susceptible that this film is unfit for them to see.[24]

The attacks were nasty and personal. But they were not just directed toward the censors or their banning of *The Birth of a Nation;* they were hostile to the censorship process itself.

The film remained banned in Kansas during Capper's term of office but not without a state supreme court case, *State of Kansas, ex rel. S. M. Brewster v. L. M. Crawford et al.* Attorney General Brewster had to continue to defend his stance in prohibiting the film from the state during his term of office. In February 1916, while the film was causing enormous controversy, Brewster composed a fourteen-page typewritten statement defending his decision, claiming that the film was "immoral . . . a slander on the character of public men during the Civil War times . . . and not true to history."[25] The Kansas Supreme Court case involved the Board of Censorship's reexamination of *The Birth of a Nation* in early 1917. Brewster's statement was made in answer to a suit pending in the district court testing the right of the Board of Censorship and the Appeal Board to reject the picture. On May 5, 1917, the film was reexamined by the Board of Censorship, and after some discussion, it was announced that after certain eliminations had been made, which the board detailed, the film would be passed. The proposed changes were mailed to the Epoch Producing Company, along with the film, on May 7. On May 9, a new order was mailed to the film's producers with quite a different message. It read, "The Board of Review of Motion Pictures, Kansas, hereby order the recall of the film 'The Birth of a Nation' for re-examination, and we are giving you the official thirty days' notice. In the meantime, of course, there must be no exhibition of the picture in the state."[26] This meant that the board

24. "Our Censors of Morals," *Concordia Blade,* n.d., in ibid.
25. "Brewster in Line," *Topeka Journal,* February 26, 1916, Clipping File, KSBR, KSHS.
26. *State of Kansas, ex rel. S. M. Brewster v. L. M. Crawford et al.,* in *Kansas Reports,* no. 103 (Topeka: State Printer, 1919), 76–69. The Board of Censors officially changed its name to the Board of Review earlier in the year. This was accompanied by a change in staff that may have led to the board's decision to revisit the film.

wanted to see the film for another examination, even though the film had been approved just two days before. Capper had been infuriated with the overturn of the original decision and demanded that the board "reexamine" the film, pressuring to keep the film banned from the state.

The State of Kansas took the company to court. The motion picture company refused to comply with the order under Section 17, Chapter 308, of the Kansas Laws of 1917 (a revised censorship statute), which said the Board of Review (Censorship) had the right to demand the film to be returned if reexamination was determined to be an appropriate action. The Epoch Producing Company questioned the "appropriateness" of the examination and would not return the film.

The defendants, under the counsel of attorney L. M. Crawford, pleaded that the film had been approved and alleged that members of the board were satisfied with the decision until they had been influenced adversely "by certain prominent and influential" persons to recall the picture. The defendants pleaded that this unyielding outside pressure was ordering the members not to reexamine the film but to reject it in its entirety. The "overwhelming influence" referred to was indeed Capper.

For many years, including those following his two terms as governor, Capper discouraged the distribution of *The Birth of a Nation* for both political and personal reasons. In 1917, while he was still governor, he drafted a letter to his newly staffed Board of Review in which he explained his position: "The only way to make that picture moral . . . is to eliminate everything after the title." He continued to state that it was immoral and debasing to picture General Ulysses S. Grant as a "roughneck," to picture Thaddeus Stevens as a "tyrant and habitué of Negro hovels," and to "pervert history by saying the South was right and that the North was wrong. . . . To do anything that would tend to stir up race and class hatred . . . borders on treason." Capper was fully aware that an African American man had been lynched in Olathe earlier in the year.[27]

Obviously, the release of the film in Kansas would also seriously damage the extent of Capper's authority over his administrative agencies, as he had openly expressed his disgust over the film. It was revealed during the trial that the Board of Review had changed its mind on approval of the film after receiving letters from Capper and his private secretary, Charles Sessions.[28]

---

27. Capper to Mrs. J. M. Miller, May 10, 1917, Box 11, File 45; "Lynching at Olathe," Box 12, File 90, General Correspondence, both in Capper Papers, KSHS.

28. "Capper Got Busy," *Topeka Journal*, June 22, 1917, Clipping File, KSBR, KSHS.

The plaintiff, the State of Kansas, was headed by Attorney General Brewster. The state declared that the board members were simply doing their job and decided to have another look at the film. The court considered each point and argument, and the majority of the justices found that the film certificate had been approved, and, therefore, under law, the film could be recalled for reexamination. The court found that this was a decision that could affect public morals, so it could be required by mandamus to supply the film to the board. The Epoch Producing Company was required to give the film back to the Board of Review. Shortly after the court decision, *The Birth of a Nation* was again banned from exhibition in the state.

Capper's influence was pervasive enough that the Kansas Supreme Court gave the Board of Review the judicial decision it needed to once again prevent *The Birth of a Nation* from exhibition. According to information released in 1924, Capper told the board never to review the film again. He instructed the board not to let the movie be made public no matter how many scenes were removed. During his term of office, he received a vast quantity of correspondence concerning the possible exhibition of the film. Most of it was in favor of Capper's decision. In one letter, John R. Shillady, secretary of the NAACP, claimed, "This picture is emphatically objected to by the colored people of this country who regard it as inimical to them and as tending to accentuate and engender race prejudice and race hatred." Capper responded to Shillady, "You need have no uneasiness about this picture being exhibited in Kansas. . . . *The Birth of a Nation* has not been exhibited and will not exhibit in Kansas as long as I have anything to say about it."[29]

By 1919, *The Birth of a Nation* had been seen by more Americans than any other film. Its popularity remained consistent, with continuous showings across the country. Roughly 5 percent of the American population had seen the film by 1919, a feat unmatched by any other film at the time.

Governor Henry J. Allen inherited *The Birth of a Nation* problem when he took office the same year. Now with Capper out of the way, distributors once again submitted the film to the Board of Review. But their hopes were dashed when Allen, a Republican, told W. D. Ross, "So far as my influence is concerned in Kansas, the picture will not be admitted to the state."[30]

---

29. John R. Shillady to Capper, October 10, 1918; Capper to Shillady, October 17, 1918, both in Box 11, File 45, Capper Papers, KSHS.

30. W. D. Ross to Henry J. Allen, February 19, 1920; Allen to Ross, February 24, 1920, both in Records of the Governor's Office, Correspondence Files, Governor Henry J. Allen, Box 15, Motion Picture Board, 1920 File, Archives Department, KSHS (hereafter cited as Allen Papers).

Between 1919 and 1921, several educators attempted to show the film in college classrooms. When Professor M. L. Smith of the Kansas State Normal School requested permission to show the film to his students, Allen, not the Board of Review, denied his request. He told Smith, "It is a powerful picture, but it undoubtedly has an unfortunate racial effect for the very reason that it is powerful."[31] During his term of office, Allen remained under constant pressure to allow the film in the state. The film's immense popularity, coupled with the fact that Kansas was the only state to still not allow the film to be exhibited, made Kansas, in the words of one board member, "the butt of many jokes." There were rumors that some of Allen's staff members were offered bribes by motion picture distributors to try to influence the governor to change his mind on the matter. The local distributors saw an immense economic opportunity and were willing to try almost anything to get the film exhibited. It is significant to understand that for all practical purposes, this decision was no longer that of the board but that of the governor.

The Birth of a Nation remained in the collective conscience of the American people as the country entered the 1920s. The state of Kansas, and the United States as a whole, had undergone a resurgence of racial unrest beginning with the end of World War I. The Ku Klux Klan had been reestablished and swiftly swelled its ranks throughout the nation. In 1915, there were only a few hundred members of the Klan in Kansas, but by 1923 membership had leaped to sixty thousand. The Klan had become a powerful yet radical political force in the state. *The Birth of a Nation* was attacked by some opponents as part of a campaign to stimulate the growth of the Ku Klux Klan. Those who opposed the film feared that the exhibition of the film in Kansas could further increase the political clout and membership of the Klan.

As the 1922 election approached, some Kansans were concerned about the growth of the Ku Klux Klan. Governor Allen said that it was the "greatest curse that comes from a civilized people," and he did his best to combat the organization. Leo Oliva claims that "Kansans were especially attracted to its anti-foreign, anti-Jewish, anti-Catholic, and anti-Negro prejudices because they needed someone to blame for the failure of their moral experiments."[32] Allen eventually brought suit against the Klan, and the crusade was carried on by the attorney general. The prosecutors and the courts had trouble keeping

31. Allen to M. L. Smith, June 7, 1919, Box 15, Motion Picture Board, 1919 File, Allen Papers, KSHS.
32. Oliva, "Kansas," 265.

witnesses who were willing to testify against the Klan because of threats and pressure, and the campaign proved to be unsuccessful. William Allen White, the nationally known Kansas newspaper editor, denounced the Ku Klux Klan.[33] He argued, "The whole trouble with the Ku Klux Klan is that it is based upon such deep foolishness that it is found to be a menace to good government in any community,"[34] By the early 1920s, one out of every four Kansans was African American, Jewish, or Catholic, and they found themselves under increased harassment by the Klan.[35]

Jonathan M. Davis, a Democrat, took office as governor in 1923. Davis faced a difficult political situation upon his election. The Ku Klux Klan had gained immense political power in a short amount of time. By 1923, Klan candidates had been elected in Pittsburg, Fort Scott, Wichita, Emporia, and Kansas City, as well as a number of smaller towns.[36] Kansas Klansmen belonged to both the Democratic and the Republican parties. Davis not only faced a Republican legislature but also had to please the Democratic Party and the radical Ku Klux Klan, which held significant power. Navigating this political terrain proved difficult.[37]

Davis was pressured by the Ku Klux Klan and the film exchanges to review the Kansas decision regarding *The Birth of a Nation* early in his term of office. In a confidential letter to Gertrude A. Sawtell, chairperson of the Kansas Board of Review of Motion Pictures under Davis, the governor inquired about the film's previous and current status. Mrs. Sawtell replied, "It is my understanding that this film was approved by the former members of the board and through the wishes of Ex-Governor Capper the approval was withdrawn and the film has stood rejected since then. At the time the approval card signed by the members of the board was destroyed and a rejection card made."[38] The letter clearly demonstrated Capper's immense influence on the Board of Review and its decisions. Both Capper and Allen, by using their influence to restrict *The Birth of a Nation*, had limited the independence of the board as a nonpolitical agency. Davis continued in this tradition, using the film in a way to benefit his own needs.

---

33. Griffith, *Hometown News*, 227.

34. Johnson, *William Allen White's America*, 343.

35. David Chalmers, *Hooded Americanism*, 144.

36. Ibid., 145.

37. Robert W. Richmond, *Kansas: A Land of Contrasts*, 225–26.

38. Gertrude A. Sawtell to Jonathan M. Davis, May 12, 1923, Records of the Governor's Office, Correspondence Files, Governor Jonathan M. Davis, Box 21.2, File 6, Archives Department, KSHS (hereafter cited as Davis Papers).

In early June 1923, the press was notified by the distributors that the film might be granted permission to be exhibited in the state. This was obviously a publicity stunt to garner support for the film. A flurry of activity followed the announcement. Anti-*Birth* forces mobilized much more quickly than they had in 1915. Various branches of the NAACP sent telegrams and letters to Davis in hopes that the film would not be permitted to be shown. The NAACP sent letters from the national office, state offices, and city offices in Wichita, Lawrence, and Kansas City, Kansas, protesting the film and asking that Kansans not have to be "outraged by this nefarious display of human viciousness." Other black organizations emphatically pushed to deny access to the film for Kansans. The Wichita Ministerial League, an organization of African American ministers, wrote Davis, telling him that *The Birth of a Nation* "is absolutely capable of arousing racial malice and ill-will."[39] The action by African Americans in the 1923 controversy was much more overt and vocal than in 1915. This immediacy of action by the African American community was probably triggered by the race riots that had wounded the nation from 1919 to 1921 and by the fact that the film could be used to inspire even more Kansans to join the Ku Klux Klan. Fearing that black rights would be limited even more severely by the growth of the Klan, African American Kansans fought against public exhibition of the film.

They were joined in protest by white citizens. Joseph Taggart, a prominent Kansas City, Kansas, attorney, sent a confidential letter to Davis pleading with him to "prevent that nasty criminal exhibition from being seen by young people in the state." More than six hundred Kansans signed a petition that asked the governor not to allow the film to be presented in Kansas. Many citizens thought that the film was wrong, even though the Klan had permeated many facets of life in their communities and the film had been extremely popular throughout the country. The state of Kansas was divided over the issue of allowing the film to be exhibited. Many Kansans believed that the film was socially undesirable because it was antiblack and racist; thus, the film was immoral because it encouraged racial prejudice. Many other citizens believed that the film was historically accurate and a wonderful piece of socially acceptable entertainment. G. A. Kubach, proprietor of the Lyric Theater in Abilene, claimed, "Many of my patrons have come up to me and

39. James A. Spears, secretary of the Wichita NAACP, to Davis, June 14, 1923; B. C. Rannavalona, secretary, and W. L. Hutcherson, assistant secretary, Wichita Ministerial League, to Davis, December 3, 1923, both in ibid.

said—what a shame this wonderful picture has been shown all over the country and we have been deprived of seeing it in our State." S. E. Schwahn, manager of the Strand Theater in Salina, argued, "Surely this picture should be
passed on the merits of the picture and as I have viewed it several times I have
been unable to see wherein it should be held out of this State."[40]

Despite vigorous action by many Kansans against the film, theater managers anxiously anticipated increased profits if the film passed the Board of
Review. W. D. Fulton, manager of the De Lure Theater in Hutchinson,
inquired about the film's possible showing: "From all reports I have heard and
from the attitude of the general public it seems to me that the logical thing to
do would be to let the public see this great picture. . . . [I]t is the duty of the
Board to pass or reject this picture on its own merits with no outside influences to interfere." Theater owner H. A. McClure of Emporia also eagerly
awaited the decision of the board. He commented, "We have a natural pride
in presenting the masterpiece of the screen in our theater and are very anxious to show the greatest of all Griffith productions."[41] The Klan never publicly came out in support of the exhibition of the film, but one can easily
speculate that *The Birth of a Nation* would only help swell its ranks.

The film was finally approved by the Board of Review in the fall of 1923.
By that time, there was no Appeal Board, so the decision was final. As
expected, there was an outcry of protest. A special meeting of the NAACP
assembled in Metropolitan Hall in Topeka on December 5, 1923, to discuss
what action to take. A committee was appointed to protest the decision.
The protest was based on the following premises: "1. The distortion of facts.
2. The general immoral nature and corrupt practices depicted therein. 3. The
demonstrated effect of this exhibition in engendering racial bitterness, antag-
onism and strife. 4. The wide-spread desire of the citizens of this state to
foster and promote interracial good will, co-operation and mutual security."
Protests and petitions flowed into the office of Kansas attorney general
Charles Benjamin Griffith. Members of the clergy, professors, military personnel, and private citizens from Kansas City, Fort Scott, and Arkansas City
angrily arrived to protest the decision. The attorney general told the various
groups that he would discuss with the Board of Review the advisability of
passing such a picture. He told protesters to ask the officials of their respec-

40. Joseph Taggart to Davis, June 8, 1923; G. A. Kubach to Davis, October 30, 1923;
S. E. Schwahn to Davis, October 31, 1923, all in ibid.
41. W. D. Fulton to Davis, November 2, 1923; H. A. McClure to Davis, October 19, 1923, both
in ibid.

tive cities to pass ordinances forbidding the appearance of the picture. The attorney general stated, "I am amazed the board passed it, and still more amazed that Governor Davis says he sees nothing objectionable about it."[42]

Immediately, the press demanded to know if the decision to allow the exhibition of the film in the state was that of the Kansas Board of Review or that of Governor Davis. A confusing controversy developed over Davis's role in the decision. In the summer of 1923, Davis sent a letter to Gertrude Sawtell, Board of Review chairwoman, regarding the film. Davis wrote, "I write this letter to inform you that it is my wish that the board of review refrain from reviewing the picture called *The Birth of a Nation*. If you do review it, do not allow it to be exhibited in Kansas. I am satisfied that the picture tends to cause race hatred. We cannot have any of that in the state."[43]

C. W. Slater of Oklahoma City had exclusive distribution rights for the film in Kansas. In early June 1923, Slater appeared at the headquarters of the Board of Review asking for a date for review of the film. Apparently, Slater was going to have the film passed by the board using any means necessary. The *Kansas City Times,* on June 7, 1923, reported that Slater had attempted to bribe the members of the board to get his film passed. When that did not work, Slater sent a personal letter to Governor Davis in which he stated:

> You are wrong in your harsh criticism and hasty decision and condemnation of this picture, especially since you write that you have never seen it. It certainly cannot represent your high ideals of justice, to condemn without even a trial, and I am asking you to *withdraw* your orders *both written and verbal* to the State Board of Review. I ask you to instruct the Board to receive this picture and to pass it or reject it, just as they do all other motion pictures, strictly in accordance with the laws governing the showing of motion pictures in Kansas.[44]

It is unknown whether Davis had seen *The Birth of a Nation* prior to this letter. In September 1923, the governor, at the request of the promoters of the film, screened the movie in Kansas City, Missouri, before it came to the Review

42. "Showers of Protest Greet Governor Davis," *Topeka Daily Capital,* 6 December 1923, p. 1, Clipping File, KSBR, KSHS.

43. "Davis Hasn't Announced Reason for Changing His Mind on *Birth of a Nation*," *Topeka Daily Capital,* January 20, 1924, in ibid.

44. C. W. Slater to KSBR, June 11, 1923, Box 2, File 6, Administration of Governor Jonathan Davis, 1923–1925, Subject Files—Censor Board and *Birth of a Nation* Controversy, KSHS; Slater to Davis, July 27, 1923, Davis Papers, KSHS.

Board. After viewing the film, Davis stated, "I told the members of the board that I had seen the picture and thought it could be censored and admitted to Kansas. I told them, however, to use their own judgment in the matter."[45]

Several rumors in the statehouse said that the governor sent a personal emissary from Topeka to Kansas City with instructions to pass the picture. Carl J. Peterson, state bank commissioner, was alleged by the *Topeka Daily Capital* to be the emissary. Both Davis and Peterson denied the story. Davis did admit that he had had a conversation with the Board of Review after he had seen the film and before the board made its decision. Obviously, Davis's opinion was important enough for the censors to change their minds on allowing the highly controversial film to be exhibited.[46]

One can only speculate as to why Davis made such a dramatic change in opinion concerning the film. Possibly, he did not consider *The Birth of a Nation* racist or offensive enough to prevent it from being seen. He might have made a political move to get the backing of the Ku Klux Klan in Kansas, which now greatly outnumbered African Americans in the state. He could have received a bribe from Slater to allow the film to be exhibited. Whatever the reasons behind the decision, it was a dramatic one.

Former governor Henry J. Allen summed up his feeling on Davis's decision: "In my four years' administration every influence from that of the practical politician to the use of money was brought to bear to an effort to induce me to permit this picture to be shown in Kansas . . . There is only one reason 'The Birth of a Nation' is to be shown in Kansas, and that is commercial. . . . The action of Governor Davis is sordid and inconsiderate. . . . This is the very worst hour since the Civil War to show it."[47] By late 1923, the Klan looked unstoppable in Kansas. The only public figure to condemn the organization was *Emporia Gazette* editor William Allen White who was literally risking his life to defeat the political and social power of the Klan.

As *The Birth of a Nation* was exhibited across the state, cities such as Wichita and Junction City passed ordinances to prevent the exhibition of the film. These ordinances did not hold up in federal district court, and restraining orders were placed on cities that passed such laws. Numerous citizens

45. "Governor Says He Didn't Order Movie Censor Board to Pass 'Birth of a Nation,'" *Topeka Daily Capital,* December 12, 1923, Clipping File, KSBR, KSHS.
46. Ibid.
47. "Won't Stop Film," *Topeka State Journal,* December 4, 1923, Clipping File, KSBR, KSHS.

across the state protested such action, but according to the court decision, the film could be legally exhibited anywhere in the state of Kansas based on the action of the Board of Review.[48] The NAACP also led a campaign to have the permission revoked, but its efforts were to no avail. *The Birth of a Nation* played successfully throughout the state in 1924 and 1925, despite protests.

The case of *The Birth of a Nation* is a classic example of film censorship, both governmental and nongovernmental, violating the First Amendment right of free speech. Exhibiting to a mass audience a motion picture that clearly presents racial prejudice and a distortion of American history was a true dilemma for Kansans. The problems regarding *Birth* were extremely critical because of the widespread belief that the film could incite racial prejudice and increase the membership of a vigilante terrorist organization, namely, the Ku Klux Klan. Balancing constitutional freedoms while protecting the American people from the incitement to racial violence remains a critical problem today.

A large number of Kansans supported the censorship of *The Birth of a Nation*. These citizens, both black and white, organized campaigns to keep the film out of the state. However, a biracial group was never organized to fight the film; the races worked separately. Despite this lack of cooperation, Kansas was progressive in race relations compared with many other states.

The story of *The Birth of a Nation* has several paradoxes. Although a large segment of the Kansas population supported banning the film because of racism, the Ku Klux Klan, with its doctrine of racial hatred, continued to grow. It was not until the successful national campaign of several prominent newspapermen (primarily William Allen White) to expose the Klan in 1924 and 1925 that the organization lost much of its steam. Additionally, although the majority of citizens in the state did not actively support motion picture censorship, many believed that a picture as controversial or dangerous as *The Birth of a Nation* should not be allowed in the state.[49]

The Birth of a Nation was a crucial political issue in the administration of Kansas governors Arthur Capper, Henry Allen, and Jonathan Davis, and all three exerted pressure on the Kansas Board of Review. The motion picture board became a political and sociological tool of the governors, enabling

48. "Show 'Birth of Nation,'" *Topeka Daily Capital,* January 1, 1924, in ibid.
49. Gerald R. Butters Jr., "The Kansas Board of Review of Motion Pictures and Film Censorship, 1913–1923."

100 **Banned in Kansas**

them to use the board to appeal to blocs of voters and, in some cases, to follow their own moral consciences.

The Kansas State Historical Society exhibited *The Birth of a Nation* in 1962 with little fanfare or response. Yet in the 1980s, the film evoked a great emotional outcry, demonstrating that many of the attitudes and prejudices that existed in 1915 were still there and that, as a society, citizens were much more aware of racism in the media. In the spring of 1986, the Granada Theater in Kansas City, Kansas, attempted to show the film as part of a revival series of classic films. Various political protests by black organizations and threats of physical violence against the theater manager, Bob Maes, and his family convinced the manager not to exhibit the film to the public. Censorship, in one form or another, still existed.

Five

The Battle Lines Are Drawn, 1916–1917

The Birth of a Nation was not the only controversy that Governor Arthur Capper, superintendent of public instruction W. D. Ross, and censors Festus Foster and Carrie Simpson faced in 1916. Motion picture censorship found itself under assault by Kansans, primarily by those citizens involved in the film industry. Kansas, one of the first states to implement such legislation, experimented with censorship through a process of trial and error. But this practice was having definite economic consequences, and industry members were willing to fight.

The *Mutual Film* decision had been a major victory for advocates of motion picture censorship. Maryland became the fourth state to enact a formal film censorship process in 1916. As Laura Wittern-Keller argues, in the period 1916–1922, "most states flirted with the idea of state censorship, some seriously and some for the political advantage of the sponsoring legislator."[1] The city governments of Louisville, Kentucky; Los Angeles; and Kansas City, Missouri, all considered municipal censorship boards. This call for censorship culminated in Congressman Dudley Hughes of Georgia introducing a bill that would create a federal motion picture commission in the Bureau of

---

1. Wittern-Keller, "Freedom of the Screen," 55.

Education in the Department of Interior that would examine, censor, and classify all films that crossed state borders.[2] Hughes telegrammed Governor Capper at the beginning of the year regarding the effectiveness and operation of censorship in the state. As Capper explained to the Georgia congressman, "State censorship has superseded municipal censorship. No figures are available as to attendance, but moving picture houses are increasing daily under censor law. State censorship is proving satisfactory and the censorship idea is generally approved by Kansas people."[3] Hughes's bill was defeated, but throughout the 1910s and into the 1920s there were frequent attempts to establish federal motion picture censorship.[4]

Capper's reply to Hughes was indeed a rosy description of the actual state of affairs. By January 1916, the motion picture industry in Kansas was organized and ready to do battle with the Board of Censorship. The *Topeka State Journal* explained, "Disgusted and distinctly peeved by the action of the state motion picture censor board, Kansas exhibitors are preparing to wage an energetic fight on the ruthless slashing and rejection of pictures by censors."[5] As the year progressed, industry men accepted the inevitability of the censorship process but believed that it must be a "logical and rational system," in their view. The goal of the industry was for a repeal or revision of the 1915 censorship legislation.

The industry had three primary objections to the way things were being handled. First, in the minds of the industry men, there appeared to be little logic in how the censors were deciding what to ban and what to allow to play in the state. Big-budget, respected pictures such as *Carmen* and *The Birth of a Nation* were banned, whereas more sensational films like *The Lure, The House of Bondage,* and *Damaged Goods* (all produced in 1914) were allowed to play.

The synopsis of *Damaged Goods* would appear to describe the very type of film that Kansas censors wanted to keep out of the state. The picture, an American Film production, was an enormously successful motion picture that was released on the states' rights market in September 1914 and continued to be rereleased until 1919. The sexually provocative nature of the film

2. Jowett, *Film: The Democratic Art,* 122.
3. Telegram from Capper to Dudley Hughes, January 20, 1916, Box 37, File 20, State Agencies—Moving Censorship Appeal Commission, Capper Papers, KSHS. A number of municipalities had experimented with film censorship before the Kansas Board of Motion Picture Censorship was created in 1915. These cities included Wichita.
4. Randall, *Censorship of the Movies,* 13.
5. "Move to Topeka," *Topeka State Journal,* January 26, 1916, Clipping File, KSBR, KSHS.

was surely the attraction. The protagonist of *Damaged Goods* is law student George Dupont. After an attempted seduction by a married family friend, George becomes sexually curious. He beds a prostitute, contracts syphilis, and decides to commit suicide, just when the woman of the night reappears in his life. She explains that she contracted syphilis from a respected, wealthy man but was turned away from numerous hospitals for treatment. She then decided she would seek revenge by trying to bed as many wealthy men as possible so she could spread the dreaded and deadly disease. She is eventually helped by Dr. Clifford, an expert in the treatment of venereal disease. Dupont goes to the good doctor, but he is warned not to marry for two years during the treatment. In a particularly graphic scene, George is shown syphilitic victims in a hospital ward, including imbecilic children. George does not listen to the doctor's advice, marries, and has a child. The child is diagnosed with syphilis, and George dramatically walks into the sea, to kill himself.[6]

The industry men, although happy to make a bundle off a feature like this, could not understand why this film would be accepted and other more respected films rejected. Perhaps the answer lay in the film's pedigree. *Damaged Goods* was originally a play by Eugène Brieux that was staged in New York City in 1913. The production was endorsed by many in the medical establishment and supported by powerful members of New York society. The stage play attempted to lift the veil of secrecy from any discussion of venereal disease. The film, apparently, was made for a serious purpose—to educate, instruct, and warn, rather than titillate.[7]

The second major complaint of the film men was the lack of organization on the part of the board. Theater owners and distributors often had a difficult time determining which films were passed and which were rejected by the board. The board itself had difficulty keeping track of their decisions. A good example was the case involving J. J. Marshall of Manhattan. He was arrested for exhibiting the film *Despair* (1915). The Reverend Foster was the individual who ordered the arrest. The film was rejected by the state censors on December 6, 1915. Eight days later, it was submitted to the Appeal Board, and the majority of the members approved the film. It was listed in the

6. Hansen, *American Film Institute Catalog, 1911–1920*, 183. During this period of time, a "states' rights production" meant that an individual obtained the exclusive right to exhibit a film in a state from the production company or an exchange. States' rights films were often timely, such as cinematic depictions of sporting events or those of a sensational nature that were often barnstormed across a state.

7. Eric Schaefer, *Bold! Daring! Shocking! True! A History of Exploitation Films, 1919–1959*, 22–23.

monthly bulletin as an approved film. Nevertheless, Marshall was arrested following the Appeal Board's decision.[8]

A similar foul-up took place in Cherryville. Foster told theater owner S. A. Davidson not to show a film that was advertised for that evening. Davidson could not get any new films on that short notice, so he had to close the theater. A few days later, he discovered that the film had actually been approved by the Board of Censorship.[9]

The third major complaint of the industry in Kansas involved the cost of censorship and the economic motivation behind the process. By December 1, 1915, the Board of Censorship had collected $14,164 in fees and spent $2,778. This was a net profit of $11,385—in only a seven-month period. This made the board appear much more as a revenue producer than a regulatory board.[10]

Throughout 1916, representatives of the motion picture industry in the state began using every means necessary to fight what was believed to be an unjust economic burden. The first victory came in April when two film projectors were installed in a basement room of the statehouse. A large asbestos screen was put in place, and after more than one year of activity, the Board of Censorship would no longer be a traveling act, moving from theater to theater, but would actually have a home. Prior to this, exchange men had to rent out theaters so that films could be inspected. This cost was removed now that films could be screened in the statehouse.[11]

The Board of Censorship's new screening room was shut down, though, shortly after it went into operation. When Paul McBride, state labor commissioner, viewed the new censor room, he immediately closed it. The room was in an out-of-the-way part of the subbasement of the building, and McBride conceived it would be a virtual death trap for Foster and Simpson. Besides having a large leaky sewage pipe in one corner of the room, the outfit was not set up for fire safety, a real danger in 1916 when film stock was highly flammable. Under the current conditions, in the event of an explosion or fire, no one could escape from the subbasement without following a narrow, winding walkway of more than three hundred feet. McBride closed up shop until safety conditions could be dramatically improved.[12]

8. "Move to Topeka," *Topeka State Journal,* January 26, 1916, Clipping File, KSBR, KSHS.
9. Ibid.
10. *Topeka Daily Capital,* December 5, 1915, in ibid.
11. "Prepare Room for Censors," *Topeka Daily Capital,* April 20, 1916, in ibid.
12. "Kansas Must Observe Own Law—McBride," *Topeka State Journal,* April 21, 1916, in ibid.

One of the major strategies in fighting what was considered to be the "absurdity" of film censorship was using the press. This was often in the context of a newspaper or trade publication that ridiculed the process or demonstrated some of its peculiarities. The *Concordia Blade* reported in its January 29, 1916, edition that Attorney General Brewster laid down some "kissing rules" for motion picture screens in Kansas after "mature deliberation." The paper reported that the following were determined to be the appropriate lengths allowed for different types of kisses, and both the Board of Censorship and the Appeal Board would follow these rules: "First sweetheart or stolen kiss . . . three feet. Second sweetheart kiss . . . fifteen feet. After marriage of a year . . . twenty feet. After five years . . . six feet" (one foot equals one second of screen time).[13] Obviously, the article was tongue-in-cheek, but it added to the feeling that standards of public morality could not be measured and statistically regulated like a train schedule.

The press liked to compare the simple values of Kansas with the more sophisticated mores of the East Coast or Europe. In February 1916, the *Kansas City Star* ran an article titled "Topeka and Paris Morals in a Clash." The article described the controversy over the film *Madame la Presidente* (1916) that was rejected by the Board of Censorship but overruled by the Appeal Board. Foster publicly branded the film as "immoral," and the *Star* lightheartedly pitted the censor against Miss Anna Held, the star of the film. *Madame la Presidente* was a typical French farce involving mistaken identity, a drinking party, and the morality of women. Foster was scandalized by the movie and launched into a diatribe against the picture: "Of course, the people will like the picture, but it has a dangerous effect on the morals of the young. It misrepresents the married man and will have a tendency to shake the confidence that women have in their husbands. . . . That film would make almost any married woman suspicious of her husband and the young girl her sweetheart."[14]

Foster then adopted an argument that reiterated a basic premise for creating motion picture censorship in the state in the first place: the preservation of the purer, cleaner morals of Kansas citizens and protection from the looser, more culpable morals of big-city folk. Foster claimed, "At least fifty percent of the men in Kansas are as virtuous as the purest woman. Not one man out

13. "Movie Kiss at Fault," *Concordia Blade,* January 29, 1916, in ibid. Apparently, couples were required to be less passionate the longer they were married!
14. "Topeka and Paris Morals in a Clash," *Kansas City Star,* February 13, 1916, in ibid.

of ten would flirt with a married woman. They are above such things. I have great confidence in the morality of the Kansas man. . . . It is the purpose of the Kansas censors to put the ban on anything that is harmful. It is better that our people know nothing of the wicked ways of the world. . . . Why should our young be educated into the ways of the fast class of people?"[15]

This was becoming an increasingly difficult thing to do as the war years began. In 1915, a new breed of film developed that portrayed a strikingly different type of woman—the vampire or, simply, the vamp. The vamp was a woman gone astray, a parasitical creature that would figuratively suck the life out of American manhood.[16] These films reflect the significant tensions that existed in American culture over the "New Woman." In contemporary society, this New Woman wanted the ability to vote, to receive an education, to perhaps have a career before marriage, and to live a freer existence than her nineteenth-century sisters. On a more radical level, this woman might also want the ability to smoke and drink and become romantically or sexually involved with the man of her choice. A set of vamp films foreshadowed the seismic cultural changes that would occur during the 1920s in regard to gender roles.

When *A Fool There Was* was released in January 1915, it was a box-office smash. Starring arguably one of the first motion picture stars, Theda Bara, the film established Fox as a major motion picture company. In the film, Bara is a vampire, a woman who ruins honorable men by seducing them with her mystical charm and overt sexuality. The vamp illustrates the power of female sexuality in a period in which gender expectations were changing rapidly. The vampire is not a femme fatale; instead, she is a supernatural creature with an irresistible sexual lure who despicably drains the blood out of men in a spiritual sense by seducing them, then destroying them.[17] In *A Fool There Was,* the Vampire, Bara, sets her sites on John Schuyler, an important American diplomat to England.[18] Schuyler is sent overseas on a passenger liner on which the Vampire conveniently is also traveling. They meet and she orders, "Kiss me, my fool," wherein Schuyler's fate is promptly sealed. He abandons his family, moves in with Bara, ruins his reputation, and throws away his career. Thus, *A Fool There Was* exemplifies a fallen-man genre rather than a fallen-woman motif. In the film, the viewer is introduced to other male characters, usually in

15. Ibid.
16. Janet Staiger, *Bad Women*, 147.
17. Two excellent sources on the life and screen persona of Theda Bara are Genini, *Theda Bara;* and Eve Golden, *Vamp: The Rise and Fall of Theda Bara.*
18. Bara's character was literally named "the Vampire."

No actress's films were as heavily censored by the Kansas State Board of Review as Theda Bara's. Her cinematic depictions of wicked female sexuality infuriated the Kansas censors. (*A Fool There Was*, 1914) (Permission granted by Photofest)

a transient state, who have thrown away their lives for the sexual allure of Bara. As Schuyler becomes more addicted to the Vampire, he begins to drink heavily. Even his wife's attempts to save him from the moral depravity of his seductress are worthless. In the final scene, the fool, Schuyler, collapses, and Bara, wearing a black velvet gown and string of pearls that Schuyler paid for, mockingly throws rose petals at his body exclaiming, "Kiss me, my fool." There is no happy conclusion or reunified family in this film; Schuyler is assumed dead, his family ripped apart, and the Vampire triumphant. *A Fool There Was* was absolutely high melodrama, but it riveted audiences in 1915. The film played to juvenile audiences but simultaneously addressed issues suitable for an adult audience. Fox staged a remarkable publicity campaign for Bara, attempting to conjoin her real life with the roles she played on the screen.

Theda Bara's vampire was exactly the type of woman that the censors of Kansas did not want children to see on the screen. Bara's name evoked a rampant wicked sexuality, and any film with her named attached underwent undue scrutiny by the Kansas Board of Censorship. One such film was *The Devil's Daughter* (1915), based on a Gabriele D'Annunzio play. In this film, Bara plays Giacando Dianti, a woman who vows to wreck the lives of men after her own lover deserts her. The film was promptly banned in Kansas. *Gold and the Woman*, a 1916 Fox production starring Bara, contains the themes of suicide, forced marriage, infidelity, and miscegenation. It was also rejected by the Kansas censors.[19]

The Kansas Board of Censorship considered Theda Bara anathema to the state for the rest of the decade. In one three-month period in 1918, almost half of the films outright rejected by the censors were Theda Bara pictures.[20] They included *The Clemenceau Case* (1915) and *Salome* (1918). What was so despicable about Theda Bara pictures to start an all-out crusade by Kansas moralists to ban them from the state? For one, Bara's portrayals of female wickedness eclipsed the early cinematic ideals of puritanical female innocence personified by actresses such as Lillian Gish and Blanche Sweet. Bara's vamps were simply much more interesting to look at. Perhaps as a symbol of the decline of the ideal of American womanhood, Bara's half demons broke every code of feminine domestic morality—they were willing to cause men to abandon their jobs, wives, and children. And they were able to do it with sex

19. "Complete List of Motion Picture Films Presented to the Kansas State Censors, January 1–April 1, 1916," Review Cards/Copy Cards/Action on Submitted Films, Box 58-5-4-5, Records of the KSBR, KSHS.

20. Ibid., report no. 6, July 1–September 30, 1918, KSHS.

appeal—a relatively new concept in American cinema. William Fox was more than willing to exploit Theda Bara's sexuality to make a tidy profit—and he unleashed a gang of imitators who were all too willing to supplant her perch as "lead vamp." Because of Bara's scanty costumes and roles modeled on immorality, Ronald Genini argues, "The Kansas Board of Censors perpetually went gunning for her films."[21] Bara represented an icon that threatened traditional gender roles in Kansas society, and the censors were determined that they were going to keep these portrayals out of the state. Although women's groups across the country often protested against Bara's pictures, Kansas had the legal mechanism of the Board of Censorship to ban them from the state.

The relationship between the press and the film industry was indeed complicated. Trade publications such as the *Motion Picture News* and *Moving Picture World* included numerous editorials condemning motion picture censorship. The motivations of the local Kansas press, though, are more difficult to discern. One of the controversies concerning the Board of Censorship that the press fueled took place in the summer of 1916. Surprisingly, it appeared in Capper's *Topeka Daily Capital*. Apparently, once the Board of Censorship began viewing films in the statehouse subbasement in the spring of 1916, they began having visitors. Attorney General Brewster began to comment on his surprise in discovering the presence of young teenage girls and children at the exhibition of films being censored. This meant, of course, that the youngsters could have watched any "immoral" or "obscene" thing, since the film had not yet been edited for such material. Brewster's remarks were apparently aimed at the Reverend Foster who allowed his sixteen-year-old daughter and her friends to come to the screenings. In fact, the *Topeka Daily Capital* reported, "His daughter often accompanies him to the office, witnessing all the pictures, whether good or bad." The *Daily Capital* reported that there were often more people in the room other than the projectionist and the two censors—sometimes as many as two dozen. A producer editorialized, "It seems queer that young girls and children are allowed to attend the exhibition of pictures which the censors will not allow the people of Kansas to witness because of the immorality featured as one of the leading roles. . . . It is unfair to the producers to allow a crowd assemble in the rooms where the censoring is done and see the picture which we are going to book in the theaters in Topeka and Kansas."[22]

21. Genini, *Theda Bara*, 64.
22. "Girls and Tots See 'Bad' Films," *Topeka Daily Capital*, July 7, 1916, Clipping File, KSBR, KSHS.

One may question why Capper's newspaper and the attorney general were willing to display such concerns publicly; this problem simply could have been take care of internally. Foster attempted to explain himself several days later, claiming that his daughter was twenty years old, not sixteen, and that she had been in his office for only half of an afternoon. Foster blamed industry men for the public controversy. He claimed, "I don't think for a minute that Brewster meant that careless remarks as a public criticism of me. But the film men are making a strenuous fight against the law and seize every opportunity to make its operation ridiculous or harmful."[23]

The controversy over Foster and Simpson allowing outsiders into their projection room reflected two overwhelming themes of 1916 in regard to the Kansas Board of Censorship. First, the Board of Censorship and the Appeal Board were displaying increasing divergence in terms of what they considered to be respectable on the screen. This split of opinion was causing possible political damage for Governor Capper and his administration, which was public knowledge. Second, the industry increased its fight against the 1915 censorship legislation now that it was newly organized in a professional manner and in agreement regarding the importance of demanding that some changes be made. These two themes will be explored.

As 1916 began, the Board of Censorship continued to reject motion pictures in their entirety but more commonly asked for scenes to be edited. The Appeal Board, though, increasingly began to overrule the Board of Censorship over some very influential motion pictures, including the previously discussed *Madame la Presidente* and Theda Bara's *Gold and the Woman*. As the year continued, the number of films overruled became substantial. For example, between April 1 and July 1, 1916, the board rejected twenty-two films, yet the Appeal Board overruled it in all but five cases. There was a dramatic difference between what the Appeal Board found objectionable and what the Board of Censorship found objectionable. By the end of the year, the Appeal Board overturned the ban on more than fifty films that had been rejected. One of the significant features of this phenomenon had to do with the amount of time it took the governor, secretary of state, and attorney general to review films banned by the Board of Censorship that were then contested by film companies. By the end of the year, Capper was sending his private secretary, Charles Sessions, to view the films because he simply did not have the time. In the attorney general's "Twentieth Biennial Report," issued on

23. "Foster Defends Work of Moving Picture Censors," *Topeka Daily Capital,* July 8, 1916, in ibid.

November 20, 1916, Brewster made a revision of the legislation on "Moving-Picture Censorship" the top priority. Calling the Appeal Board an "unnecessary burden imposed upon the governor, the secretary of state and the attorney general," he suggested that the provision on appeal be stricken from the law or the appeal be vested in some other body.[24]

The matter was also becoming politically problematic for the governor. In May 1916, the Wyandotte County Woman's Christian Temperance Union wrote the governor explaining that "we give our hearty support to the Board of Censorship [yet] we feel that when this board decides unfavorably upon a film then the Appeal Board should be very careful in this decision." Charles Sessions, Capper's secretary, felt the need to respond. He explained, "It would be impossible for the appeal board to promise to sustain every decision of the board. That would be equivalent of saying there would be no appeal board. . . . [I]f the board was given no authority except to affirm the decision of the censors, the courts would knock down the law in a hurry." Kansan Hattie Sparks wrote to Capper about the same matter. She claimed, "Many complaints are coming to us of objectionable films that are passing the Board of Appeals of Moving Picture Films after having been rejected by the Board of Censors. Would you kindly give this your attention believing as me that moving pictures are a great educational force either for good or bad and feeling the need of a higher standard?" In September 1916, Capper wrote to the Reverend Willis L. Goldsmith and expressed his true feelings on his responsibility as an Appeal Board member: "I am in favor of rigid censorship. I am of the opinion that one of the most ridiculous laws a legislature ever enacted is that which makes the Governor, Attorney General and Secretary of State an appeal board. If these three officers should attempt to carry out the spirit of the law it would take most of their time to look at pictures. . . . I shall insist that the next legislature repeal that provision of the censorship law."[25]

If Capper was upset with the censorship apparatus in the state, the motion picture industry was furious. The motion picture industry in Kansas was given a window of opportunity to defeat film censorship. This opportunity came about as the result of a critical Kansas Supreme Court opinion on an

24. "Attorney General's Twentieth Annual Biennial Report," November 20, 1916, Box 58-5-4-6, Records of the KSBR, KSHS.

25. Daisy Miller to Capper, May 3, 1916, Box 4, Capper Papers, KSHS; Sessions to Miller, May 8, 1916; Sparks to Capper, April 20, 1916; Capper to Reverend Willis L. Goldsmith, September 2, 1916, latter three in Box 37, File 20, General Correspondence—Alphabetical File—State Departments—Moving Picture Censorship Appeal Commission, Capper Papers, KSHS.

oil-inspection fee. The court held that although inspection of oil was constitutional, the fee charged was excessive in that it allowed the state an unreasonable profit. The court said that the state could charge only for police
inspection, with a reasonable margin to protect against inspecting at a loss.
Since the Board of Censorship had made a thirteen thousand–dollar profit in
its first nine months of operation, this crucial decision would surely have an
impact on the financial windfall of film censorship.[26]

Direct action was taken in February 1916, when the Universal Film Company wrote a check for the inspection of its films and marked it paid under
protest. It was understood that other film exchanges would follow Universal's
lead.[27] In the middle of March, producers from all over the nation colluded
and paid their censorship fees under protest. According to state law, not one
dollar paid under protest could be turned in to the general revenue fund of
the state.[28] As it stood, if a public official turned this money in to the general
revenue fund, he was likely to be held responsible and sued.[29]

This form of economic warfare would prove effective. The goal of the
protest was to take the matter to court and allow a judge to decide. Using the
oil-inspection case as precedent, the industry had a good chance of winning.
As the *Topeka State Journal* reported, there will be "no love and friendship
spirit when the movie producers and the state censorship department enter the
court." In his "Twentieth Biennial Report," the attorney general commented
that he had brought suit in the Kansas Supreme Court asking that the superintendent of public instruction be directed to pay into the state treasury the
money received under protest. This was the first issue that the attorney general
commented on in his report, reflecting its overall importance.[30]

The industry men also decided to use moviegoers to press their case. The
Topeka State Journal reported in March 1916 that the next plan of strategy was
to withhold some of the better features from the state with the hopes that avid
filmgoers would complain to their elected representatives, demanding change
in the legislation. The paper reported, "None of the really big films are now
coming to Kansas. The really high class attractions on the screen in this state

26. Capper to Goldsmith, September 2, 1916, Capper Papers, KSHS.
27. "Film Companies Now Plan to Attack Law," *Topeka Daily Capital,* February 22, 1916, Clipping File, KSBR, KSHS.
28. "Real Protest by Reel Men in Film Realm," *Topeka State Journal,* March 13, 1916, in ibid.
29. "Kansas Men Pay Censor Fees 'Under Protest' and Plan Test in Courts," *Motion Picture News,*
April 22, 1916, 2354.
30. "Real Protest by Reel Men in Film Realm"; "Attorney General's Twentieth Biennial Report for
Fiscal Year June 30, 1915–June 30, 1916," KSBR, KSHS.

are old productions and news has been sent to Topeka that Kansas movie fans will take such offerings as producers care to send and make the most of it." Whether the leading film companies were deliberately holding back quality films is highly doubtful. Motion picture companies were directly competing with each other for box-office revenue, and they would not consider withholding a film for political purposes when they could not trust their rivals to do the same. There was simply not that much collusion in the industry. It was by nature a competitive business. The *Journal* also claimed that a number of film stars had vigorously protested against Kansas censorship.[31]

What was important was the tone of the rhetoric. As the year progressed, both sides became more combative in their stances. In February, *Moving Picture World* reported on the activities of Mrs. Cora G. Lewis, a member of the Kansas State Board of Administration of Educational Institutions. Lewis, apparently, had decided that the state needed to begin to censor film music also since "most of the music heard at picture shows is demoralizing to the musical sense of the children and renders them unfit to absorb appreciation of the best music in the schools."[32] Kansas was increasingly being portrayed as a state full of cranks.

All of this frustration poured out when the Kansas Amusement Association and the Exhibitor's League of Kansas held their annual convention in Wichita on March 20–21, 1916. The organizations decided to carry the fight into politics. The strategy was to have every candidate for the legislature vote for the repeal of the censorship law; those who refused would be opposed by the movie men. Superintendent Ross had a very public political challenge for his office at this convention. Professor E. Lawrence Payne of Emporia spoke to the film men and promised them a square deal if they elected him to office, which made him a friend of the exhibitors.[33] J. W. Binder, secretary of the Motion Picture Board of Trade, was the special guest at the convention, and it was his organization that led the fight to end censorship in Kansas. Similar campaigns were being waged in Ohio and Pennsylvania, the only other states to have motion picture censorship at the time. This is significant

---

31. "Real Protest by Reel Men in Film Realm."

32. "Kansas Educator Now Wants to Censor Music," *Moving Picture World*, February 12, 1916, 996.

33. "Local Men Await Move in Censorship Fight," *Topeka Daily Capital*, March 28, 1916, Clipping File, KSBR, KSHS. Payne was a professor of mathematics at Kansas State Normal School in Emporia. He did not win the election—Ross was state superintendent of public instruction from 1912 to 1919.

because traditional film histories have portrayed the motion picture industry as having censorship "imposed" on it, indicating helplessness and inadequacy. On national, state, and local levels, theater owners, exchange men, and producers were willing to fight attempts to restrict their product.

By April, fifteen out of sixteen exchanges were paying their censorship fees under protest. This left the Kansas Board of Censorship with only $286 to operate on—not enough to cover costs. Although the industry was hopeful about the oil-inspection precedent, they were also nervous because they had lost the crucial *Mutual Film* decision.[34]

That month, the Amusement Association of Kansas announced that it would use film screens in an attempt to repeal the censorship legislation. The plan was to have every screen in the state carry picture editorials and appeals to the voters of the state to elect members to the legislature who were pledged to repeal the movie censorship law. The *Topeka Daily Capital* claimed, "The movie men are not seeing an amendment to the law, a reduction of the censor fee or anything of that sort. They want the law repealed entirely."[35]

In August, the semiannual convention of the Amusement Association of Kansas and the Motion Picture Exhibitor's League met in Topeka. By the time of the convention, the primaries for the 1916 election were over. The organizations were optimistic. They claimed that they clearly knew how candidates stood on the censorship issue prior to the meeting. More than five thousand dollars was budgeted by the organizations to combat censorship. At its meeting, the Motion Picture League voted to affiliate with the National Association of the Moving Picture Industry. The primary motivating force was money. The national organization had budgeted two hundred thousand dollars to fight film censorship in the four states that had it (Maryland had recently passed such legislation). Film men immediately began working out the figures in their heads—it would mean roughly fifty thousand dollars for the state, or more than three hundred dollars per legislative district.

The August meeting of the Motion Picture Exhibitor's League and Amusement Association of Kansas was a seminal event in Kansas film history. As the *Topeka State Journal* reported, "It was not until last year that the amusement association of Kansas was organized and the film companies began having an active part in the convention." This meeting demonstrated

34. "Movie Men Pass Buck to Brewster," *Topeka Daily Capital,* April 4, 1916, in ibid.
35. "Movies Propose to Force Repeal of Censor Law," *Topeka Daily Capital,* April 14, 1916, in ibid.

the professionalism in organization of the industry in Kansas. It came at a crucial time—shortly before the election, when a bitter campaign was being waged against censorship in the state and a second battle over Sunday closings was being fought in Wichita (more on this later). It also occurred during a period of immense structural change in the industry. Storefront nickelodeons were on their way out; exhibitors were building elaborate picture palaces to appeal to middle-class audiences with disposable income. The *Journal* reported, "Nickelodeons (jitney theaters) are becoming a thing of the past. It won't be long until every movie house in Kansas will demand ten cents for admission."[36] The industry was consolidating, and complete vertical integration emerged by the late 1910s. Studios also moved to Hollywood, where abundant sunshine, a variety of landscapes, and scales of production proved advantageous for film producers.

The city of Topeka received some of the collateral benefits of the film exhibitors' organizational efforts. For the first time, Kansas had film stars come to the state capital (although minor ones). On August 23, 1916, a parade was held in downtown Topeka and a "Grand Ball" held at the Garfield Hotel so that local residents could ogle "girl beauties and men models in the flesh."[37] Film celebrities included Richard Travers (Essanay), Leota Lorraine (Universal), Ethel Quinn (Pageant), Marie Davis (Vitagraph), and Katharine Bush (Universal).

The meeting was also a turning point in the censorship debate. It had become clear both to Governor Arthur Capper and his administration and to individuals in the motion picture industry that a revision or repeal of film censorship legislation had to be a priority in the next legislative session that met in early 1917. Capper, of course, wanted the termination of the Appeal Board. Most film industry men wanted a complete negation of film censorship, but some were also becoming pragmatic in the debate. The rhetoric was still vicious. E. R. Pearson of Kansas City, a member of the executive committee of the Amusement Association of Kansas, claimed that the Reverend Foster had received his appointment simply because he had campaigned for Ross in the primary.[38] But some film men concurred that if the repeal of censorship was not successful at the next legislative session, then some other form of censorship, other than the present system, needed to be put into place. Suggestions

---

36. "Movie Men Are Preparing for a Bitter Fight," *Topeka State Journal*, August 22, 1916, 1.
37. "Stars in Topeka Will Attend Big Ball in Garfield," *Topeka State Journal*, August 23, 1916, 1.
38. "Movie Men Are Preparing for a Bitter Fight," *Topeka State Journal*, August 22, 1916, 1.

were made that the censors not be "petty political officers" but "critics." Fred J. Herrington, former president of the Motion Picture Exhibitor's League of America, exclaimed, "If you look for evil, you will find evil. That is where the Kansas censorship board falls down. Composed of an ex-minister and two church people, it looks for evil in the pictures and finds it. You can go down-town and look in the store windows or on your street and find evil."[39]

The battle against censorship in the state was not the only film conflagra-tion that summer. A much more localized yet equally heated event took place in Wichita. Motion picture exhibitors still could not show films on Sunday there. The largest city in Kansas was one of the last locations to enforce blue laws against this popular form of entertainment. In late May, local theater operators launched a campaign and hired legal talent to combat the enforce-ment. On May 29, eight exhibitors filed papers in the district court seeking to restrain the city commissioners and the chief of police from enforcing the ordinance against film screenings on Sunday. The petition to the court alleged that the Sunday ordinance was void because the commissioners did not have the legal authority to adopt it, that it was a violation of the Kansas Constitu-tion, and that it infringed on the rights of citizens as outlined by the United States Constitution. On June 3, a public demonstration for Sunday pictures was held at the Palace Theater, where an overflowing crowd attended the rally. The Reverend Leon Milton Birkhead, pastor of the First Unitarian Church in Wichita, presided over the event. He spoke to the effect that he was in favor of clean, uplifting films on Sunday. He was followed by several well-known citizens from Wichita.[40]

The opposition was also well organized. Fifty Wichita churches organized a united front to maintain the Sunday blue law. They hired O. A. Keach, a prominent local attorney. He was assisted by three men from the Public Morals Committee of the Ministerial Alliance. The alliance was invited to send members to the June 3 event but declined, arguing that it was "a ques-tion of law which the courts must decide [and] debating it will have no effect one way or the other on the decision of the court."[41]

As the summer continued, the battle intensified. The city commissioners stood firm on the ordinance and enforced the Sunday-closing law. The theater

---

39. "Movie Men Told Kansas Censors Search for Evil," *Topeka Daily Capital*, August 23, 1916, 1.
40. "Exhibitors Fight to Gain Sunday Opening Right in Wichita," *Motion Picture News*, June 24, 1916, 3913.
41. Ibid.

managers challenged the commissioners' interpretation of the law, questioning why the baseball field and Wonderland Park, an amusement location, were not closed on Sunday. This restrictive interpretation would have pleased the Wichita Ministerial Alliance, which adopted strong resolutions against all secular uses of the Sabbath, including participation in any sports and games.[42]

In August 1916, exhibitors of Wichita took up a petition campaign to open up the question of Sunday movies to a referendum. Only 3,145 signatures were needed for the drive; the exhibitors garnered more than 6,000. When the referendum was held in September, it was an overwhelming loss for the theater managers. Only 1,678 voted for Sunday movies, while 10,680 voted against it.[43] Why did the campaign fail? This is particularly curious considering the success of the petition campaign. Simply put, the churches were very active and highly efficient in their opposition.

This efficient opposition by the churches reflected a larger trend in Kansas society in 1916. Many citizens actively supported governmental control over motion pictures. While the film industry in the state was fighting against censorship and even while Governor Capper was frustrated with the current system, some Kansans believed that the state was not going far enough. On September 20, 1916, the Central Association of Congregational Churches closed its two-day annual convention advocating a more stringent moving picture censorship law with the loophole of the Appeal Board removed.[44]

Although the governor received a number of letters protesting the overall quality of motion pictures, even after film censorship was put in place, he was more likely to receive complaints from citizens about individual films. One such example was *The Black Fear* (1916). A morality tale about the dangers of the big city, it involved a brother and two sisters who move to the city to find work. The young man begins working for a villainous manager who exposes him to various dens of iniquity in the town; the boy eventually dies from a drug addiction. The manager attempts to rape the younger sister, and the older sister shoots him dead. Mrs. Laura Rhodes, president of the Wellington chapter of the Woman's Christian Temperance Union, was shocked that the film passed the Board of Censorship and wrote the governor concerning the film.

42. "Film Men in Wichita, Kansas, Threaten Ouster Proceedings against Commissioners," *Motion Picture News,* July 15, 1916, 254.

43. "Exhibitors Lose Sunday Opening Vote in Wichita, Kansas," *Motion Picture News,* September 23, 1916, 1873.

44. "More Rigid Censors," *Topeka State Journal,* September 21, 1916, Clipping File, KSBR, KSHS.

"I think you will agree with me that a picture with the scenes laid out in houses of ill fame, gambling halls and opium dens, have little to recommend."[45]

As the election of 1916 neared, many moving picture men believed that film censorship should be a major campaign issue. F. L. Klitz, manager of the Kansas City branch of the Mutual Film Corporation, claimed that censorship was tightening and that it was becoming harder to get his pictures passed by the Board of Censorship (which tended to contradict Mrs. Rhodes's view). The manager of the World Film Branch in Kansas City concurred. He argued that exhibitors were clamoring for films with "more meat in them" and that they would not submit to such stringent censorship much longer.[46] Apparently, he was willing to exhibit more controversial films if they brought in audiences.

In December 1916, *Moving Picture World*, a national trade publication, reported that "exhibitors of Kansas feel that the recent election has put them in a much better position than ever before, in reference to the censorship law." The paper explained that candidates for the legislature were put on record as to their position on censorship in almost every district in the state. In a large number of districts, those in favor of changing the law were swept to victory. The publication reported that "some of them favor abolishing censorship altogether, others favor a radical modification of the law, others the placing of censorship elsewhere than the department of education."[47] Clearly, the publication took an upbeat approach to the elections. In fact, many Kansas film men became resigned to censorship and adopted a more moderate approach.

Arthur Capper was reelected governor and W. D. Ross was reelected superintendent of instruction in November 1916. By the end of the year, Capper publicly advocated a change in the censorship law but not a total repudiation of motion picture censorship. *Moving Picture World* claimed that he was "widely recognized as so fair and just that exhibitors had absolutely no complaint against him. Indeed he has rather been considered the best possible man to help the exhibitors in their troubles."[48]

When the newly elected legislature met in early 1917, motion picture censorship was on its mind. A number of suggestions were made during the ses-

---

45. Mrs. Laura Rhodes to Capper, December 1, 1916, Box 37, General Correspondence, Capper Papers, KSHS.
46. "Unjust Censorship Conditions in Kansas Arouse Ire of Exchangemen," *Motion Picture News*, November 18, 1916, 3160.
47. "Now for the Kansas Censor Law," *Moving Picture World*, December 2, 1916, 1367.
48. Ibid.

sion designed to lessen some of the hardships that the censorship process was causing distributors and exhibitors. One such consideration was moving the headquarters of the Board of Censorship to Kansas City, Kansas. There it would be conveniently located closer to the exchanges of Kansas City, Missouri, where Kansas theater owners received most of their films. This would significantly reduce a major cost for distributors—the transportation of films to Topeka for review.[49]

On one of the last days of the legislative session, March 9, 1917, the Kansas legislature passed a new motion picture censorship law. This piece of legislation was important because it laid the foundation for motion picture censorship in the state for almost fifty more years. An in-depth look at the bill is necessary in order to understand how the body attempted to deal with some of the previous problems of the Board of Censorship in its first two years of operation and how the legislature attempted to adopt a system that was palatable to those with an economic interest in the motion picture industry. The legislature had a number of constituencies it had to try to please with this new bill, including church organizations, social workers, and other advocates of film censorship and film distributors, producers and, exhibitors who had been economically burdened by the process in the period April 1915–March 1917.

The Moving Picture Law of 1917 repealed sections 10774–81 of the General Statutes of 1915 that had created the original board.[50] In a sense, the legislature was starting over. The first major change was the name of the board. No longer known as the Kansas Board of Censorship, the body was now known as the Kansas Board of Review. There were several rationales for this change. First, the term *censorship* was objectionable in a republic; it smacked of governmental control over free thought and speech and, therefore, had a negative connotation. *Review* was a much more palatable word, as it did not imply direct governmental interference in the transmission of ideas but denoted a "lighter" approach to the matter. It was still a censorship board, but the semantics of this phrasing was pure public relations on the part of the legislature. The National Board of Censorship had transformed itself into the National Board of Review in 1915. Although the board had lost a lot of respect among moralists in the nation, it was still one of the leading national forces in delivering "cleaner" motion pictures to the American public and obviously had an impact on the Kansas name-change decision.

---

49. "Kansas May Lower Censor Fees," *Moving Picture World*, February 10, 1917, 893.
50. Moving Picture Law, chap. 308, in *Session Laws of 1917*, in *General Statutes of Kansas*, 1917.

The 1917 legislation dealt with the makeup of the board, a matter almost completely neglected in 1915. The superintendent of public instruction was completely taken out of the equation. The Kansas Board of Review was now directly responsible to the governor. To be a reviewer, one had to be a resident citizen of the state and "well qualified by education and expertise." The board now consisted of three members, with one individual designated as chairman. The three censors were given staggered terms of office of one, two, and three years; following this interval, all censors were to serve three-year terms. The governor also reserved the right to remove a censor for "incompetency or neglect of duty," a procedure that would be indirectly used several times.[51] If a censor left before his or her term of office expired, the governor had the right to appoint a new censor, but the board would continue to operate as normal, even if there was a vacancy. The chairman received an annual salary of eighteen hundred dollars a year, while the other censors received fifteen hundred dollars each. Traveling expenses were also reimbursed by the state.

The Kansas Board of Review was charged with inspecting all films but was also given the additional responsibility of examining all folders, posters, and advertising materials used in connection with the exhibition of motion pictures. As the industry matured, promotional materials became more elaborate. In 1917, silent film–era advertising followed a pattern established by nineteenth-century circuses and traveling shows in Kansas. Paid newspaper ads were still relatively small, but there was a heavy emphasis on large, colorful posters.[52] Because these materials were often seen by members of the public who might not even see the film, it was considered doubly important that they be censored. In the 1915 legislation, the censors were deemed to approve films that were "moral and proper" and to disapprove of films that were "sacrilegious, obscene, indecent, immoral or tend to corrupt morals."[53] The 1917 wording matched almost verbatim the 1915 legislation, except the word *sacrilegious* was dropped.

One of the major criticisms the Board of Censorship had faced was confusion over whether films had been approved by the Board of Censorship or the Board of Appeals, or both or neither, which the 1917 legislation attempted to rectify. Each approved reel had to be stamped by the board and furnished

---

51. Ibid., sec. 3.
52. Richard Koszarski, *An Evening's Entertainment: The Age of the Silent Feature Picture, 1915–1928*, 36.
53. Article 8, Section 10774–81, Superintendent of Public Instruction, in *General Statutes of Kansas*, 2197–99.

with the statement, "Approved by the Kansas State Board of Review." This approximately five-foot short snippet was to be shown at the beginning of each film. The board was also required to keep all records of examinations, noting which films had been approved and which had been disapproved (and the reasons for it).

The sheer growth of the industry and the increased length of many films meant that it would take more than two individuals to carry out the day-to-day operations of the board and to administer the office. The Board of Review was given the right to hire clerks, inspectors, operators, and other employees if approved by the governor.

One of the most significant changes that the 1917 legislation made was moving the board from Topeka to Kansas City, Kansas, a decision that pleased the film exchanges. The transportation costs of delivering films to the board would now be greatly reduced.

The legislature also attempted to stop the lawsuit that was winding its way through the courts regarding the funds "paid under protest." Examination fees remained at two dollars a reel. This money would go into the state treasury, and the salaries and expenses of the board would then be appropriated by the state government. The board reserved the right to lower the examination fee if revenue from censorship fees was greater than overall costs. This was a goodwill gesture on the part of the legislature. On the other hand, the legislature also gave itself the right to take all funds "paid under protest" and use them to fund current censorship.[54]

One of the major changes in the 1917 legislation had to do with the appeal process. The Appeal Board was completely terminated, although an appeal process remained. Film corporations could contest decisions in the district court of Wyandotte County within sixty days of the board's decision, but contesting a decision did not suspend the action of the board. For example, if Questionable Film A had been rejected by the Board of Review and then contested in court, it was not allowed to be exhibited before the court's decision. The board was also given the right to reexamine films, giving thirty days' written notice to the owner of the film.[55]

All fines and punishments for violating the act remained the same with one exception: individuals who exhibited advertising, posters, or printed matter not approved by the board could now also be fined or imprisoned.

54. Moving Picture Law, chap. 308, in *Session Laws of 1917*, in *General Statutes of Kansas*, 1917.
55. Ibid., secs. 15, 17.

The 1917 legislation was a turning point in the history of film censorship in the state. Through a two-year period of trial and error, the legislature, prompted by Governor Capper and the motion picture industry, had created a system of censorship more palatable to all concerned. From 1915 to 1917, motion picture exhibitors and distributors had contested a system that appeared haphazard, inefficient, and conflicted. The 1917 legislation was written with these concerns addressed. Although many film men in the state may have personally and professionally disliked motion picture censorship, they had recognized that it was there to stay. As a result, the film industry and the state government would no longer be as hostile toward each other. There would still be disputes, but they were handled in a more diplomatic, often private way.

Advocates of film censorship were also pleased with the maintenance of the Board of Review in their state. Despite attempts to eradicate screen control, film censorship was now institutionalized through a permanent regulatory body. The Board of Review would find itself challenged in new ways as the decade ended. The entrance of the United States into World War I would make the board more politically sensitive. Like almost every aspect of life in the United States, the Board of Review and the state motion picture industry would find itself profoundly impacted by the war. A fundamental shift in American mores and morals would also be vividly displayed in motion pictures in the period 1917–1919, and this would also bring new challenges to the board.

Six

World War I and the Struggle against Sin, 1917–1919

Kansas's adoption of the Board of Review of Motion Pictures coincided with the U.S. entrance into World War I in April 1917. It would prove to be a transformative time for both the state and the film industry. Governor Arthur Capper argued that his responsibilities as governor "were quadrupled by the entrance of the nation into the war."[1] Not only was he responsible for managing the economic resources of the state, but he also had never-ending requests for his presence at patriotic meetings. He simply did not have the time to manage the new board the way he had worked with the Board of Censorship. The termination of the Appeal Board could not have come at a more opportune time for the governor.

In March 1917, shortly before the United States declared war, the Board of Review was involved in a controversy concerning the censorship of army recruiting films. A clause in the new legislation said that the board at its discretion could grant special permits for exhibitions of educational, charitable, or religious films without a fee. During the preparedness movement, a series of films representing army life had been furnished to the recruiting officer in Topeka. The idea was that he could use the films to encourage enlistment and

1. Socolofsky, *Arthur Capper,* 99.

inspire patriotism. He was told that if the films were to be exhibited in Kansas, they had to be reviewed and an accompanying fee had to be paid. H. P. Dillon of Topeka was furious about this, and as a concerned citizen he felt it was his duty to pay the fee. He wrote a furious letter to Capper, protesting in the first line, "Your censor board is an ass." Arthur Capper, unaware of the board's actions, immediately instructed it that a fee did not have to be paid since the film was "the property of the Federal government and the interest of the function was national defense."[2]

The Kansas Board of Review was forced to operate under new circumstances once the United States entered the war. Ever mindful of patriotism and national duty, the Board of Review found it had to walk a fine line on political and international matters. Much of this work was preemptively completed by the Committee on Public Information (CPI), which President Woodrow Wilson established on April 13, 1917. Wilson created the CPI to promote the war domestically while publicizing American war aims abroad. The Committee on Public Information was led by journalist George Creel who recognized the value of moving images on the screen. He created the Division of Films within the CPI to promote the war through the cinema. This division was used by the U.S. government to disseminate propaganda supporting the war and U.S. war aims on a massive scale. With the weekly American filmgoing audience in the millions, Creel believed movies were an effective way to spread the message. Hollywood producers, many of them immigrants who wanted to gain respectability and support their new homeland, wholeheartedly supported the war effort through this cooperation. Films that were considered anti-American or anti-Ally were prohibited by the committee through official wartime censorship. Therefore, the Kansas Board of Review did not have to review a significant number of motion pictures that were politically sensitive because they had to clear the CPI first.

There was a new staff in the newly created Kansas Board of Review. The state government had changed the makeup of the board with the passage of the new legislation. Mrs. J. M. Miller was made chairman, with Mrs. B. L. Short and Carrie Simpson accompanying her. Censor Festus Foster was gone. The all-female board would have significant personality clashes with the makeup of this staff. Although things were relatively subdued in 1917, they

---

2. H. P. Dillon to Capper, March 22, 1917; memo from Capper to Kansas Board of Censorship, March 26, 1917, both in Box 11, File 45, General Correspondence, Numerical File, 1917–1918, Capper Papers, KSHS.

would intensify with the board's longevity. The initial cause of this fractious fighting was the Board of Review's decision to reexamine and then approve the infamous *The Birth of a Nation*. As demonstrated in Chapter 4, Arthur Capper made them "rethink" this decision. This action obviously displeased the governor, and finger-pointing by the board members immediately began. On May 11, 1917, Mrs. Short wrote Charles Sessions, Capper's private secretary, arguing, "[Mrs. Miller's] statement to you does me an injustice. . . . I did not—at *any time* stand for the approval [of *The Birth of a Nation*] and only concurred with the majority when we thought in certainty of a [lawsuit]." The censors apparently feared losing their newly obtained positions because Mrs. Miller wrote Sessions three days later claiming, "There's a rumor here this morning that there may be a change in the Censor Board."[3] Apparently, the vultures were already circling, as individuals were dropping by the Kansas City, Kansas, office seeking these possible governmental positions.

Part of the board's frustration may have been its inadequate working conditions. The City of Kansas City was to provide the board offices free of charge, but that meant it received the space that no one else wanted in the basement of the Old City Hall. Miller wrote the governor in October that they had no heat in their present offices, with the exception of one standing radiator in the projection room and little electric stoves in the outer office.

World War I impacted every facet of motion picture life—the subject matter in films, exhibitions patterns, distribution, and the organization of the industry. The industry seized the opportunity to aid in the government's efforts to rally the American people.[4] Since it was difficult for motion picture companies to obtain actual war footage, it was in the realm of the popular feature film that the American public became aware of how horrible the war actually was. This was a politically challenging task for filmmakers, as the nation underwent a psychic transformation in the period 1914–1917 from nonintervention to preparedness to full support of the war effort.

Throughout this era, there was always a strong pacifist contingent that included many Kansans. Pacifism was equated with treason by superpatriots once the United States entered the war. Motion pictures that smacked of this sentiment could receive a backlash. One such film that created controversy in the state was *The War Brides* (1916). The film was a political allegory set in an

3. B. L. Short to Sessions, May 11, 14, 1917, in ibid.
4. See Craig W. Campbell, *Reel America and World War I: Film in the United States, 1914–1920*; Andrew Kelly, *Cinema and the Great War*; and Peter C. Rollins and John O'Connor, eds., *Hollywood's World War I: Motion Picture Images*.

The World War I melodrama *The War Brides* (1916) had a strong pacifistic message that infuriated some superpatriotic Kansans. (Permission granted by Photofest)

imaginary kingdom. Four brothers are drafted into war, leaving their mother, sister, and Joan, the wife of the eldest brother. The women receive news that all four men were killed in a great battle, and Joan contemplates suicide but chooses to save the life of her unborn child. The government issues a directive that all unmarried women must marry soldiers that are going off to war in order to provide future manpower. Joan is disgusted by this and becomes an activist against the edict. She is sent to prison and escapes. When the king visits her town, she leads a group of women to meet him, vowing that she will not bear her child unless the war ends. The king tells the women that there will always be wars, so Joan shoots herself, committing suicide. She becomes a heroine for the other women, and they elevate her body over the crowd, vowing they will continue the struggle.[5]

Dr. Clarke Mangun wrote Capper about *The War Brides* and maintained that it was a "well-staged argument and emotional appeal against war. There

5. Hansen, *American Film Institute Catalog, 1911–1920,* 999–1000.

is no question about liberty, justice or humanity." What Mangun did have problems with was the film's advocation of "peace at any price." He proclaimed, "As a citizen of this State and one who is offering his life on the altar of his country, I protest against this insidious form of treason. The only excuse of such a picture is to make war ineffective." The film, which was released in November 1916, was caught in a time vacuum in which pacifism was no longer acceptable to the mainstream public. The film was produced while the nation was still neutral but released while the country was careening toward active participation in the war. There was still a strong peace movement in the United States in 1916. But once the war began, as demonstrated by the doctor's words, pacifism or criticism of the war was equated with disloyalty. He argued that "characters presented in uniform [in the film] tended to discredit the uniform, particularly of officers and the death fest was characterized as a 'Great Victory.'" Mangun had serious concerns with how the film specifically dealt with women. He claimed that in the picture, "women who bear children were characterized as 'Brood Mares' and 'Breeding Machines.' . . . I protest against my wife and mother as well as those of other soldiers being classed with those who are held up to public infamy because they reared sons who offered to fight for this country." Mangun was astounded that the film could have been passed by the Board of Review. He begged Capper to keep such films out of the state and to use his influence to keep them out of the nation.[6]

Exhibition patterns were also strongly influenced by the war. The Committee on Public Information launched a successful program known as the Four Minute Men. This army of volunteers gave brief speeches wherever they could find an audience. The purpose of the Four Minute Men was to assist the various departments of the government in the work of national defense during the war by presenting messages on subjects of vital national importance to motion picture audiences during intermissions. Kansas enthusiastically responded to this outburst of patriotism. Arthur Capper strongly supported the program and received a number of letters of request on how to apply to or volunteer for such a program. One such individual was S. C. Orr of Manhattan. A Civil War veteran and pioneer schoolteacher, Orr was eager to participate in the Four Minute Men.[7]

6. Clarke Mangun to Capper, n.d., Box 11, File 45, General Correspondence, Numerical File, 1917–1918, Capper Papers, KSHS.
7. S. C. Orr to Capper, September 4, 1917, in ibid.

Mr. C. W. Myers was Kansas state chairman of the Four Minute Men. The organization really began to coalesce in an effective manner in the last six months of the war. One of the subsections of the Four Minute Men was a group called the Alien Squad. These were all enlisted men, but they were either foreign born or natives of countries against which the United States was presently fighting. Arthur Capper was apparently moved and very supportive of this group of loyal Kansans. After hearing them speak in September 1918, Capper wrote, "On every head there were expressions of admiration for their spirit and devotion and for their determination to do all in their power—to die if need be—in support of the cause of liberty and justice to the preservation of which their adopted country has taken up. . . . Their presence and their participation in this program . . . has made a profound impression."[8]

Large numbers of servicemen were stationed for training in Kansas. It became necessary for military leaders to consider how to provide proper amusement for the men. Thousands of army personnel were at Camp Funston (now Fort Riley) in 1917–1918. A large amusement zone was created in order to provide entertainment facilities for the fifty thousand men stationed there. Several moving picture theaters were included in this amusement zone. Camp Funston was off the beaten path and transportation facilities to larger towns and cities were woefully inadequate, so providing this entertainment zone was essential to morale. The concern that army personnel had was with the Sunday closing law that was still haphazardly enforced in the state. Governor Capper, realizing that Sunday was the only day many of these men had to catch a film, waived the law for the necessity of keeping spirits up.[9]

The governor and his administration were not alone in their concern for the unification of the American people in the war effort. When the Motion Picture Exhibitor's League held its annual meeting in October 1917, its principal concern was not film censorship, as it had been in the previous two years, but patriotism.[10] Part of this change was the industry's grudging acceptance of motion picture censorship under the 1917 legislation. One exchange manager said that "since the law is on the Kansas books, and the board has to obey it,

8. Capper to C. W. Myers, September 18, 1918, Box 11, File 45A, General Correspondence, Numerical File, 1917–1918, Capper Papers, KSHS.

9. W. P. Montgomery, captain inspector, Camp Funston, to Capper, "Sunday Entertainment for Troops at Camp Funston," October 23, 1917; Capper to Montgomery, October 26, 1917, both in Box 16, File 28, War Correspondence of Capper, Numerical File, 1917–1918, KSHS. Capper may have also made this decision considering reports coming to him that venereal disease rates were climbing at Fort Funston (Socolofsky, *Arthur Capper*, 100).

10. "Kansas Exhibitors Meet," *Moving Picture World*, November 3, 1917, 676.

we can see that our best interests be in assisting the board in the administration of the law in the best interests of the industry. We are saving ourselves a lot of grief that would be involved in hopelessly securing the annulment of the law."[11] Members of the legislature, ever mindful of economic gain, helped expedite the process for the film men who had been frustrated the past two years. Samuel Clasen, a member of the Kansas House of Representatives, ran a truck back and forth between Kansas City, Missouri, where the exchanges were located, and the Board of Review on the Kansas side. He took the films to be censored in Kansas, stayed while the board reviewed them, reported to respective producers if there was any controversy around a film, and then ran the films back to Kansas City, Missouri, so they could be redistributed back over the state line.[12]

One would assume that with the war raging in Europe and with thousands of American men dying, the political content of motion pictures would be the prime target of the Kansas Board of Review. This turns out not to have been the case. When one examines the films that were rejected by the board, there is one consistent theme: sexual indiscretion. Other than *The Birth of a Nation*, the film that created the most uproar was *The Easiest Way* (1917), starring Clara Kimball Young. She portrays Laura Murdock, a struggling actress who accepts the assistance of a wealthy broker with the understanding that she will become his mistress. Laura falls in love with a penniless reporter while performing in stock in Denver. She becomes torn between a life of financial security with the broker and an uncertain existence with the reporter. She eventually decides to end her life by jumping into a river. The young reporter learns of Laura's fate, and she dies in his arms, asking for forgiveness.[13]

The Kansas Board of Review examined the film on July 2, and it was rejected. The Mid-West Photoplay Corporation attempted to get the board to review it again or to suggest certain changes or eliminations but was unsuccessful. *Variety* admitted that "the back stage detail is shown devoid of all glamour, [especially] her entry into the Bacchanalian orgies." The dialogue was also offensive to the censors. When Laura says to her maid, "Doll me up, Annie—I'm going over to the Montmarte and then to hell," the board members must have been shocked. Apparently, the board felt that the film was totally unredeemable and chose not to cooperate with the company. The

11. "Kansas Exhibitors Aided by Censors Co-operation," *Moving Picture World*, January 18, 1919, 340.
12. "Kansas State Board Gets Down to Routine," *Moving Picture World*, April 28, 1917, 664.
13. Hansen, *American Film Institute Catalog, 1911–1920*, 235.

Mid-West Photoplay Corporation responded by bringing mandamus proceedings in the Wyandotte County District Court to compel the board to approve the film and to pay the company eighty-five hundred dollars for its rejection of the picture. On review, the Wyandotte County District Court reversed the Review Board, but the Supreme Court of Kansas reversed the lower court. Chief Justice William Johnston wrote that the court "is not warranted in substituting its judgment for that of the board."[14] Thus, the Board of Review was becoming institutionalized as a regulatory body in Kansas and given judicial protection.

Several other sexual themes led to outright rejection by the Board of Review. One of them was illegitimacy. *The Devil's Prize* (1916), a Vitagraph feature, involved a status-conscious young man named Arnold St. Claire who decides to marry a wealthy woman, even though his former lover Myra is pregnant. Myra quickly marries another man to give her child the cloak of legitimacy. Meanwhile, her husband's uncle finds out about Arnold's indiscretions and decides to expose him, but Arnold murders him before he can. Arnold dies of fright when he finds out the police are after him, and Myra's husband begins choking their child to death when he finds out the truth. All of the death, illegitimacy, and child abuse were too much for the censors—they rejected the film entirely.[15]

White slavery was also off-limits by the censors, even though *Traffic in Souls* (1913), the film that popularized the genre, had been passed by the previous board. *Is Any Girl Safe?* (1916), a Universal feature that had gone on the states' rights market, involved two pimps who procure women into the white-slavery trade until they realize their mistake and end up marrying two of the victims. *Variety* reported that the film was a special release that was rushed on the market to take advantage of the white-slavery investigation that was conducted by the New York County District Attorney's Office.[16]

Nudity was also completely off-limits. *Purity* (1916), an American Film Company release, pushed the boundaries of screen exploitation with its blatant female nudity. In the movie, a young woman poses nude as an artists' model in order to help her boyfriend, Thorton, get his poetry published. The female star was Audrey Munson, a young woman who was the model for the

14. Review of *The Easiest Way*, *Variety*, April 13, 1917, 26; "Midwest Photoplay Sues Kansas Board," *Moving Picture World*, August 25, 1917, 1260; Reports of the Kansas Supreme Court, 1917, vol. 102, p. 356, *Mid-West Photo Play Corporation v. State*.

15. Hansen, *American Film Institute Catalog, 1911–1920*, 463.

16. Review of *Is Any Girl Safe? Variety*, September 8, 1916.

noteworthy sculpture that adorned the Panama and Pacific Exposition. *Variety* reported that she walked around the camera every three hundred feet wearing "mostly a smile." The film had a number of nude scenes, and *Variety* claimed that the audience would get about "eighteen good peeks at the girl, in just the same state of undress as she would be on entering the morning tub." The film was a huge moneymaker, and exhibitors fell all over themselves to obtain a print of the release. But *Purity* never played in Kansas.[17]

The censors were particularly sensitive about film subjects that approximated real-life events, especially if they contained sex and violence. *Redemption* (1917) starred the infamous Evelyn Nesbit-Thaw and her son Russell Thaw. A great deal of the plot bore a strikingly similarity to Nesbit-Thaw's own life. Her husband, Harry Thaw, killed architect Stanford White, his wife's former lover. Part of Thaw's defense was that White had taken advantage of Evelyn while she was quite young. Nesbit-Thaw capitalized on the fame she obtained from the notorious event, one of the first court sensations of the new century. The board was apparently uncomfortable with the scandalous woman and her attempt to capitalize on this misfortune.

Woman and the Law (1918), a Fox feature, bore a similar fate. The story was based on a murder case in which Blanca de Caulles shot her former husband, John Longer de Caulles, on August 2, 1917. Shortly after the birth of his son, John had an affair with a woman with a disreputable reputation. His wife divorced him, and they shared joint custody of their son. John decided one day that he would not return his son to his former wife, and she shot him dead. The film was so thinly disguised that the characters' names were almost identical. Blanca de Caulles became Blanquetta del Castillo in the film version. *Variety* remarked that "while such a thing is perfectly legal, the whole thing is utterly morbid and mercenary and degenerates into a cheap, mawkish, melodramatic tale."[18]

One of the consistent themes in the history of the Kansas Board of Review is that the agency often "filled in the gaps" regarding the regulation of screen content. For example, in the World War I years, the Committee on Public Information appeared to have removed all politically sensitive material from the screen, thus saving the Kansas board from making decisions on such content. This was not the case, however, with material that was sexual in nature

17. Review of *Purity*, *Variety*, July 7, 1916, 25.

18. Hansen, *American Film Institute Catalog, 1911–1920*, 1054; review of *Woman and the Law*, *Variety*, March 15, 1918, 43.

or that tended to push the boundaries of what was considered "morally appropriate." As a result, in the period 1917–1919, the Board of Review spent most of its time and energy censoring such material. One finds a similar pattern with the establishment of the Production Code Administration in 1934. When an external agency (outside of Kansas) censored screen material, it was left up to the Kansas censors to cut anything it may have missed.

As the war continued, the film industry in Kansas was greatly impacted by changing economic and political realities. The high cost of film stock greatly reduced the number of film producers in the market. Production costs escalated, and fewer films were manufactured. Another significant cause of the drop in product was the almost complete cessation of imported foreign films. European-manufactured motion pictures, especially French productions, had continued to make up a significant, if dwindling, part of the American market before the war began. The advent of World War I in 1914 almost completely stopped this trade and led to American monopolization of the domestic market and the domination of the international market.[19]

One unrelated phenomenon that was impacting the Kansas film industry during the World War I years was that the number of theaters in the state was dropping. Smaller venues were being replaced in many towns and cities with larger, more elaborate, and more ornate theaters meant to appeal to a middle-class audience. The conversion of the Grand Theater in Topeka to a cinema house was an example of this attempt to engage a bourgeois audience.

In July 1918, the Board of Review issued an annual report that is revealing in its language and themes. It allows us to understand the challenges the board faced and the values that the censors held at the end of the war. In 1918, the Kansas Board of Review was reviewing an average of twenty films a day. More than $19,000 was collected in censorship fees, and $15,401 was spent on disbursements.[20] Although this still led to a profit, it did not give the impression that the board was a revenue-producing machine like its predecessor.

The board recognized that it was walking a fine line in its decision making. It argued that the reviewers "tried to give to the state a class of films free of immoralities and possessing artistic and educational values," yet it did not want to "destroy the legitimate industry of the vast film concern." Unlike the

---

19. See Larry Wayne Ward, *The Motion Picture Goes to War: The U.S. Government Film Effort during World War I*.

20. KSBR Annual Report, 1918, Box 58-5-4-5, Review Cards/Copy Cards/Actions on Submitted Films, KSHS.

previous board, the Board of Review members attempted to adopt a consistent set of standards, choosing to eliminate "those things that tend to debase morals or establish false standards of conduct."[21] The censors argued that their goal was to advance the interest of "Better Films." This was a politically wise move since Governor Arthur Capper was a member of the Clean Pictures and Play League of America that was also dedicated to the promotion of "better films."[22] During this tumultuous period in which they lived, the censors argued that they were looking for films that were "clean," "wholesome," and "heroic" (as ambiguous as these words might be).

The Kansas Board of Review, in its annual report and its daily work, advocated reconstruction over rejection. Far fewer films were rejected in their entirety when the new board came into place. Instead, the members would suggest eliminations and changes that would make the film acceptable for a positive clearance. One example was *Tyrants Fear* (1918). The film was initially rejected in its entirety, but the board suggested that if the following changes were made, it might be approved:

Eliminate titles "You are as cold as ice," and "The girls at the North Star, they warm a man's blood."

Eliminate scenes of Christmas drunkenness.

Eliminate scenes and titles regarding game with Dorothy Dalton as stake.

Eliminate scenes of man dragging her upstairs.

Eliminate title referring to a man living openly with Dorothy Dalton.

Eliminate title "If I do this, what will you do?" and the response, "Anything."[23]

The film was eventually approved after it was "rebuilt." It was this spirit of cooperation that made the review process more palatable to movie men in the state.

In this report, the board listed three broad categories of subject matter that were consistently causing them difficulty: crime, sexuality, and slapstick comedy. The Board of Review despised motion pictures that depicted crime and

21. Ibid.

22. Clean Picture and Play League of America to Capper, February 5, 1917, Box 11, File 45, General Correspondence, Numerical File, 1917–1918, Capper Papers, KSHS.

23. "Complete List of Motion Picture Films Presented to the KSBR for Action from April 1, 1918 to June 30, 1918," Records of the KSBR, List of Films Reviewed, Box 58-5-4-5, KSHS.

specifically went after serials that they claimed were nothing more than a "succession of crime[s] [with] impossible feats." The primary objection that the board had with these films was that they were teaching a generation of children how to participate in criminal activity. Claiming that these pictures made the "strongest possible impression" on the "plastic minds" of youth, the censors were praying for the day when "this class of picture has reached the limit through a waning public sentiment."[24] Although the individual members of the Review Board may have disliked serials, they actually did not censor them heavily.

This was not true of the "sex pictures" that the censors frequently condemned. The board hated films like *The Checkmate* (Mutual Film Corporation, 1917), in which a young country girl goes to the city to pursue a life of excitement, aligns herself with a fast crowd, becomes the mistress of a wealthy bachelor, and, of course, is dumped by the young man. In rejecting the film, the board criticized it and other films that depicted "the betrayal of young girls and unsuspecting women." The reviewers did not accept the rationale of industry men that they were simply depicting the world the way it really was. They claimed that "pictures that deal with the vice of the underworld are ofttimes presented for the purposes of commercial gain."[25]

The board also condemned slapstick comedies that "cause censors sorrow and vexation of spirit." Such comedies were routinely censored by the board but seldom rejected in their entirety. The board claimed that many such films were of "such disgusting character, of vulgar situations and evil suggestiveness that we have protested long and loud against [their] production." But the board was also hopeful, commenting that some recent comedies were relatively free of these conditions and generally funny.[26]

The Kansas Board of Review published a weekly bulletin that reported all pictures submitted for censorship and then explained whether they had been approved or rejected and what eliminations needed to be made. To guarantee that a film had been reviewed, a certificate or approval tag was placed on each picture following the main title that read "Approved by the Kansas State Board of Review." The board was receiving reports that exhibitors were removing or not including these approval tags in the motion pictures they were exhibiting.

24. KSBR Annual Report, 1918, Box 58-5-4-5, KSHS.
25. Hansen, *American Film Institute Catalog, 1911–1920,* 742; KSBR Annual Report, 1918, Box 58-5-4-5, KSHS.
26. KSBR Annual Report, 1918, Box 58-5-4-5, KSHS.

They believed that it was necessary once again to send out a traveling censor, like the work the Reverend Foster had completed, to guarantee that the exhibitors were showing films that actually had been approved by the board.[27]

In its annual report, the board, in summation, argued that its work had won the general approval of the "better class" of Kansans. The board claimed that it had received letters of commendation from fellow citizens of the state, particularly from women's groups. Certainly, the reviewers had the support of Arthur Capper. In a letter to a constituent, he claimed that the 1917 law "had been an unqualified success. Beyond question it has improved to a remarkable extent the quality of pictures now offered for exhibition in this state." Capper was pleased with not only the censorship process but specifically the work of the Kansas Board of Review. He claimed that "during the first year our law was in operation a great many complaints were received because pictures contained objectionable features and were shown in picture houses. During the past year not more than two complaints of this kind have been received in this office. I do not know of any stronger endorsement of the censorship policy than that."[28]

Not everything was perfect among the board members. Intraboard politics were starting to cause difficulties. Ray Gandy, the film projectionist for the board, was demanding an increase in salary.[29] Mrs. B. L. Short, the censor who received the one-year appointment, was scrambling for recommendations out of fear that she would lose her job.[30] The stenographer for the board was also anxious to gain full-time employment.

The major rupture the Board of Review faced was with the citizens of Salina. By May 1918, the municipal government of that city was preparing to close all places of amusement, including motion picture houses, during the war. The rationale given was that the time and money expended in such places should be given to worthier causes. This was a clear example of the "superpatriotism" that gripped some Americans during the war and the impact that it could have on the motion picture industry. One of the motivating factors behind this unusual decision was that a contingent of Salina residents believed that the board was sleeping on the job. Specifically, they were outraged by the exhibition of three films: *A Daughter of the Gods* (1916), *Cleopatra* (1918), and *Thaïs* (1917). *A Daughter of the Gods* has the reputation

27. Miller to Capper, January 9, 1918, Box 11, File 45, General Correspondence, Numerical File, 1917–1918, Capper Papers, KSHS.
28. Capper to Luttie L. Jackson, April 24, 1918, in ibid.
29. Miller to Sessions, January 10, 1918, in ibid.
30. A. S. Clinton to Capper, February 11, 1918, in ibid.

of being one of the first American films ever made with a nude scene. Swimming star Annette Kellerman disrobes quite frequently in the film. She also delivers a provocative dance as a member of a sultan's harem. The Fox film had been passed by the previous Board of Censorship, but apparently the eliminations they demanded were reinserted. *Cleopatra*, a Theda Bara feature, was passed by the Board of Review with certain eliminations. A major box-office smash from Fox, the epic film has Bara as the Egyptian seductress. She makes frequent costume changes in the film, usually into scandalously brief outfits. Bara's exposure of skin wreaked havoc with censors across the nation. The Kansas censors apparently cut out the most flagrant exposures of flesh but came to the conclusion that these eliminations may have been added back in. They asked for a reexamination of the film playing in Salina.[31] *Thaïs* had a more respectable reputation. A quality Goldwyn picture, the film was based on an opera by Anatole France (pseudonym of Jacques Thibault) and starred operatic star Mary Garden. Perhaps the problem that Salinians had with the film was that Garden played a courtesan who decides to become a nun. Even Mrs. Miller, chairman of the Kansas Board of Review, said, "The dramatic feature of this picture is so fine and the setting so gorgeous and magnificent we have received most favorable comments upon it from a number of people who have seen it." Miller guessed that it was the "character depicted by Mary Garden in this play before her reformation and her scant attire in the last reel [that were] considered objectionable features by some people."[32]

As the war came to a close, the Board of Review and the Kansas motion picture industry found that they had an unexpected yet serious matter on their hands. Early in the morning of March 11, 1918, a young private reported to the army hospital in Fort Riley, Kansas, complaining of a number of symptoms including fever, sore throat, and headache. Dozens of other soldiers followed him into the hospital that morning. By the end of the week, there were more than five hundred soldiers in the hospital. Forty-eight of these men died, and no one knew why.[33] Kansas ended up being ground zero for the influenza epidemic of 1918 that ended up killing more than six hundred thousand Americans. It was the worst epidemic the United States has ever faced. The fall and winter of that year were times of fear and horror for the American people; they were afraid of going into crowds and catching the

---

31. Miller to Capper, April 27, 1918, in ibid.
32. Miller to Capper, May 27, 1918, in ibid.
33. "Influenza 1918," *The American Experience* videotape, program description, PBS/WGBH, 1999.

A Daughter of the Gods (1916) was one of the first American films with a nude scene. The Kansas Board of Review demanded that this scene be cut from Kansas prints. (Permission granted by Photofest)

disease. For theater owners, it was devastating to their business. Many of them closed their theaters, never to reopen. The closure of their theaters was not just voluntary due to a lack of patrons. In the fall of 1918, the Kansas state government issued a statewide quarantine that included motion picture houses. Arthur Capper wrote E. A. Van Doran, owner of the Victoria Theater in Hiawatha, about his loss: "I have your letter of October 26th in regard to the loss which will be sustained by moving picture houses by reason of the state-wide quarantine. I realize this is a serious matter to the moving picture men and I have great sympathy for them. I would like to help them if it was within my power."[34]

In November 1918, Arthur Capper was elected U.S. senator from Kansas. He would cease to play the role as the most influential impetus behind, and supporter of, motion picture censorship. His influence would not be totally negated; even when he was not governor, he strongly discouraged allowing *The Birth of a Nation* into the state. But he turned the reins of power over to Henry Allen, a Republican editor who shared many of his political sympathies. A Capper biographer describes Allen as an "aggressive, outspoken Wichita newspaperman."[35]

In 1919, Kansans held one of three perspectives on the Kansas Board of Review and film censorship. They were either apathetic about the entire process, which may have been the majority of citizens; they believed the board was too harsh in its judgments on films; or they believed that the board was too lax. Newly elected Governor Allen definitely fitted into this final category. In March 1919, shortly after his inauguration, his private secretary, Clyde M. Reed, wrote to Mrs. Miller to explain the governor's views on the board's work, "The entire motion picture law seems to be a dead letter, except that some of the films are being viewed by the Board. Neither the Film Companies, the exhibitors or the patrons have any respect for the law or the way it is being administered. Probably more complaint has come to me over the state as regarded motion picture censorship than any other single thing in which the administration is interested." Claiming that the new administration would be an "actively efficient" one, the secretary claimed that the board, based on the evidence they had submitted to the newly installed governor, was being too lenient. They were letting in bad films, not enforcing the pres-

34. Capper to E. A. Van Doran, October 28, 1918, Box 11, File 45, General Correspondence, Capper Papers, KSHS.
35. Socolofsky, *Arthur Capper*, 145.

cnt censorship law in regard to inspecting tags, allowing rejected films to be exhibited, and not ensuring that film companies actually removed board-mandated eliminations from movies before they were screened.[36]

Enforcement was apparently the major issue for Allen. Miller explained to Reed that former attorney general Brewster had pursued a policy of having the law enforced without prosecution if possible. This kept relations with the film industry on a more positive note and was less accusatorial. She further explained that the board subscribed to a number of the state's newspapers, watching theater ads closely, and when an uncensored or rejected film was advertised, the board notified the exhibitor by telephone or telegram and called the film exchange that distributed the film, notifying them that they had to substitute another movie.[37]

Miller quickly attempted to protect her position. Pleased that Governor Allen was taking an active interest in film censorship she noted the problems that had occurred once the board's offices were moved to Kansas City: "As a matter of fact I believe the state offices were glad to have the office removed to Kansas City and to be rid of the annoyance of having the work done in Topeka with its many disagreeable features," such as the Appeal Board, angry exchange men, and potential lawsuits. But Miller argued that by being located in Kansas City, so close to the film exchange offices, they were in the virtual lion's den of abuse. "[We are] in the midst of the enemies of censorship and every influence has been antagonistic to the role of the Board."[38]

To ensure her job, Miller went into action. She hired Leonard Vaughn, a World War I veteran, to serve as a temporary traveling inspector. Apparently, he was well qualified in Miller's view, since "he has had clerical training and is a Christian." He found three violations of the censorship law in his first few months of work, and cases were pending against theater managers and distributors. Miller explained the difficulty of working with county attorneys. They were reluctant to bring suit against exhibitors for failure to show approval tags or for running uncensored or condemned films because the theater owners were usually "good and law-abiding citizens" who were often hoodwinked by the Kansas City, Missouri, exchanges. It was also difficult to bring charges against the film exchanges because they were across the state

36. Clyde M. Reed to Miller, March 20, 1919, Box 15, File 2, Correspondence—Subject File, 1919–1923, Allen Papers, KSHS. Reed became governor in 1929 and U.S. senator from Kansas in 1939.
37. Miller to Reed, March 19, 1919, in ibid.
38. Miller to Reed, March 27, 1919, "Motion Picture Board," in ibid.

line in Missouri and could be prosecuted only through the federal court. Miller realized that she would have to work carefully with the present attorney general to enforce the law. But she also realized that film exchanges were often not intentionally breaking the law. The fault often occurred because they were serving a large territory contiguous to Kansas, and in the rush of doing business, Kansas copies were often interchanged with others. Films were frequently sent out on long circuits, and the tags were torn off in transit or by irresponsible operators who did not want to display the censorship tag. To illustrate that the Board of Review was preoccupied with not just enforcement but actual censorship, she explained to Reed that in the past month, eighteen films had been rejected, a record by Kansas standards.[39]

In the midst of Allen and Reed's crackdown on the board, an old familiar figure intervened. The Reverend Festus Foster, former censor, wrote Governor Allen in April 1919. Whether this letter was the response to an inquiry by the governor or simply the reverend volunteering his views as a good citizen is not known. But Foster gave his honest views on the problems that motion picture censors faced in the state:

> The matter of passing on pictures to be offered the public is too important a matter to be done hastily and without undue consideration. I often passed on from 40 to 60 reels in one day. I submit that it is physically impossible to do satisfactory work at this great speed. Say nothing of the physical strain on the eyes—the nervous strain is too great to permit careful work. And greatest of all perhaps in the need for some form of "liaison" between the Board of Review and the public which it serves. If each member of the board would make from two to four trips a year, inspecting the theaters and meeting the teachers and preachers and club women of the state, the work would soon become the pride of the state.[40]

Governor Allen was apparently concerned with the work of the Review Board. A fascinating and confidential work schedule written by an unknown individual came to the governor's office that illustrated the censors' actual day of labor. On June 2, Miller came and worked from nine to eleven alone. Mrs. Short did not arrive until eleven. Mrs. Miller left to do errands, and Short worked alone all afternoon. Simpson did not show up the entire day. On June 6, Miller and Simpson worked from ten till noon and then closed the office

39. Miller to Allen, May 17, 1919, in ibid.
40. Festus Foster to Allen, April 4, 1919, in ibid.

for the rest of the day. This work schedule was obviously not constructed by a member of the board; a handwritten comment on the bottom of the page claims, "[They] condemn pictures before they see them."[41]

A letter from Miller to Allen demonstrates the governor's scrutiny of the board's work. Miller wrote that after discussing their "plan for inspection . . . we want you to see our methods of work. What we are accomplishing as well as what we are not accomplishing." She continued, "We want you to understand this intricate piece of state machinery from an inside view and we want suggestions from you so as to bring about better and more definite results."[42]

There were also new frustrations over screen content. The development of the Theda Bara–like sex film was an important factor in fanning the flames of increased censorship. The disastrous influenza outbreak of 1918–1919 and the sudden lack of audience interest in war films meant that many studios began looking at other options to outdo each other. By 1919, this often led to making more "adult" pictures. Board of Review member B. L. Short claimed that part of this new frankness was due to the intensity and fervor of the war. She explained that "we allowed many phrases to go through, while the war was on, that would have been eliminated under ordinary circumstances. But we feel that the line should be drawn somewhat more strictly now." Short advocated the elimination of all swearing and strong language in motion picture titles. She claimed, "There is not the same necessity for keeping high strung to a high pitch of emotion with reference to the war and foreign and domestic affairs."[43]

Solicitor G. W. Butts was flabbergasted by what he considered to be the frank, immoral lessons that these new "sex pictures" were teaching young women. "Thousands of girls receive their first thrills of sex knowledge in the movies. Every step taken, showing the unfaithfulness of women, [is] vividly portrayed. . . . This showing gives girls and wives the idea, and belief, that they are, and will be, immune from punishment, for this immorality. . . . This thought in girls and women, is a prime factor in our divorce evil."[44] Butts seemed not to care much about the impact of these films on young men; his fear was the influence that this new class of films was having on young

41. Box 15, File 2, Allen Papers, KSHS.

42. Miller to Allen, July 2, 1919, "Motion Picture Board—1919," Box 15, File 2, Allen Papers, KSHS.

43. "War over Stop Swearing Says Kansas Censor Body," *Moving Picture World*, January 18, 1919, 314.

44. G. W. Butts to Allen, July 10, 1919, Box 15, File 2, Subject File, Allen Papers, KSHS.

women. Butts must have been referring to enormously popular new pictures like Cecil B. DeMille's *Old Wives for New* (1918) and Gloria Swanson's star-making turn in *Don't Change Your Husband* (1919).

The horrors and terrors of World War I, the sheer loss of humanity and hard-hearted coldness of the calamity, forced film producers and audiences to face the realities of the new world they lived in. World War I had caused seismic shifts in gender relations, work patterns, political sensibilities, and the economic structure of the nation.[45] Motion pictures that attempted to reflect, in a modern way, this new reality often ran into the brick wall of censors who wanted to shield audiences, particularly the young, from this new frankness. Two motion pictures ran into this problem in Kansas in the immediate postwar period. They were *The Spreading Evil* (1918) and *The Unpardonable Sin* (1919).

The Spreading Evil was a morality tale that warned of the dangers of syphilis. In the film, Dr. John Carey convinces philanthropist Jules Le Mayne to finance German chemist Emil Hatsell's search for a cure for syphilis. His research is successful, but after the death of his patron he breaks his pledge to give the cure to benefit humanity and instead confers with a New York pharmaceutical profiteer. They plan on selling the miracle cure at a price that only the wealthy could afford. Hatsell's son Karl represents his father in New York. He is engaged to be married but has a bachelor fling in which he contracts the deadly disease. Dr. Carey meets the elder Hatsell in Holland, where he tells him of his son's fate. Hatsell selfishly refuses to give Carey the formula but decides to go to New York himself to aid his son. Hatsell is killed in a submarine explosion in the Atlantic Ocean, a fatality of the war. Karl, his son, commits suicide by walking into the ocean to join his father. At the end of the film, American scientists discover a cure that is superior to the German cure (of course). In the epilogue, Secretary of the Navy Josephus Daniels appears to present James Keane, producer, with a letter of endorsement for the film.[46] *The Spreading Evil* was one of a series of sex-hygiene films that was released in the immediate post–World War I era.[47]

The imminent homecoming of millions of soldiers from overseas meant that the disease, which could easily be contracted by soldier-prostitute relations, could be brought home to American women. Many welcomed the frank treatment of the delicate subject matter. *Variety* reported, "Only a short

45. Lynn Dumenil, *Modern Temper: American Culture and Society in the 1920s*, 9–11.
46. Hansen, *American Film Institute Catalog, 1911–1920*, 880.
47. Schaefer, *Bold! Daring! Shocking! True!* 25.

time ago an educated film of this undoubted value of *The Spreading Evil* would not have been permitted by the authorities. To be sure, it is pathologically educational and not suitable for smaller children but the time has come for parents to place before the offspring of both sexes the need for enlightenment on a subject hitherto tabooed for purely prudish reasons."[48]

Well, not for the Kansas Board of Review. It reviewed and condemned the film twice, not because it did not think the film would be enlightening for young people but because it thought the film would be detrimental. Miller claimed, "The ruined life of the young girl who was thrown out into the world (and gave the younger Hatsell syphilis) and became a menace seemed particularly objectionable and in all pictures we object to this special feature." Miller recognized that there would be a flurry of pictures with this similar theme and that if the Board of Review approved of this film, it would be difficult to construct an argument against the upcoming features. Film historian Eric Schaefer documents that three armed-service training films—*Fit to Fight* (1918), *The End of the Road* (1918), and *Fit to Win* (1919)—all dealt with venereal disease and displayed graphic footage of the physical ravages of the illness. Whereas earlier sex-hygiene films (such as *Damaged Goods*) had dealt with sexually transmitted diseases strictly in terms of morality, the public release of these three films to a general audience after the war led to a backlash against sex-hygiene pictures.[49] Miller and the board were part of a larger movement to end the production and distribution of this type of film.

The *Unpardonable Sin*, starring ingenue Blanche Sweet, is about rape. The film involves Dimny Parcot, a woman who attempts to find her family in Belgium following a German attack in the war. Dimny's sister Alice is "ravished" by a German colonel (*ravished* was postwar terminology for rape), and Dimny is attacked by the same despicable man. The film is pathologically anti-German. *Variety* claimed that the film showed the "unspeakable brutality and bestiality of the Huns during the invasion of Belgium." The trade publication acknowledged the difficulty the film might have passing certain censorship boards, claiming, "There seems to be some question whether the censors would pass the depiction of brutal ravishment." The Kansas Board of Review would not pass the film, despite its popularity. Miller reported, "People who saw it when shown in its original form in Kansas condemned it

48. Review of *The Spreading Evil*, *Variety*, November 22, 1918, 48.
49. Miller to Reed, May 10, 1919, Box 15, File 2, Subject File, Allen Papers, KSHS; Schaefer, *Bold! Daring! Shocking! True!* 28–30.

severely and commended us for our action in barring it from Kansas." The board acknowledged that it had been too lenient in its first year of operation, 1917, and that they were "striving constantly to be more discriminating and are rejecting more films outright than formerly instead of mutilating them by numerous cuts for the reason exhibitors do not want cut pictures and they usually come back to haunt us."[50]

The Unpardonable Sin caused additional problems for the censors because the exchange men who represented the film put undue pressure on the Kansas Board and the governor's office to pass the film. Miller acknowledged that two gentlemen, messengers Park and Nathan, called on the board's office and used persuasion and threats to try to get the censors to reverse their decision. The gentlemen clearly violated Section 2 of the 1917 law in their efforts to bring sufficient pressure on the women to secure their approval of the film. These actions were reported to the governor's office.[51]

The war had an incredible impact on every facet of American life, including race relations. Tens of thousands of African Americans served their country overseas in World War I. Many of these soldiers witnessed racial conditions in Europe that were much less restrictive and more humane than those in the United States. These men (and women) went home with high expectations. If they had helped make the world "safe for democracy," then they expected equal rights at home. African Americans began to organize and demand protections they were guaranteed under the Constitution. Instead, they suffered a sharp increase in lynching and some of the worst racial violence of the twentieth century, including in Chicago in 1919 and Tulsa in 1921.

In the early part of 1919, an incident took place at a Wichita movie theater that was indicative of this new spirit. In many Wichita movie houses, African Americans were relegated to the balcony or were completely excluded from the theater. In late February or early March 1919, four African American women sat on the lower floor of a Wichita theater. When an usher discovered their presence, he asked them to go to the balcony. They refused, and an argument ensued. Each woman later filed a fifteen thousand–dollar lawsuit against the theater for discrimination. *Moving Picture World*, when reporting on this incident, reflected the hardened racism of some Kansans: "Kansas exhibitors are up against the Negro problem good and hard. . . . If the demand

---

50. Hansen, *American Film Institute Catalog, 1911–1920*, 972–73; review of *The Unpardonable Sin*, *Variety*, May 9, 1919, 52; Miller to Reed, June 27, 1919, Box 15, File 2, Subject File, Allen Papers, KSHS.

51. Miller to Reed, June 27, 1919, Allen Papers, KSHS.

[to desegregate] is made to stick the exhibitors might as well close their houses. Black and white won't mix in Kansas."[52]

The Kansas Board of Review of Motion Pictures was facing a very different world as it entered the decade of the 1920s. The moving picture was an integral part of American life, but American life had substantially changed from nickelodeon-era simplicity. Motion pictures in the postwar years would reflect the adult concerns that millions of audience members held. Americans still went to the "pictures" for sheer entertainment, but film producers and directors were now pushing the envelope in what would be considered acceptable amusement. The response would be an unprecedented outcry for public control of the powerful medium.

52. "Kansas Theaters Face Negro Problem," *Moving Picture World,* March 8, 1919, 1342.

Seven

The Roaring Twenties, 1920–1927

By the end of World War I, the American film industry dominated the world market. Motion picture production was the fifth-largest industry in the United States, and film stocks were among the most valuable on Wall Street.[1] Motion pictures were far from being a simple diversion for the working classes as they had been at the beginning of the century. Filmgoing was one of the most popular and influential forms of recreation in the United States. Movie idols such as Mary Pickford, Charlie Chaplin, and Douglas Fairbanks Sr. were part of a constellation of national heroes and heroines celebrated in the mass media. Motion pictures delivered messages about consumption, leisure, and identity that helped transform the American public. These "messages" were not always readily accepted by the American people, but the medium could not be ignored, even by citizens who considered films a noxious form of entertainment. Motion pictures were helping to mediate the national debate over sexuality, gender roles, capitalism, and class in the 1920s. The Kansas Board of Review was an active participant in that debate, attempting to control what images were seen on the state's screens. For better or worse, the Board of Review was influential in restraining cinematic representation.

1. Burl Noggle, *Into the Twenties: The United States from Armistice to Normalcy*, 172.

The 1920s began with controversy on many fronts for the Kansas Board of Review. These included bitter intraboard fighting, the release of a spate of frank "mature" films, and the reissuing of *The Birth of a Nation*. As the decade progressed, however, censorship became more of an established, if not consistently abnormal, process.

On July 1, 1920, the board issued its annual report. The report, in many ways, reflected the lethargy of the board. The members claimed that they worked five and a half days a week, but this was not reflected in their actual job performance reviews. A great deal of the language of the 1920 report, in fact entire paragraphs, was lifted from the 1917 report. Certainly, the postwar board was operating under dramatically changed conditions. The differences in the two reports are perhaps what is most revealing. Motion picture censorship in Kansas was a more complicated and businesslike matter in 1920 than it had been in 1915. Whereas the 1915 board employed two censors, the 1920 Board of Review had three censors, a stenographer, an operator and assistant operator, an inspector, and a janitor on the payroll. Whereas the 1915 board was clearing more than ten thousand dollars a year in net profit, the 1920 board was more than two thousand dollars in the red. Chairwoman J. M. Miller's comments in the report that "the work is self-sustaining and it does not cost the state a cent to maintain it" were simply false.[2]

Miller and the board began the decade by continuing the tradition of criticizing the unholy triumvirate of the crime film, the sex picture, and the slapstick comedy genre. There was some added language in their report that reflected changing themes and interests. Regarding the crime film, the censors added, "A large number of pictures deal with the underworld, scenes of robbery, Chinese opium dens, brutal murders, assignation houses, white slavery and kindred themes [that] contribute the major parts of some films."[3] The Kansas censors were preoccupied with censoring scenes of specific locations associated with immorality such as brothels and drug chambers. This became a major theme concerning their work in the early 1920s.

The board's frustration with crime films reflected a sentiment expressed in the national press. In March 1921, P. W. Wilson, American correspondent of the *London Daily News*, wrote an essay in *Current Opinion* titled "The Crime Wave and the Movies." In this piece, Wilson questioned the contribution of

2. KSBR Annual Report, 1920, Box 58-5-4-5, Review Cards/Copy Cards/Action on Submitted Films, KSHS.
3. Ibid., 4.

motion pictures to criminal behavior. He ended his essay, "In the movies, as in the Psalms, you often have the wicked man flourishing on the green bay tree and the young folks are inclined to ask, if he got away with it on the big scale, why may not others try their hand in a modest way?"[4] Other editorialists also questioned the impact of cinematic criminal behavior on the "feeble" mind.

Concerning sex pictures, the board members said, "The protest that has been made against this class of pictures by the Kansas Board, as well as by every censor board in the country, and which is registered by rejecting them outright or requiring the elimination of bad scenes, has brought down upon censorship in general, and the censors in particular, a veritable storm of condemnation by those persons who have been exploiting the same."[5]

The censors were truthful in their description of public clamoring for renewed motion picture censorship. Virtually every state in the United States and numerous municipalities had censorship proposals before their legislatures and city councils in the early 1920s, although only two additional states, New York (1921) and Virginia (1922), actually instituted censorship boards. Although that meant that only six states had motion picture censorship boards, the action of the New York legislature in establishing a licensing system for movies was an especially hard blow for the industry. New York represented one of the major markets in the United States, and the industry had mounted a vigorous challenge to the licensing scheme. The National Board of Review was considered by many advocates of film censorship as worthless by this time in its attempt to "clean up" movies.

One of the major causes of this renewed interest in motion picture censorship was that a social revolution of major significance was taking place in the post–World War I period. This convulsion in morals challenged established religious and cultural beliefs. Defenders of traditional morality castigated scandalous new women's fashions and the openness and frankness with which young people talked about sex. The postwar attempt by studios to find an audience reflected many of these new values concerning gender roles and sexuality. Whereas the vamp roles of Theda Bara in the World War I era were looked upon as an aberration of female sexuality, many postwar women looked upon sexual freedom as a newly won right. This new genre of "sex pictures" was coupled with the explosion of the star system in which actors and

---

4. P. W. Wilson, "The Crime Wave and the Movies," 323.
5. KSBR Annual Report, 1920, Box 58-5-4-5, Review Cards/Copy Cards/Action on Submitted Films, KSHS.

actresses were glorified as role models.[6] Concerning the early 1920s, Richard Randall has argued, "The medium already had a well established reputation for excess, and in the postwar years it found a permissive climate in which this vice could flower."[7] The period was one of extremely rapid change, and the film industry both reflected and contributed to this seismic shift in mores.

Threatened by attempts to enact censorship at the municipal, state, and federal levels, in 1916 the industry formed the National Association of the Motion Picture Industry (NAMPI). One of the primary goals of the organization was to stem the threatened tide of censorship and attempt to give films protection under the guise of the First Amendment. In February 1921, industry journalist Benjamin Hampton wrote a series of articles in which he argued that "unless producers and exhibitors cleaned their own house and cleaned it thoroughly, there might not be much house left."[8] Motion picture executives condemned Hampton's message but also seriously listened to his warning. They had become convinced that unless immediate steps were taken to rid the screen of some of the worst abuses of content, governmental censorship might do it for them. NAMPI fought long and hard against the attempt to legislate film licensing in New York, and the association's failure forced industry leaders to reexamine their approach.

The Kansas Board of Review, meanwhile, was attempting to deal with this new film fare. In 1920, for the first time in its history, the board published a written guide of standards regarding what content would be eliminated from motion picture screens in the state. It is important to examine this document because it served as a working guideline for the board:

A. Pictures should be clean and wholesome, whether for entertainment or amusement, and all features that tend to debase morals or influence the mind to improper conduct should be eliminated.

B. No comedy which ridicules any religious sect or peculiar characteristics of any race of people should be shown.

C. The dress of comedy characters must be condemned when used for evil suggestion.

D. Infidelity to marriage ties must be condemned.

E. A display of nude human figures must not be shown.

6. See Dumenil, *Modern Temper*, 134, 138.
7. Randall, *Censorship of the Movies*, 15.
8. Jowett, *Film: The Democratic Art*, 156.

F. Bar-room scenes with drinking, gambling and loose conduct between men and women, should be eliminated when possible, and at all times should be abbreviated, as also social drinking and cigarette smoking.

G. Crimes and deeds of violence, with an undue use of guns, revolvers and knives, and criminal methods, such as give instruction in the committing of crime through suggestions, should be eliminated or abbreviated.

H. Prolonged and passionate love scenes, when suggestive of immorality, will not be approved.

I. Prolonged scenes of roadhouses, dance halls and houses of ill fame must be eliminated. Vulgar and suggestive dances by seminude dancers, especially those of the underworld, must not be permitted.

J. Pictures having for their theme white slavery and the allurement and betrayal of innocence will not be approved.[9]

What is important about this list of Kansas standards is that within a year, under the guise of NAMPI, a conference of top film directors adopted a code known as the Thirteen Points or Standards. Film historian Garth Jowett notes, "Basically, this series of resolutions condemned the production and exhibition of certain types of film or film content known to be most frequently censored by the existing censorship boards."[10] Out of sheer desperation (and the threat of more impending censorship), the industry attempted to improve its image through public relations. The correlation between these Thirteen Points and the ten Kansas standards for censorship was not accidental; the directors must have used the Kansas standards, along with other state censorship guidelines, to formulate their resolutions. By adopting state standards of censorship, studio heads were hoping to head off the costly process of reediting their films. Among those things that the directors agreed they would try to avoid were "white slavery," "illicit love affair[s]," "scenes which exhibit nakedness or persons scantily dressed," "demonstrations of passionate love," "stories which make drunkenness or gambling attractive," "stories and scenes which may instruct the morally feeble in methods of committing crimes," and "stories or scenes or incidents which offend religious belief."[11] The Kansas standards had been influential in serving as a guideline by which the industry would attempt to self-censor. Although the industry

9. KSBR Annual Report, 1920, 10, KSHS.

10. Jowett, *Film: The Democratic Art*, 157.

11. The Thirteen Points of the National Motion Picture Industry—1921, ibid., 465.

adopted the Thirteen Point regulations, they did not establish any enforce-ment machinery to guarantee that the studios would abide by the content regulations, indicating that the Thirteen Points were little more than a pub-lic relations ploy. The promotion of the Thirteen Points and their actual adoption were two very separate things.

The Kansas Board of Review continued to deal with problems related to the inspection process. In 1920, the board demanded that all films that were to be delivered to their office had to be well wrapped and contained in metal cases that had been approved by them. They also required that film companies guar-antee the number of duplicates and prints they would make of the examined film and then swear that they would be identically cut to the film being exam-ined. The board, in this 1920 report, clearly laid the blame for violation of the censorship law on the film exchanges. But as the censors explained to the gov-ernor, the exchanges were outside the state borders and beyond law enforce-ment's reach. The board acknowledged how this crippled their process: "Every interest of the motion-picture industry is united in a constant effort to defeat or cripple censorship. But there is no apparent indication at the present time, in the general class of films being released, that the necessity for having a cen-sored supervision over them has decreased."[12]

In the early 1920s, Governor Henry Allen found himself increasingly involved in matters of motion picture censorship. As governor of one of only a handful of states in the nation that had censorship, his views on the subject were frequently sought by government officials. Kansas governors were looked upon as "authorities" on governmental film censorship by other offi-cials. In early 1920, as the Massachusetts legislature was considering film censorship in its state, it wrote Governor Allen asking about the impact of the phenomenon in Kansas. His answers reflect a savvy knowledge of the film industry. When asked how the theater business had fared since Kansas adopted censorship, Allen responded, "The volume of business in the presen-tation of motion pictures has decreased in the past few years, however, we do not think this is due to censorship, you understand the pictures nowadays are presented on a much more elaborate scale than ever before, therefore, it costs more to produce this class of pictures. Speaking from a standpoint of public patronage to the moving picture theater, I believe that more people are attending the theaters to day than ever before." Attorney Henry L. Shattuck, a member of the Massachusetts legislature, wrote Allen about his opinion on

12. KSBR Annual Report, 1920, 6, KSHS.

the effectiveness of film censorship and his concern that it might become a political football. Allen's secretary responded, "The board is generally endorsed by the state and we feel that it has had strong influence in maintaining high standards. There has been no tendency to use it as a political weapon. In fact, no films have ever come before it which were of a political nature."[13] Allen's secretary, C. M. Reed, must have conveniently forgotten about *The Birth of a Nation*.

Allen supported censorship in Kansas but recognized that the vast majority of complaints to his office were about the board being too restrictive. On September 20, 1920, he wrote to Emporia professor E. D. McKeever, "I think I have had one hundred letters within the last year picking on the board, and yours is probably the third or fourth that has complained the board was too liberal." Allen remarked that most of these letters pointed out that movie patrons in Colorado and Missouri were given an opportunity to see "a class of moving picture art which Kansas is deprived of because of the severity of our censorship."[14]

Governor Allen had completely lost faith in the National Board of Review by 1920. He claimed that it "passes everything and does not seek to establish a standard." He believed, therefore, that it was the state's responsibility to "select pictures that are least offensive." Governor Allen and the members of the Kansas Board were disgusted with recent films that had attempted to get approval in the state. Allen argued that "one of the greatest troubles with the moving picture business is the rotten product of the producer."[15]

What was this "rotten product"? Specifically, what types of films were the governor and the board trying to keep out of the state? What subject matter offended them particularly? Between January 1, 1920, and December 31, 1921, the Kansas Board of Review rejected 47 films in their entirety and demanded eliminations in 334 others. There were four main genres of films and other related subject matter that the censors objected to or frequently forced eliminations of. The first was the wildly popular genre of slapstick. Chairwoman Miller, in particular, hated this brand of comedy. In 1919, several complaints came in regarding the Mack Sennett short *Never Too Old* (1919). The board passed the film with several eliminations, but Miller wrote Allen's

13. Massachusetts State Committee on Motion Pictures to Allen, February 9, 1920; Reed to Henry L. Shattuck, November 24, 1920, both in Box 15, File 3, 1919–1923, Correspondence, Allen Papers, KSHS.
14. Allen to E. D. McKeever, September 14, 1920, in ibid.
15. Ibid.

private secretary about slapstick comedies in general, "There are decidedly few of this class of picture I would pass if I were to consult my own preference." She said, "The general public clamors for them and exhibitors are eager to procure them so we try to make them as clean and decent as possible."[16]

The second genre that caused the censors frustration was films with criminal activity. Chairwoman Miller wrote a concerned citizen that "it is safe to say that nine tenths of the pictures censored are of the underworld or deal directly with crime. We try at all times to eliminate everything that shows the actual committing of the crime and that makes it attractive and educational." These were problematic films for the censors. The Vitagraph film *Trumpet Island* (1921) was a source of much criticism in the state. Governor Allen wrote Miller personally, explaining that he had heard a lot of complaints about the film and that it was apparently "one succession of blood and thunder after another." Allen had not seen the film but questioned how the board could have possibly passed it. He suspected that the film was shown without the forced eliminations removed. Allen explained in the letter that he had attended a good-size luncheon of men in Wichita and that the speaker was addressing the "boy question." The speaker was criticizing the exhibition of pictures with gunplay and banditry. The matter bothered Governor Allen enough that he instructed the board to "discuss this . . . and write me somewhat in detail just the process of determination which you use in passing on a picture full of wild-west scenes, gunplay, robberies etc." Several days later, Allen wrote a fellow Kansan, "I think [the censors] have reached a better standard on the sex problem than they have on the banditry problem."[17]

And then there was the "sex problem." Of all the subject matter most critiqued and condemned by the board, the depiction of impressionable young women being led to immorality, or sexually liberated young women having a good time, frustrated them the most. This genre of "sex picture" was routinely rejected in the period 1920–1921. Examples included *Sex* (1920) with Louise Glaum (Theda Bara's successor) as the queen of the Frivolity Theater and self-centered vamp who steals other women's husbands; *Sacred and Profane Love* (1921), a woman who spends all night with a concert pianist; *The Day She Paid* (1919), a Universal feature about a woman who has a premarital affair; and *Flames of the Flesh* (1920), about a woman who is ruined by an

16. Miller to Reed, March 4, 1919, "Motion Picture Board," Box 15, File 2, Allen Papers, KSHS.
17. Miller to Ewing Herbert, February 8, 1921; Allen to Miller, April 9, 1921; Allen to Leon Nusbaum, Dolan Mercantile Company, Atchison, April 14, 1921, all in "Motion Picture Board," Box 15, File 4, in ibid.

older man and seeks revenge on him by attempting to seduce both of his sons. Postwar movies projected a new version of womanhood that emphasized women's physical freedom, energy, and independence.[18] This imagery of the "New Woman" offended moralists who believed that women were on their way to ruin. The *Central Christian Advocate* of Kansas City argued, "The reputation of Sodom and Gomorrah is not lower than that of Hollywood."[19]

Displays of partial nudity in films was problematic for the censors. They rejected Famous Players-Lasky's *Idol of the North* (1921) because of its location (a Yukon dance hall) and its dancing girls. *Variety* reported that star Dorothy Dalton appeared as a star performer in a mining-camp dance hall "with bare shoulders and abbreviated skirts."[20]

The Board of Review's taboo on depictions of bars, saloons, or the imbibing of alcohol also led to some unusual choices. By 1920, the entire nation was following the Kansas example and participating in prohibition. *Law of Nature*, a 1919 feature, was pure prohibition propaganda. It illustrated the miseries and heartaches caused by alcohol consumption and drunkenness. One would suspect that the dry state of Kansas would want such a film to be exhibited in its borders, but that was not the case. Films in Kansas could not show locations where alcohol was frequently consumed or the pleasure (or destruction) caused by drinking, so the film was not allowed in the state, regardless of what the message might be.

The women on the Kansas Board of Review were not alone in their call for the increased regulation of films. By 1921, the call for various forms of governmental censorship had reached a crescendo. A multiplicity of municipalities considered film censorship. By 1922, censorship bills were introduced in thirty-two states. Each board would seemingly have its own standards. The renewed call for censorship threw the industry into a panic. The various film studios combined their efforts to create the Motion Picture Producers and Distributors of America (MPPDA). They selected Postmaster General Will Hays to accept the presidency of the new organization and began a program to clean up the movies. Hays immediately began a campaign to end any talk about federal censorship and defeat the passage of the state censorship bills. He promised industry self-regulation that was viable and enforceable. He was successful in stemming the tide of censorship and was able to stop some of the

18. Dumenil, *Modern Temper*, 134.
19. Quoted in "Movie Pictures Morals Attacked and Defended," 505.
20. Review of *The Idol of the North, Variety*, May 20, 1921.

worst abuses of film content.[21] Between 1923 and 1928, forty-five censorship bills were introduced in state legislatures. All forty-five bills were defeated.[22]

While the Kansas Board of Review was battling film content, Governor Henry Allen experienced numerous problems with the personnel of the board. In 1919, the state legislature amended the 1917 law to raise the salaries of the board chairperson to twenty-one hundred dollars and the individual censors to eighteen hundred dollars. This amount of money was barely enough for an individual to survive on without some other form of assistance; no head of household who was supporting a family could have entertained the notion of holding the job.[23] Gender dictates of the time, therefore, helped indicate that the position of "reviewer" was geared toward women since they were not thought to be the primary breadwinners in most households.

Allen became acutely aware of the personnel problems in early 1920 with a letter from Lucille Dill Russell, a former stenographer for the board. The purpose of Russell's letter was to protect the job of her friend Hallie Tucker, the board's secretary. Russell described the working conditions of the board as "more deplorable than when I was employed there." Russell claimed that her primary responsibility while employed for the board had been transcribing the personal correspondence of Mrs. Miller. She described the relationship among the three censors as intolerable. She claimed, "You no doubt know of the jealousy which exists among the Board members. . . . I have even heard a member of the Board express her opinion of the other member in language quite unbecoming." Apparently, throughout 1919, each censor made individual trips to Topeka to speak to the governor personally and complain about the other members of the board. Each of the censors jockeyed to protect her own position, obtaining letters of recommendation and commendation from women's civic groups. One example is a letter from the Kansas City, Kansas, Parent Teachers Association that "resolved that we highly commend the faithful and conscientious work of Mrs. Miller and Mrs. Short of the Kansas State Board of Review."[24] Carrie Simpson was conveniently left out.

Allen inquired about using the services of a politically connected woman, Mrs. Myra Williams Jarrell, in mid-1920. She ended up doing substitute

21. Ruth Vasey, *The World according to Hollywood, 1918–1939*, 30–31.
22. Randall, *Censorship of the Movies*, 17.
23. State Laws of Kansas, 1919, chap. 284, sec. 29, *Session Laws, 1919*, 394.
24. Lucille Dill Russell to Allen, January 27, 1920; Kansas City, Kansas, Parent Teachers Association to Allen, April 25, 1920, both in "Motion Picture Board," Box 15, File 2, Allen Papers, KSHS. Russell had left employment for the board when she married.

work for the board. Allen thought highly of Mrs. Jarrell and explained that he was "immediately impressed with the fact that a woman of your particular capability could be of great service for us." But Allen also frankly explained that he was outlining a reorganization of the board, something "more constructive and business like than that which we have now." This fitted the business community's obsession in the 1920s with administrative efficiency. Allen explained that he did not have any problems with the individual censors "except that they do fuss a lot." When Mrs. Jarrell showed up at the Kansas City, Kansas, offices of the board, the female censors were surprised and a little frightened. Allen wrote Jarrell, "Unfortunately they are all worried about their jobs, because I have been rather frank in expressing my discontent with the manner in which they quarrel together."[25]

Apparently, the three women stayed on Allen's mind because the very next day he wrote an associate commenting on their qualities for the job, "Mrs. Miller—choice of the board of the Women's Federation. Mrs. Short—club woman of Kansas City—both listed as cranks by state exhibitors and moving picture manufacturers. Miss Simpson—regarded as more liberal; all three of them are well educated Christian women of average intelligence."[26]

Allen became convinced that the solution to the personnel problem was a man at the helm. He recognized this would be a difficult option considering the low salary paid to the chairperson. Perhaps letters like one from Galena theater owner N. W. Huston influenced him: "Get rid of some of the petticoats on the board. There is no reason why there should be three women on the Board of Censors. One would be a-plenty." By the summer of 1920, Allen was frank with Miller about his decision on male leadership. He explained to her, "I haven't found my man yet. I have investigated two men since I talked to you, both of whom I thought would do, but upon further investigation I concluded that neither of them was just what we need."[27]

That "man" ended up being Dwight Thatcher Harris, a World War I veteran who took over the board chairmanship on January 20, 1921. Miller and Short stayed on the board as censors, but Simpson was on her way out. She had served on the board since its inception, almost six years, and was the one sign of continuity in the operation. She did not leave on good terms. Letters in Governor Allen's files imply that she had some type of "relationship" with

---

25. Allen to J. F. Jarrell, September 13, 1920, in ibid.
26. Allen to McKeever, September 14, 1920, in ibid.
27. N. W. Huston to Allen, March 20, 1920; Allen to Miller, August 16, 1920, both in ibid.

the Universal Film Exchange in Kansas City, Missouri. Certainly, Simpson had gained a reputation by 1921 of being the most liberal of the three female censors. Whether this was a clandestine relationship or simply sabotage on the part of Miller and Short is unknown. But Harris wrote Allen on the morning he began work, "Miss Simpson turned over her keys to me and departed shortly after I came. Not, however, without informing me that Senator Rolla Coleman had told her that he would 'make 'em pay the tax' at the next legislature." Miller and Short, realizing their precarious condition, demonstrated "the very kindliest spirit of co-operation and courtesy" to Harris as he began his job.[28]

There had been other personnel controversies during Miller's chairmanship. One major incident involved the employment of projectionist Leroy A. Edmunds. The Theatrical Stage Employees and Moving Picture Machine Operators was the local union for film projectionists in the Kansas City area. Miller attempted to hire a union employee, but the board could not meet the pay demands of the union, which then refused to allow any of its members to work there. The board hired three nonunion operators, but they were all forced to quit because of intimidation. The union was furious about the appointment of Edmunds. J. G. Campion of the union claimed that the disgruntlement was over the board's continued insistence on hiring nonunion men. African American organizations in Kansas City claimed that the union was fighting for Edmunds's dismissal because of racial prejudice. In the intensely white-hot climate of postwar racial violence and strife, African American organizations were trying to protect their own. The Kansas City Kansas Negro League wrote Allen, "The real reason [for] the complaint is his race. . . . He is our only representative connected with the Board." In October 1920, Reed, Allen's secretary, wrote to Miller, "I don't know of anything about this situation personally but feel that it might not be a good political move to make any change which would give rise to a feeling about colored people that they are discriminated against."[29] One may question Henry Allen's motives. Was he afraid to lose the African American vote, or was he sincerely concerned about race relations with the dramatic rise of the Ku Klux Klan in the state?

The hiring of Harris as chairman was Allen's first step in putting the board on a more solid footing. One additional consideration was moving the board's

28. Dwight Thatcher Harris to Allen, January 20, 1921, in ibid.
29. Miller to Allen, October 7, 1920; J. G. Campion to Allen, October 13, 1920; Kansas City, Kansas, Negro League to Allen, October 1, 1920; Reed to Miller, October 4, 1920, all in ibid.

office from Kansas City back to Topeka. The problem was not the accou-
trements of the office but the proximity to the Kansas City, Missouri, film
exchanges. The censors frequently complained that they had no room to hold
conferences in private. Allen acknowledged that "my present understanding is
that the bars are all down and the representatives of the producers swarm into
the office and the exhibition room." Allen sent an emissary to the Kansas City
offices in the spring of 1921 to observe working conditions. F. W. Roberts
reported, "I am persuaded that the reviewing room should be closed to all visitors except those invited by the Board to come in." Roberts believed that
agents and exchange men should absolutely be barred from the reviewing
process and that the board's votes should be taken in private.[30] The board's
headquarters remained in Kansas City, Kansas, until its demise in 1966.

Allen's frustration was quite evident. He was ready to suggest legislation in
early 1921 to reorganize the board in a more effective manner. He explained
to Charles Sheldon, a writer for the *Christian Herald*, "The great difficulty
with our Board of Review in Kansas is that the present members have not
been able to establish a standard." Sheldon, a very influential Social Gospel
reformer in the early twentieth century, had complained about the films that
were playing in Topeka that winter, and he was presently in New York City,
meeting with film producers. Allen explained to him, "Censorship really
ought to begin with a creator of the film because when the films now come to
our board, the only question is the elimination of those that are most evil."[31]

Complaints regarding films continued to pour into Allen's office. They
were typically of two varieties. One type was a broad, sweeping condemnation of all contemporary films. Allen's patience with these letters, usually
written by club women, was thin. He said, "The general complaint is that pictures aren't as good as they ought to be, because there's nothing constructive
in general criticism." The second type targeted a specific film. One of the
costliest and most newsworthy films of 1922, Erich Von Stroheim's *Foolish
Wives*, caused problems for Allen and the censors. Advertised as the first mil-
lion-dollar picture, the director and star appears as a fraudulent count who
seduces married women while extorting money from them. In the film set in
Monte Carlo, Von Stroheim is assisted by two fake princesses who live in
depravity in a huge mansion. Swimming in Von Stroheim's cynicism and
contempt for American values, *Foolish Wives* was bound to run into problems

---

30. Allen to C. N. Prouty, January 26, 1921; F. H. Roberts to Allen, May 31, 1921, both in ibid.
31. Allen to Charles Sheldon, January 26, 1921, in ibid.

with various censorship boards. The film was passed by the Kansas Board of Review by a vote of two to one. After a number of letters to the governor's office about the picture, Allen demanded to know from Harris what had happened. Apparently, *Foolish Wives* caused a lot of discussion on the board. Even Harris, the negative vote, argued, "It is cunningly devised, skillfully directed and subtly put across." Harris, realizing the importance of the picture, viewed it on five occasions. After forcing a number of eliminations, Short and Miller argued that they could not "conscientiously condemn it," and the film played in Kansas.[32]

Allen was governor during a politically and economically turbulent period in Kansas history. The prosperity of the war years quickly led to labor strife and the Red Scare. Allen had to contend with labor disputes on an unprecedented scale in Kansas history. In 1919, the United Mine Workers began to strike during the deadly cold of winter. This led to Allen's infamous statement, "It is the duty of government, and it has the inherent power, to protect the people whose welfare is dependent upon it. . . . If government is to mean anything, then its obligation is to prevent innocent people from being the victims of a fuel famine, which, in the course of events, is both unnatural and unnecessary."[33] A spate of strikes occurred during Allen's administration, including a paralyzing railroad strike in 1922. The strikes led to Allen's creation of the Kansas Court of Industrial Relations. The purpose of the court was to prevent such management and labor quarrels in the future.

Much of the blame for increased union activity was placed on the supposed rise of bolshevism. Conservatives fueled the flames of the Red Scare, arguing that there was a distinct relationship between bolshevism and labor agitation. When moving pictures attempted to depict these occurrences, censorship of the political sort occurred.

Under Harris, the Kansas Board of Review rejected films on political grounds on a scale unprecedented during the board's early history. In 1921, the wives and mothers of striking Kansas miners began a march in Cherokee County. Known as the "Amazon Women," they were eventually stopped by National Guardsmen. In January 1922, the board rejected a film based on this incident titled *The Marching Amazons of the Kansas Coal Fields* on the grounds that it would "corrupt morals." Specifically, the board objected because the film

32. Allen to Mrs. T. A. Rogers, chairman, Rosetti Circle, Winfield, March 6, 1921, in ibid.; Harris to Allen, March 28, 1922, "Motion Picture Board," Box 15, File 5, Allen Papers, KSHS.
33. Miner, *Kansas*, 248–50.

contained scenes of "1) unlawful assembly; 2) a worker compelled to kiss an American flag and promise to quit work; 3) a soldier is attacked and chased by a small crowd of women."[34] There was no nudity, obscenity, or criminal activity in *The Marching Amazons*—it was censored strictly for political reasons.[35]

A similar event occurred over the film *The Contrast*. The film was produced by New York's Labor Film Services. It was a class-conscious melodrama that depicted poor West Virginia coal miners fighting management. The miners had to overcome lockouts and the murder of union leaders. The newly established Federal Bureau of Investigation (FBI), led by J. Edgar Hoover, was determined to prove the connection between bolshevism and the radicalized postwar labor movement. In December 1921, Dr. William Sausele of the Kansas City, Missouri, branch of the Bureau of Investigation, U.S. Department of Justice, called on Dwight Thatcher Harris over this specific film, which he called "Soviet propaganda." *The Contrast* was to be shown at 711 Central Avenue in Kansas City, Kansas, by the Friends of Soviet Russia. The FBI was particularly concerned because a packinghouse strike in both Kansas and Missouri was occurring at the time. The film had not been submitted to the board, but Harris expected that there would be no intention of doing so. Titles in the film included:

1) Down with Capitalism
2) Why Wait?
3) You Are Many, They Are Few
4) Long Live the Dictatorship of the Proletariat
5) Long Live the Third Internationale
6) You Have Nothing to Lose but Everything to Gain
7) All Power to the Workers[36]

Harris wanted to personally go to the location where the film was supposed to be exhibited and stop the screening. He made it publicly known that the film was banned from the state, even though none of the members of the board had ever seen it. One prolabor newspaper claimed that the Kansas cen-

34. Harris to Allen, March 17, 1922, "Motion Picture Board," Box 15, File 5, Allen Papers, KSHS.
35. See Ann Schofield, "The Women's March: Miners, Family, and Community in Pittsburg, Kansas, 1921–1922," 159.
36. Harris to Allen, December 19, 1921, "Motion Picture Board," Box 15, File 4, Allen Papers, KSHS.

sors banned the film because "the board felt that the exhibition would inspire class antagonisms that would be damaging to the public interest."[37]

Unions went ballistic in response to Harris's decision. Wichita Contract Lodge no. 1543 vigorously protested the move. The Wichita International Boiler Makers claimed "no public officer has the right to interfere with or abridge the channels of education." The International Alliance of Theatrical Stage Employees and Moving Picture Machine Operators, Local 414, claimed that the board's denial of *The Contrast* demonstrated that the board was "inefficient, in-as-much as it functions for certain political and capitalistic interests and to the detriment of the masses."[38] Allen received more negative correspondence about the banning of *The Contrast* than any other governor received about any other film in the 1920s.

But that was not all. Harris and the Kansas Board of Review were also actively censoring newsreels, particularly those that were critical of Prohibition. They rejected a Fox News film that called for a repeal of the Volstead Act under the argument that it corrupted morals. As Harris said, "Candidly I wouldn't put my name on an approval card on that Fox propaganda for booze for a good many dollars. Not in the Sunflower state."[39]

The ugly rhetoric of the Ku Klux Klan was also reinforcing ethnic, racial, and religious prejudice across the state. The fight against "modernism" and "urbanism" that was preached by the Kansas Klan synthesized with the fight to reinforce the Sunday blue laws. Perhaps as many as forty thousand Kansans were members of the Klan in 1922. Allying themselves with religious organizations, there was a reinvigorated movement to close theaters on Sunday. By 1922, the enforcement of blue laws had become a distinctly local issue, although there was legislation on the state books prohibiting Sunday exhibition of moving pictures. The Reverend Ira M. Benham of the First AME Church in Leavenworth argued, "There is a substantial lot of people who want [the strict enforcement of Sunday blue laws] done. The membership of the Protestant churches and a lot of people who are not church people want it done." Then, mimicking Klan prejudice, Benham, in a litany of

37. AFI News Service quoted in *Los Angeles Citizen,* September 23, 1921.
38. Wichita Contract Lodge no. 1543 to Allen, n.d.; Wichita International Boiler Makers to Allen, January 31, 1922; International Alliance of Theatrical Stage Employees and Moving Picture Machine Operators, Local 414, to Allen, January 25, 1922, all in "Motion Picture Board," Box 15, File 5, Allen Papers, KSHS.
39. Harris to Allen, January 17, 1922, in ibid.

religious bigotry, explained, "Of course, the Catholics, most of them, and the Jews would likely be against it. And all the underworld of course would be against it. They destroy the morals of the city."[40]

On June 30, 1922, several months before statewide and national elections, the board issued its biennial report. It is uniquely a product of its time and a reflection of the anxieties that existed regarding motion pictures and Hollywood.

By the summer of 1922, seven states—New York, Pennsylvania, Virginia, Ohio, Maryland, Florida, and Kansas—had enacted film censorship legislation. Other states were presently considering it. Harris, the author of the 1922 document, described the relationship between the motion picture industry and the public in combat terms. He noted that film censorship had always been fiercely attacked by the film industry. "High-priced employees of the united industry have gone from one end of the country to the other protesting against what they call 'political' censorship. These employees cry 'Clean the pictures from within' and make promises of what is to be done for Better Pictures."[41]

Harris was clearly talking about the formation of the MPPDA and the hiring of its president, Will Hays. Making the fight against film censorship a crusade for the First Amendment, Hays was able to successfully defeat proposed censorship legislation in Massachusetts. One of the primary reasons Hays was brought on board the MPPDA was as a public relations man. The industry suffered through a series of scandals in 1921–1922, including the mysterious death of director William Desmond Taylor, the quickie divorce and remarriage of Mary Pickford, the drug addiction and eventual death of star Wallace Reid, and, in the most sensational case, the rape and murder trials of Fatty Arbuckle. Harris reported on these infamous activities in his 1922 report: "Scandals have been uncovered in the motion picture actor's colonies, and films produced that drew nation-wide protest against their exhibition. From the production centers of the films comes news of murder [Taylor], orgies [Arbuckle], drug addiction [Reid] and libertines. At least one of the most notorious characters [Arbuckle] was suspended from the industry for a few months and then 'forgiven' within the industry."[42] What was clear by the summer of 1922 was that not only were

---

40. Ira M. Benham to Allen, April 14, 1921, in ibid. For Governor Allen's relationship with the Klan, see Patrick G. O'Brien, "'I Want Everyone to Know the Shame of the State': Henry J. Allen Confronts the Ku Klux Klan, 1921–1923."

41. KSBR "Biennial Report," 1922, Box 58-5-4-5, Review Cards/Copy Cards/Action on Submitted Films, KSBR, KSHS.

42. Ibid.

Hollywood films to be put on trial but so were the moral characters of actresses and actors who performed in them. Prior to 1921–1922, the fight over censorship had been distinctly about film content. Now, that discussion expanded enormously to include the private lives of those individuals who worked in Hollywood. In December 1922, Will Hays worked with Fatty Arbuckle in an attempt to resuscitate the latter's career. There was a virulent reaction to this attempted reinstatement on the part of much of the American public. Harris would have neatly fitted into this camp.

Since motion picture censorship was being attacked for being "anti-American" by those in the industry and by defenders of free speech, Harris defended his cause and his livelihood, claiming, "The right of a state to bar from its territory the salacious picturization of lascivious story is as logical as the right of the nation to bar from its mails the transmission of pictures and obscene messages." Harris made a veiled reference to the nineteenth-century Comstock Law that had made it illegal to send any "obscene, lewd, or lascivious" book or pamphlet through the mail. He justified his practice of censoring motion pictures through this historical precedent.[43]

Like Hays, Harris was a firm believer in public relations. In the 1922 report, he informed the legislature that complaints against individual films were given careful attention. If there were sufficient complaints against a film, it would be recalled and reexamined. Harris was practical, though, while addressing the public: "In the consideration of hundreds of films it is of course impossible for this Board to receive the unanimous approval of the public." He then added a corollary to the old Progressive rationale for censoring films: concern for the children. He argued that there were films suitable for adults and ones suitable for children. Not all films passed by the board could or should be seen by children.[44] Several years previously, the board had begun compiling lists of films available for children, churches, and Sunday school programs. This was an indication that the board believed that certain films were suited for certain age groups.

In November 1922, Kansans elected Democrat Jonathan McMillen Davis to the governorship. With the election came a clean sweep of the board. When Davis was inaugurated in 1923, he followed the practice of partisan politics, appointing Mrs. Gertrude Sawtell as chairwoman and Mrs. Luther Swensson and Mrs. Eleanor Tripp as fellow censors. Following the departure

43. Ibid.
44. Ibid.

of Harris, the Kansas State Board of Review of Motion Pictures would be an all-female enclave for the rest of its history.[45]

With no veteran members on the board, the new appointees faced some challenges. In the board's 1924 report, it claimed, "Our greatest trouble has not been with the dramatic releases of the bigger and better established film companies but with the vulgarity prevalent in one or two reel comedies."[46]

This was the board that was pressured by Governor Davis to admit *The Birth of a Nation* in the state after an eight-year exclusion. In 1922, the Ku Klux Klan in Kansas had reached the height of its power. The Klan actively fought against "modernism," "urbanism," Jews, Catholics, and African Americans.[47] The Klan and its racial politics had an immeasurable impact on the state. The Klan's fight against "modernism" and "urbanism" borrowed earlier Progressive Kansas rhetoric about the moral "threat" of the big city. Racial matters were very much at the forefront of the actions of the Ku Klux Klan and the Kansas Board of Review, as reflected in the censorship of the films of director Oscar Micheaux.

Oscar Micheaux was one of the preeminent and most prolific African American directors of the 1920s. He made a number of provocative films in the decade that challenged racial norms and castigated the nation for the various ways in which African Americans were second-class citizens. Micheaux's filmic depictions included lynching, the lack of employment opportunities, segregation in transportation, mob violence, rape, inferior educational facilities, and false imprisonment. One of Micheaux's most common themes was that of miscegenation. He favored very light-skinned African American actresses, and the "threat" of interracial romance was a common trope in his oeuvre. As a result, Micheaux was one of the most castigated filmmakers of the 1920s in Kansas. His films *The Dungeon* (1922), *The Virgin of the Seminole* (1923), and *Son of Satan* (1924) were all banned. Other "race films," movies by African American directors for black audiences, were also rejected, including Reol Production's *Burden of Race* (1921).

A witch hunt over alleged film scandals would destroy the careers of a number of stars during the 1920s. This was not just a phenomenon of 1921–1922. Much of the impetus behind this blacklisting came on the local

45. Laura Wittern-Keller demonstrates that in the Pennsylvania, New York, and Virginia boards, the majority of censors were women ("Freedom of the Screen," 73).
46. KSBR "Biennial Report," 1924, Box 58-5-4-5, KSBR, KSHS.
47. Miner, *Kansas*, 252–53.

and state levels. Kansas newspapers were all too willing to publicize the sinful but intriguing exploits of Hollywood stars. One such incident involved actresses Mabel Normand and Edna Purviance. On New Year's Day 1924 they were guests of oil magnate Courtland Dines. Mabel's chauffeur got into an argument with Dines, pulled out a revolver, and shot him, although not fatally. The scandal was a major story in Kansas and across the nation. Immediately following the event, the *Topeka State Journal* ran a headline, "Film Queens Questioned in Hollywood Shooting," with photos of both Normand and Purviance.[48] The shooting coincided with the release of Purviance's *Woman of Paris* in which she portrays a kept woman. The United Artists feature passed the Board of Review before the Dines shooting with several eliminations. The Kansas censors objected primarily to scenes of women smoking cigarettes and sexually suggestive behavior.[49] In an unusual move, the Motion Picture Theater Owners of Kansas, Inc., wrote Governor Davis asking the Board of Review to ban films starring the two actresses. The argument behind such a dramatic decision was to "avoid the moral effect it might have on the public that the theatres of Kansas glorify and make heroines of questionable characters."[50] The real motivation may have been fear of a crackdown by the Kansas legislature and the Kansas Board of Review on motion picture exhibitors.

In late December 1923, Kansas attorney general Charles Benjamin Griffith had the board consider a request to ban all films that Mabel Normand starred in. The attorney general wrote that the rationale behind his decision was a result of Normand's connection with the murder of William Desmond Taylor. Normand had spent less than an hour with the director the evening before his death. Even though she was never considered a potential suspect in the shooting, the press gleefully jumped on the story. The police discovered that Normand had a two thousand–dollar-a-month cocaine habit, and the actress was portrayed as simply another example of the evil and sinful side of Hollywood.

The board of its own accord banned all films of Mabel Normand and were deciding on Purviance when they wrote the governor on the matter. Davis did not accept the censors' rationale for banning two actresses when they were not even guilty of any crime. He wrote to the board, "I really cannot see

---

48. "Film Stars Land," *Topeka State Journal*, January 1, 1924, 1.
49. "Complete List of Motion Picture Films Presented to the KSBR for Action, July 1, 1923–December 31, 1923," Box 58-5-4-9, KSBR, KSHS.
50. Motion Picture Theater Owners of Kansas, Inc., to Davis, January 8, 1924, Box 2, File 5, 1923–1925, Davis Papers, KSHS.

Due to her scandal-ridden private life, many of Edna Purviance's films were banned from Kansas in the mid-1920s. (*A Woman of Paris*, 1923) (Permission granted by Photofest)

why the Board should take any action except in regard to the pictures, not taking into account the person's appearing in the picture. The pictures, themselves, it seems to me, are what count, but perhaps they should be scrutinized a little more closely if the persons appearing in them are of bad repute. In the days of the stage, actors and actresses whose reputations were unsavory appeared in plays that were of the best, with the full approval of the public."[51] Davis clearly wanted the board members to reconsider their censoring of an individual's private life rather than just film content.

Davis was savvy regarding the Hollywood proposition that there is no such thing as bad publicity. He wanted the board to be open-minded in its consideration of individual films but claimed, "I have been trying to avoid giving any publicity of any kind that would cause people to be curious to see pictures that are labeled wrong." Davis knew that Kansas citizens would gladly hop the border to Missouri, Oklahoma, or Colorado to view a scandal-tinged motion picture if it was "banned in Kansas." Perhaps Davis best stated his opinion in a letter to disgruntled Kansan Mrs. George Pierson, who wanted Normand drawn and quartered. "I want to say that I do stand for clean pictures, and I have been making a fight for clean people, as far as possible but cannot be guided by rumors or newspaper talk and it is certainly contrary to our American ideals and thoughts to make snap judgment on everything."[52]

By the middle of January 1924, the board had arrived at the decision to ban all films of Mabel Normand from the state and was waiting to gauge the fallout regarding Edna Purviance. Even the rereleases of old, wildly popular Charlie Chaplin films, with his costar and friend Mabel Normand, were banned from the state.[53]

Normand's career went into a free fall after these scandals. She became the feminine icon of Hollywood immorality since she was directly or indirectly involved in the Dines's shooting, the Taylor murder, and the alleged Arbuckle rape case (she was at the hotel party where the incident allegedly occurred). Both she and Purviance became scapegoats for the wrath of the celebrity-hungry public.

Normand and Purviance were not the only stars to have their careers dashed by questionable behavior and newspaper-driven scandal mongering.

51. Davis to Sawtell, January 14, 1924, in ibid.
52. Davis to Mrs. George Pierson, Independence, Correspondence File, Box 21.2, File 5, Censor Board and Board of Review, 1923–1925, Davis Papers, KSHS.
53. Sawtell to Davis, January 11, 1924, in ibid.

As previously mentioned, the Fatty Arbuckle case was perhaps the biggest story in Hollywood in the early 1920s and was a primary rationale why Hays was called in to head the MPPDA and to clean up the film capital. Arbuckle, at the time one of Hollywood's most popular and highly paid stars, was accused of raping starlet Virginia Rappe at the St. Francis Hotel in San Francisco. Arbuckle had to defend himself in three well-publicized trials, and the comic was never found guilty of the crime. But on April 18, 1922, Will Hays, in conjunction with studio heads, made the decision to stop the distribution and exhibition of all films starring Arbuckle. Even though this ban was rescinded later that year, on December 20, the damage was done. Women's groups across the nation, including the state of Kansas, were enraged by the negative publicity and demanded that Arbuckle be persona non grata on the screen.[54]

In the spring of 1926, as Arbuckle attempted to resuscitate his career, the Kansas Board of Review was caught off guard. The board received a promotional newsreel titled *Screen Snapshots* that depicted various film celebrities. One of these "stars" was Fatty Arbuckle. When the scandal originally broke in 1921, the board had decided to completely ban any depiction of the rotund star from the state. The board wrote the governor that this ruling had not been rescinded, and clips of Arbuckle in the newsreel would be eliminated.[55]

By the mid-1920s, Kansas had gone movie crazy. Not only was film exhibition a major business in the state, but the cultural influence of the medium was astounding. In 1924, Topekans had their choice of a number of theaters that played motion pictures, including the Cozy, Orpheum, Isis, Novelty, Gem, and Best.[56] Going to the movies was a primary diversion for both urban and rural Kansans. The *Topeka Daily Capital* had three full pages of motion picture news and advertising for local theaters in its March 3, 1925, edition. In 1915, film news (with the exception of *The Birth of a Nation*) was largely nonexistent in the daily Kansas newspapers, and theater advertising rarely consumed more than a half page. By 1925, film theater advertising was a major source of revenue for urban Kansas newspapers. Editors also clearly recognized that stories concerning film stars, or regarding new releases, sold additional newspaper copies. In 1925, Kansans could swoon over Latin lover Rudolph Valentino in *Cobra* or cheer on action-adventure star Douglas Fair-

54. Koszarski, *An Evening's Entertainment,* 207.
55. Emma Viets to Ben S. Paulen, April 2, 1926, Correspondence, Box 3, File 13, Subject File—Censor Board, 1925–1929, Paulen Papers, KSHS.
56. *Topeka Daily Capital,* January 1, 1924, 12.

banks Sr. in *Don Q, Son of Zorro*.[57] One could also view a popular new genre of "sex picture" that promoted scandalous behavior in its advertising copy but seldom delivered on the real product. With titles like *Flaming Youth* and *Flaming Passion,* producers were capitalizing on the youth-driven cultural and sexual revolutions of the 1920s to sell more tickets. In March 1925, the Orpheum Theater in Topeka exhibited the film *East of Suez* starring screen siren Pola Negri. The advertising copy for the film in the *Topeka Daily Capital* read, "Out where there ain't no Ten Commandments. Scarlet nights in an atmosphere charged with disregard for conventionality. Pola with her glorious natural appeal fights a terrific battle against odds planned by sensual steeped Orientalism."[58]

By the mid-1920s, motion pictures were having a significant impact on American culture. Heralding both the new postwar standards of morality and contributing to its development, motion pictures were "the" form of entertainment for more than fifty million Americans weekly. Motion pictures reflected and were a part of the culture of the Roaring Twenties. The screen archetype of the flapper—the newly liberated modern woman—was a staple in current films. As early as 1923, Colleen Moore in *Flaming Youth* depicted this standard of fun-loving woman. Actresses like Moore and Clara Bow had "it," a sexuality that was all-American and nonthreatening, unlike the screen vamps of the previous decade.

The rapidly changing cultural landscape made Will Hays take action. When he took over the reins of the Motion Picture Producers and Distributors of America, he established the Committee on Public Relations that was an advisory board on public demands and moral standards. This committee often served as a shield for directors and producers who were willing to push the envelope a little more every year with depictions of sexuality and scandalous costuming.

The Kansas State Board of Review had to contend with these trends on the American screen. They were in constant contact with the other six state censorship boards in the country. Between June 1, 1924, and May 31, 1925, the board viewed 1,929 films. Only 18 percent of these films were required to have eliminations made before they were allowed in the state. A total of 755 scenes and titles were cut from that year's pictures. In the period July 1,

57. *Topeka State Journal,* November 21, 1925, 14.
58. *Topeka Daily Capital,* March 3, 1925, 5.

1926–June 30, 1927, 2,399 films were examined by the board. Only 9 percent of all films were forced to have eliminations made, and only 411 scenes or titles were cut. Thus, as the decade progressed, either the vast majority of films had screen content that was deemed appropriate for Kansas viewers, and the percentage of these films increased over time, or the board was simply becoming more lenient. In 1924, the board stated, "It would, of course, be virtually impossible to avoid offense to certain types of persons who attend motion picture exhibitions, seemingly with the sole desire to find something about which to complain. We have received many communications from this class of people."[59] This statement is remarkable in that it reflects a significant change in stance and attitude among the members of the board. During the 1910s, this breed of motion picture viewer was often driving the censorship process. These viewers were seriously listened to, and films were often recalled based on the influence of and the number of complaints about a particular film. By late 1924, these reluctant filmgoers were often depicted as cranks.

A second important change in stance was reflected in the 1924 biennial report. The board stated, "Naturally, all films approved by the board are not suitable for the entertainment of children."[60] This qualification would have shocked the Kansas Progressives who initiated this censorship process. The protection of children was one of the major rationales for adopting the censorship process in the first place. Thus, the censors were clearly approving films deemed appropriate only for adults but not classifying films as such. Apparently, it was a responsibility of parents to determine which films were for adults only. One of the principal reasons for the longevity of the Board of Review was its ability to adapt to new standards of morality or new constituencies.

This is not to say that all adult-oriented films sailed by the board. An examination of such films is in order. Thomas H. Ince's production of *Anna Christie* (1923) was heavily edited by the board. *Anna Christie* is the story of a streetwalker who is taken in by her father, who is unaware of his daughter's profession. The father, an old coal-barge commander, is determined to keep his daughter away from sea life. Anna meets a sailor, and they promptly fall in love. Her new suitor and father argue over Anna's future. Angrily, Anna reveals her past life, and both men leave her. In true Hollywood fashion, a reconciliation with both men takes place in the end. The First National pro-

59. KSBR "Biennial Report," for the biennium ending June 30, 1926; for the biennium ending June 30, 1928; for the biennium ending June 30, 1924, all in Box 58-5-4-5, KSBR, KSHS.
60. Ibid., for the biennium ending June 30, 1924.

duction, considered a prestige picture on the East Coast, included material considered "unsuitable" for Kansas moviegoers. Scenes of alcohol consumption and female smoking and suggestive dialogue ("She's a sweet good girl; yes, she is") were exorcised from the screen.[61]

Flaming Youth (1923), another First National picture, was the epitome of Roaring Twenties hedonistic youth culture gone wild. Although the board approved the film, it forced the studio to eliminate scenes of drunken men and women, specifically a provocative scene in which young people disrobe and plunge into a swimming pool. A number of concerned citizens wrote Governor Davis about the supposed debauchery of *Flaming Youth*. Women's clubs questioned the board's judgment in allowing the film into the state in any manner. Films like *Flaming Youth* were *the* pictures to watch for teenagers, and the peer pressure to view such hot films was overwhelming. Lilla Day Monroe, editor of the *Kansas Women's Journal,* explained it to Governor Davis this way:

> It seems a terrible thing to put these pictures out and have all of them talked over by our high school students. It was reported to me by different mothers that the high school students talked about the matter to one another and were crazy to go and see the picture. Of course, some did go and tell the others and then all wanted to go. It was a very unfortunate thing. I very much feel that there is a united effort to break down the morale of our youth in this country. I think it is much more serious than many people want to believe.[62]

During the 1920s, exploitation became a recognized and distinct category of motion pictures. As Eric Schaefer discusses in his book *Bold! Daring! Shocking! True! A History of Exploitation Films, 1919–1959,* exploitation films became a separate category of cinema despite the fact that the term had been bandied about at an earlier date. He argues that exploitation films contained the following features: their primary subject was a forbidden topic, they were cheaply made with extremely low production values, they were distributed independently and exhibited in theaters not associated with the major studios, and there were relatively few prints of these films circulating at any one time.[63] Exploitation films were not hard-core pornographic films, although

---

61. Kenneth Munden, ed., *American Film Institute Catalog of Motion Pictures Produced in the United States: Feature Films, 1921–1930,* 19–20; "Complete List of Motion Picture Films Presented to the KSBR for Action, July 1, 1923–December 31, 1923," Box 58-5-4-5, KSBR, KSHS.

62. Lilla Day Monroe to Davis, February 20, 1924, Box 2, File 5, Davis Papers, KSHS.

63. Schaefer, *Bold! Daring! Shocking! True!* 36.

such stag movies did make the rounds in clandestine ways. Exploitation films first began to be exhibited (or they were attempted to be exhibited) in the state in the 1920s and would prove to be attention grabbers for small-town and big-city audiences through the 1960s.

Exploitation films, deemed as sex-hygiene pictures, were problematic for the board. One such film was *Some Wild Oats* (1919).[64] The film dealt with victims of syphilis but was condemned for its "coating of vulgar humor."[65] The Topeka Health Department exhibited the film, after initial approval by the board. Governor Davis took the unusual step of having a special screening of the picture for a committee of club women, selected by Mrs. Lilla Day Monroe. The group decided that the film should be shown only to medical school students, so Davis requested that the film not be admitted to the general commercial motion picture trade. Going around the board's decision was an unusual step, perhaps demonstrating Davis's loss of trust in its decision-making process. Lilla Day Monroe wrote the governor about the matter: "Now as to this picture—'Some Wild Oats.' I do not remember one spiritual or sweet line in the whole thing. The only lesson that youth would carry is that, 'You'll be all right if you get the right doctor.' This is a vicious untruth. If you could rid the State of the entire sex-hygiene program you could get the people back to a wholesome normalcy and clean mindedness you would be doing an inestimable amount of good for our people."[66] Although Monroe may have been considered a crank by board members, she was a politically well-connected citizen and a force to be reckoned with or Davis would not have taken this unusual step. Her opinion did matter.

The pressure of the women's clubs was significant enough for the board to recall another "educational" picture, *The Miracle of Life* (1926). The film concerned a newly married couple, Blair and Janet Howell, who are compatible on every issue but one—he wants children, whereas she prefers her freedom. When Janet learns that she is pregnant, she calls on a friend who suggests a doctor that will perform an abortion. Prior to her obtaining an abortion, Janet has a dream in which Blair finds out about the procedure, divorces her, remarries, has children, and leaves her a bitter, lonely old woman. She comes to her senses following the dream and decides to keep the child. The censors wrote to Mr. J. A. Epperson, manager of the Pathe Film Exchange. They explained

64. Exploitation films often circulated ten to twenty years after they were originally released.
65. Edward Weitzel, review of *Wild Oats, Moving Picture World*, August 9, 1919, 882.
66. Monroe to Davis, August 2, 1924, Box 2, File 5, Davis Papers, KSHS.

that the board could order a reexamination of any film or reel approved by it upon giving twenty days' written notice to the owner of the film.[67] The recall of *The Miracle of Life* was a victory for Kansans who considered abortion immoral and not a subject for motion pictures.

Women's clubs remained the strongest supporters of motion picture censorship in Kansas and among the board's most vocal critics. When the board "seemed" too lenient, there were other constituencies in the state that they had to listen to. Such a population was the large number of Roman Catholics in Kansas. The lack of Catholics on the board led to a lack of sensitivity regarding Catholic religious beliefs. A 1923 Inspiration feature, *White Sister,* created such a problem. The film's story line involves an Italian woman (Lillian Gish), who, thinking her sweetheart (Ronald Colman), has been killed in a war in Africa, becomes a nun and works in a hospital. Two years later he suddenly appears again and endeavors to make her break her vows and marry him. She refuses to do so. On the surface, the film would seem unproblematic because the nun maintains her vows. But the very hint of a nun having a romantic life outside the sisterhood was apparently too much to take, and complaints poured into board headquarters. The board explained the rationale of their initial decision of passage to Governor Davis: "There was nothing immoral or objectionable in the picture although we thought at the time that it would only appeal to Catholics. We felt that we could not reject a film from a religious standpoint and there was nothing in this to cause it to be rejected."[68]

The Board of Review also had to contend with differing standards of morality based on geographic location. Residents of Kansas City, Kansas, who had easy access to the swinging lifestyle and jazz-filled clubs of Kansas City, Missouri, could be considered a little more worldly than residents of rural Kansas. This often led to battles over what was considered acceptable for the state as a whole. In 1929, Fulton theater owner Charles R. Smith wrote the governor about a picture he had exhibited, *The Bridge of San Luis Rey* (1929). Seldom did a motion picture owner write to complain about a film, but apparently Smith either had to accept the film as a result of block booking or accepted the film blindly without viewing it first. Smith described the MGM production, based on a Thornton Wilder play, as "the Rottenest, filthiest, vulgar picture I have ever run." He questioned how "any Censor

67. Munden, *American Film Institute Catalog, 1921–1930,* 516; KSBR Minutes, March 22, 1926, Box 8, KSHS.
68. Sawtell to Davis, August 20, 1924, Box 2, File 5, Davis Papers, KSHS.

Board composed of women could sit—and look at a dance put on by Lily Damita and let it go before as a decent picture is beyond me." The governor asked the board for an explanation. Miss Emma Viets, chairwoman at the time, explained that *The Bridge of San Luis Rey* was a "heavy picture" and that it "might not be a good box office attraction in a small town." But Viets asked the governor to understand the context of Damita's dance. As a fiery Spanish dancer, "a waif transformed into a theatrical queen," she performs a dance of the eighteenth century, albeit a "sensational" one."[69] Content was not an excuse in a small town in Kansas, though—vulgarity was vulgarity.

By the mid-1920s, the Kansas Board of Review of Motion Pictures had become an entity tied to the political patronage of the governor. Democratic governor Jonathan M. Davis served in office from 1923 to 1925. During his term, Mrs. Gertrude Sawtell served as chairwoman of the Kansas State Board of Review, with Mrs. Luther Swensson and Mrs. Eleanor Tripp assisting her as fellow censors.[70] In November 1924, Ben Sanford Paulen, a Republican, was elected governor, and a restructuring of the board was made. Miss Emma M. Viets became chairwoman, with Mrs. Walt Haskell and Miss Fern Bauers-feld assisting her.[71]

By the mid-1920s, the board had become exclusively a female domain, reserved for those who were politically connected. Board members did not always serve an entire gubernatorial term of office, due to illness, an impending marriage, or other family circumstances. Board members often cut their term of service short. Myra Williams Jarrell resigned her board position in early 1927. She explained to Governor Paulen, "Dabbing in politics has its drawbacks as well as its charm. My family is my first consideration. I feel that I cannot do my full duty to my family and at the same time give to the work of a public office the attention it should have."[72] During a period of time in which a woman's primary responsibility was still perceived to be that of wife and mother, Jarrell's decision is understandable. Even with the wild antics of flappers and wanton women of the movies, marriage and family were often the goals for such enigmatic figures.

69. Charles R. Smith to Reed, April 1929; Viets to Dora Louck Miller, assistant to Reed, n.d., both in Box 1, File 4, Records of the Governor's Office, Correspondence Files, 1929–1931, Reed Papers, KSHS (hereafter cited as Reed Papers).
70. KSBR "Biennial Report," for the biennium ending June 30, 1924, Box KSHS.
71. Ibid., for the biennium ending June 30, 1926.
72. Jarrell to Paulen, January 3, 1927, Correspondence File, 27-09-05-05, Records of the Governor's Office, Correspondence Files, 1925–1929, Paulen Papers, KSHS (hereafter cited as Paulen Papers).

More often than not, positions on the board were reserved for women who had actively contributed to a governor's campaign or whom the governor had to reward for some other past (or future) political aid. In late 1925, dozens of letters began pouring into Governor Ben Paulen's office, pleading for the extension of the commission of Fort Scott board member Mrs. Lizzie Hughes Storkhoff. Attorney C. J. Morton, pleading Storkhoff's case, wrote, "I have been intimately acquainted with Mrs. Storkhoff and the Hughes family of Ft. Scott for over 30 years. They are all staunch Republicans; have always worked for the party during the campaigns and have given of their funds to assist in carrying on the campaigns from time to time." William Bass, principal of Chanute Senior High School, explained the political connections of former teacher Storkhoff: "She has one brother who is a prominent Republican in Bourbon County, another who is Superintendent of Schools at Parsons and one who is Principal of the High School at Independence."[73]

Being a member of the board was certainly not financially lucrative. In 1925, the chairman made twenty-one hundred dollars a year, and board members made eighteen hundred dollars. But there were other "perks." Members kept in touch with censorship boards in other states, and this often meant frequent travel. In 1925, Emma Viets attended the Fourth National Motion Picture Conference in Chicago. She returned and reported to Governor Paulen, "I listened very attentively and gained much information on the idea of Federal Censorship and I still believe that State Censorship is preferable."[74]

Viets had significant problems with growing loopholes in the censorship apparatus. The first issue revolved around the Kansas State Board of Review's legal right to censor advertising motion pictures, that is, films designed specifically to sell a product. In March 1928, Viets asked Governor Paulen to have the attorney general draft a written opinion in regard to this matter. The chairwoman insisted, "It has always been the policy of the Board to require all MOVING PICTURE FILMS to be approved or disapproved by this Board."[75]

A more serious issue, in regard to the board's ability to control screen content in the state, involved nonprofit exhibition of motion pictures. The availability of inexpensive 16-millimeter motion picture projectors (such as Bell and Howell) in the 1920s meant that churches, fraternal organizations, and social welfare organizations could have easy access to motion pictures. Viets

73. C. J. Martin to Viets, January 22, 1925; William Bass to Paulen, January 19, 1925, in ibid.
74. Viets to Paulen, February 15, 1926, in ibid.
75. Viets to Paulen, March 1, 1928, in ibid.

claimed that the Board of Review was "besieged with letters" claiming that "a film of this nature which is displayed *without charge* does not come under the censorship law."[76] Viets, of course, disagreed.

Three distinct strategies of avoiding the censorship board particularly annoyed the Board of Review. First, there were obvious contraband films, many of them pornographic or of the striptease variety, making the rounds in the state and being exhibited in male-only settings. Outside the parameters of respectable society and usually with deliberate evasion of the authorities, it was difficult for the Board of Review to get access to this type of film. The second instance involved social service organizations, who in the name of education and good health exhibited films free of charge, as a service to their clients. These films often involved childbirth, sexuality, contraception, or venereal disease. One particular instance took place on February 28, 1928, when Viets sent the board's chief clerk, Nira M. Robinson, to report on the exhibition of *The Story of Life* at the local Young Women's Christian Association. The third issue for the board members was the attempt by independent producers and distributors (usually of exploitative products) to screen films that had been disapproved or seriously cut by censors before welfare or social service organizations. One such example was Samuel Cummins's *Naked Truth* (1924). Viets argued that Cummins's films "have been rejected by every state having legal censorship and many cities will not permit the picture to be shown." Enforcement remained a major priority for the chief censor. The film was one of the earliest exploitation blockbusters in the nation. *The Naked Truth* was a compilation film, including scenes from a number of earlier movies, showing the horrors of venereal disease. Cummins was one of the leading exploitation film producers in the country, and his films had a notorious reputation.[77]

The period 1926–1929 also witnessed a revolution in the motion picture industry with the introduction of sound. This process did not take place overnight with the introduction of Al Jolson's *Jazz Singer* (1927). Instead, it took place in fits and starts, and Kansas is an excellent case study of the impact that "talking pictures" had on the entertainment form. In 1927, a matinee show in Topeka would cost between ten and thirty-five cents and an evening show from a dime to seventy-five cents.[78] In late 1927, you could catch a rerelease of *The Birth of a Nation* at the Grand, a Zane Grey story at

76. Ibid.
77. Ibid.; Schaefer, *Bold! Daring! Shocking! True!* 62.
78. *Topeka Daily Capital,* April 3, 1927, B18.

the Orpheum, or a Lon Chaney picture at the Jayhawk.[79] The similarity of these films is that they were silent pictures, accompanied by a piano or a small musical group.

Everything began to change in Topeka in the year 1928. Touring acts of symphony orchestras that accompanied major studio releases became de rigueur by the late 1920s. Cecil B. DeMille's blockbuster *The King of Kings* (1927) arrived in Topeka in February 1928 with a touring symphony orchestra. Seat prices varied from fifty cents to a dollar ten, a relatively steep price for a Topeka theater at that time.

The Grand Theater, the premier motion picture theater in Topeka, became the first wired for sound. The Grand closed in late August 1928 and reopened on September 17. The theater promoted its groundbreaking new form of entertainment to Topekans by exclaiming, "See! Hear! A Quality Sound Picture—the Complete Program in Sound—the Marvel of the Age for Eye and Ear." The opening bill included Al Jolson in *The Jazz Singer* and several Vitaphone acts, such as Hugh Herbert in *The Prediction* (1927) and Fred Waring's Pennsylvanians, the Famous Collegian orchestra. On opening day, the *Topeka State Journal* pointed out that this was not the first time Topeka movie patrons had "heard voices from the flickering shadows of the silver screen."[80] More than fifteen years earlier, in 1912–1913, Thomas Edison's experimental talking pictures had been presented in the very same site.

The advent of sound motion pictures in Topeka created a great deal of excitement, and the Grand management pulled out all the stops to whip up enthusiasm for the changing medium. They took out a half-page advertisement in the September 17, 1928, *Topeka State Journal* that read:

OPENING TONIGHT 7 AND 9

VITAPHONE

AND

MOVIETONE

SEE—HEAR

AL JOLSON

IN

THE JAZZ SINGER

GRAND THEATER

THE HOUSE OF COMPLETE SOUND

79. *Topeka Daily Capital*, October 2, 1927, B17.
80. *Topeka State Journal*, September 15, 1928, 10, 11.

The managers of the Grand were also savvy in their investment in sound equipment. They installed machinery for presentation of both Vitaphone and Movietone sound pictures. Vitaphone carried sound on a separate disc, whereas Movietone had sound on a small track on the extreme left-hand side of the filmstrip. The latter was the technology that studios would accept as standard in the 1930s.[81] The conversion to sound was a costly process for the theater, an investment of somewhere between ten and twenty thousand dollars.

Despite the popularity of *The Jazz Singer,* the Grand changed its bill every week, perhaps wanting to meet the eager demands of filmgoers. Certainly, the Grand Theater's attendance spiked with the introduction of such films in 1928. The week following the run of *The Jazz Singer,* the theater screened *Glorious Betsy* (1928) with Dolores Costello and Conrad Nagel.[82] In October 1928, the theater presented *Wings* (1927), the first motion picture to win the Academy Award for Best Picture. *Wings* had originally been made as a silent film, but with the remarkable success of early talkies like *The Jazz Singer,* General Electric technicians worked with Warner Brothers studio heads to make a special version of the film with music and sound effects.[83] One could hear "thundering propellers . . . the distant din of combat . . . the staccato notes of the machine guns . . . the howl of planes fully in action" in this new version of the film.[84] Although this touring road show of *Wings* was not a talking picture with full vocal accompaniment, as we enjoy today, it was an important step in the eventual transition to sound. The Grand Theater promised, "Every dramatic turn of action is enhanced by the marvelous synchronized musical skill and the skilled use of sound." *Wings* was accompanied by several Vitaphone acts. Vitaphone was Warner Brothers's patented process of recording and reproducing sound on film.[85] In 1927, Vitaphone became the trademark for Warner Brothers sound films. Warner Brothers began producing "shorts" in 1927 with comedians such as Joe E. Brown and featuring musical acts such as Sissle and Blake.

In early 1928, Warner Brothers made the commitment that all thirty-four of their films produced in the period 1928–1929 would be using the Vitaphone process.[86] The company agreed that these films would have not only musical scores but talking sequences too. One of the first of these films was

81. *Topeka State Journal,* September 17, 1928, H3.
82. *Topeka State Journal,* September 22, 1928, 11.
83. Donald Crafton, *The Talkies: American Cinema's Transition to Sound, 1926–1931,* 134–35.
84. *Topeka Daily Capital,* October 7, 1928, B17.
85. Crafton, *The Talkies,* 70–87, 101–26.
86. Ibid., 113, 115.

Michael Curtiz's production *Tenderloin* (1928), starring Conrad Nagel and Dolores Costello. Unlike *The Jazz Singer*, which had brief talking sequences, *Tenderloin* was shot as a silent film with four talking sequences, lasting a little less than fifteen minutes. The film opened at the Grand Theater in November 1929. Apparently bought out by the Paramount chain in late 1928, the theater ran a full-page ad of the studio's upcoming sound releases in the January 26, 1929, *Topeka State Capital*.[87]

By late 1928, the writing was on the wall—if you were going to survive in the motion picture business in Topeka, you had to find some way to bring sound to your theater. By March 1929, three of the five film theaters in Topeka had sound films. The Grand was billed as the theater "where the screen speaks." The Gem was the "House of Talkies," and the Novelty was the "Home of the Matchless RCA."[88] The introduction of sound to motion pictures playing in Kansas had a direct impact on the dissemination of news. Those theaters that were converted began adding talking newsreels to their bills. The Grand added Fox Movietone News immediately upon the conversion to sound.

The Novelty was a unique theater in Topeka, holding on to the vestiges of the past while simultaneously adapting to the future. The theater converted to sound in February 1929, using the RCA Photophone system. It also promptly raised its prices. The Novelty was part of the Keith-Orpheum vaudeville circuit, and the management boasted that the Novelty was the "Only Theater in Kansas Presenting Legitimate Vaudeville and Talking Pictures." On March 9, 1929, the theater screened *Lucky Boy* (1929) with George Jessel (who would have been comfortable in either medium).[89]

The Gem Theater was an excellent example of this transition to sound. The theater was closed completely during the month of March 1929 so that "talking equipment" could be installed. The Gem reopened the first week of April with a bang, showing *The Land of the Silver Fox* (1929), starring the canine star Rin Tin Tin. The Gem proclaimed, "It will be the first time Topekans have heard the voice of the dog star."[90]

Neither the Jayhawk nor the Orpheum had sound films in early 1929, and it was hurting the box office of these smaller Topeka theaters. The Orpheum began to discount ticket prices just to bring in patrons.

87. *Topeka Daily Capital*, January 26, 1929, 11.
88. *Topeka Daily Capital*, March 31, 1929, A3.
89. *Topeka State Journal*, March 9, 1929.
90. Ibid.

By the spring of 1929, sound films were all the rage in Kansas. The Novelty Theater, "Where Sound Sounds Best," screened *Syncopation* (1929), billed as "America's First Great Screen Extravaganza." The film was really a low-budget RKO musical starring the radio personality Morton Downey and featuring Fred Waring and the Pennsylvanians, but the advertising copy for the film demonstrated audience approval and excitement over this new, evolving form of motion picture. *Syncopation* was displayed on a "100% Mammoth All-Talking Screen," allowing audience members to watch the musical stars "Talk, Sing, Play and Howl."[91]

By May 1929, all of the major theaters in Topeka had converted to sound. This conversion process across the state often depended on a number of economic and demographic factors. In Kansas City, Kansas, for example, motion picture theaters were small neighborhood businesses such as the Gaintior, Seventh Street Theater, Art, Tenth Street, Pershing, Electric, and the Home. Downtown Kansas City, Missouri, received all of the first-run box-office films, and then they often filtered down to second- and third-rate theaters like those in Kansas City, Kansas. If one wanted to hear Al Jolson sing, Fanny Brice wisecrack, or John Gilbert speak, one would cross the river and go to one of the grand picture palaces on Main Street. Most Kansas City, Kansas, theaters converted to sound in the spring of 1929.[92]

Wichita, more geographically isolated, could draw Kansans from hundreds of miles due to its unique setting. Wichita had its share of large picture houses, but the Greater Palace was the only one that converted to sound in 1928. In September, one could attend the Greater Palace and see Colleen Moore in *Lilac Time* (1928). Other Wichita theaters had to scramble not to lose all of their audience to the Greater Palace. The Uptown ran *Uncle Tom's Cabin* (1927) in September 1928, augmented by a special synchronized version of the original musical score as performed by the symphonic orchestra of the Roxy Theater in New York and the Dixie Jubilee Singers.[93]

Most rural areas in Kansas did not get sound films until well into the 1930s.[94] It was a good thing for the Kansas State Board of Review that talking pictures did not spread even more rapidly. The board was caught completely off guard by the wildly popular phenomenon in motion picture presentation and had neither the institutional nor the legal apparatus to deal

91. *Topeka Daily Capital,* April 7, 1929, B19.
92. *Kansas City Kansan,* January 10, 1929, 7.
93. *Wichita Beacon,* September 23, 1928, A4.
94. *Goodland News Republic,* August 30, 1928.

with sound films. The period from 1928 to 1934 would be a turbulent era for the Kansas Board of Review. The conversion to sound, the death of chairwoman Emma Viets, provocative new Hollywood film fare, and the Great Depression would plague the board yet also ensure the necessity of its existence in the minds of many Kansans. The period 1928–1934 is considered a particularly tumultuous time in the history of Hollywood; technological, economic, and personnel issues all plagued the studios. But all of these challenges also faced the film industry on a localized level, and the state of Kansas was no exception.

Eight

The Challenge of Sound, 1928–1934

The period 1928–1934 was one of tumultuous change for the residents of Kansas and for the motion picture industry within the state. The onslaught of the Great Depression challenged all Kansans in economic, political, and psychological ways. Americans began to question the basic structure of society and, perhaps, even God, as falling agricultural prices, drought, unemployment, wind and dust, bankruptcy, and searing heat plagued the state. For the Kansas State Board of Review, these years were an immense challenge, as the board faced technological, legal, and moral hurdles to maintain its viability as an entity. During this period of tumult, as Hollywood responded to falling attendance by spicing up motion pictures, the need for the board seemed even more apparent in the minds of many citizens. When sound motion pictures were first introduced to the state of Kansas, the Board of Review was ill-prepared to deal with the phenomenon. It did not have sound equipment in its office in Kansas City, Kansas, and there was serious questioning over whether the board had the legal right to censor the audible part of a film.

By the fall of 1928, just as sound films were beginning to appear in Topeka and Wichita movie houses, the Board of Review was desperately looking for a new headquarters. The dilapidated fire station where the board was located was inappropriate for work. One possible solution was Memorial Hall in

Kansas City, Kansas. The central location of the hall and its nearness to the Missouri River that separated the state from Missouri, where the exchanges were located, seemed to be a desirable fit. The mothers of deceased World War I veterans loudly rejected this proposal, though, believing that it was blasphemous that their sons' memories would be honored in the same building where potentially scandalous motion pictures were being censored.[1] The public clamoring made the board look elsewhere. The gravity of the matter peaked with an inspection of the board's offices by W. A. Elstun, state fire marshal. Elstun sent copies of his report to both chairwoman Emma Viets and Governor Paulen. He warned, "I am writing to advise that our inspection disclosed the fact that the building is very dangerous and unsafe for occupancy."[2] The likelihood is that Viets invited the inspector. For years, the censors had complained about their office being a firetrap with insufficient heat and badly deteriorating construction. Inspector Elstun, who found badly cracked walls and floors separated from walls, recommended that "the building be vacated at once" since "it is now unsafe to occupy."[3] By the end of the month, preparations had been made to move the headquarters to the Wyandotte County Courthouse, but that plan also fell through. It was not until two years later, 1930–1931, that the Board of Review offices moved to the new fire department building in Kansas City, where they were located for the rest of the board's existence.[4]

The difficulty of working in a potentially dangerous office was made more problematic by the rapidly changing circumstances of film production. By spring 1929, dozens of Kansas theaters had invested in the equipment necessary to exhibit sound motion pictures. But the guardians of Kansas screen morality did not have the proper equipment to view such films when completing their censoring duties. Chairman Viets wrote Attorney General William Smith in April 1929 explaining the Board of Review's predicament. She claimed that the board could review scenes and written titles but "knew nothing of spoken titles." Viets questioned the attorney general whether the board "had the right to censor the reproduced voice."[5]

The issue appeared to overwhelm the board. Four days later, Viets wrote directly to Governor Clyde Martin Reed and stated that "quite a discussion is

1. Frank Ryan, Secretary of State, to Viets, September 28, 1928, Box 27-09-05-05, 1925–1929, Paulen Papers, KSHS.
2. W. A. Elstun to Paulen, October 5, 1928, in ibid.
3. Howard Payne, City Clerk of Kansas City, Kansas, to Viets, October 28, 1928, in ibid.
4. Hazel Myers to Reed, June 8, 1930, Box 9, File 5, Reed Papers, KSHS.
5. Viets to William Smith, June 8, 1930, in ibid.

raging over the question 'Have the Censors a right to censor the voice, the dia-
log in connection with the Motion Picture?'"[6] The issue was also plaguing censorship boards in New York, Pennsylvania, Maryland, and Virginia. In Ohio, a
lower court decided that the state censors could not censor the voice. In New
York, there was an injunction against the deletion of the reproduced voice.

The attorney general's reply came later in the month. He had to make his
decision based on the 1917 legislation that had revised the structure and purpose of the board. Attorney General Smith recognized that "in 1917, nobody
in the legislature had ever dreamed of the advances that the art was to make in
the past twelve years and did not contemplate extending the censorship to the
spoken word." Smith pointed out that the 1917 legislation defined film as "an
apparatus for reproducing photography and nothing else" and concluded that
the powers conferred upon the Board of Review "do not include the power to
censor the spoken word, no matter how recorded."[7] This placed the board in
an enormous quandary. The aural aspect of a film—be it voice, music, or sound
effect—was becoming an increasingly integral part of the motion picture. It
left open the possibility of numerous audible instances that might offend
an audience, including "obscene" noises, cursing, racial or ethnic slurs, or provocative dialogue. Censoring sound films was also a much more difficult and
cumbersome task than censoring silent ones. Censoring a silent film meant
explaining specifically to the distributor the scene or title in a reel that must be
cut. This was frequently done so that continuity would not be disturbed. Forcing censorship on a sound production, though, brought untold hardship upon
the distributing company. Since Movietone films had separate discs, it made it
extremely difficult if not impossible to take the needle from the disc during the
censored scene and then replace it exactly at the correct spot where the vocal
and visual aspects matched. The Vitaphone process was less of a problem but
still led to striking examples of where the film had been cut—much more visible than when a silent film had been edited.

Governor Reed became aware of the insurmountable problem this created
for distributors. He wrote chairwoman Viets that the "exhibitors in Kansas
are entitled to a reasonable degree of protection. I, therefore, doubt the advisability of the Board opposing films which must suffer eliminations to the
extent that render their commercial utility a matter of considerable doubt. In

6. Viets to Reed, April 8, 1929, in ibid.
7. Smith to Viets, April 25, 1929, Box 7, File 3, in ibid. The Pennsylvania Supreme Court ruled
that sound film was no different from silent film and could be censored.

such cases I think the Board should flatly reject the picture."[8] Governor Reed's comments, made in May 1929, are enlightening. First, the gist of his comments included the presumption that the Board of Review would censor sound films sometime in the future. The overall success of sound films meant that it appeared they would become a permanent part of the entertainment. Second, it clearly led to his suggesting a binary system of censorship in which "questionable" films, which might have been easily edited in the silent era, were now to be rejected in toto. Governor Reed was clearly interested in protecting motion picture exhibitors, but this decision placed an additional burden on distributors, and especially producers, who may have found their multimillion–dollar investments flatly rejected by the state censors.

This anticipation of the ability to censor sound films in the future was also evident in the board's revision of fees for examination. By early 1929, film exchanges were submitting one- and two-reel talking pictures, as well as reels of songs and instrumental music and filmed vaudeville acts. These sound acts were examined for a price of two dollars a reel, despite the fact that the board did not have the technology to hear such films. Studios continued to produce silent films until 1930; the board remedied the situation that year. Equipment for sound films was installed in the board's office (probably happening simultaneously with the office move). Negotiations began with the officials of the Theatrical Stage Employees and Moving Picture Machine Operators Union. The two sides concluded a settlement that gave the operator, George Williams, a flat salary of three hundred dollars a month with a flexible work schedule, due to the changing demands of the board. By 1930, the board had reduced its viewing schedule from ten o'clock until noon and one to three o'clock on weekdays and ten till noon on Saturdays.[9]

Sound films also put additional strain on the actual censors. Not provided with a script, the women had to listen closely for language they considered undesirable or for double entendres they considered uncouth. In October 1930, the board decided that "owing to the necessity of entire concentration on sound pictures . . . no one should be admitted to [the] viewing room when a picture is being shown."[10]

In 1930–1931, the Kansas state legislature took up the matter of spoken dialogue on the screen, giving the Board of Review the right to extend its

8. Reed to Viets, May 18, 1929, Box 7, File 1, in ibid.
9. KSBR Minutes, August 14, 1930, Box 58-5-4-14, KSHS.
10. KSBR Minutes, September 3, 1930, in ibid.

censorship duties to include all aspects of talking films. Senate Bill no. 384 gave the board the right to "examine films, reels, *including subtitles, spoken dialogue, songs, other words or sounds,* folders, posters and advertising matter used in connection therewith to be exhibited or used in Kansas." The legislature gave the board the right to censor screen content that was "cruel, obscene, indecent or immoral, or such as tend to debase or corrupt morals." In anticipation of a future scandal, the legislature curbed the board's ability to censor "strictly pictorial news of the day," commonly referred to as newsreels.[11]

The desire of the Kansas legislature and the Board of Review to censor screen dialogue was not a condition limited to the state. The transition of American motion pictures to sound set off a struggle by those who wanted to control the social effects of the new art form. Effie Angler, head of the Chicago censor board, claimed, "Very often a written remark will not be offensive. The voice can change the entire meaning of a statement and we have to be on the watch constantly for . . . double meanings."[12] A renewed debate over film censorship took place in the late 1920s and early 1930s as local clergy, social service agencies, editorialists, audiences, and critics argued over who should monitor the new boundaries of screen sound.

In 1926, Will Hays had appointed Colonel Jason Joy to head the Studio Relations Committee (SRC) of the MPPDA. The committee was to read scripts and scenarios with the purpose of advising producers of potential problems with local and state censorship boards. Joy was to form liaisons with church groups, social reformers, and women's groups in order to head off any further attempts at governmental censorship. It allowed Hays once again to make the claim that Hollywood had cleaned house.[13]

Joy examined the regulations of the censorship boards across the nation, and in October 1927 he produced *The Don'ts and Be Carefuls*. This was an attempt to summarize censorship prescriptions for the regulation of screen material. Five of the "don'ts" included topics often covered in exploitation films, such as drug trafficking, nudity, white slavery, venereal disease, and sex hygiene.[14] This list coincidentally came out the very month that *The Jazz Singer* was opening. By 1931, more than one-third of all Americans lived in an area controlled by state or municipal censors.[15] With the advent of sound,

11. State of Kansas, Senate Bill 384, in *Session Laws, 1931,* in *General Statutes of Kansas,* 1931.
12. Frank Walsh, *Sin and Censorship: The Catholic Church and the Motion Picture Industry,* 47.
13. Vasey, *World according to Hollywood,* 31–34.
14. Schaefer, *Bold! Daring! Shocking! True!* 147.
15. Crafton, *The Talkies,* 469.

the monetary cost of censorship for the studios went up exorbitantly. Hays made it a policy since heading the MPPDA to try to stifle any further censorship legislation.

The transition to sound turned the studio system on its ear. It has been well documented that a number of film stars were not able to successfully make the transition due to a foreign accent or a voice that was not pleasant or did not match the screen persona they had crafted. The demand for dialogue and for actors who could successfully recite this dialogue led the studios naturally to the New York stage, a source for screen material for years. The New York stage, however, had conventions that would make the hair curl on the heads of the Kansas screen censors. Topless showgirls, four-letter words, sexually provocative dialogue, and adult subject matter were becoming de rigueur on stage. As movie theaters became wired in larger cities in 1928–1929 and in smaller towns in the early 1930s, it became recognized that what would play in New York might not be acceptable in Kansas. The Hays Office (as the MPPDA became popularly known) found itself increasingly under attack, as sound both boosted film attendance and threatened renewed censorship. In January 1929, Hays begged the members of the MPPDA to avoid the spread of censorship by cleaning up their pictures.[16]

The stock market crash of October 1929 also made industry investors nervous. Censorship simply added to costs, as studios were often forced to reedit or even reshoot or rerecord motion pictures to make them palatable to local and state censorship boards. The banks and investment houses that financed the Hollywood studios wanted continued profit and looked upon anything that impeded the free circulation of films as economically dangerous. Although it seemed impossible that state and municipal censorship could be defeated in 1929–1930, motion pictures could be sanitized so that there would not be a question of whether they would pass censorship boards. Hays approached Father Daniel Lord, a Jesuit priest at St. Louis University, to draft a production code for the industry. With the aid of devout Catholic Martin Quigley, the publisher of the *Motion Picture Herald*, the code was presented to film industry executives in February 1930 and accepted the next day. Studio executives did not plan to actually implement the Production Code, though, making it similar to other public relations ploys of the MPPDA. In the 1920s, this was simply another "sincere attempt" to clean up the movies.

16. Ibid., 472.

The Code recognized the challenge that sound presented to the medium. The preamble to the Code read, "During the rapid transition from silent to talking pictures [motion picture producers] realized the necessity and the opportunity of subscribing to a Code to gain the production of talking pictures and of re acknowledging the responsibility."[17] The Production Code, based on the Quigley-Lord philosophy of the morality of entertainment, contained three working principles:

1) No picture should lower the moral standards of those who see it.

2) Law, natural and divine, must not be belittled, ridiculed nor must a resentment be created against it.

3) As far as possible, life should not be misrepresented, at least not in such a way as to place in the minds of youth false values on life.[18]

The Production Code included a list of words, subject matters, and scenarios that were not to appear in motion pictures. The Code revolved around morals, particularly Catholic morals. It was a sophisticated document, a long and deep treatise on the relationship among moral philosophy, entertainment, aesthetics, and reform. Film historian Gregory D. Black argues that there was a common objective that the Catholic supporters of the Code shared with Protestant film reformers: "They all wanted entertainment films to emphasize that the church, the government, and the family were the cornerstones of an orderly society; that success and happiness resulted from respecting and working within this system."[19]

But there was a definite fundamental misunderstanding between Lord and his Catholic supporters, on one hand, and Hays and the producers, on the other. The Catholic supporters of the Production Code (including Martin Quigley) believed that screen content and dialogue would finally be controlled, whereas producers often just ignored the document altogether. Hays could argue that the industry was practicing self-censorship while MPPDA reviewers were allowing almost anything to get by.

The Code originally promised real change in Hollywood. Colonel Joy was bumped from being a consultant to the studios to being the enforcer of the Code. Although film company presidents in New York initially supported

17. Ibid.

18. Leonard J. Leff and Jerald L. Simmons, *The Dame in the Kimono: Hollywood, Censorship, and the Production Code from the 1920s to the 1960s*, 10.

19. Gregory D. Black, *Hollywood Censored: Morality Codes, Catholics, and the Movies*, 39.

Joy, as attendance fell off due to the effects of the Depression, they became concerned about increasing box-office revenues, no matter what the means. The period 1929–1934 has been described by film historians as the pre-Code Hollywood era, and the frankness and adult subject matter in these movies are often shocking to contemporary audiences who nostalgically, though incorrectly, view the early talkies as innocent and pure.

Another crucial element was that not all film producers were members of the MPPDA; therefore, they would not have to subscribe to the Production Code. States' rights films of the 1920s and 1930s were often exploitation movies that promoted "sex hygiene" or exotic (read: topless) locales. As the mainstream industry began to determine what subjects were salacious and would not be allowed in major studio productions, a window of opportunity opened up for producers of exploitation films. If exploitation producers focused on subjects forbidden by the majors, they were almost guaranteed an audience. There was almost a direct parallel between MPPDA self-censorship and the rise of the exploitation film industry.[20]

As the Depression worsened in the years 1930–1934, moving picture producers, whether Hollywood based or independent, were willing to do almost anything to bring in desperately needed audiences. Pre-Code Hollywood films may have pushed the limits of sex and violence on the screen, but if this is what the box office demanded, cash-strapped studios were all too willing to provide audiences with the thrilling product. By the early 1930s, producers were no longer crying freedom of expression but economic survival when it came to producing adult-film fare.

By 1931, it had become evident to many critics of the industry that the Production Code was not working. Colonel Jason Joy and his successor on the Studio Relations Committee, Dr. James Wingate, did not have "the fortitude and vision to enforce" the Code.[21] The cooperative spirit between the studios and the Studio Relations Committee had dissipated. It was very difficult to prove that Colonel Joy's Studio Relations Committee was effective at all; there was little proof that objectionable material had been prevented from getting to the screen. The laxness of the SRC was an open secret in Hollywood; no studio producer took the Production Code seriously. The content of motion pictures, the rise of crime and gangsterism, and the long, steep slide

20. Schaefer, *Bold! Daring! Shocking! True!* 8.
21. Thomas Patrick Doherty, *Pre-Code Hollywood: Sex, Immorality, Insurrection, and American Cinema, 1930–1934,* 8.

into the Depression created a type of moral panic about American social behavior. Before the Production Code, censors could be criticized for being arbitrary or impulsive in their decision making. With the Production Code and its explicit guidelines, studio executives looked like charlatans. Under the Code, Hays understood that studios would be responsible for implementation. It was not mandatory for studios to submit scripts to the Studio Relations Committee. In 1929, only 20 percent of all film scenarios were sent to Joy.[22] If there were questions about whether a completed film adhered to the provisions of the Code, a jury, composed of various studio heads of production, would decide upon the suitability of the film. This became an unworkable and ineffective scheme, though, because these studio executives were very reluctant to decide against one of their own since it might come back to haunt them in a future decision on one of their films.

In October 1930, Hays hired Joseph Breen to oversee publicity for the Production Code. Breen, a politically conservative Catholic with deep religious convictions, was opposed to public discussion of moral issues such as divorce or birth control.[23] Whereas Colonel Joy had been conciliatory with studio heads, Breen understood that these men were a tough bunch and needed to be whipped into shape. Breen was openly sympathetic with Catholic crusaders who wanted to clean up films. He believed that there was no decency in Hollywood. He told the Jesuit weekly *America*, "[Nobody] cares a damn for the Code or any of its provisions. . . . I've heard it sneered and laughed at."[24]

As 1932 continued and as reformers demanded that Hollywood change its ways, studios continued to dish out provocative fare by the likes of individuals such as Mae West. *McCall's* published a series of excerpts that year of Henry James Forman's *Our Movie-Made Children*. Based on research by the Payne Fund Studies, Forman sensationalized and bastardized the research by selling hot copy that told parents that moving pictures were making their children into sex delinquents and criminals. This was exactly the "research" that reformers had been waiting for. By the end of the year, nearly forty religious and educational organizations were calling for federal regulation of the film industry.[25] In March 1930, a bill had been introduced into Congress that would have made the film industry a public utility and forced studios to pay the salaries of federal regulators. Although the bill did not pass, a groundswell

22. Leff and Simmons, *Dame in the Kimono*, 8.
23. Black, *Hollywood Censored*, 38–39.
24. Tino Balio, *Grand Design: Hollywood as a Modern Business Enterprise, 1930–1939*, 54.
25. Ibid., 56.

of support for federal censorship by 1932 had made the situation threatening for studio executives.[26]

In the first half of 1933, as the unemployment rate reached 25 percent and banks closed nationally, a number of studios teetered on the brink of bankruptcy. By early 1933, weekly attendance figures were off 40 percent from 1929, and 20 percent of all American movie houses had closed their doors.[27] As newly inaugurated president Franklin Roosevelt called for greater federal regulation of industry under the National Recovery Act, many Catholics and reformers hoped that the Production Code would become law. Others believed that the Catholic Church needed to take action against the sinful screen. As Laura Wittern-Keller points out, censorship began as a Progressive reform but far outlasted the Progressive era. She argues, "By the 1930's, massive societal pressure, largely from organized religion, maintained censorship's appeal. As the progressive impulse faded, Catholics stepped to the forefront of censorship."[28]

By early 1934, Catholic leaders had formed the "Legion of Decency," an organization that was designed to unify Catholics behind a national protest plan against motion pictures. The goal of the Legion was to intimidate producers into cleaning up screen content.[29] Joseph Breen supported the Legion of Decency for moral reasons and because he saw the distinct possibility of career advancement if the Catholic threat was successful. Breen and Quigley wanted to get rid of the production heads' jury and replace it with a board that would have teeth.[30]

On June 13, 1934, the Studio Relations Committee was renamed the Production Code Administration (PCA), with Joseph Breen as its director. Studio executives must have recognized that a Catholic boycott of films would be economically devastating and that it would be in their best interests to develop a Production Code enforcement mechanism. Under the new scheme, the producer jury was eliminated. Every film had to abide by the Production Code and be passed by the Production Code Administration. Every PCA-approved film would be given a certificate, and all of the member studios had to agree not to exhibit films without this certificate.[31]

26. Crafton, *The Talkies*, 474.
27. Leff and Simmons, *Dame in the Kimono*, 28.
28. Wittern-Keller, "Freedom of the Screen," 21.
29. See Walsh, *Sin and Censorship*.
30. Raymond Moley, *The Hays Office*, 87.
31. See James M. Skinner, *The Cross and the Cinema: The Legion of Decency and the National Catholic Office for Motion Pictures, 1933–1970*.

What did any of this have to do with the state of Kansas? Well, as Holly-wood successfully made the transition to sound and increasingly began to test the limits of acceptable screen content, the Kansas Board of Review found its "necessity" enhanced. Although the percentage of films that the Board of Review banned or censored continued to drop throughout the 1920s, the board's scissors were resharpened in 1929 and used frequently throughout the pre-Code era, as the censors were extremely busy "protecting" Kansans from immoral Hollywood influences. The period 1929–1934 was simply an era of intense activity on the part of the board, as it was tested by the challenging films that Hollywood was distributing. This era was one in which Hollywood seemed to lack any serious content-regulation mechanism, and the Kansas Board of Review attempted to fill that void.

An overview of the content areas that the censors of the Kansas Board of Review addressed in this critical period is necessary. Borrowing the divisional scheme of Thomas Patrick Doherty in his influential book *Pre-Code Holly-wood: Sex, Immorality, Insurrection, and American Cinema, 1930–1934,* this analysis will examine trends of the censors' shears, as they pertain to dialogue, screen personalities, scenarios, and genres.

Doherty comments on the difficulty these censors must have faced, as they too were adapting to the new medium of talking pictures. For the Kansas censors, they no longer simply had to cut scenes but had to listen closely for both explicit dialogue and subtle implications within the world of film. Motion picture censors "patrol[led] the diegesis, keeping an eye and ear out for images, language and meanings that should be banished from the world of the film."[32] The easiest task was to simply cut a snippet of an exposed breast or a "dirty" word. The difficulty lay in the censors' analysis of the morality of the text and determining whether there were subversive lessons and hidden meanings in the narrative of the film.

The period 1930–1934 also formed a nexus between some convulsive movements in American culture, and this was demonstrated through the motion picture medium. First, the pre-Code era began during the most eco-nomically catastrophic period in American history. All of the optimistic values of Roaring Twenties culture—rugged individualism, unbridled capitalism, American exceptionalism—were brought into question by the plummeting of the American economy. Just as motion pictures got a voice, characters on the screen could challenge the bedrock of American morality. The disillusionment

32. Doherty, *Pre-Code Hollywood*, 10.

and social upheaval unleashed by the Depression led to radicalism, despair, and cynicism—which often came out on the screen.

Second, the motion picture industry had spent millions of dollars converting from a silent medium to a synchronized sound cinema during the late 1920s. This not only meant heavy investment in studio equipment but also led to tremendous expenditures in rewiring theaters for sound. Just as the studios found themselves cash-strapped and vulnerable, the stock market crashed in October 1929. As talking films did booming box-office business, some studio production heads believed that more talking would lead to higher financial rewards. "Fast talking, wisecracking, and double entendres" became standard in the early sound era.[33]

Third, as the studios and theater chains began suffering financially from the downturn in attendance as the Depression worsened, new genres were developed, expanded, or transformed. In contrast to the nostalgic stereotype of happy, singing, upper-class, wholesome, escapist fare during the Depression years, many films explored the darker recesses of the troubled mind—stressing the violent, macabre, brutal possibilities of human nature. Gangster films, fallen-woman films, and horror films were all immensely popular in the pre-Code era.

I will stretch the traditional chronological definition of the "pre-Code film" to fit the unique conditions that the Kansas Board of Review censors faced in the state. The period 1928–1930 was an era of strong leadership under long-time censor Emma Viets. She and her fellow censors appeared to be more stringent in regard to screen content. They also were on the board during a chaotic period when many motion picture theaters in the state had sound but the board still did not have the technology to view such motion pictures. Sound added an entirely new dimension to the responsibilities of the censors, and they appeared to take a very cautious approach to their responsibilities.

The period 1931–1934 was just as erratic but for different reasons. The sudden death of chairwoman Viets left the board rudderless just as the Depression was bearing down on the state and the motion picture community was testing the boundaries of acceptable sound-screen material. The board experienced a circulating membership from 1931 to 1934 that contributed to this instability and led to some unusual condemnations and omissions in this pivotal era.

Emma Viets had first been appointed as a censor by Governor Jonathan Davis in 1923. Upon his election in 1924, Republican Ben Paulen appointed Viets to chair the Kansas Board of Review. Viets was the only member of the

33. See Crafton, *The Talkies*, 463–79.

previous board to survive Paulen's "housecleaning." The other censors and the secretary, stenographer, and inspector were all asked for their resignations upon Paulen's inauguration. Viets, therefore, was the only experienced member of the board, and she proved to provide strong leadership and guidance during her chairwomanship between 1924 and 1930. Viets was the leader of the board through the administrations of three governors, and her unexpected death in 1930 came at a time when the board desperately needed a firm hand and guidance.

In the period 1928–1930, Viets and the board faced a number of motion pictures that demonstrated the excesses of the Roaring Twenties. In this period, more than twenty major studio releases were banned from the state, and dozens more were heavily edited. Viets and the board attempted to strongly contain such "hedonism" and "vulgarity" from the motion picture screen in Kansas, particularly when a combination of sex and alcohol was depicted. One such film was the First National release *The Mad Hour* (1928), penned by Elinor Glyn. Glyn was deemed the "high priestess of sex" during the 1920s, as a number of her sizzling novels were filmed for the screen.[34] *The Mad Hour* starred Sally O'Neill as Cuddles Magrue, the daughter of a cabdriver. Cuddles is determined to have a life of luxury despite her plebeian upbringing. After a gin party, she marries wealthy lounge lizard Jack Hemingway, played by Daniel Reed. They move into the Ritz, and Jack's father promptly disinherits him. In order to maintain his and Cuddles's lifestyle, Jack becomes involved with a group of criminals. Cuddles is wrongly implicated in one of their robberies and is promptly sent to jail, where she gives birth to a son. When she is finally released from prison, she discovers that Jack has annulled their marriage and is being remarried. In despair, she commits suicide. The film was too much for the Kansas censors. Despite the fact that the film was a strong morality tale against vice and alcohol, Viets and her fellow censors may have understood all too well the probable appeal of the movie. A reviewer in *Variety* wrote, "The stewing up in the early part is the morality tale, of how young girls booze in roadhouses when college boys have enough money to buy it, but here the booze, the stews, the party and the marriage in the middle of the night may intrigue the sticks."[35] The Board of Review apparently concurred and banned *The Mad Hour* from the state.

34. Jerry Vermilye, *Films of the Twenties*, 164–66.
35. Munden, *American Film Institute Catalog, 1921–1930*, 470; review of *The Mad Hour*, *Variety*, April 18, 1928.

A similar theme, how the consumption of alcohol could lead to bad decision making and sexual impropriety, was explored in Fox's *Red Wine* (1928). In the film, Charles Cook, a rigidly moral, upright married man is taken out on the town by some friends and becomes involved in a wild party in a restaurant where he eventually blacks out. His friends, in jest, arrange it to make it look as if he has been unfaithful to his wife, Alice. The next night Charles takes Alice to the same restaurant for their anniversary dinner, and he finds he has a lot of explaining to do.[36] The combination of drunkenness, sexuality, and wanton behavior was too much for the board, and *Red Wine* was never screened in public theaters.

Between 1928 and 1930, a number of the films condemned by the board were not "talking pictures" but films that had musical scores or sound effects added to originally shot silent films. This was an important transitional phase for motion pictures in the late 1920s, as studio production heads believed that any oral addition would bring in audiences.

The Viets-led board also disapproved of films that dealt with illegitimacy. Such a picture was the Windsor production *Her Unborn Child* (1930), an early talking film. The movie involved the illegitimate background of one of the romantic leads, an unexpected premarital pregnancy, and the contemplation of abortion. These unsavory sexual elements were deemed inappropriate for Kansas audiences, and the film was condemned.

The testing of a young woman's "purity" and attempts to take her virginity were also forbidden subjects on Kansas screens. In the First National comedy *Why Be Good?* (1929), a young woman is taken to a disreputable roadhouse to test her virtue, and she protests to her suitor. In the Chesterfield production *The House of Shame* (1928), a romantic triangle ends with a wife and her husband's employer in a relationship that appears to be condoned since the husband is a no-good scoundrel and "deserves to be killed in the end." The Warner Brothers' Vitaphone release *Madonna of Avenue A* (1929) involved prostitution, illegitimacy, and suicide.[37] All three motion pictures were promptly banned from the state by the Kansas State Board of Review. These motion pictures of the early sound era gave indication to larger trends that would burst forth in the early 1930s.[38]

The first of these films was the Fox Movietone feature *Girls Gone Wild* (1929). The film was an early example of the rising tide of violence and

---

36. Munden, *American Film Institute Catalog, 1921–1930*, 642.
37. Ibid., 473.
38. Disapproved Features and Shorts, 1929, Box 35-6-5-12, KSBR, KSHS.

disrespect for the law that would become key themes in the wildly popular gangster genre of the early 1930s. In *Girls Gone Wild,* a wealthy Babs Holworthy dumps Buck Brown when she figures out that he is the son of a cop who would not help her fix a speeding ticket. Babs decides to slum one night and attends a street dance in a rough neighborhood. She flirts and dances with a notorious bootlegger who is suddenly killed by a member of a rival gang. Buck manages to rescue Babs, but they are then both kidnapped by the mob. In a chase scene, Buck is thrown from a car and is able to rescue his former girlfriend with the aid of his father's gun. Perhaps the most disturbing element for the members of the Kansas Board of Review was the presumption that this film would appeal to a young crowd. *Variety* agreed: "*Girls Gone Wild* proceeds on the premise that the adolescent high school crowd and their doings are just about the most vital happening in the world."[39] Certainly, the violence, gunplay, and fast living of *Girls Gone Wild* were much more exciting that anything happening in small-town Kansas, and the censors were fearful that such pictures might lead adolescents to engage in such behavior.

The two Fox features *The Cock-Eyed World* and *Hot for Paris* were 1929 sequels to the popular film *What Price Glory?* (1926). The original film starred Edmund Lowe and Victor McLaglen as First Sergeant Quirt and Captain Flagg. Raoul Walsh directed both sequels, with *The Cock-Eyed World* released in August 1929 and *Hot for Paris* in December 1929. Both films were demonstrations of the frankness with which pre-Code films would deal with sexuality. *The Cock-Eyed World* reteams Flagg and Quirt, who constantly argue over their women. As world travelers, they have women in Russia, New York City, and the "Tropics." *Hot for Paris* stars Victor McLaglen as John Patrick Duke, "a sailor fond of women and liquor."[40]

Both films caused an enormous stir among the censors. *Parents Magazine* described the first film, *The Cock-Eyed World,* as a "boisterous comedy of life as it is lived by certain types of U.S. Marines. . . . It is loud, crude, tough, loutish and decidedly vulgar in spots." Complaints flowed into Governor Clyde Reed's office regarding the film. Kansas citizen William H. McCamish described the movie as "highly suggestive and [a] salacious production." He contended, "It is misnamed, however; a more appropriate name would be the 'sex life of the marines.' My son is between 16 and 17. He wanted to see the picture, because he has heard so much about it and that it has drawn such

39. Review of *Girls Gone Wild, Variety,* April 24, 1929.
40. Munden, *American Film Institute Catalog, 1921–1930,* 364.

Girls Gone Wild (1929) exemplified the violence, gunplay, and fast living that Kansas censors wanted eliminated from the screen in the 1920s. (Permission granted by Photofest)

crowds. His mother also has heard much about it from other mothers and she said he ought not to go." McCamish claimed the real problem was that the Kansas Board of Review had passed the picture. He argued that the film "depicts the sex life of the marine. It does not depict any of the discipline or any of the educational advantages or teach any lesson of loyalty or patriotism. There is no moral to the play—just immorality. The prominent theme is the idea that married women receive the marines with open arms and in their bedrooms at all ports, mostly at night."[41]

In a response to McCamish's complaint, Governor Reed wrote that the "Censor Board mentioned this picture on a visit to my office and I gathered the impression it would not be permitted to be shown in Kansas." The governor

41. *Parents Magazine*, November 1929, 32; William H. McCamish to Reed, November 23, 1929, Box 9, File 5, Reed Papers, KSHS.

explained that he called Chairman Viets, and she informed him that the picture had been rereviewed and the objectionable features had been eliminated. She also explained, though, that the attorney general's ruling had restricted the board's censoring the sound part of the picture, so the oral dialogue remained intact.[42]

Within a matter of months, though, the legal landscape had apparently changed. *Hot for Paris* was disapproved by the Board of Review on January 10, 1930. The justification was that "many actions were deemed by the board to be obscene and indecent."[43] On February 1, a revised film was presented to the board, and *Hot for Paris* passed this time. More than eight hundred feet of film had to be eliminated for the film to be accepted. An examination of required cuts by the board reveals that both visual scenes and spoken dialogue were cut by the censors. The board required the elimination of phrases such as "I'll always say yes, sir" (spoken by a woman) and "Look before you sleep."[44] The required eliminations were extensive; every reel had numerous scenes, snippets of action, and dialogue cut. Almost all of these cuts had to do with double entendres of a sexual nature or a sexual situation in general. The Fox Company agreed to make new discs for the picture to conform to the cuts made in the "sound on film" prints so there would not be any blank film where the eliminations were made. The board also demanded that Fox not advertise *Hot for Paris* as a successor to the notorious *The Cock-Eyed World*, although the teaming of Walsh, Lowe, and McLaglen confirmed that it was a sequel.[45]

Hot for Paris had never been submitted to the Studio Relations Committee of the MPPDA for approval. Will Hays had purposefully set up the Studio Relations Committee in an attempt to self-censor. Studios were supposed to cooperate by submitting all scripts derived from a literary source to the SRC for approval before going into production. Maurice McKenzie wrote Jason Joy on November 9, 1929, "Fox's picture *Hot for Paris* is finished and I understand that it is hotter than *The Cock-Eyed World*. Of course we were not consulted during the writing of the script nor during its production."[46] The SRC censorship report on the film claimed that *Hot for Paris* lacks "story value and con-

42. Reed to McCamish, November 25, 1929, Box 9, File 5, Reed Papers, KSHS.

43. Myers to Reed, February 3, 1930, in ibid.

44. "Eliminations to Be Made—*Hot for Paris*," Box 35-6-24, "Features and Short Subjects," KSBR, KSHS.

45. Myers to Reed, February 3, 1930, Box 9, File 5, Reed Papers, KSHS.

46. Maurice McKenzie to Jason Joy, November 9, 1929, *Hot for Paris* file, MPPDA Files, Academy of Motion Picture Arts and Sciences (AMPA), Margaret Herrick Library, Beverly Hills.

tains no particular value to fortify it against the excessive and unnecessary vulgarity which runs rampant throughout the entire picture."[47] Jason Joy claimed that it was "a very vulgar picture."[48] When Hays had established the SRC and Joy issued the *Don'ts and Be Carefuls*, film producers were encouraged, but by no means obligated, to follow the guidelines set forth. Clearly, by 1929, self-censorship by Hollywood was not working. Sexuality and other material of a disreputable nature led to a winning box office, and producers were increasingly reluctant to conform to guidelines set forth by the MPPDA. But the industry could still give the excuse to the press and the government that it was regulating itself, when, as *The Cock-Eyed World* and *Hot for Paris* prove, it was not. Even when these films were eventually approved by the Kansas Board of Review, they were seriously truncated versions.

The acclaimed Paramount production *Applause* (1929) was indicative of the cynicism that would creep into and then overwhelm many pre-Code films. *Applause*, directed by Rouben Mamoulian, tells the story of blowsy, washed-up burlesque queen Kitty Darling, played by Helen Morgan. The screenplay was an adaptation by Garrett Ford of Beth Brown's popular novel of the same name. In the opening shots, Mamoulian establishes the tawdriness of the burlesque world that Darling inhabits by depicting worn-out musicians and shapeless, gray chorus girls. A very pregnant Kitty passes out onstage and gives birth to her daughter, April, in her dressing room. In order to protect her daughter from the dangers of the theater world, Kitty sends April to a convent where she is given a strict upbringing. Kitty continues her sad career and becomes involved with a cruel, unscrupulous comedian, Hitch, who persuades Kitty to bring her daughter to the city to earn her living in the show. Hitch makes a play for April when she returns to New York City. In return, the young girl joins the burlesque chorus. Kitty, convinced that she has failed as a mother, commits suicide in her dressing room. April decides the stage will not be her life, and she takes off to marry a young sailor. Donald Crafton has described *Applause* as a "realist film [that] provided glimpses of the gritty lives of marginalized people."[49] SRC chairman Jason Joy praised the film at the time of its release, stating that it was "intelligently directed and extremely well photographed."[50] He claimed, though, that *Applause* had a

---

47. Censorship Report on *Hot for Paris*, November 22, 1929, in ibid.
48. Joy to Will Hays, December 6, 1929, in ibid.
49. Donald Crafton, *The Talkies: American Cinema's Transition to Sound, 1926–1931*, 17.
50. MPPDA file on *Applause*, AMPA.

Applause (1929) was indicative of the cynicism that would creep into many pre-Code films. The movie was banned from Kansas. (Permission granted by Photofest)

"touch of . . . realism which makes it a rather sordid subject for general consumption. The dialogue causes a great deal of unfavorable comment. The costumes worn by members of the chorus are reproductions of typical burlesque costumes and as such are very brief and sexy." Joy pointed out that the dialogue violated the *Don'ts and Be Carefuls*. These violations included the phrases "dirty double-crossin' broads," "everybody in the whole damn house," "two damn high hat," and "some God forsaken farm."[51] After the film was completed, the SRC had warned Paramount that the film had potential censorship problems. On September 18, 1929, the SRC wrote the studio, "We are inclined to believe that it would be profitable to cut . . . four or six scenes which in our opinion do not materially add to the value of the picture. . . . [T]hese scenes are those in which the anatomy of Helen Morgan and/or the showgirls are most intimately revealed."[52]

51. Censorship Report, in ibid.
52. SRC to Paramount, September 18, 1929, in ibid.

There was also concern at the SRC that the film would offend Catholics. When Hitch argued with Kitty about taking April out of the convent, she argues, "Why there's a coupla dames in the show that's as good Catholics as anybody." Also, later in the story when Hitch tries to force his attentions on April, she pushes him away, and he says, "I've met babes like you before St. Cecilia."[53] This potential Catholic backlash was enough of a concern that the SRC decided to use subterfuge. Paramount agreed that on sound films, the dialogue would be blurred so that the word *Catholic* would not be distinguishable. When sound-on-disc prints were shown, Paramount notified every exhibitor to turn down the feeder at that particular point to eliminate the word *Catholic*.[54] The SRC and Paramount, therefore, were passing the buck, giving the responsibility to the exhibitor. It is safe to say that many exhibitors across the country did not have the time to patiently wait for this word of dialogue to appear. In Kansas, it did not make a difference because *Applause* never played. The state of Pennsylvania and the Chicago censor boards also demanded many eliminations before the film could be screened.[55] Filmed before the Depression, *Applause* was indicative of the more adult, cynical attitude of many pre-Code films.

Girls Gone Wild, The Cock-Eyed World, Hot for Paris, and *Applause* were all transitional films in several respects. They were early talking films that demonstrated the "rough vernacular and sophisticated wordplay" that could be utilized effectively in films only with spoken dialogue.[56] Although all of these films were shot before the stock market crash, they foreshadowed the rough-and-tumble life of Depression-era America with gunplay, sex, and contemptible, manipulative behavior. The films also pushed boundaries of acceptable screen fare and tested local and state censors.

The death of Emma Viets on April 26, 1930, left a tremendous hole in the Kansas Board of Review. Governor Clyde Reed promptly elevated censor Hazel Myers as chairman. Mrs. L. S. Bearce and Miss Minnie Henderson remained as censors. The board became a revolving door, though, with Jessie Hodges and Zelma Redmond replacing Henderson and Bearce in 1931. During the pre-Code years of 1930–1934, Kansas had a total of nine censors.[57] Just as the Great Depression was making its full impact on Kansas and

53. MPPDA file on *Applause*, AMPA.
54. McKenzie to Joy, November 20, 1929, in ibid.
55. Censorship Report, in ibid.
56. Doherty, *Pre-Code Hollywood*, 17.
57. They were Emma Viets, Mrs. L. S. Bearce, Hazel Myers, Minnie Henderson, Jessie Hodges, Zelma Redmond, Mae Clausen, Mrs. R. W. Stubbs, and Mrs. L. H. Chapman.

provocative, adult screen fare was being presented by producers, the board appeared rudderless. Two theories can be introduced here. First, Myers simply did not have the same leadership skills as her predecessor. The second is that the board was confronted with such a dazzling array of mature, violent, oversexed fare that it found it difficult to establish standards.

The board members found themselves "courted" by more industry executives at this more than any other period in its previous history. In February 1932, the Kansas City Film Board of Trade gave a luncheon at the Hotel Muelbach in honor of the Kansas State Board of Review. The film board, of course, expressed its desire to cooperate in every way with the Board of Review and invited the members of the board to visit the exchanges.[58] In May 1932, the censors were guests at a banquet hosted by the Motion Picture Theater Owners Association at the Jayhawk Hotel in Topeka.[59] In June, Elbert G. Rhoden, division manager of the Fox Theater of Kansas City, Missouri, entertained the censors at a luncheon at the Riveria.[60] This type of socializing with industry types was absent during the 1920s.

Myers had difficulty reining in her staff. A controversy arose in February 1931 when inspector Lizzie Robinson signed and circulated a pamphlet attacking the motion picture industry. She did not inform the board, and chairwoman Myers considered her actions insubordinate. Robinson signed the pamphlet not as a private citizen but as an "inspector for the Kansas State Board of Review," giving it an air of being sanctioned by the board. Myers was furious and called Robinson in for a special meeting with the board on February 24. Robinson spoke in double-talk. She claimed that her husband or daughter must have signed the pamphlet, and then she admitted that she had been insubordinate. She claimed that she had signed the pamphlet as a private citizen but not as inspector yet claimed that she did it to rile up the masses. Robinson argued, "I understand that the WCTU are intending to put a bill in and I thought that some of the facts would help the bill. The general public is getting wonderfully stirred up about pictures. . . . Preachers in several towns took Sundays to preach against picture shows. There is a bitter sentiment against shows in general."[61]

It is necessary to examine the Kansas Board of Review's actions on submitted films from the death of Viets in April 1930 until the formation of the

58. KSBR Minutes, February 2, 1932, Box 58-5-4-14, KSHS.
59. KSBR Minutes, May 26, 1932, Box 58-5-4-15, KSHS.
60. Ibid., August 2, 1932.
61. Myers to Lizzie Robinson, Minutes, February 24, 1931, Box 58-5-5-15, KSBR, KSHS.

Production Code Administration in July 1934. The decisions of the board on various films appear disjointed and confusing, as if the standards adopted (and readopted in 1930) applied only in particular cases.

One wildly popular genre that emerged in this era was the gangster film. As Al Capone and John Dillinger made nationwide headlines and created an alternate antihero for struggling, unemployed Americans, the screen appropriated these charismatic criminals. As Thomas Patrick Doherty explains, "No motion picture genre of the pre-Code era was more incendiary than the gangster film." The three films that cast the mold for the gangster genre were *Little Caesar* (1930), *The Public Enemy* (1931), and *Scarface* (1932). Although the Kansas Board of Review allowed the first two films to be exhibited in the state, *Scarface* was completely banned. The film was released at a time when the question of censoring films was receiving renewed focus by civic organizations. The popularity of *Little Caesar* and *The Public Enemy* put the gangster genre in the spotlight. *Scarface,* on the other hand, *Variety* claimed, "contains more cruelty than any of its predecessors. It bumps off more guys and mixes more blood with rum than most of the past gangster offerings combined. . . . It isn't for children to see. And its pretty strong for adults." Apparently, the Kansas Board of Review agreed. They banned the film on the premise that it "tends to debase morals" and was "Crime Education."[62]

There were many private citizens who were concerned about the rash of gangster films. Will Hays received a letter signed "Disgusted." He wrote, "You are responsible for the morality of our films. Such pictures as *Little Caesar* and other gang pictures are more destructive to the morality of the people and civilization of our country than any other single force today. The public expects you to censor these movies."[63]

As real-life gangsters began to face their eventual demise, studios quickly attempted to cash in on the newsworthiness of their destruction. *Dillinger—Public Enemy no. 1* (1934) was a short biopic that chronicled the notorious gangster's life. Not yet captured, Dillinger was a man on the loose. This cinematic glorification of the gangster was banned by the Board of Review, even after his death. Similarly, the short *Retribution of Clyde Barrow—Bonnie Parker* (1934), filmed after the famed couple's violent death, was banned from the state for reasons that it was "cruel" and "tended to debase morals."[64]

---

62. Doherty, *Pre-Code Hollywood,* 139; review of *Scarface, Variety,* May 24, 1932; Disapproved Features and Shorts, Box 35-6-5-12, KSBR, KSHS.
63. "Disgusted" to Hays, February 17, 1931, *Scarface* file, MPPDA, AMPA.
64. Disapproved Features and Shorts, Box 35-6-5-12, KSBR, KSHS.

Another genre that received great popularity in the early 1930s was the horror film. The approach of the Kansas Board of Review was again scatter-shot. Although *Dracula* (1931) and *The Mummy* (1932) created no problems for the board, *Frankenstein* (1931) was anathema to the lady censors. A Production Code Administration member wrote Carl Laemmle of Universal, "We have seen your picture *Frankenstein* and believe it is satisfactory under the Code and unless some of the official censor boards consider it gruesome, reasonably free from censorship action."[65] Well, this staff member underestimated the ladies on the Kansas Board of Review. The film was originally banned from the state for reasons of "cruelty" and that it "tended to debase morals." Specifically, this included claims by the censors that the film was blasphemous. They argued, "Blasphemy is a crime of the common law, as well as generally by statute, a tendency to a breach of the peace and being a public nuisance or destructive to the foundations of civil society."[66]

The board demanded that if the film was to be admitted to the state it would have to be extensively recut. Every reel was ordered to have entire scenes cut, greatly shortening, if not destroying, the story line. A detailed list of the cuts demanded by the board is included in the Appendix. The board appeared to reject the Frankenstein monster in its entirety, forbidding close-ups of the creature. In the MPPDA file on *Frankenstein*, an unnamed MPPDA staff member argues, "As you will readily see, these deletions destroy all the dramatic power of the picture and Junior [Laemmle] requests you to do anything you can to have these cuts reconsidered." Apparently, the PCA went to bat for Universal because Joy's "résumé" on December 11, 1931, explains, "We have seen the Universal picture *Frankenstein* and then talked for a half hour with the Kansas censors for the purpose of persuading them to lift the ban on this production. Following this, we talked with Joe Breen in New York who will follow through with it."[67] The growing importance of Breen in the overall PCA framework was becoming apparent. Breen had the tenacity and the skill to deal with tough studio heads and sensitive censorship boards. Whether Breen actually made the trip to Kansas City is unknown, but within six days, he, somehow, was able to convince the Kansas State Board of Review to reverse its decision on *Frankenstein*. Jason Joy wrote Will

65. Fred W. Beetson to Carl Laemmle, MPPDA file on *Frankenstein*, AMPA.
66. Correspondence, Governor Harry H. Woodring, 1931–1933, Box 24.14, File 6, Woodring Papers, KSHS (hereafter cited as Woodring Papers).
67. Joy résumé, December 11, 1931, MPPDA file on *Frankenstein*, AMPA.

The Kansas Board of Review was extremely bothered by *Frankenstein* (1931). It took the intervention of future PCA head Joseph Breen to convince the censors to allow the horror film to be allowed in the state. (Permission granted by Photofest)

Hays in December 1931 with thoughts of a preemptive strike on this new genre by asking, "Is this the beginning of a cycle which ought to be retarded or halted?"[68]

The board also forced the distributors of *Dr. Jekyll and Mr. Hyde* (1932) and *Island of Lost Souls* (1933) to make extensive cuts to their completed products before the films would be admitted to the state.[69] The censors demanded that a lengthy and graphic scene in which Hyde strangles one of his victims, including close-ups of both of them, be removed.[70] Jason Joy wrote Bud Schulberg of Paramount in December 1931, "The censors may overlook the horror of the Hyde makeup, though we are frank to say we cannot estimate what the reaction will be to this or the other horror pictures."[71]

There were many issues that the Kansas Board was not willing to overlook for *Dr. Jekyll and Mr. Hyde* or *Island of Lost Souls*. Surprisingly, the Kansas censors had no problems with Tod Browning's exploitative *Freaks* (1932). Whereas *Frankenstein*, *The Mummy*, and *Island of Lost Souls* all contained a type of fantastic horror about imaginary creatures, *Freaks* depicted the abnormality of human genetics—legless, armless, and mentally disturbed people were shown—along with Siamese twins, dwarfs, and hermaphrodites. The film is still shocking today, and it is amazing that the board had no problem with the film given the hue and cry that erupted in many parts of the United States concerning the production.

"Sex films" were also a dominant genre in the pre-Code era. Capitalizing on lax MPPDA standards and desperate for box-office revenue, the studios resorted to the old warhorse of cinematic sexuality in an attempt to bring in audiences. Sex films were often censored, rather than outright banned from the state, but there were some notable exceptions. First National's *Five Star Final* (1931), a newspaper film, was banned for much of its suggestive dialogue. Censors objected to a contest editor telling a coworker, "I hear your wife is going to have another baby. She will wear herself out one of these days." They also eliminated a remark from one of the leads when he yelled, "Take it and shove it up his . . . ," as he flings a phone through a glass door.[72] The German film *Maedchen in Uniform* (1932) was banned from Kansas for its implied lesbian content. *Variety* claimed there was a "whispering campaign

68. Ibid., December 16, 1931.
69. Action on Submitted Films, 1932–1933, KSBR, KSHS.
70. MPPDA file on *Dr. Jekyll and Mr. Hyde*, AMPA.
71. Jason Joy to Bud Schulberg, December 1, 1931, *Dr. Jekyll and Mr. Hyde* file, MPPDA, AMPA.
72. Kansas eliminations, MPPDA file on *Five Star Final*, AMPA.

that managed to get started to the effect that the picture has to do with the subject of mannish femmes."[73]

Sexuality on the screen appeared to offend the Kansas censors in two distinct ways—regarding the overtly adult treatment of a sexual theme or in the guise of double entendres. The Greta Garbo feature *Susan Lenox: Her Fall and Rise* (1931) fit the first category. Garbo stars as Helga, a woman born out of wedlock. Forced into an engagement with a loutish farmer by her uncle, Helga escapes the night before her impending marriage. She runs away through a heavy rainstorm to the house of Rodney Spencer, played by Clark Gable, and the two fall in love. She has to run away again, as her uncle and fiancé attempt to find her. Helga realizes that in order to survive, she must use her sexual power over men. Censors rejected dialogue that implied Helga/Susan was a whore. In reel 5, when Rodney rediscovers Helga/Susan and figures out her game, he exclaims, "I should have paid you off. Thrown a few dollars on the bureau. That's the kind of language you understand." Shortly later, he angrily tells her, "You will go from one man to another like all the other women of your kind of the gutter." Helga/Susan replies, "Gutter, but I'll make it a worthwhile gutter."[74] The Board of Review forced the elimination of this type of dialogue.

Yet the board passed with few or no eliminations highly controversial adult-themed films with blatant sexual content such as Marlene Dietrich's blockbuster *The Blue Angel* (1930), Clara Bow's comeback vehicle *Call Her Savage* (1932), and the Jean Harlow potboiler *The Red-Headed Woman* (1932). All three of these films, along with countless others of the pre-Code era, lured audiences with their overdose of sin with a dash of redemption. And the Kansas Board of Review tended to have few problems with the material.

The double entendre or wisecrack was personified by the mistress of mischief Mae West, who became a huge box-office success in the early 1930s with her sultry brand of saucy language. Although her films caused outrage among the advocates of screen censorship, the Board of Review had few complaints with her movies. West's breakthrough film, *She Done Him Wrong* (1933), required only five eliminations by the board, whereas her follow-up film, *I'm No Angel* (1933), required a mere three. Yet the non-West Universal comedy *Love, Honor, and Oh, Baby!* (1933), which utilized male wisecracks, was heavily edited by the censors when they ordered the extensive deletion of dialogue.

---

73. Disapproved Features and Shorts, Box 35-6-5-12, KSBR, KSHS.
74. Action on Submitted Films, Box 58-5-4-5, KSBR, KSHS.

One sexual theme the board was consistent about was any hint of bestiality. *Ingagi* (1931) hinted at a sexual relationship between African women and
jungle apes. Pure exploitation, disguised as a travelogue, the film was shot in
California, not the "Dark Continent." Producers marketed the film to the
stag audience. The Board of Review forced numerous eliminations on the
completed film, but uncensored versions kept popping up at fraternal organizations and men's clubs. One such illegal exhibition took place on June 11,
1931, when an unexpurgated version was shown at the Abdallah Temple in
Leavenworth. Herman Silverman, distributor of *Ingagi*, was arrested by the
county attorney, and he promptly pleaded guilty. The film critic of the *Kansas
City Star* exclaimed, "*Ingagi* is an affront to public decency."[75] The continu-
ally changing standards of the Kansas Board of Review, coupled with differing standards in other states and municipalities, were giving producers and
distributors fits. In 1932, Edward M. Barrows stated, "We have so wide a
field for varying opinion that the producers complain that the censorship
boards rarely make the same cuts in a picture. What Kansas censors think is
harmful to morals, Ohio censors may pass without a murmur, while Pennsylvania will discover immoralities that neither of them thought of. This reduces
the whole concept to absurdity."[76]

By early 1934, the wishy-washy policies of the board were solved by external forces. The growing demands of the Roman Catholic Church's Legion of
Decency, the bipartisan support of new film censorship legislation across the
nation, and the renewed condemnation of the medium by ministers on the
pulpit forced the industry to take action. On July 12, 1934, the MPPDA
made two substantial changes to the Production Code. They abolished the
Producer's Appeal Board and the Studio Relations Committee and replaced
them with the Production Code Administration, controlled by Joseph Breen.
Breen's forceful and combative personality made him an excellent character
to challenge the bombastic studio heads. For the first time, self-regulation
became a reality in Hollywood. A noticeable change in screen content
emerged. The *Topeka State Journal* reported on this phenomenon in its
December 29, 1934, edition. Claiming that 1934 was the "year of the clean-
up," the newspaper reported, "The immediate results of the screen reform
wave were the abandonment of a few projected screen stories, the revision of

75. MPPDA file on *Ingagi*, AMPA.
76. Schaefer, *Bold! Daring! Shocking! True!* 141.

several completed films . . . and a naturally more discriminating selection of future screen stories."[77]

While the Kansas State Board of Review wandered aimlessly in its regulation of screen content, Joseph Breen and the Production Code Administration solved its problems. Breen's PCA closely watched for objectionable screen material, closely monitored the writing of scripts, and reviewed completed films. The PCA did the job of the Kansas Board of Review by having Hollywood send fewer objectionable films to the state. Although Breen was able to deny seals to studio films that violated the Code, he wielded little control over exploitation films that were distributed without the seal. This became the primary responsibility of the Kansas Board of Review following 1934.

Throughout its history, the Kansas Board of Review responded to changes in content in motion pictures and to industry self-regulation or the lack of it. During the period 1920–1934 while the film industry was maturing into the studio system, industrial self-regulation was minimal. From 1934 to 1948, the Production Code Administration of the MPPDA made industry self-regulation a reality. That eased both the responsibility and the criticism of the Kansas Board of Review, as they found much of their work now completed by the PCA.

77. "Film War in 34," *Topeka State Journal,* December 29, 1934, A4.

Nine

An Age of Maturity? 1934–1948

The Production Code Administration held a tight rein on the motion picture industry in the period 1934–1948. With strict enforcement of the Production Code, chair Joseph Breen was able to cause a seismic shift in tone, subject matter, and genre in a matter of months in late 1934. As Shirley Temple skyrocketed to stardom that year, producers began to look for more "wholesome" film entertainment. With the Legion of Decency acting as watchdog, the PCA was able to strengthen its grip over the filmmaking process.

Three factors helped shore up the power of the PCA. First, until the late 1940s, the motion picture industry was a vertically integrated oligopoly. Studios controlled the production, distribution, and exhibition of their films. The five major studios—MGM, Warner Brothers, Paramount, Universal, and RKO—owned more than 70 percent of the first-run movie theaters in cities with a population of greater than one hundred thousand.[1] According to the MPPDA, the only films that could be exhibited in those theaters were those with a Code Seal of Approval. This also meant that independent filmmakers and distributors had a limited outlet for their films. It was their films that would prove to be the most problematic to the Kansas Board of Review.

1. Randall, *Censorship of the Movies,* 219.

Second, family films began to yield considerable profits for the film industry in the period 1934–1948. The rise of wholesome, youthful actors such as Temple, Judy Garland, Mickey Rooney, and Deanna Durbin moved the industry away from the sensationalism of the pre-Code era. By the mid-1930s, the film industry had begun to work more closely with radio, using the medium as a way to sell motion pictures rather than considering it a direct threat to its livelihood. There developed a relatively peaceful coexistence between the two enormously popular forms of entertainment. Without much competition from other entertainment fields, the film box office continued to rise from 1934, reaching its peak in 1946. The financial rebounding of the motion picture industry in late 1934 dovetailed with the strengthening of the PCA enforcement and the investment in family fare.[2]

Third, the PCA headed off renewed threats of governmental censorship by 1935. This was considered an enormous success by Will Hays and Joseph Breen. Discussion about local, state, and federal censorship virtually came to a halt, as religious and civic groups recognized the "effectiveness" of the PCA. As the PCA grew in power, state censorship boards tended to see their overall influence decline. The September 30, 1936, issue of *Variety* reported that movie censorship boards across the nation were nervous about losing their jobs since there was a remarkable change in film content, making their positions less necessary.[3]

During the 1930s, motion picture theater owners found themselves facing new challenges, as their audience dried up due to unemployment and economic insecurity. It is a common myth that the majority of motion picture theaters were forced to close during the Great Depression due to falling attendance. A case study of Topeka in this period proves this not to have been the case. The city emerged in 1936 with more theaters than it had had in 1929. This does not mean that Kansas theater owners were not hurting. They tended to react to the Depression in one of three ways: by dropping their price of admission, cutting back on advertising, or temporarily closing their doors. By 1933, the Gem, a second-rate Topeka theater, was offering prices of twenty-five cents for adults and ten cents for children. The Grand, the most prestigious of the Topeka theaters, charged adults thirty cents for matinees and forty cents for evening performances.[4] By 1934, newspaper advertising

2. Jowett, *Film: The Democratic Art*, 281–83.
3. *Variety*, September 30, 1936, 3.
4. *Topeka State Journal*, October 25, 1933, 7.

by film theaters was down to a minimum, barely a fraction of the space bought by theater owners in the late 1920s. The *Topeka Daily Capital* and the *Topeka State Journal* suffered from this loss of revenue. Theaters also changed hands more frequently or temporarily closed in the period 1930–1935. By mid-1936, though, as the industry began to recover from the devastating effects of the Depression, film advertising became prominent once again.

It is difficult to get a clear picture of the day-to-day operation of the Kansas Board of Review in the period 1934–1948 due to the paucity of records dealing with the board's work. One of the major problems, discussed in the previous chapter, was the constant change in the membership of the board. There were six separate chairwomen in the period 1930–1940. The constant change in the leadership and membership of the board makes it difficult to see a clear pattern of continuity in these years. From the administration of Arthur Capper (1915–1919) through Harry Hines Woodring (1931–1933), there is ample evidence of correspondence between the governor and the Board of Review. But beginning with the administration of Alfred Mossman Landon (1933–1937), there is scant extant correspondence with the board. The records of Governors Walter Augustus Huxman (1937–1939), Payne H. Ratner (1939–1943), and Andrew F. Schoeppel (1943–1947) also offer few clues to the relationship between the governors and the board.

Clearly, the board appointments continued to be politically motivated. In February 1934, Governor Landon appointed Mrs. W. R. Stubbs, widow of a former governor of the state, to the Board of Review. Living in Lawrence, Mrs. Stubbs had been active in women's club affairs for years.[5] In June 1937, Mrs. Zelma Redmond of Kansas City was named by Governor Huxman to the state censor board. She was the wife of Edward L. Redmond, former chairman of the Wyandotte County Democratic Central Committee.[6] Republican governors appointed Republican loyalists, and Democratic governors appointed Democratic supporters—it was part of the state game of partisan politics.

There were other factors involved that impacted the scarcity of records concerning the board. Clearly, the Great Depression and World War II were far weightier subjects for the governors of this period. The Great Depression had devastated the state, and the New Deal had a tremendous impact on Kansas farmers and laborers.[7] World War II also brought extraordinary eco-

5. *Topeka Daily Capital,* February 2, 1934, Clipping File, KSBR, KSHS.
6. *Kansas City Times,* July 1, 1937, Clipping File, KSBR, KSHS.
7. See Paul Bonnifield, *The Dust Bowl: Men, Dirt, and Depression;* and Pamela Riney-Kehrberg, *Rooted in Dust: Surviving Drought and Depression in Southwestern Kansas.*

nomic and social change to Kansas as the state became an arsenal for democracy.[8] But one must also remember that the period 1934–1948 was the golden age of the Hollywood studio system, and the influence of the cinema on urban and small-town Kansas life was perhaps greater than it had ever been. Both film production and attendance increased in this era, and one would assume that the records of the board would also increase. It is possible that as the Board of Review became more established as a state agency and as the citizenry accepted film censorship as a fact of life, there was less need to correspond with the governor. Perhaps a simple phone call in the 1930s or 1940s would solve the issue at hand; thus, there would be no written record. Another theory is that since the Production Code Administration was regulating content before it made it to the screen, there may have simply been less contention with the board's responsibilities, thus, less correspondence. An examination of the documentation of this period reflects that the board had much more contact with the state attorney general, a real sign of things to come after 1948.

A great deal of the Kansas Board of Review correspondence from 1934 through 1942 dealt with changes in the laws and rules under which the board operated. In 1937, chairwoman Mae Clausen had to deal with a delicate matter of film-operator "double-dipping." The Board of Review was audited annually, and personnel were required to sign a statement saying that none of the board equipment was used by any of the staff for personal revenue. Film projectionists were signing this statement but committing perjury in the process. Since the 1920s, when the board required eliminations in a film, the projectionists would take the reels to a nearby theater, make the required eliminations, and return the film to the board for approval. The film projectionists would then be paid by the distribution company for their work as well as drawing their monthly board salary. This led to the projectionists getting a type of double salary. Technically, it was not against the law until the projectionists began using the board equipment to do the cutting.[9] Kansas state budget director Don E. Symes proposed that the board offer to have the projectionists do the cutting for a fee that would then be turned over to the state. The union projectionists, of course, would not do this without an increase in salary, which they promptly got. The amount negotiated was the difference

8. See Patrick G. O'Brien, "Kansas at War: The Home Front, 1941–1945."
9. Clausen to Don E. Symes, Kansas state budget director, September 3, 1937, File 115, Attorney General Opinions, KSHS.

between their salary and the funds they were getting from the distribution companies.[10] This issue demonstrates that the Kansas Board of Review was recognized as an established, permanent part of the state bureaucracy by the 1930s. No longer did state film associations attempt to eradicate the board. The ethical concern over projectionist "double-dipping" illustrated political concern with "clean government."

Chairwoman Clausen also made other important contributions to the board. Three days after Clausen became chair of the board in April 1937, Mrs. Carlotta Chapman suggested that Section B of Rule 10 of the board rules be revised and strengthened to read as follows: "Ridicule, adverse criticism or abuse of any religious sect or peculiar characteristics of any race of people or any public official or law-enforcing officer will not be approved."[11] The motion was unanimously approved by the board, although it is not known what the mitigating circumstances were that would cause this change. In 1939, Clausen had the board add Rule 10 in Section H of the rules and regulations of the board. She wrote in April 1939, "Within the last year a new situation had arisen through the production of several pictures dealing entirely with child-birth. The Board feels that it should have a rule protecting them in case the subject is handled in a manner which they deem not suitable for public showing." Rule 10 said, "Ridicule or facetious remarks about motherhood or scenes pertaining to childbirth will be disapproved."[12]

One such example of this type of film was the 1938 feature *The Birth of a Baby*. The film was produced by the American Committee on Maternal Welfare. In the sober, unsensational film, Mrs. Burgess explains menstruation to her teenage daughter by showing her medical-book diagrams. Her daughter-in-law Mary confesses her ignorance of her own body and admits that she may be pregnant. Mary tells her husband, John, that she will see the family doctor the next day. Dr. Wilson, who confirms Mary's pregnancy, explains the process of childbirth. During the next seven months of Mary's pregnancy, Dr. Wilson and his nurse, Julie Norton, emphasize proper maternal care. There is no hospital in Mary's hometown, so she gives birth to a baby girl at home with the doctor and nurse attending.[13]

---

10. Symes to Clausen, September 9, 1937, in ibid.
11. KSBR Minutes, April 8, 1937, Box 58-05-04-14, KSHS.
12. Ibid., April 28, 1939.
13. Patricia King Hansen, ed., *American Film Institute Catalog of Motion Pictures Produced in the United States: Feature Films, 1931–1940*, 168.

Variety explained that the film was "sociologically and medically of great value" and has "commercial merit too."[14] Joseph Breen wrote to Francis Harmon, one of the leaders of the sponsoring organization, on December 31, 1937, explaining that "the policy of the PCA had been at all times not to allow any suggestion of abortion, or even any discussion with regard to it. In the case of the pictures cited above *[An American Tragedy* and *Where Are Our Children?]* in which some reference or discussion was permitted, such references or discussions were almost invariably deleted by political censor boards." The film was clearly meant to be informative and educational but was certainly bound to have trouble with municipal and state censorship boards. The film received the endorsement of many social service and medical organizations, though. Even the savvy *Variety* argued that *The Birth of a Baby* was "informative educationally" but advised "its showing [only] under restricted auspices, such as medical schools, hospital organizations, maternity welfare outfits and the like." The Legion of Decency claimed that "the production has considerable merit from the medical, educational, social and technical points of view."[15] The Legion even claimed that "the film is moral in theme. The Legion does not criticize the sincere ultimate purposes of the organization which are listed as sponsoring this picture." The problem the Legion had with the picture is that they could not control audience reception or guarantee the proper moral perspective that the Legion (and, supposedly, the film's sponsors) wished to preach. The leaders of the Legion acknowledged, "Adequate and satisfactory audience controls are very difficult to obtain in theatrical exhibitions. . . . The theatre is not popularly accepted as a clinic, consultation office or classroom." The Legion of Decency, therefore, deemed that *The Birth of a Baby* was unsuitable for entertainment and inappropriate for general theatrical exhibition. *The Birth of a Baby* was soundly rejected in Kansas, and censorship boards in New York, Pennsylvania, and Ohio also denied the exhibition of the film. Despite the ban, the film was still exhibited at independent theaters across the nation, much to the consternation of the Legion of Decency. In Minneapolis,

14. Review of *The Birth of a Baby, Variety,* March 9, 1938. As Laura Wittern-Keller points out, more than 150,000 mothers and children died in childbirth each year in the 1920s and 1930s ("Freedom of the Screen," 138).

15. Joseph Breen to Francis Harmon, December 31, 1937, MPPDA file on *The Birth of a Baby,* AMPA; National Legion of Decency pamphlet, MPPDA file on *The Birth of a Baby,* AMPA; "Birth Began as Commercial Film," *Moving Picture Daily,* April 12, 1938, 1, 7; "*Life* Banned for *Birth of a Baby* Picture," *Motion Picture Herald,* April 16, 1938, 18; "White House Drops 'Birth' Show Plans," *Moving Picture Daily,* April 19, 1938.

216	**Banned in Kansas**

where it wowed audiences, the film grossed more than eleven thousand dollars in one week. *Life* ran a spread on the film in its April 11, 1938, issue. The highlight of the film, an actual delivery of a female child, was covered with photos in the magazine. In a number of cities, copies of the magazine were pulled and the issue banned. First Lady Eleanor Roosevelt announced that she would exhibit the film at the White House, but plans were dropped only four hours later. Apparently, political concerns of the administration forced the reversal of the decision.[16]

The *Hollywood Reporter* in its April 12, 1938, issue argued that *The Birth of a Baby* "caused a number of producers to announce pictures of a similar nature." Suddenly, *Childbirth from Life* (1938), *Life* (1938), *The Birth of a Child* (1938), and *Childbirth* (1940) appeared. Obviously, it was this activity on the part of independent studios that caused the Board of Review to revise its rules and regulations. *Her Unborn Child* was still being exploited by exhibitors more than ten years after its initial release. The distributors attempted to have it approved by the PCA so that it could be distributed nationally. Breen wrote the distributor in 1939, "The basic objection to the picture is that it presents illicit sex, without the necessary compensating moral values." The PCA rejected *Her Unborn Child* for three basic premises, "1) the sin of the young principals throughout is treated as a youthful mistake rather then a reprehensible transgression. 2) numerous and sustained discussions of the right and wrong of abortion, birth control, etc., are thoroughly and completely unacceptable. 3) the advocacy of abortion by the mother per se, in spite of the fact that the doctor condemns her suggestions."[17]

Motion pictures that were produced by major Hollywood studios were relatively safe from the shears of the Kansas censors, unlike exploitation features. From late 1934 through 1939, relatively few films were disapproved in toto by the board. The number of films in which eliminations were required also was reduced substantially. This was evidence of the effectiveness of the PCA. In July 1934, it ordered eliminations in twenty-six films. In November 1934, it ordered eliminations in twenty-three films. In the two-month period of January–February 1936, the board only asked for minor eliminations in two films. It was common in the period 1936–1938 for months to go by before the board decided to pull out the scissors.[18]

16. *Hollywood Reporter*, April 12, 1938, 3; Breen to Weiss, distributor, September 25, 1939, MPPDA file on *Her Unborn Child*, AMPA.
17. "Films Reviewed," July, November 1934, January, February 1936, Box 58-5-4-5, KSBR, KSHS.
18. Clausen to Mrs. F. M. Lynn, October 5, 1937, in ibid.

The entire process had become businesslike by 1937. As Clausen explained to a concerned Kansas City, Kansas, resident, "The pictures, which we preview daily, are furnished us by a representative of the Kansas City Film Board of Exchange, which is made up of all the major film companies such as Universal, Paramount, Fox, United Artists, Metro-Goldwyn-Mayer [MGM], RKO, Columbia, Monogram, Republic and many others. At the conclusion of the day's work, the pictures we have screened and passed are distributed to the various exchanges, which are located at 17th and 18th Wyandotte Street, known as 'Film Row.'"[19]

There were only a handful of films that the board banned in the post-1934 period. From July 1, 1935, to June 30, 1936, no film was deemed unpresentable to Kansas film audiences. From July 1, 1936, to June 30, 1937, only two pictures were rejected.[20] The majority of films banned in the period 1934–1948 were exploitation films, a genre of film that flourished during the heyday of the Production Code Administration and Hollywood self-censorship. Exploitation films were usually shot very quickly and very cheaply with the intention of exposing a topic forbidden by Hollywood films. Exploitation films were often recycled movies, either rereleased with an entirely new title several years after their initial release or compiled from old and new footage. Many producers and distributors defended the integrity of their films by pointing out the "square-up," the "prefatory statement about the social or moral ill the film claimed to combat."[21] Square-ups served as both an apology or excuse for the material about to be displayed on the screen and as a warning to audiences that they were going to see something unique and might be shocked. Exploitation films often came in both hot and cold versions. Hot prints could be shown in states or municipalities without censorship boards. The hot version might include nudity and suggestive or graphic scenes. Cold versions, which were prevalent in Kansas, were self-censored versions that played in territories in which distribution might be difficult. That does not mean that "hot" versions did not sometimes play on Kansas screens. Producers would usually edit out suggestive scenes before submitting them to the Kansas Board of Review for approval and then readd them for distribution.

19. "Complete List of Motion Picture Films Presented to the KSBR for Action, report no. 36, July 1, 1935–June 30, 1936"; "Complete List of Motion Picture Films Presented to the KSBR for Action, report no. 37, July 1, 1936–July 1, 1937," both in ibid.

20. Schaefer, *Bold! Daring! Shocking! True!* 56–57, 69–71.

21. Ibid., 99.

Exploitation films were usually distributed in the states' rights system. Sometimes the production company would distribute the films that they had shot, and sometimes they would sell the states' rights to an individual who then owned the rights to exhibit the film in a given region. It was common for the distributor to change the name of the film they had acquired just in case the audience had already had access to the product. With a name change, it would be difficult to know. Many of these films were "roadshowed." This means that the films "traveled" across the state, with a great deal of fanfare and ballyhoo before the film was presented. Since few prints of such exploitation films existed, they often played for a limited time in second-run theaters across the state. Kansas was a perfect venue for such exploitation films due to the rural nature of the state and lack of entertainment attractions (particularly those with adult themes) in many localities.[22]

Advertising for such films often put the distributor into direct confrontation with the Board of Review, since such films often used blatant sex and nudity, unusually aberrant or forbidden images, or themes of an exposé nature to sell their product. Exploitation films were screened in theaters that were not associated with the major studios and were often the theaters of last resort for many audience members. Due to the subject matter, many audience members might see exploitation features in theaters that they would not normally attend. The exhibition of exploitation films was a way that desperate theater owners could draw spectators.[23]

Some definite themes emerged in the types of motion pictures that the board found offensive in the late 1930s. The Board of Review had difficulty with independent exploitation films that combined criminal activity, sexuality, and drug abuse. One such example was the feature *The Pace That Kills* (also known as *The Cocaine Fiends* or *Cocaine Madness* in its 1937 reissue). The film was initially denied a PCA code of approval.[24] It was rejected by the board in February 1937 but accepted with eliminations after it had been resubmitted in September of that year. *The Pace That Kills* was a lurid tale of cocaine addiction, gangsterism, opium dens, premarital sex, kidnapping, and suicide. Unlike the morality tales of the 1920s that illustrated the glamorous hedonism of the Jazz Age only to teach the protagonists a lesson in the end,

22. Ibid., 105.
23. Vincent Hart to Bert Kulick, May 15, 1936, MPPDA file on *The Pace That Kills*, AMPA.
24. Hansen, *American Film Institute Catalog, 1931–1940*, 1604–5; "Dope Picture Only for Morbid-Minded," *Hollywood Reporter*, December 19, 1935.

The Pace That Kills was more of a ghastly crawl through the sewers of Depression-era cynicism, sin, and corruption without a "proper" moral to be taught. The *Hollywood Reporter* claimed, "The picture is grimly realistic and thoroughly unpleasant. It uses the fear motive on warning parents and young people against the dangers that lurk just around the corner."[25]

The board may have eventually approved the film, with eliminations, because of one of the film's themes. *The Pace That Kills* contrasts a serene, pure, pastoral country life (Kansas) with the vice and corruption of the big city. The film depicts the drug trade as an exclusively urban phenomenon and warns rural youth of the dangers of urban life.[26]

Gambling with Souls (1936), a Jay Dee Kay production, was banned entirely from the state. An exploitation quickie, the film was "loosely based" on Thomas Dewey's destruction of a vice ring in New York. The drama involved Mae Miller, who is drawn into a gambling addiction. Married to a doctor who conducts medical research, Mae hides her habit from her husband and ends up ten thousand dollars in debt. She finds out her friend Molly, who introduces her into this life of degradation, is running a sex exchange through a local gambling establishment. Women who can no longer pay their debts are forced into this life by the racketeering club owner. Mae is forced to prostitute herself. Her sister Carolyn also gets trapped into this life of sin and gambling. She becomes pregnant, has a botched abortion, and dies. Mae ends up shooting and killing the club owner. *Variety* said this about *Gambling with Souls:* "Money is the goal of this sex piece and it'll get it for those houses who can stand the rap." The trade publication acknowledged the difficulty the picture would have getting by censorship boards and predicted that "managers will have a tough time selling the idea that the sole purpose is to present a moral."[27]

One of the chief difficulties in getting the film passed by the Board of Review was its clear-cut exploitation angle in regard to camera work. One reviewer claimed that the camera work was sensationalistic, "with shots when they're [women] only in stepins, chorines in the floor shows, strip shots with the stripper out of the camera range and throwing shoes, stockings, unmentionables into the scene."[28]

25. Schaefer, *Bold! Daring! Shocking! True!* 227.

26. Hansen, *American Film Institute Catalog, 1931–1940,* 728; review of *Gambling with Souls, Variety,* May 19, 1937, 23.

27. Review of *Gambling with Souls, Variety,* May 19, 1937, 23.

28. Hansen, *American Film Institute Catalog, 1931–1940,* 119.

All-black cast pictures were also scrutinized by the Board of Review. The Harry Popkin–produced *Bargain with Bullets* (1937) was one such example. Although all-black independent film productions had virtually ceased with the introduction of sound, race films began to make a comeback in the mid-1930s. In the 1930s, African American and white producers of all-black films tended to use traditional Hollywood genres in which to develop their stories. *Bargain with Bullets* was a unique feature in that it was a gangster film that featured songs. It was not an unusual phenomenon in 1930s race movies to have the narrative of the story frequently interrupted by musical interludes that featured black performers. *Bargain with Bullets* featured Ralph Cooper as Ed "Mugsy" Malone and Theresa Harris as Grace Foster; they were two acknowledged stars of all-black cinema.[29]

Bargain with Bullets had something in common with *The Pace That Kills* and *Gambling with Souls* besides being initially rejected by the Kansas Board of Review. All three films were also initially rejected by the Production Code Administration, severely limiting the theaters in which they could be exhibited. In June 1937, the PCA rejected *Bargain with Bullets* "in toto," citing "gangster themes, detailed crimes, offensive sex and undue glorification of the character Mugsy."[30] On September 30, 1937, Joseph Breen wrote Ralph Cooper, producer and star of the film, and explained to him "that we cannot issue our certificate of approval for this production as it stands since it clearly falls under the ban of pictures showing 'American gangsters armed and in violent conflict with the law.'" Breen claimed that "the letter of the Code is violated by numerous details while the general flavor and atmosphere of the picture violates the spirit of the Code."[31]

The film was severely edited and granted certification by the PCA four days later. After this certification, Breen warned Cooper that "some political censor boards, in all probability, will be inclined to do additional cutting of some of the scenes [including] the final gun battle." Breen accurately forecast what happened in Ohio and Kansas, where the film was cut to shreds. Even *Variety* argued that "it is a bang bang gangster thriller of the most unadulterated type . . . full of murders, all of them revoltingly cold-blooded and hardly excusable by those loose codes known as gangster ethics."[32]

29. Ibid.

30. Breen to Ralph Cooper, September 30, 1937, MPPDA file on *Bargain with Bullets*, AMPA.

31. Ibid., October 5, 1937; review of *Bargain with Bullets*, *Variety*, September 18, 1937.

32. Hansen, *American Film Institute Catalog, 1931–1940*, 2344–45; List of Films Reviewed, 1938, Box 58-5-4-5, KSBR, KSHS.

The Wages of Sin (1938) appeared as a resurrection of the "girl gone wrong" vogue of pre-Code cinema. Clearly reflecting the realities of the Depression, the film features Constance Worth as Marjorie, a hardworking yet frazzled laundress who must support her entire lazy family on her meager salary. When her worldly coworker, Florence, invites Marjorie on a double date, she begins a downward spiral after being introduced to alcohol, marijuana, and a bad man—Tony. Tony intimidates Florence and Marjorie's employer into firing them, and the girls become desperate. Marjorie begins to shack up with Tony who promises her marriage but leads her into a life of sexual slavery when she is trapped into becoming a hotel call girl. By the conclusion of the film, Marjorie shoots and kills both Tony and his new female victim. The combination of common-law marriage, pimps, prostitutes, brothels, firearms, and marijuana was too much for the Board of Review to take, and the film was banned from the state.[33] The film was also rejected in Ohio, whereas Maryland and the Chicago censor board demanded major deletions.[34]

As the 1940s began, gangsterism continued to be taboo among the censors. A unique compilation documentary, *American Gang Busters* (1940), was banned from the state in 1940. The film was a virtual who's who of the criminal world of the 1920s and 1930s. *American Gang Busters* combined newsreel footage, stills, and reenactments as the film traced the lives, activities, and bloody ends of notorious criminals, including John Dillinger, Pretty Boy Floyd, Clyde Barrow, Machine Gun Kelly, and Bruno Richard Hauptmann.[35] The film was silent except for a voice-over that emphasized and praised the work of the FBI and other law-enforcement agencies.[36] As the PCA claimed in its analysis of the film, "The culprits receive their due punishment."[37]

Despite the fact that the film clearly carried the theme that crime does not pay, the Kansas censors were not going to chance it by allowing the film to be exhibited to its probable audience—young male teenagers. One of the elements of the film that may have disturbed the censors were actual scenes of John Dillinger's body in the morgue and Pretty Boy Floyd after he had been shot. The censorship boards of both Ohio and New York forced the producers to eliminate these scenes before *American Gang Busters* could play in their states.[38]

---

33. MPPDA file on *The Wages of Sin*, AMPA.
34. Review of *American Gang Busters*, *Variety*, March 27, 1940, 14.
35. *Motion Picture Herald*, March 30, 1940, 62.
36. Analysis chart, MPPDA file on *American Gang Busters*, AMPA.
37. MPPDA file on *American Gang Busters*, AMPA.
38. Review of *The Fight for Life*, *Variety*, March 6, 1940, 18.

Motion pictures that were in any way related to sex education were promptly banned by the Kansas Board of Review. The censorship board flatly rejected such motion pictures, regardless of their intent or potential audience. The film with the highest pedigree was Pare Lorentz's *Fight for Life*. By 1940, the time of the film's release, Lorentz was acknowledged as one of the finest documentary filmmakers in the United States. Films such as *The Plow That Broke the Plains* (1936) and *The River* (1937), which Lorentz produced for the federal government, drew enthusiastic critical praise and did remarkable box-office business for documentary pictures.[39] His third film, this one feature length, was *The Fight for Life*. The film was based on author Paul de Kruif's book of the same name. The film was produced by the United States Film Service, and, therefore, it was exempt from review by the Production Code Administration.[40] This did not keep the PCA from completing an analysis chart on *The Fight for Life*. The organization claimed that the social significance of the film was an "appeal for greater knowledge of abstinence, abolition of slums and better conditions and food for the poor." But the PCA was obviously worried because the government-sponsored film showed scenes of "the delivery of babies . . . labor pains. . . hypodermic needles and blood transfusions," things you definitely would not see in a motion picture under the auspices of the PCA.[41] The film covers the problems of pregnancy and childbirth among the nation's poor. The bulk of the film was shot in the Chicago Maternity Center and in the tenement homes of expectant mothers, the majority of whom are on relief. The *Motion Picture Herald* was not enthusiastic about the sobering film. A reviewer claimed, "The depiction of the sordid and poverty stricken aspects of the patients' homes may be utilized by the advocates of artificial birth regulation." A reviewer in *Film Daily* agreed to an extent, saying that "the picture is grim, never humorous." The reviewer acknowledged, however, "But at all times [the picture is] true to life as it shows maternity the hard way under unfavorable conditions in slum areas." Advertising for the picture warned, "Every girl thinking of marriage—Every woman thinking of motherhood. Must see CHILDBIRTH (The Fight for Life)." Morris Fishbein of the *Journal of the American Medical Association* agreed with the Kansas censors, though: "I doubt if such a picture should be shown to young children or even girls of a high school age. . . . There is one important criticism; it is of the uni-

39. Hansen, *American Film Institute Catalog, 1931–1940*, 630.
40. Analysis chart, MPPDA file on *The Fight for Life*, AMPA.
41. Ibid.

versal glumness and sadness of practically every woman shown." The Kansas Board of Review eventually relented and allowed the film to be exhibited "under written request . . . to Medical Societies, Nurse Training Classes, Social Welfare Training Classes and Universities for the use in Medical Classes."[42]

Mom and Dad (1945) did not have such impressive credentials as *The Fight for Life* but also found itself banned. Produced by Hygiene Productions, the film was cleverly exploited by producer Kroger Babb who continued to successfully distribute the film throughout the 1950s.[43] According to Babb, the film made somewhere between forty and one hundred million dollars internationally. Film historian Eric Schaefer claims that *Mom and Dad* was "the most successful sex hygiene film in history [and] the biggest pre-1960 exploitation film of any kind." The film focuses on a young girl, Joan Blake, who leads a relatively sheltered life due to her puritanical mother, Sarah. Mrs. Blake promptly gets Carl Blackburn, a progressive-minded teacher, fired from Joan's high school when he begins lecturing on "social and moral hygiene." Conveniently, for the purpose of the plot, Joan gets pregnant. She is seduced by big-city slicker Jack Griffith, who impregnates her and then promptly dies in an airplane crash. This leaves Joan confused, panicky, and suicidal. The film treads the line between informational and exploitative. In a lengthy foreword written by the producers in the beginning of the film (following "The Star Spangled Banner"), they state, "Ignorance is a sin and knowledge is power." They argue for sex education for the nation's youth. Babb's exploitative strategies included having a sex-hygiene expert speak during the intermission of the film, segregating the audience by sex and warning, "You may faint but you'll learn the facts."[44]

The Story of Bob and Sally (1948), another exploitation feature, was produced due to the enormous success of *Mom and Dad. Bob and Sally*'s release also coincided with the publication of Alfred Kinsey's *Sexual Behavior in the Human Male*, leading to an unprecedented public discussion of human sexuality.[45] The film was a social drama with documentary overtones meant to relate certain facts of sex education to its audience. The documentary footage

42. *Motion Picture Herald*, March 16, 1940, 34; *Film Daily*, March 18, 1940, MPPDA file on *The Fight for Life*, AMPA; *Motion Picture Herald*, October 19, 1940; MPPDA file on *The Fight for Life*, AMPA.

43. Patricia King Hansen, ed., *American Film Institute Catalog of Motion Pictures Produced in the United States: Feature Films, 1941–1950*, 1595.

44. Schaefer, *Bold! Daring! Shocking! True!* 197.

45. Elaine Tyler May, *Homeward Bound: American Families in the Cold War Era*, 100–101.

in *Bob and Sally* was graphic for its time, including shots of "reproductive organs, menstruation, conception, development of the human embryo, normal and Caesarian childbirth, and the treatment and cure of venereal diseases, including examples of the three stages of syphilis."[46]

PCA chair Joseph Breen wrote George Bale of Universal International in 1949 informing the movie man that *The Story of Bob and Sally* was "a clear-cut violation of the Code, on at least three basic grounds, 1) it is a story dealing with sex hygiene and venereal disease; 2) It contains the dramatic element of abortion; 3) It is basically the story of illicit sex and pregnancy 'without sufficient compensating moral values' which are necessary with a story of this kind." The *Hollywood Reporter* claimed that *The Story of Bob and Sally* "treats emotional and health problems tastefully and intelligently" and that the "script is extremely well written." *Variety* contended that the film "was a fresh expose of what venereal diseases do and shows some amazing real-life glimpses of bodies in various stages of affliction." Like *Mom and Dad*, the film was shown to sex-segregated audiences, and a doctor or expert was on hand to lecture on sex hygiene. *The Story of Bob and Sally* never played in the state of Kansas; it was banned by the Board of Review. The rationale was that it contained "suggestive lines, nude figures and too much sex."[47]

Elaine Tyler May has argued that "wartime . . . caused such a massive unleashing of sex in all its forms that postwar experts realized that repression was no longer possible. . . . The goal was now to teach young people already indulging in 'petting' how to keep sex under control."[48] Certainly, during World War II the military attempted to educate its personnel about the potential dangers of sexual activity. But the Board of Review was clearly on the side of Kinsey's critics, believing that such talk about sexuality, whether it was in cinematic or literary form, should be banned.

The Kansas censors established a pattern between 1938 and 1948: motion pictures that dealt with pregnancy, childbirth, or sex education were not going to be allowed to be exhibited in the state regardless of their intention or the pedigree of the agency behind the film's production. There was clearly an element of exploitation that was present in the exhibition of a number of

46. Hansen, *American Film Institute Catalog, 1941–1950*, 2336–37.
47. Breen to George Bole, Universal-International Studio, January 20, 1949, MPPDA file on *The Story of Bob and Sally*, AMPA; review of *The Story of Bob and Sally*, *Hollywood Reporter*, May 5, 1948; "*Bob and Sally* Frank Story of Sex and Ills," *Variety*, May 5, 1948; MPPDA file on *The Story of Bob and Sally*, AMPA.
48. May, *Homeward Bound*, 100–101.

these films; undocumented commentary at the time acknowledges that the vast majority of these films' audience members were men, some of whom, it can be suspected, went for thrills rather than the educational or informative content of the motion pictures. But the banning of such "sex ed" pictures from Kansas also has a troubling dimension to it. The Kansas Board of Review was attempting to keep young men and women in the dark when it came to knowledge about their bodies and reproductive capacities, and this was occurring at the very time that World War II was geographically displacing people, separating young couples, and throwing men and women together into new social situations. Venereal disease and premarital pregnancy were very real problems in Kansas in the war and postwar years, and the actions of the Board of Review in not allowing such pictures on the screen may have had an impact on young people's lives who may have still been ignorant of the facts of life. The Kansas Board of Review's actions were prescient of a trend in the late twentieth century in Kansas when social conservatives attempted to ban sex education from the public schools.[49]

In the period 1934–1948, the Kansas Board of Review took it upon itself to keep "immoral" exploitation features off of state screens. The board's attempt to withhold information, not just control content, appeared in other perhaps more questionable forms in this period. Chairman Hazel Myers revisited an old issue during her term of office. One major question plaguing the board was whether universities and colleges could exhibit films that had not been screened by the censors. In 1934, Myers asked the attorney general whether films owned by the University of Kansas and distributed by their Department of Visual Education should be approved by the board. Attorney General E. E. Steerman argued in the negative—these films owned by the university were property of the state; therefore, they did not have to be censored.[50]

The censoring of newsreels became an explosive issue for the board. It was one thing to withhold information on sex education from citizens, but to attempt to control the news was a clear trampling of the First Amendment. Technically, the Board of Review did not have the legal right to censor such newsreels—as was clearly stated in the board's rules and regulations.[51] In March 1934, though, the board censored an entire episode of *March of the*

49. For more information on sexuality during World War II and the immediate postwar years, see Allan Berube, *Coming Out under Fire: The History of Gay Men and Women in World War II;* and John D'Emilio and Estelle B. Freedman, *Intimate Matters: A History of Sexuality in America.*
50. G. E. Steerman to Myers, September 7, 1934, File 115, Attorney General Opinions, KSHS.
51. KSBR Annual Report, 1932, Box 58-5-4-5, KSHS.

Years, a newsreel in which President Franklin Roosevelt upholds his decision to repeal Prohibition. The rest of the nation may have had free access to alcohol after FDR's election, but the censors appeared determined to keep Kansas dry. Kansas remained dry despite the repeal of the national Prohibition. The state constitutional amendment on Prohibition was not repealed in Kansas until 1948.[52]

A 1925 amendment to the board's rules specifically banned the board from censoring newsreels. An incident in 1937 demonstrated the board's ignorance of the rules and led to an incident that aroused national attention. In April, the board ordered stricken a political speech by Senator Burton K. Wheeler (D-MT) in a *March of Time* newsreel. In the speech, Wheeler criticizes President Franklin Roosevelt's attempt to "realign" the Supreme Court. The deleted dialogue reads as follows: "You can say that the privilege of appointing postmasters will not be accorded me. You can say that I'll get no more projects for my state. You can say what you do please but I say to you and to Mr. [Postmaster General James A.] Farley and to everybody else, that I will vote against this proposition because it is morally wrong; it is morally unsound, it is a dangerous proceeding."[53] Wheeler was clearly referring to the political damage that would be done to him if he did not go along with President Roosevelt's court-packing scheme.

Mae Clausen, chairwoman of the board, wrote T. R. Thompson, branch manager of RKO Radio Pictures, and explained, "We feel [Wheeler's] dialogue is partisan and biased, therefore the Board made the decision to cut the material." Louis de Rochement, producer of the *March of Time* segment, commented that "to the best of our knowledge this is the first time that a statement on a national political issue by an accredited authority like a U.S. Senator has been censored from the screen by a state Board." The newsreel segment had surveyed the controversy over Franklin Roosevelt's Supreme Court plan and offered speakers who opposed the plan, including Wheeler, Senator Carter Glass (D-VA), and Senator Bennett Clark (D-MO). The producer claimed that the cuts would "distort the impartiality of *March of Time*'s complete review of the Supreme Court controversy."[54]

Governor Walter Huxman was immediately thrown into the political firestorm. Senator Wheeler, mistakenly believing that Governor Huxman was

52. "List of Films Rejected and Approved as Rebuilt, April to November 1934," Box 13, Governor Alf Landon Papers, 1933–1937, KSHS.
53. Undated article, "Says Censors Ban Wheeler Court Talk," Clipping File, KSBR, KSHS.
54. Ibid.

behind the Board of Review decision, argued that he "ought to qualify the Governor of the state for the dictatorship of the United States." Clausen immediately came to Huxman's defense: "Governor Huxman knew nothing of the matter and gave me no suggestions or instructions."[55] The governor did not realize the seriousness of the matter and downplayed its possible political ramifications. He said that he knew nothing about the picture and "would be happy to entertain an appeal from anyone who feels he has been aggrieved or injured by the action of the state agency." Clausen stood her ground, though. "I am ready to stand back of my decision and shall file a report on the matter to Governor Huxman if he requests it. The censor board, under regulations creating it, is not limited to a strict interpretation of the nature of deletions."[56] This indeed was a troubling statement. Did Clausen believe that she and the other board members had carte blanche to delete anything from Kansas motion picture screens that offended them morally or politically? Was Clausen not aware that she was forbidden from censoring newsreels by state law? Yet she felt little need to explain herself since she did not have to abide by or explain any "strict interpretation."

Representative E. A. Briles of Stafford County saw a hot political issue and demanded that Governor Huxman rescind the board's decision regarding the newsreel. On a radio talk show over WIBW, Representative Briles, a newspaper publisher, argued that if the censorship board was allowed to censor newsreels, it was only a short amount of time before radio and newspapers would be placed under rigid censorship. The *Topeka Daily Capital*, in its April 19, 1937, issue, published a transcript of Briles's complete remarks on the radio show.[57]

Governor Huxman had not expected such a hue and cry. The Board of Review was usually out of the limelight. By April 20, the issue had become serious enough that the board was forced to reverse its previous decision and allow Wheeler's speech to play unedited. Clausen realized that she was in hot water. She told the press, "All three members are happy to have again reviewed this film and render a new decision. We are sincerely sorry if our first decision has caused embarrassment to anyone."[58] This did not occur

55. Ibid. Governor Woodring appointed Clausen on January 11, 1932. She remained on the board through the administration of Republican governor Capper. Although she caused Democratic governor Huxman a great deal of controversy, she stayed on in her role on the board through 1939.

56. "Huxman Out of Film Case," *Kansas City Star,* April 17, 1937, Clipping File, KSBR, KSHS.

57. "Demands Huxman Rescind Action of Censor Board," *Topeka Daily Capital,* April 19, 1937, Clipping File, KSBR, KSHS.

58. KSBR Minutes, April 21, 1937, Box 58-5-4-5, KSHS.

without some of the members of the press getting in some good Clausen-bashing. The *Topeka Journal* called her a "clinkety-clank wooden shod New Dealer Marcher."[59]

The controversy over the *March of Time* newsreel also reawoke Kansans to the fact that they had a motion picture censorship board. An April 22, 1937, editorial in the *Topeka Journal* summarized the feelings of many who were only negligibly aware that such an operation existed:

> Kansas became rather accustomed to deleted pictures depicting crime. Movie boards learned it was good politics and in keeping with the state's moral tone and tendency to protect picture patrons from scenes where something resembling a rugged hard liquor bottle appeared on the dining room table or sat next to the catsup and bitters in the bar. Pictures of ladies in the raw also came in for more or less dressing up before going out for public gaze in the show houses. But anything dealing with public issues or expressions of public men or displaying spot news of the day, ran without question or not more than most casual inspection. Well that was the rule of the day until Mrs. Clausen got her hands full of scissors.[60]

During the World War II years of 1941–1945, the board continued its review process. But with the Production Code Administration and the Office of War Information (OWI) reviewing films before they reached the state, there was often little for the board members to do. The Office of War Information had been created by an executive order signed by Franklin Roosevelt in June 1942 in an attempt to bring a number of overlapping propaganda agencies in the federal government together under one bureau.[61] Roosevelt realized the importance of motion pictures to the propaganda war and had the OWI work as a liaison with the motion picture industry.[62] The Kansas Board of Review now had two agencies screening films before they reached the state border. For example, in April 1941, the board reviewed 224 films and asked for eliminations in only 3 of them.[63]

During the war years, the censors continued to object to certain dialogue. For example, in Preston Sturges's *The Lady Eve* (1941), the censors forced the

59. "Movie Board in Limelight," *Topeka Journal*, April 24, 1937, Clipping File, KSBR, KSHS.
60. "Kansas Political Gossip," *Topeka Journal*, April 22, 1937.
61. Thomas Patrick Doherty, *Projections of War: Hollywood, American Culture, and World War II*, 27–28.
62. Thomas Schatz, *Boom and Bust: American Cinema in the 1940s*, 269.
63. List of Films Reviewed, April 1941, Box 58-5-4-5, KSBR, KSHS.

removal of the following dialogue: "Girl: 'But mama, it makes me puke.' Father: 'Puke.'" In a 1942 Three Stooges short, the censors deleted the word *sexy*. In Sturges's *Miracle of Morgan Creek* (1944), they forced the elimination of a short scene in which Trudy tells Norval that "some sort of fun lasts longer than others."[64]

The board was consistently prudish about pregnancy, forcing a cut in *Mr. Skeffington* (1944) when Fanny says, "Soon I'll be all swollen and puffy and ugly. I don't want anyone to see me like that, I couldn't bear it."[65]

Violence or the threat of violence also made the censors squeamish. In *The Mark of Zorro* (1940), the censors cut out a scene in which Tyrone Power thrusts a sword through the heart of Basil Rathbone. In *Tiger Hunt in Bengal* (1941), they eliminated a scene in which a boa constrictor was shown around the neck and shoulders of a man.[66]

The board was restrictive in its examination of race films during the war years. Much of this activity was due to the popularity of jitterbugging or other dancing that the censors believed was sexually suggestive. In *Murder on Lenox Avenue* (1945), the censors eliminated "vulgar dances." In *It Happened in Harlem* (1945), an entire dance sequence in reels 1 and 2 was removed. In the classic all-black film *Cabin in the Sky* (1943), a scene was eliminated in which Georgia Brown throws herself in Little Joe's lap with one leg over his shoulder.[67]

The popular new dance forms of the 1940s such as jitterbugging, performed by many young people and servicemen home from leave, made the censors nervous. In the Universal film *Model Wife* (1940), a jitterbug scene was axed. In *My Wife's an Angel* (1943), a scene was eliminated in which a dancer was astride the neck of a male partner.[68]

By far, the most censored form of motion picture during the war and early postwar years was not a full-length film or a newsreel—it was "soundies." Soundies were strictly a phenomenon of the 1940s for the motion picture industry.[69] They were short three-minute films that were exhibited in coin-operated viewing machines. They were originally filmed in a 35-millimeter format, then reduced to a 16-millimeter format for the projecting machine. These machines were usually made of walnut and stood seven feet high so

64. Ibid., April 1941, 1942, 1944.
65. Ibid., 1944.
66. Ibid., 1940, 1941.
67. Ibid., 1945, 1943.
68. Ibid., 1940, 1943.
69. Klaus Stratemann, *Duke Ellington: Day by Day and Film by Film*, 97.

that the screen met the viewer at eye level, with the speakers underneath. These coin-operated machines were like visual extensions of jukeboxes and were enormously popular during the war years. Interest in such machines was created at the 1939 world's fair in New York City. Commercial loop machines at the fair showed the possibility of the new medium. For ten cents, a viewer could see one of eight different films on a reel. It was impossible to go specifically to the film you wanted to see—you might have to go through several preceding films to find your desired choice.

"Soundie" machines were found in train stations, bars, bus depots, restaurants, bowling alleys, cocktail lounges, drugstores, dance halls, and hotels. By the summer of 1940, more than a dozen independent companies were producing these short films; however, by late 1941, when the machines came to the attention of the Board of Review, most companies had dropped out due to competition, and the dominating company in the industry became the Mills Novelty Company of Chicago, the second-largest producer of jukeboxes in the United States. By December 1941, the month that the board took it upon itself to censor these films, more than four thousand of the company's "automats," or soundie machines, were dispersed across the nation.[70]

Why did the Kansas Board of Review give itself the right to censor these short films? They were not motion pictures in the traditional sense, particularly in relationship to their short length, the location where they were displayed, and their typical subject matter. Why did the motion picture censors decide to take on this medium and not attempt to censor television as it began to impact Kansas homes in the late 1940s? The answer is undoubtedly in the subject matter. Most soundies were precursors to the modern music video. They showcased bands, jazz combos, singers, musicians, and vaudeville acts in musical numbers that patrons could usually dance to. More than two thousand soundies were produced between 1940 and 1947. They are valuable historical records today due to the racial dictates of the time; many African American musical performers never made it to Hollywood films, but they did make it to the soundies. These short films often depicted dancers in suggestive or provocative styles that the censors hated. They also featured cheesecake scenes or depicted scantily clothed women. The "worst" of the bunch included striptease, burlesque, or bathing suit segments specifically intended to attract wartime military personnel on leave.[71]

70. Ibid., 98.
71. Ibid., 99.

The Kansas Board of Review's shears came out when soundies came to the state. The titles of three November 1943 soundies indicate the moral decorum of the subject matter: *Take It Off, G-Strings,* and *Close Shave.* All three were banned from the state. A March 1945 soundie titled *A Woman's a Fool to Think Her Man Is All Hers* was disapproved of entirely because of "obscene jokes, a strip tease, indecent dancing and scantily clothed girls." Supposed "vulgar" dancing or the costumery (or lack of it) on women became the most frequent reason that soundies were banned from the state. The following is a list of soundies that were not allowed to play in Kansas:

I Want My Rib (1941)
Are You Havin' Any Fun? (1942)
Close Shave (1942)
Dance of Shame (1942)
G-Strings (1942)
Hawaiian Holiday (1942)
I Would Like to Know You Better (1942)
Swing Shift Swing (1942)
Take It Off (1942)
Don't Get around Much Anymore (1943)
Escort Girl (1943)
Gertie from Bizarte (1943)
Jungle Jamboree (1943)
La Conga Si Fue (1943)
My Man (1943)
Rhythm in My Heart (1943)
Slender, Tender, and Tall (1943)
Swing Woman (1943)
Tin Pan Alley Cat (1943)
By the Beautiful Sea (1944)
Dance Revels (1944)
I Want to Be Bad (1944)
I Was Born 'neath the Light of the Moon (1944)
Sunday Sinners (1944–1945)
Broken-Hearted Blues (1945)
Princess Papaya (1945)
Digga Digga Do (1946)
Happy Cat (1946)
Moitle from Toidy Toid and Toid (1946)
She Looks Cute in Her Bathing Suit (1946)

Tune of Luna Park (1946)
You Never Know (1946)

By 1947, the novelty of soundies had pretty much run its course. Unlike contemporary video productions in which musical artists appear in short films to promote their latest recording, the music industry in the 1940s saw soundies as more closely tied to the filmmaking industry than the sale of records. The machines were then stored away and many of the short films were later sold to television.

World War II shook up the traditional morality and mores of Americans, and a new frankness was shown on screen in the postwar years.[72] The Kansas State Board of Review always had to be on guard in attempts to circumvent its authority. Two occurrences illustrate this point. In March 1945, there was an attempt to screen the race film *A Woman's a Fool* at the Dunbar Theater in Wichita. The film had been "bootlegged" into the state and had never been submitted to the Board of Review. Apparently, there had been telegrams and letters of protest about the anticipated film in the city among the African American population, and the Board of Review kept the film out.[73] In 1946, a board inspector found a nudist-colony picture on a reel ready to be run at a midnight show in an Olathe theater. The board took the reel back to the office in Kansas City and did not return it.[74]

Howard Hughes's film *The Outlaw* (1943) was one of the most notorious films of the 1940s. Hughes independently produced the western, so the screenplay was not required to be submitted to the Production Code Administration review board for approval. Hughes decided to submit the script anyway. PCA chair Joseph Breen wrote Hughes of the major difficulties the review board had with the script. The problems included "illicit sex" and several scenes of "undue brutality and unnecessary killings." They also warned about "questionable angles or postures" of the female lead.[75]

When the PCA later screened the completed film, Breen discovered that Hughes had ignored most of the PCA's recommendations and had fully exploited leading lady Jane Russell's bountiful breasts to the fullest. Breen wrote Will Hays, "In my more than ten years of critical examination of

72. Eugenia Kaledin, *Daily Life in the United States, 1940–1959: Shifting Worlds*, 59.
73. Frances Vaughn to W. F. Turrentine Jr., secretary to Governor Andrew Schoeppel, March 20, 1945, Correspondence of Schoeppel, 1943–1947, Box 37, File 8, Schoeppel Papers, KSHS.
74. Ibid., August 23, 1946.
75. Leff and Simmons, *Dame in the Kimono*, 114.

motion pictures, I have never seen anything quite so unacceptable as the shots of the breasts of the character of Rio. . . . Throughout almost half the picture, the girl's breasts, which are quite large and prominent, are shockingly emphasized, and, in almost every instance are very substantially uncovered."[76] The PCA issued a seal of approval to *The Outlaw* on May 23, 1941, but only when Hughes agreed to a number of deletions.[77]

The film opened in a single theater in San Francisco on February 5, 1943. Hughes had withheld the film's release in order to build a groundswell of interest in Jane Russell. After a remarkably successful public relations campaign, Russell became a bona fide celebrity without having been in a single motion picture. When the film was finally released in early 1943, the reaction of the reviewers was largely negative, and that of the audience was unexpected—they laughed in sections of the film that were not supposed to be funny. Hughes promptly withdrew the film.[78]

In 1946, Hughes attempted to promote his investment once again. Perhaps he was encouraged by the acceptance of new adult fare like *The Best Years of Our Lives* (1946) and risky features like *The Postman Always Rings Twice* (1946) that were released at the end of or immediately after World War II. Hughes promoted *The Outlaw* in 1946 on star Jane Russell's mammillary assets. Billboards, magazines, newspapers, and radio advertisements asked provocative questions like—"How Would You Like to Tussle with Russell?" And "What are the Two Great Reasons for Jane Russell's Rise to Stardom?" In New York, a skywriter spelled out "The Outlaw" followed by two huge circles, each dotted in the center.[79] The PCA was furious with Hughes's advertising campaign and promptly withdrew the seal from the film. The Legion of Decency gave the film a C, or Condemned, rating. Many theater owners were nervous to screen the feature, and an estimated 85 percent of the nation's theaters shut out the film. Public interest in *The Outlaw* was remarkable, though, and theaters that chose to play the film did booming box-office business.

It was this type of notoriety and scandal that *The Outlaw* carried when United Artists attempted to distribute the film across Kansas. It was not until August 1947, more than six years since the film had been shot, that the Kansas Board of Review approved the film with eliminations. Jane Russell's character, Rio, was the object of most of the required deletions. The censors demanded

76. Internal memo from Breen to Hays, MPPDA file on *The Outlaw*, AMPA.
77. Dawn B. Sova, *Forbidden Films: Censorship Histories of 125 Motion Pictures*, 235.
78. Leff and Simmons, *Dame in the Kimono*, 124–25.
79. Ibid., 136–37.

Howard Hughes's film *The Outlaw* (1941) carried a scandalous reputation when United Artists attempted to distribute it in Kansas in 1947. Kansas censors were most concerned with the "overexposure" of Jane Russell's body. (Permission granted by Photofest)

that "views of Rio actually removing shoes and stockings as she sits on the side of the bed be eliminated." They also removed "all closeup views of Rio with her breasts exposed as she bends over the bed" and "closeup views, side views of Rio standing over bed."[80] These two features—Rio's breasts and her proximity to a man lying in bed—were too much for the censors to take.

In the summer of 1947, the *Topeka Daily Capital* ran a feature on the Kansas Board of Review. Arguing that the board had "more power than the Hays Office ever thought of having," the author gave insight into the day-to-day operation of the board and their duties. *Daily Capital* staff member Saralena Sherman explained that the board had to "keep the film representatives from taking them into court on charges of being biased, acting under pressure or forcing an undue hardship." She argued that they "are not just censoring

80. List of Films Reviewed, Features and Short Subjects, Box 35-6-5-3, KSBR, KSHS.

for a selected group of Kansans—but passing on entertainment for every 'Tom, Dick and Harry' and Tom doesn't always like what Dick does and seldom what Harry prefers." They also had the duty to "define what is vulgar, profane or harmful to minors."[81]

At the time of the article, the three state censors were Marion Vaughn (Bonner Springs), Mrs. J. R. Stower (Kansas City), and Mrs. Bertha Hall (Merriam). It is important to note that these three women were exclusively from the northeastern section of the state, probably because of their close proximity to the board's headquarters in Kansas City. Stower had been on the job for ten years, Vaughn for seven years, and Hall for two years. Sherman wrote that the women censored films while sitting in overstuffed easy chairs with side tables next to them that contained buzzers. The buzzers were to be used anytime the censors faced an objectionable scene. The projectionist would then mark the spot in the film that was questioned. The censors averaged three to four features a day, not including newsreels, cartoons, and so on. The censors agreed that their major problem at the time was bootleg pictures—films that illegally passed over the state borders and were screened without the seal of approval of the Board of Review. The board also closely paid attention to films that were ballyhooed as "adult-only" shows. The women recognized that these films were more widely distributed since the war, a clear indication of the social impact of the war on traditional morality. The board had recently picked up a film in Olathe in which four young women went camping in the Northwest woods in the nude.[82]

The year of 1948 is widely recognized as a watershed year in American film history. In that year, the Supreme Court ruled in *United States v. Paramount*, an antitrust case against the eight major studios and the theater circuits. The Court ordered the major studios to divest of their interest in theater ownership, which the Court equated with monopolization of the industry. Production and distribution of films were now to be separated from exhibition. Until 1948, a majority of first-run theaters in the nation were owned by the major Hollywood studios. The Supreme Court, in effect, issued a divorce decree. Although the case was that of an antitrust nature and did not directly pertain to the censorship of motion pictures, Justice William O. Douglas wrote in the decision, "We have no doubt that moving pictures, like

81. "They Govern Your Movies," *Topeka Daily Capital*, August 3, 1947, Clipping File, KSBR, KSHS.
82. Ibid.

newspapers and radio, are included in the press where freedom is guaranteed by the First Amendment."[83] This was a grand refutation of the 1915 *Mutual Film* decision that had granted state and municipalities the police power of censorship. It appeared as if the Court was now out to protect films from censorship under the guise of the First Amendment. As the major studios lost control over where their films could be exhibited, the Code began to lose one of its major enforcement powers. Theoretically, it was now much easier for motion picture theater owners, independent of the power of the studios, to exhibit the type of films they wanted.

In the late 1940s and early 1950s, as the cold war deepened and the fear of communism took its toll on Hollywood, the release of a film without the Production Code Administration's seal still bore a stigma. Theater owners feared being boycotted by the Legion of Decency or some other religious or social welfare organization. The *Paramount* decision also had the effect of opening up an outlet for foreign films. The importation of foreign films reflected the changing nature of the postwar marketplace. Many of these films were not submitted to the PCA for approval, and their adult-oriented content often challenged prevailing norms in American society. As television became a nationwide phenomenon in the late 1940s and early 1950s, the Hollywood studio system was threatened, and industry leaders began resorting to new techniques to draw audiences back into the theaters. This included the loosening of the Production Code standards.

The Kansas Board of Review would find itself under attack from 1948 on. From 1920 to 1948, while the Hollywood studio system was at its height, the Board of Review was recognized as a legitimate regulatory agency by the majority of Kansans. There was little if any talk of abolishing the board. During these years, when industry self-censorship through the Production Code Administration was strong and when the Office of War Information dealt with film fare that might be politically or internationally sensitive, the board was primarily involved in keeping exploitation features off of Kansas screens. From 1948 on, the board would have to deal with two challenges: the increased adult-film fare that was attempted to be distributed and screened in the state and fellow Kansans who believed that the board had become obsolete, an archaic remnant of the past.

83. *United States v. Paramount* 334 U.S. 131, 166 (1947).

Ten

The Moon Is Blue over Kansas, 1948–1954

In 1946, two experienced Kansas politicians ran against each other for governor. Frank Carlson, Republican, beat Harry Woodring, the Democratic nominee. Woodring had been governor during the early years of the Depression. But Kansas was a very different place in 1946. Carlson campaigned against what he labeled as a "Truman-perpetuated New Deal Administration in Washington D.C." Carlson was a reflection of the new Republican insurgency following the longtime popularity and control of both the nation and the Democratic Party by Franklin Roosevelt. Carlson served two terms as governor, from 1947 to 1950, and these were years of great change in the state of Kansas. World War II had just ended, and millions of servicemen were returning home from points all around the globe. Americans began to enjoy a wave of unprecedented prosperity. Money that had previously been allocated to the war effort could now be spent on civilian causes, and Carlson initiated programs that substantially increased building construction in Kansas.[1] Construction began on state office buildings, highways, and universities. The

1. Library/Archives Division, Finding Aid, State Agency Records, Governor's Office, Governor Frank Carlson, KSHS.

previous twenty years had been years of austerity due to the Depression and World War II, but now Kansas was ready to build and expand.

Historian Craig Miner argues that in the immediate post–World War II years, "there was heavy pressure to be 'modern' and to live down the legacy of Kansas 'provincialism' in the state."[2] This sentiment was perhaps best reflected in the passage of an amendment that ended the constitutional prohibition of liquor in 1948. The Kansas legislature had approved an amendment repealing prohibition, which voters endorsed in the election of 1948. Governor Carlson signed the Kansas liquor-control bill that repealed a dry law that had been on the books since the 1880s. For much of its history, the Kansas State Board of Review had worked hand in hand with organizations such as the Woman's Christian Temperance Union that wanted to prohibit visual, primarily entertaining, depictions of alcohol consumption and inebriation in the state. During the 1910s and 1920s, the Board of Review had removed scenes involving alcohol from literally hundreds of motion pictures. But temperance and prohibition seemed to be a quaint reminder of the past —not the image that the progressive, modern, economically vital state wanted to display before the rest of the nation. The Kansas Board of Review of Motion Pictures was beginning to look like an anachronism, a legacy from the state's past when puritanical guardians attempted to legislate and control morality. From 1948 on, the Kansas Board of Review would find itself under increased attack. Not only would the decisions of the board be questioned, but the very existence of censorship itself would be debated. What was surprising was not the relentless attacks on the board but the fact that motion picture censorship would actually last until 1966.

The motion picture industry was also undergoing enormous changes in the post–World War II years. The year 1946 was the peak year for film admissions in the United States, following the wartime boom of massive attendance. A long decline then began, reflecting changing cultural and social trends, namely, the postwar baby boom and subsequent nesting and the introduction of television.[3] Perhaps the biggest shock to the industry was the Supreme Court decision in the *Paramount* case, handed down in May 1948. In the 1930s and 1940s, the Big Five movie studios—MGM, Paramount, RKO, Twentieth Century Fox, and Warner Brothers—had seemingly per-

2. Miner, *Kansas*, 324.
3. Brian Neve, *Film and Politics in America: A Social Tradition*, 81.

fected the studio system. One of the keys to success of the studio system was that a firm would control the film's production, distribution, and exhibition. Actors, directors, and writers all worked for the studios, usually under long-term, multiple-year contracts. The studios had realized that if they could control distribution and exhibition, this would create a guaranteed outlet for their product. The Big Five did not own all of the theaters in the country, but they did own the largest, most centrally located first-run establishments. The Department of Justice brought suit against the Big Five in the 1930s, concerned that vertical integration was monopolistic. There were two major concerns. First, small film producers might not get their films shown because the Big Five controlled exhibition; certainly, their products would not be exhibited in studio-owned theaters. The second concern was that independent theaters might not have access to the same quality products as the studio-owned theaters, putting them at a competitive disadvantage.

There was direct evidence of this attempt to restrain trade in Kansas. Glen Dickinson was one of the most significant independent theater-chain owners in the state. In the spring of 1947, he decided to close the Dickinson Theater in Mission. He wrote Governor Carlson that the rationale behind this decision was that the "major film producing companies . . . have steadfastly refused to serve us pictures quick enough after first run to make the theater profitable." The major chains were deliberately holding back their products from Dickinson until they could squeeze all of the profit out of them and then finally deliver the film. Dickinson was able to rally enormous support for his cause. Dozens of letters flooded Carlson's office, substantiating Dickinson's charges. Businessman John W. Halbert explained to the governor that the Fairway Theater, east of the Dickinson on Highway 50, was one of the major competitors to the Mission Theater. The Fairway was owned and operated by the Fox Film Company, which in turn was owned and operated by the Twentieth Century Fox Film Corporation. The Fairway Theater, therefore, ran first-run Fox features to overflowing crowds. Halbert, a clear supporter of Dickinson, complained, "As an American citizen, I would like to know why such conditions exist. It seems these large Corporations, have entire control of the picture industry." Dickinson supporter Amelia Ulrickson echoed this sentiment: "Obviously it's a game of 'squeeze out' detrimental to my business as well as the businesses of all owners and the patrons we serve in this community." The closure of the Dickinson Theater was harmful not only to Glen Dickinson and his staff but to all businesses that surrounded the closed theater that had made money off their close proximity to the entertainment forum. As "people were standing in line for seats" at the Fairway, Mission businesses suffered.[4]

The overwhelming response to the boarding up of the Dickinson forced a response from Carlson's attorney general, Edward Arn. He explained to the governor the technicalities of the present case and that the "court granted injunctive relief intended to give independent theaters such as the Dickinson a fair opportunity to compete with the major companies in licensing films. However, the provisions of this judgment relating to film distribution practices have been stayed pending appeal by all parties to the Supreme Court," which was not argued until the fall of 1947. The attorney general noted that the Antitrust Division had been in touch with Dickinson about the possibility of involvement in this class-action lawsuit. The theater owner would have to wait until the spring of 1948 for the Supreme Court to make its ruling.[5]

In the meantime, Glen Dickinson resorted to extreme measures to bring spectators to his theaters. Whether it was an act of economic desperation or he was fighting the system of screen censorship in Kansas was unclear; he may have been attempting to do both. In 1948, the theater-chain owner attempted to have three controversial films exhibited in the state, only to be denied permission each time. In January, Dickinson submitted the classic 1930s gangster film *Scarface* to the board, only to be told no. The next month, he submitted the Czech film that had made Hedy Lamarr a star—*Ecstasy* (1933). Although the film was fifteen years old, it included a nude swim and a romp in the woods by Lamarr. The combination of nudity, foreignness, sexuality, and stardom made *Ecstacy* "indecent" in the eyes of the Board of Review. Later in the year, the distributor submitted *The Love Life of a Gorilla* (1937), a compilation exploitation film produced by schlockmeister Samuel Cummins. One of the implications of the film was that black women had sexual intercourse with gorillas. The board condemned the film because of the theme of "the mating of women with wild animals and because of nude figures in the picture."[6]

Dickinson would not have to seek out such films following a pivotal Supreme Court case in the spring. The *Paramount* decision in May 1948

4. Glen Dickinson to Carlson, April 20, 1946; John W. Halbert, Food Bank, to Carlson, May 2, 1947; Amelia Ulrickson, Mission, to Carlson, May 2, 1947; Halbert to Carlson, May 2, 1947, all in Correspondence of Governor Frank Carlson, 1947–1950, Box 27-13-07-04, File 1, Carlson Papers, KSHS.

5. Acting attorney general to Carlson, June 12, 1947, Papers of Governor Frank Carlson, Box 40, File 1, Carlson Papers, KSHS.

6. List of Films Reviewed, 1948, Box 58-05-04-05, KSBR, KSHS.

forced the studios to divest their theatrical chains. The Court had found that the major studios had conspired to fix ticket prices, fix patterns of runs at theaters, and force block booking (in which the studios told theater managers "you take all of our films or none of our films," meaning they would have to accept an inferior product). In a seven-to-one ruling, the Court found that the major studios had unreasonably restrained trade and were ordered to divest. RKO signed the first consent decree with the Department of Justice in November 1948, with the other major studios following suit in 1949. The process of block booking was also eliminated.

Perhaps as a reflection of changing times, in 1948 the Kansas legislature revised the "General Rules and Regulations" of the Kansas State Board of Review. A brief overview of the statutes suggests the board's perceptions and legal restrictions. Article 18-1-14 gave the board the opportunity to screen "all advertising material used in connection with the exhibition of films."[7] Following the prurient display of Jane Russell's cleavage in *The Outlaw*, racy advertising, and other exploitation strategies, this was considered necessary. The board was instructed to review, approve, and certify all films except those that were "cruel, obscene, indecent or immoral such as tend to debase or corrupt morals."[8] A growing legal controversy over the meaning of *obscenity* or *immorality* forced the board to develop somewhat more precise definitions on what was deemed "cruel, obscene or immoral." The new regulations stated:

a) said film or reel expressly or impliedly presents as undesirable, acceptable or proper patterns of behavior, acts relating to sex which constitutes felonies or misdemeanors under the law of the state.

b) either the theme or its manner of presentation, or both, presents sex relations as desirable, acceptable or proper pattern of behavior between persons not married to each other.

c) it portrays explicitly or in detail an act of adultery, fornication, rape or seduction.

d) it portrays nudity or a simulation thereof, partial nudity which is sexually immoral, sexual relations of any kind, or actual human birth, or if it presents scenes portraying sexual hygiene, sex organs, abortion, methods of contraception or venereal disease.

7. KSBR, Article 1, General Rules and Regulations, *General Statutes of Kansas*, 1949, 51–103.
8. Ibid., 18-1-21.

These regulations conformed to what the board had previously been subscribing to. It was also necessary for the board to define what "tends to debase
or corrupt morals." This included:

> a) the theme or manner of its presentation is of such a character as to
> present the commission of criminal acts or contempt for law as consti-
> tuting profitable, desirable, acceptable, respectable or commonly accepted
> behavior.
>
> b) if it advocates or teaches the use of, or the methods of use of, narcotics
> or habit forming drugs.[9]

During the 1940s, one category of films that brought out the censors'
shears was the Mexican imports that served the state's Spanish-speaking
community. Despite the fact that none of the censors understood Spanish,
they found plenty of visual scenes to eliminate. These films were distributed
by the Azteca Film Distribution Company. In 1945, the company's film
Santa was banned because of "scenes laid in [a] house of prostitution, many
immoral and indecent views and nude pictures on the wall." In 1949, *Pasiones
Tormentasas* was refused entry into the state because of "indecent acting, costumes and [a] vulgar plot."[10]

Exploitation films continued to be the bane of the Board of Review in the
period 1948–1952, as states' rights distributors attempted to repeatedly exhibit
their films in Kansas. *The Story of Bob and Sally* was disapproved by the board
in 1948, 1952, and again in 1957 because of "low moral theme[s] throughout,
suggestive lines, nude figures and too much sex." In 1951, chairwoman Frances
Vaughn wrote Governor Edward F. Arn about the picture *Street Corner*. The
1948 feature had been disapproved by the board "because of scenes of childbirth and nudity." *Variety* claimed, "*Street Corner* is a sex picture with real
exploitation possibilities. As the sort of film that can be circused to the skies it
should make nice coin for exhibitors going for such pix."[11]

Vaughn's letter to the governor is intriguing because it describes the forces
at work in the state. By 1951, the board was not allowed to make judgments
from on high with universal acceptance; pressure from producers, distributors, and special-interest groups was slowly beginning to turn the public tide

---

9. Ibid., 18-1-22.
10. Disapproved Features and Shorts, Box 35-6-5-12, KSBR, KSHS.
11. Ibid.; review of *Street Corner, Variety*, December 1, 1948.

against motion picture censorship. Vaughn warned Governor Arn that a film company representative was about to visit him, attempting to influence him to pass *Street Corner*. Vaughn argued that the film was "almost a duplicate of the controversial *Mom and Dad*," one of the bellwether exploitation films. Vaughn noted that *Street Corner* had "scenes of actual births and about one hour's running of venereal diseases from films salvaged from the training films of the last war." Like many compilation films, the producers had haphazardly cut-and-pasted a number of previously shot films together. Bosley Crowther, film reviewer for the *New York Times*, would have agreed with Vaughn's opinion on the "intention" of the filmmakers of *Street Corner*. He said that "this film becomes the medium for a sleazy commercial enterprise in which its makers . . . must be named accomplices."[12]

Vaughn explained to the governor what had happened when the distributors of *Mom and Dad* attempted to get their film approved in the state. The makers of the movie had apparently secured the services of Major Alpha Kenna of Topeka, and he, with a group of Legionnaires, went before former governor Frank Carlson and told him that the picture had passed every censor board in the United States except Kansas. Carlson, ignorant of the legal situation of *Mom and Dad*, phoned Vaughn, upon which she had revealed the controversial nature of the film and the fact that it had been rejected in other localities.[13] Vaughn did not want this scenario to replay itself.

Film historian Ira Carmen argues that the modern period of motion picture censorship began with the pivotal Supreme Court decision of *Joseph Burstyn v. Wilson* in 1952. This crucial, precedent-setting case substantially contested the *Mutual Film* decision of 1915 that argued that motion pictures did not have First Amendment protection since they were "a business pure and simple."[14] The *Burstyn* decision began placing American motion pictures on the same constitutional footing as books and newspapers in regard to First Amendment rights. It was the first important legal challenge to motion picture censorship and would place the Kansas Board of Review in a defensive position for the next fourteen years. During the period 1952–1966, state motion picture censorship and the First Amendment right of free expression came into conflict with each other. More than ever before, moving picture

12. Vaughn to Arn, June 8, 1951, Records of the Governor's Office, Correspondence Files, Governor Edward Arn, 1951–1955, Box 7, File 1, Arn Papers, KSHS; Bosley Crowther, review of *Street Corner*, *New York Times*, December 4, 1948, sec. 9, p. 4.

13. Crowther, review of *Street Corner*, *New York Times*, December 4, 1948, 9:4.

14. Carmen, *Movies, Censorship, and the Law*, 48–56.

producers and distributors, encouraged by the *Burstyn* decision and subsequent favorable Court decisions, began to vigorously protest the prior restraint of state and municipal censorship boards. First, it is necessary to examine the operations of the board in 1952 to understand its tenable position in regard to First Amendment protections.

The Kansas State Board of Review had been in existence for thirty-seven years in 1952. It operated under both codified laws enacted by the legislature and administrative rules adopted by the board itself. Bureaucratic agencies interpret laws by writing their own rules. For most of its history, the Kansas legislature had practiced its supervisory role over the board with a hands-off approach. The Kansas legislature could have formally legislated the board's operating rules but failed to do so throughout the board's existence. This proved not to be a problem in regard to day-to-day board decision making, but following the *Burstyn* decision the legislature would pay more attention to this agency.

During the 1940s and 1950s, the typical Kansas film censor was a middle-aged, married woman who was a supporter of the current governor. The table illustrates that these trends continued in the period 1952–1966.[15] Almost all of the women were married (with the exception of Clarice McBride and Margaret Gebhart), and they all lived in the northeast quadrant of the state. The board also employed three clerks, two projectionists, and an inspector. The inspector traveled across the state, visiting more than three hundred theaters at least twice a year. If films did not have appropriate tags or were not approved by the board, they would be confiscated.

By 1950, most films were sent to the Exhibitor's Film Delivery and Service, a clearinghouse for motion pictures. The company was located near all of the major film distributors in Kansas City, Missouri. The Exhibitor's Film Delivery would pick up films from distributors; take them to the Board of Review in Kansas City, Kansas; then return them to the distributors. If there was a "problem" film that would certainly cause controversy, the producer or distributor would often accompany the film to the board headquarters.

Almost all films were screened by the board in its Kansas City, Kansas, headquarters. This became problematic during the 1950s, as Hollywood utilized a number of new technological "marvels," such as Cinerama, Cinemascope, and 3-D in order to lure audiences back into the theaters. In these cases, the board did not have the necessary equipment to properly project these

15. Thomas Michael Gaume, "Suppression of Motion Pictures in Kansas, 1952–1973," appx.

Table 1. Members of the Kansas Board of Review from May 26, 1952, through July 27, 1966

Name	Party	Home	Dates of Service
J. R. Stowers	Rep.	Kansas City	May 1952–May 1954
Frances Vaughn	Rep.	Bonner Springs	May 1953–January 1956
Bertha Hall	Rep.	Mission	May 1952–February 1955
Louise Rahner	Rep.	Kansas City	June 1954–February 1957
Mary Cook	Rep.	Leawood	March 1955–February 1958
Edna Stewart	Rep.	Kansas City	February 1956–February 1959
Frances Lysaught	Dem.	Kansas City	March 1957–May 1957
Margaret Gebhart	Dem.	Bonner Springs	June 1957
Hazel Runyan	Dem.	Bethel	July 1957–February 1960
Dorothy Frankovich	Dem.	Kansas City	March 1958–February 1961
Kitty McMahon	Rep.	Kansas City	March 1961–July 1966
Mary Trehey	Rep.	Kansas City	August 1962–July 1966
Cecile Ryan	Rep.	Kansas City	March 1960–February 1963
Clarice McBride	Rep.	Kansas City	March 1959–July 1962
Polly Kirk	Rep.	Kansas City	March 1963–July 1966

films, and the legislature would not appropriate more money to purchase it. Film distributors, therefore, set up private screenings in Kansas City, Missouri, theaters that had such equipment.[16] Attorney General Harold Fatzer initially believed that this activity was illegal. In a letter to chairwoman Vaughn, he wrote, "I do not believe you can legally perform any of [the board's] official functions outside the state of Kansas. The Supreme Court of Kansas has held on several occasions that the 'power of an officer is limited to the territory of which he is an officer.'" By the 1950s, though, the major motion picture theaters were all based in Kansas City, Missouri, and only they had this ever changing equipment. It was then concluded by the attorney general that if the actual decision making and announcement of these decisions took place in Kansas, it would be legal.[17]

16. Vaughn to Harold Fatzer, August 21, 1953, Box 58-5-04-13, File 2, KSBR Correspondence, KSHS.
17. Fatzer to Vaughn, January 5, July 26, 1954, in ibid., File 1.

Edward Arn was governor of the state from 1951 to 1955, the era in which the Kansas Board of Review found itself under direct assault by legal challenges to the state censorship apparatus. As former attorney general of the state, Arn was familiar with such constitutional challenges. During Arn's administration, McCarthyism, the Korean conflict, and the landmark case *Brown v. Topeka Board of Education* were indications that the nation and the state were being pulled in a number of directions at the same time. Although the 1950s is often regarded as a conservative decade by American historians, it was the decade in which a series of legal and constitutional challenges impacted motion picture censorship across the nation and in the state of Kansas.

The case of *Burstyn v. Wilson* is often referred to as the "Miracle" case. *The Miracle* (1948) was a forty-minute Italian film, directed by Roberto Rossellini and starring Anna Magnani. The short movie involves a single peasant girl who is made drunk and seduced by a vagrant (played by Federico Fellini). She conceives a child and convinces herself that the would-be father is Saint Joseph and that the conception is a miracle. As she tells her story to local villagers, she is taunted and forced to flee, bearing her child in a remote, desolate church. The parallels between *The Miracle* and the doctrine of the Immaculate Conception of Christ were not difficult to miss. In December 1950, the film was combined with Jean Renoir's *Day in the Country* and Marcel Pagnol's *Jofroi* and packaged as *Ways of Love*. All three films were passed by the New York State Board of Censors. The film opened at the Paris Theater in New York City on December 12, 1950. The distributor of *Ways of Love* was Joseph Burstyn, a small, independent businessman who specialized in foreign art films. Eleven days after the film opened, Edward McCaffrey, commissioner of licenses for the city, banned the *Miracle* segment, declaring it was a "blasphemous affront to a great many of our citizens." Burstyn then took legal action, securing a temporary injunction against the commissioner. On January 5, 1951, Justice Aaron Stevens of the New York Supreme Court said that no municipal official could stand in the way of a film that had already been approved by the New York state censors. All of the notoriety caused a great deal of attention, and when the film reopened at the Paris in January 1951, mobs of patrons turned out to see this controversial new film.[18] At this point, Francis Cardinal Spellman of New York became involved, condemning the film and reminding Catholics of the Legion of Decency pledge. Hundreds of Legion members and other members of Catholic organizations

18. Jowett, *Film: The Democratic Art*, 406.

then turned out to picket the Paris Theater and harass any would-be ticket holder.[19] Under threats of protest, the New York State Board of Regents then overruled its own Motion Picture Division, revoking the license of *Ways of Love*. Both the Board of Regents and the appeals court of New York upheld the concept of "sacrilegious" as a valid censorship standard.[20] Lewis A. Wilson was commissioner of education for the State of New York. The New York State Board of Regents was under his jurisdiction.

Burstyn's last hope was the U.S. Supreme Court, and he filed an appeal. On May 26, 1952, the Supreme Court unanimously reversed the New York Court of Appeals and struck down the ban on *The Miracle*. Justice Tom Clark, who wrote the opinion, carefully stated that First Amendment protection did not mean "absolute freedom to exhibit every motion picture of every kind at all times and places."[21] The majority of the justices on the Court did not condemn all movie censorship, and the implication was that a clearly drawn statute on obscenity might be permissible. But the Court found that the concept of "sacrilegious" was not an adequate standard for censorship because of its ambiguity.[22] What was critical about this decision was the Court's willingness to consider cases involving arbitrary decisions by state and municipal censorship boards. The Court did not overturn the *Mutual Film* decision but emphasized that freedom of expression was the rule, and particularly in the case of prior restraint, a state had a heavy burden to justify an exception to the rule. The decision was critical in the relationship between government and organized religion, stressing that it was not the business of government to censor screen material that might be considered distasteful to it. Clearly, the Catholic Legion of Decency had reasons to be concerned regarding its effectiveness as an organization.[23]

Over the next decade, the Supreme Court heard six more film-licensing cases, and the powers of the censors were reduced each time. In a sense, the *Burstyn* decision did not immediately determine that all state and municipal censorship was unconstitutional, but it did considerably restrain what categories of material could be censored and held such boards to stricter standards

19. Edward De Grazia and Roger K. Newman, *Banned Films: Movies, Censors, and the First Amendment*, 79–80.

20. Garth Jowett, "A Significant Medium for the Communication of Ideas: The *Miracle* Decision and the Decline of Motion Picture Censorship, 1952–1968," 265.

21. *Burstyn v. Wilson*.

22. Peter Lev, *The Fifties: Transforming the Screen, 1950–1959*, 98.

23. K. A. Harris, "Censorship in Kansas: A Dilemma," 1.

when it came to defining such concepts. The Kansas board regularly bandied about such concepts as "immoral," "obscene," or "sacrilegious"; defining such terms was indeed problematic.

The *Burstyn* decision did not change the operation of the Kansas State Board of Review overnight. But at the request of the board, Attorney General Harold Fatzer examined the impact of the *Burstyn* decision on Kansas law and the motion picture censorship process. Fatzer concluded that the sole standard of censorship under attack in the *Burstyn* proceeding was that which permitted the New York board to ban "sacrilegious films." According to Kansas legal statutes, the board was authorized to refuse licenses to the showing of films that were "cruel, obscene, indecent or immoral or such as tend to debase or corrupt morals." The statute did not anticipate the exclusion of films from Kansas theaters that were based on religious attitudes. Therefore, the Board of Review did not need to change its censorship legislation. Yet, as the attorney general pointed out, Section B of Rule 10 of the board claimed, "Ridicule, adverse criticism or abuse of any religious sect . . . will not be allowed." According to Fatzer, "it would appear that under the Burstyn case, this may not be a proper basis for censorship."[24] Thus, only one subsection of the board's unlegislated rules needed to be reversed—but it was a chink in the armor.

The board also attempted to define more clearly what was "cruel, obscene, indecent or immoral," its standard guidelines for censoring a film. The new revised code claimed that the following indications were a breach of these standards: "a) it presents as unacceptable behavior acts relating to sex which are unlawful in Kansas; b) it presents sex relations as acceptable behavior between persons not married to each other; c) it portrays nudity, sexual relations of any kind, actual human birth, sexual hygiene or contraception." The board also ruled that a film could be censored if it "tends to debase or corrupt morals" and that this occurred when "a) the theme presents criminal acts or contempt for law as profitable or acceptable behavior; b) it teaches the use or methods of using narcotics."[25]

As far as members of the board were concerned, one of the redeeming factors to come out of the *Burstyn* decision was that the Supreme Court did not declare municipal or state censorship unconstitutional. Justice Stanley Reed claimed, "Assuming that a state may establish a system for the licensing of

---

24. *General Statutes of Kansas*, 1949, 51–103; Fatzer to Vaughn, August 19, 1952, Box 7, File 2, KSBR Correspondence, KSHS.
25. Harris, "Censorship in Kansas," 1.

motion pictures, an issue not foreclosed by the Court's opinion, our duty requires us to examine the facts of the refusal of a license in each case to determine whether the principles of the First Amendment have been honored."[26]

An ominous quote in the *Burstyn* decision foreshadowed legal action for the next fifteen years. The Court quoted the 1931 decision in *Near v. Minnesota*. The Court said, "The protection even as to previous restraint is not absolutely unlimited. But the limitation has been recognized only in exceptional cases.... [I]n the light of the First Amendment's history and of the *Near* decision, the state has a heavy burden to demonstrate that the limitation challenged here presents such an exceptional case."[27] This case strengthened the notion that a "prior restraint" of the press violated the First Amendment. But the Court left a loophole, the heavy burden, as indicated in the decision. This "heavy burden" was a price that the Kansas Board of Review and other censorship boards were going to have to pay for arbitrary or heavy-handed decision-making.

There was renewed interest in the board by the press by 1953, but it was typically not favorable. A series of newspaper editorials condemned the board and its actions. An editorial in the *Ottawa Herald* called the board a "folly" and said that motion picture censorship "permitted a handful of political appointees dictatorially to impose their taste, prejudices, and ethical and artistic standards on one of the most popular forms of entertainment." This editorial was widely reprinted in newspapers across the state. The *State Journal* reported that of the 1,900 motion pictures that the board reviewed in 1952, 3 were considered unfit for exhibition and 3 were ordered censored in part. The editorial writer then explained, "It is noteworthy that one of the six suppressed [the classic Japanese film *Rashomon*] was chosen in a number of competitions as among the ten best films produced last year."[28] The board ordered the rape scene in *Rashomon* to be shortened.

The writer problematized his argument with two misleading statements. Chairwoman Vaughn wrote Oscar Stauffer of the *State Journal* on the date of the editorial's publication and explained that the board had reviewed 355 films instead of the 1,900 mentioned in the article.[29] The author also indirectly led

26. *Burstyn v. Wilson.*

27. 283 U.S. 697, 716; 51 Sup. Ct. 625, 632; 75 L. Ed. 1357, 1367; 343 U.S. 495, 504; 72 Sup. Ct. 777, 781; 96 L. Ed. 1098, 1108.

28. *Ottawa Herald*, December 10, 1952, 3; "The Censors Still Reign," *State Journal*, December 15, 1952, Clipping File, KSBR, KSHS.

29. Vaughn to Oscar Stauffer, *State Journal*, December 15, 1952, Box 58-05-04-13, KSBR Correspondence, KSHS.

the reader to the conclusion that the other films censored by the board were of high merit—they were far from it. The 3 films banned by the board in 1952 included the stalwart exploitation film *The Story of Bob and Sally*, *Latuko*, and *Hurly-Burly*. *Latuko* was a quasi documentary that featured full-frontal male and female nudity.[30] *Hurly-Burly*, advertised as "old-fashioned burlesque," was banned from the state for its numerous scenes of striptease performances that eventually led to total nudity.[31] None of these films measured up to the pedigree or timeless quality of *Rashomon*.

What led to this dramatic attack on, and questioning of, the Kansas State Board of Review? Why were private citizens, legislators, and journalists suddenly interested in the board? The Kansas Board of Review was a glaring symbol of the past attempt to control social behavior. Kansas historian Craig Miner argues that there was a deep-seated undercurrent in Kansas politics that too much governmental interference was a negative thing. In *Kansas: The History of the Sunflower State, 1854–2000*, he quotes scholar Allan Nevins. In an address titled "Kansas and the Stream of American Destiny," Nevins argued, "In cold fact, liberalism in its class sense—the maintenance of individual freedom of thought, of speech, of conscience, of economic and social action within legitimate bounds—has sometimes fared ill within Kansas."[32] Citizens were beginning to question governmental attempts to legislate morality.

Chairwoman Frances Vaughn went on the offensive. In correcting *State Journal* editorialist Oscar Stauffer, she explained, "Kansas is in line with the largest and most progressive states of the Union. New York, Pennsylvania and Ohio are among the large Eastern states who have had censorship for many more years than Kansas."[33]

Miner contends that there was "stress" in living down Kansas's puritanical past.[34] Where Vaughn saw motion picture censorship as progressive and forward looking, Stauffer condemned it as an archaic relic. Claiming that "the Hollywood code has taken so much of the human juice out of the movies as to make them nambly-pambly, this is a reflection on the three states which still continue this type of curb on freedom of living."[35] Stauffer was not a

30. Eric Schaeffer, *Bold! Daring! Shocking! True!* 284.
31. "Actions of the KSBR," Box 35-6-5-1, KSBR Monthly and Yearly Review, 1952, KSHS.
32. Miner, *Kansas*, 321.
33. Vaughn to Stauffer, December 15, 1952, Box 58-05-04-13, KSBR Correspondence, KSHS. This was an untrue statement; Kansas's board was in operation longer than that of Pennsylvania or New York.
34. Miner, *Kansas*, 324.
35. "The Censors Still Reign." This was also untrue, as there were more than three states that still had film censorship boards.

crackpot journalist; he was a giant in the industry in the state and later created the School of Journalism at the University of Kansas while sitting on the
Board of Regents. Vaughn, defending her job and her responsibilities, countered, "We believe that the motion picture house is for the entertainment of
its patrons and not for scenes of actual and Caesarean birth, for birth control
information, for venereal disease information and all of the other things
shown in a lot of these films. That information has its place but not, we
believe, in the entertainment class." Vaughn was defending the board's
actions on films like *Mom and Dad* and *The Story of Bob and Sally*. She further
explained, "We serve three purposes; we keep filth, obscenity, nudity off of
the entertainment screen where it can be witnessed by juveniles as well as
anyone who can pay the admission price of the theatre."[36] Vaughn was going
back to the old Progressive argument: "We must defend the children."

As 1953 began, one clear sign of citizen frustration with the Kansas Board
of Review came with a legislative attempt to abolish the board. Representative Milo Sutton of Emporia introduced House Bill 43 that would have
repealed the state censorship legislation. It was referred to the State Affairs
Committee, but no action was taken. At twenty-two years of age, Sutton
was the youngest Democratic legislator in the state of Kansas and one of
the youngest in the nation. He represented a new generation of politician-
journalist who questioned the suitability of film censorship.[37]

The Board of Review continued to be harsh on features that it deemed
exploitative. In April 1953, the board banned two such films—*Narcotics
Racket* and *Twilight Woman*. *Narcotics Racket* was a bottom of the barrel
exploitation film consisting of material from three 1930s films: *The Pace That
Kills* (1935), *Marijuana* (1936), and *Narcotic* (1937). This compilation film
was condemned by the board for its "lewd scenes of dope parties" and because
"the entire picture tends to debase morals." *Twilight Woman*, a Fox feature,
was banned in April because of its "sordid plot." The film was set in a home
for unwed mothers, and the plot involved baby selling and the murder of
handicapped children not considered fit for adoption.[38]

Joseph Burstyn contacted the Board of Review in the summer of 1953.
Burstyn, of course, initiated the appeal that led to the precedent-setting

36. Vaughn to Stauffer, December 15, 1952, Box 58-05-04-13, KSBR Correspondence, KSHS.
37. *Kansas House Journal*, 1953, 251.
38. "Actions Taken by the KSBR," April 1953, Monthly and Yearly Review, 1953, Box 35-6-5-3,
KSHS. It is difficult to date the production of certain films; I have included the original production
date of each film when I could verify it.

Supreme Court decision. In a letter dated June 9, the producer claimed that
fees for censorship "violated the constitutional guarantees of expression and
communication and were, therefore, void." Burstyn explained that from that
day forward, he would pay his licensing fees under protest and fight legally to
recover these funds. Chairwoman Vaughn took the matter to the attorney
general for advice on the legality of depositing checks paid under protest.
Fatzer defended the state board and sent a warning to Burstyn: "You may be
assured that the appropriate agency of the state of Kansas will take whatever
steps are necessary to resist any attack on any statute of the state."[39] Before
the conflict heated up, though, Burstyn died of a heart attack on November
29, 1953. His successors were unwilling to launch a costly legal battle to contest the licensing fees. Burstyn's strategy would be employed by most of the
major film companies in the mid-1960s, though, when the Kansas State
Board of Review would eventually be killed off.

In the summer of 1953, a matter of much greater significance would occupy
the board and the court system for the next year—Otto Preminger's film *The
Moon Is Blue* (1953). The sexy comedy raised more than a few eyebrows when
it was released in the conservative atmosphere of 1953. The film was based on
an enormously successful Broadway play that later toured the country. The
popularity of the stage play made it a natural for the movies. Preminger
believed that industry self-censorship, the Legion of Decency, and state and
local censorship were absurd, and he was willing to make *The Moon Is Blue* a
test case, particularly since it had toured the country with barely a peep.[40]

The Moon Is Blue was a turning point in the history of frankness in American film. Producer-director Otto Preminger bought the rights to the hit play
but stubbornly refused to change the racy dialogue in the script. The film
begins with an accidental encounter between a young man (William Holden)
and a young woman (Maggie McNamara) in the Empire State Building.
Holden, who is engaged to another woman, invites her to his apartment for
dinner. Holden's upstairs playboy neighbor (David Niven) and his neighbor's
daughter (Dawn Addams) periodically engage the couple in a virtual movie-
length conversation about seduction, marriage, and virginity. The most controversial aspect of the film was the dialogue; words like *virgin, pregnant,* and
seduction had not been heard in a mainstream Hollywood production before.

---

39. Fatzer to Joseph Burstyn, June 15, 1953, Box 58-05-04-13, File 1, KSBR Correspondence,
KSHS.
40. Gregory D. Black, *The Catholic Crusade against the Movies, 1940–1975*, 122.

Despite the fact that the film ended with a marriage proposal, Holden's experienced attempt at seduction and Niven's lecherous middle-aged playboy were too much for the Production Code Administration and many censorship boards. Preminger had a deal with United Artists to distribute the film with or without a seal of approval from the PCA.

The Kansas board formally banned the film on June 17, 1953. The film was condemned because of its "sex theme throughout."[41] The board determined that the "frank bedroom dialogue and many sexy words" were consistently replicated "both in dialogue and action." Finally, the board argued that *The Moon Is Blue* had "sex as its entire theme." The board applied various provisions of Rule 10 to its decision. Section A said that "pictures [were] to be clean and wholesome and [that] all features that tend to debase morals or influence the mind to improper conduct should be eliminated." Section D said that "loose conduct between men and women should be eliminated."[42]

Otto Preminger insisted that the dialogue in question was absolutely necessary in the context of the entire picture. The distributor in Kansas, Richard Biechele, attempted to negotiate a settlement in which only adults would be allowed to view the film.[43] Chairwoman Vaughn wrote that she did not think that the board had that authority, but Biechele insisted on an official opinion. Attorney General Fatzer wrote Vaughn, "You indicated that you do not believe the statutes of Kansas authorize such conditional approval of motion pictures. You are advised that we agree with your conclusion." Vaughn wrote the distributor, "Nowhere in the statutes do we find any basis for a qualified or conditional approval based upon an argument by the distributor to permit the film to be shown to adults only."[44] At this point, the distributor had two choices—to heavily edit the film (which Preminger would not allow him to do) or to bring suit against the board.

Biechele decided to file suit. In September 1953, Vaughn wrote the National Welfare Conference of the Legion of Decency that "you might be interested in our problem with the film." Vaughn decided to use the power of the Legion to back up the board's case for not allowing the film in the state. Vaughn wrote, "Father Lacy of the *Catholic Register* [a local Catholic

---

41. "Actions Submitted by the Board," June 1953, Monthly Review File, 1953, Box 35-6-5-3, KSBR, KSHS.

42. Rules Governing the KSBR, 1949, Box 58-5-4-14, KSHS.

43. Gaume, "Suppression of Motion Pictures in Kansas," 42.

44. Vaughn to Richard Biechele, July 11, 1953, Box 58-05-04-13, KSBR Correspondence, KSHS.

The Kansas Board of Review's decision to ban *The Moon Is Blue* led director and producer Otto Preminger to contest the case all the way to the United States Supreme Court. (Permission granted by Photofest)

newspaper] suggested that you might be able to give some assistance in the matter of publicity with people here."[45]

As Gregory Black illustrates in *The Catholic Crusade against the Movies*, there was even dissension in the Legion of Decency over *The Moon Is Blue*. A committee of reviewers from the International Federation of Catholic Alumnae gave the film a B rating, which meant that the film was objectionable in part for adult viewers but not condemned. This committee was overruled by Msgr. Thomas F. Little and Father Patrick J. Masterson, who gave the film a C rating—Condemned. In the summer of 1953, Legion leaders made a concerted effort to halt distribution of the film and quickly sent correspondence to local Legion directors informing them that *The Moon Is Blue* was "avowedly salacious" and "dangerous to the moral welfare" of movie audiences. The Legion

45. Vaughn to National Welfare Council Conference, Legion of Decency, September 15, 1953, in ibid.

was at the height of its campaign against Preminger and the film when Chairman Vaughn attempted to get its assistance in keeping the film from the state.[46]

On August 17, 1953, Holmby Productions, the producers of *The Moon Is Blue*, and United Artists, the distributors, filed a suit in district court, seeking an injunction or declaratory judgment to halt the enforcement of the motion picture censorship law on the grounds that the board had acted arbitrarily and capriciously and that the law was unconstitutional. The future of the Board of Review and motion picture censorship in Kansas was now at stake.[47] The suit was of a landmark nature because subsequent suits filed against the board used language and arguments similar to the one in this case.

The board's attorneys sent a letter on September 8, 1953, warning the board of the shaky legal grounds upon which it was standing and made several suggestions to protect the legitimacy of the board and of its actions. The attorneys suggested that the film be reexamined and that other governmental representatives be present, including the juvenile judge of Wyandotte County, the head of the Family Welfare Services, and representatives of the Police Department Youth Bureau and city welfare departments so they would be available as witnesses "to the probable effects of the film on children who might see it in neighborhood theaters." The attorneys also suggested that the letter of disapproval that the board would send to the producers "follow the words of the statute and should dispose of the possibility of the plaintiff's raising that question at trial."[48] The *Burstyn* decision had made state and local boards stick much more closely to the letter of the law as written in their own statutes.

The board then reexamined the film three days later under their attorney's suggestions and once again disapproved *The Moon Is Blue*. This time, however, the board changed its reasoning. In order to protect itself in court, the board found the film "obscene, indecent and immoral and as such it tends to debase or corrupt morals."[49] The board quoted the state censorship legislation verbatim yet did not mention its own rules that were not legally binding. The board had been forced to undergo a reexamination of *The Moon Is Blue*, not because it seriously considered overturning its previous ruling but in order to protect itself from charges that it had acted in bad faith. In a test case over *The Birth of a Nation* in 1918, the Kansas Supreme Court had ruled that "should bad

46. Black, *Catholic Crusade*, 126–27.

47. *Holmby Productions, Inc. v. Vaughn*, Docket no. 87493-A (Wyandotte County District Court).

48. Arthur Stanley to Vaughn, September 8, 1953, Box 58-05-04-13, 1951–1955 File, KSBR Correspondence, KSHS.

49. Vaughn to United Artists, September 17, 1953, in ibid.

faith be actually shown, relief may be had in the courts."[50] Vaughn and her attorneys clearly had to prove in court that they were not acting in bad faith.

By late summer 1953, *The Moon Is Blue* had become a cause célèbre. United Artists and Holmby Productions had taken a real gamble in releasing the film without a Production Code seal. Joseph Breen, head of the PCA, and Francis Cardinal Spellman of New York believed that the very existence of American morality was at stake if the film was allowed to be freely exhibited without the approval of the PCA or the Legion of Decency. Before the mid-1950s, it was believed that releasing a film without a seal would mean financial suicide since few theaters would risk exhibiting a condemned film. In an editorial, Spellman explained, "This picture is condemned because of the subject matter. In its substance and manner of presentation, it seriously violates standards of morality and decency and dwells, hardly without variation, upon suggestiveness in situations and dialogue. Because this picture bears a serious potential influence for evil, especially endangering our youth, tempting them to certain ideas of behavior conflicting with moral law, incite to juvenile delinquency, I am gravely concerned about its presentation." But Spellman realized that the controversy over the film was much larger than simply having a dirty picture seen by the public. He claimed:

> My concern is heightened by the circumstances surrounding the production and release of this condemned picture. This picture was avowedly produced in defiance of the system of self-regulation which the Motion Picture Industry itself has maintained for more than two decades. The producers refused to make any revisions of the film and openly spurn the Code of the American Motion Picture industry. The presentation of this film constitutes an attempt to ignore and override the moral law and to challenge the ideas of morally wholesome standards in public entertainment.[51]

State and municipal censorship boards were divided over *The Moon Is Blue*. Massachusetts, New York, and Pennsylvania approved it, whereas Kansas, Maryland, and Ohio rejected it.

Spellman's words and arguments were telling because by 1953 there appeared to be a nexus of prior restraint that the Production Code Administration, the Legion of Decency, and state censorship boards all used to justify their exis-

50. Gaume, "Suppression of Motion Pictures in Kansas," 43.

51. Francis Cardinal Spellman, "Condemned Film Overrides Moral Law, Cardinal Asserts," *The Moon Is Blue* production file, MPAA, AMPA.

tence. Spellman defended Legion boycotts of *The Moon Is Blue* because of the lack of a PCA Seal of Approval. Chairwoman Vaughn, in a letter to Time, Inc., claimed, "With the industry's self-censoring agency refusing to give a seal of approval to *The Moon Is Blue* after it submitted to them three times, what do you think of other Boards?" Clearly, Vaughn apparently thought the board's actions were contingent upon the actions of the PCA. Geoffrey Shurlock of the PCA explained to Sidney Schreiber of the Motion Picture Association of America (MPAA), "The Code states explicitly that seduction is never the proper subject for comedy. While it is true that nobody gets seduced in the course of the picture, nevertheless, the *subject* of seduction is discussed in such a way to get laughs. The same applies to the subject of virginity and chastity. We have steadfastly maintained that these subjects should not be interjected into pictures in such a way to get laughs from the audience."[52] Yet there was a significant difference between the PCA and the Kansas Board of Review. The PCA was a private self-censoring body; therefore, it was not limited by public laws. But the Kansas Board of Review was a public board that could be tested judicially.

Before *The Moon Is Blue* case went to trial, the U.S. Supreme Court, in a per curiam decision, reversed the decisions of two other state boards.[53] This would have a definite impact on *The Moon Is Blue* case in Kansas. In an Ohio case, *Superior Films, Inc. v. Ohio Department of Education,* the controversy surrounded a remake of the classic German film *M* (1931). The Ohio censorship board refused a license for the film on the grounds that it might be harmful "on unstable persons of any age."[54] The distributor, Superior Films, sued, and the Ohio Supreme Court upheld the board's decision. In another case, *Commercial Pictures Corporation v. Regents of the State University of New York,* the battle was over the classic French film *La Ronde* (1950). The regents denied the film because it was "immoral." In both the Ohio and the New York case, the Supreme Court overturned the decisions, effectively meaning that the films could play in each state. Again, the very existence of state censorship bodies was threatened by the highest court in the land because these decisions had been overturned.

By January 1954, the writing was clearly on the wall, and political officials and members of the state censorship boards knew it. Kansas governor Edward Arn, in the *Topeka Daily Capital,* commented, "It looks as if they

---

52. Vaughn to Time, Inc., undated, Box 58-05-04-13, 1951–1955 File, KSBR Correspondence, KSHS; Geoffrey Shurlock to Sidney Schreiber, Motion Pictures Association, May 11, 1953, MPAA, AMPA.

53. A per curiam decision is one in which a judicial decision is made without justification.

54. Gaume, "Suppression of Motion Pictures in Kansas," 46.

have no authority to do the thing they are designed to do." Frances Vaughn was more in a state of denial. She claimed, "I am firm in the knowledge and the belief that the Kansas Board of Review has been properly exercising the jurisdiction conferred upon it by the Kansas legislature."[55]

By coincidence, a six-state conference on censorship was scheduled on January 22–23, 1954, just four days after the *M* and *La Ronde* decisions. The conference was a direct reaction to the new state of affairs as a result of the *Burstyn* decision. Vaughn represented the Kansas Board of Review and met with censors from other state boards. Obviously, a strategy session for survival, the hearings were closed. The boards all had to revise their statutes and procedures in order to make them judicially and constitutionally sound. At the closing of the meeting, a joint statement was released claiming that recent Supreme Court decisions had in no way undone "the constitutional right of the state to exercise pre-regulation of motion pictures."[56]

The first few months of 1954 were a flurry of activity for the Kansas Board of Review. Besides adjusting its mode of operation to fit new stricter judicial guidelines, board members were preparing for a fight with *The Moon Is Blue* case. Vaughn wrote the Kansas reviser of statutes on March 5, 1954, "Our attorney has advised us that we should revise our Rules and Regulations, making them conform to the recent Decision of the Supreme Court. Enclosed is a copy of the Rules and Regulations as adopted by the Board today, March 5th. Because of the pending suit on 'The Moon is Blue' we would like to have the Rules adopted as soon as possible."[57] The new legislation varied little from the revised 1948 statutes. The one exception was the dismissal of Rule 10 that attempted to define *obscene*. It was replaced by a new definitional scheme that was presently before the New York state legislature for adoption. Part of the rationale for the January meeting of the state censorship boards was an attempt to have a unified codification of what was considered "immoral" or "obscene." The New York definition of *obscene* was adopted by the Kansas State Board of Review.[58]

A February 16, 1954, *Kansas City Star* article titled "Film Pressure Is On" illustrated the board's siege mentality.[59] In 1953, the board had reviewed 381 feature films. Of that total, only 6 were banned—*Hurly-Burly, Narcotic, A Vir-*

55. *Topeka Daily Capital,* January 19, 1954, 1.

56. *New York Times,* January 23, 1954, 11.

57. Vaughn to Kansas Revisor of Statutes, March 5, 1954, Box 58-05-04-13, KSBR Correspondence, KSHS.

58. "Law Concerning Motion-Picture Films or Reels and Censoring the Same for Public Exhibition," March 15, 1954, Box 58-05-04-13, Rules and Regulations File, KSBR, KSHS.

59. "Film Pressure Is On," *Kansas City Star,* February 16, 1954, 3.

gin in Hollywood, Twilight Woman, Violated, and *The Moon Is Blue.* The first 5 were all exploitation films, easy targets for the Board of Review. *Hurly-Burly* was a burlesque film that the Board of Review condemned. *A Virgin in Hollywood* was the cinematic equivalent of moving cheesecake photography, with numerous women modeling swimsuits, lingerie, and other provocative outfits.[60] *Narcotic* was an ancient dope film about the dangers of the illegal substance. Clearly, 6 out of 381 films, all but one of them an exploitation film, seemed to be of little threat to the state. Yet chairwoman Vaughn claimed in the *Kansas City Star* article, "The Film industry is renewing its efforts to show objectionable crime and sex movies in Kansas."[61] Was this true? Was Hollywood ready to unleash a torrent of scandalous films to a naive public?

Certainly, the motion picture industry was dramatically changing. By 1954, television had made a remarkable impact on the industry, and audiences were staying away from the theaters in droves.[62] In order to present the public with a form of entertainment that would drag them away from their television sets, the motion picture industry had developed a series of strategies. One of these was the use of technological innovations (such as 3-D and Cinemascope) to enhance the appeal of a film and to offer the movie patron an experience that could not possibly be replicated at home. The second strategy was an attempt by Hollywood to offer more adult film fare, offering themes and images that were not permissible in the medium of television.[63] *The Moon Is Blue'*s content and language were prime examples of this new strategy.

The success of *Moon* and *A Streetcar Named Desire* (1951) demonstrated there was a demand for adult screen material. The Production Code of the MPAA was slowly being whittled away. An example was the PCA's revision of its amendments on miscegenation, liquor, and profanity in 1954.[64] In a sense, this allowed the industry organization to consider the treatment of such themes if dealt with in an appropriate fashion. Part of the PCA's new laxity on film content was due to the pragmatism of Geoffrey Shurlock, successor to the stalwart defender of movie morality Joseph Breen, as new head of the PCA. Breen retired from his position in the spring of 1954.

So was Vaughn correct? Was the industry ready to unleash "crime and sex" films across Kansas? Well, the answer is yes and no. The exploitation

60. Schaeffer, *Bold! Daring! Shocking! True!* 303.
61. "Film Pressure Is On."
62. James T. Patterson, *Grand Expectations: The United States, 1945–1974,* 76.
63. Mitchell K. Hall, *Crossroads: American Popular Culture and the Vietnam Generation,* 17–18.
64. Jowett, *Film: The Democratic Art,* 415.

industry, which was still going strong in the mid-1950s, along with art films and teen pics, challenged the sense of "normalcy" of various censorship boards. By early 1954, when Joseph Breen announced his intention to resign, the Production Code seemed hopelessly outdated to many in Hollywood. Numerous critics, including Arthur Schlesinger Jr., were calling for the liberalization and modernization of the Code. Few, though, challenged the right of the Code to exist. But the multitude of "taboos" excluded from the screen, such as prostitution, abortion, miscegenation, homosexuality, and "lustful" embraces, made it difficult for writers and directors to deal with the realities of postwar America. According to Vaughn, perhaps, the world of the screen was changing dramatically in 1954. The Production Code, the Legion of Decency, and state censorship boards were being challenged by members of the film industry, public opinion, foreign motion pictures, and defenders of free speech. When motion pictures like Denmark's *We Want a Child* (1954) appeared before the board, the censors promptly dismissed it because of "a display of nude human figures" and "scenes pertaining to childbirth" and because it was "not clean and wholesome."[65] Whereas producers claimed that their film would show you "the beginning of life right before your eyes," the Kansas State Board of Review was ready to keep this knowledge in the dark.[66]

The revision of the Board of Review's rules did not save it from *The Moon Is Blue* case. The rules became effective on March 15, 1954; therefore, they did not pertain to the previous decision regarding the film. The board did use these rules to demonstrate that they had remedied any constitutional deficiencies in the previous set of rules.

The case of *Holmby Productions, Inc., and United Artists Corporation, Plaintiffs v. Mrs. Frances Vaughn, Mrs. J. R. Stowers, and Mrs. Bertha Hall, Constituting the Kansas State Board of Review, Defendants, no. 87943A,* was argued in June 1954 in Wyandotte County District Court. The film companies argued that *The Moon Is Blue* was not obscene and found judicial support for their contentions in three lower court decisions that also involved the film. The Maryland state censorship board had banned the film and was reversed by the Baltimore City Court in December 1953.[67] In January 1954, a New Jersey theater manager had been found guilty of violating an ordinance that prohibited obscene pictures. A New Jersey court reversed his conviction, and

65. List of Films Reviewed, 1954, Box 27-14-08-01, File 7, Arn Papers, KSHS.
66. Schaeffer, *Bold! Daring! Shocking! True!* 106.
67. *United Artists Corporation v. Traub,* Docket no. 295, folio 16.

the judge in the case said, "I find nothing in *The Moon Is Blue* that may be deemed as manifestly tending to the corruption of morals."[68] In February 1954, a similar event took place in Missouri. A theater owner who had been charged with exhibiting a picture that was "immoral" found his case thrown out by a lower court.[69] Judicial opinion was definitely running in favor of the plaintiffs.

The case was tried without a jury before Judge Harry G. Miller, who heard oral arguments and testimony of witnesses. Judge Miller found the statute creating the board "repugnant" because "motion pictures are protected by the First and Fourteenth Amendments to the Constitution." What had begun as a case regarding a single film now threatened the life of the Board of Review itself. The judge's opinion would make the entire censorship process unconstitutional. Moreover, Judge Miller declared that the terms *cruel, obscene, indecent,* and *immoral* that were used to judge films were "so broad and vague as to be unconstitutional."[70]

The board appealed Judge Miller's decision to the Kansas Supreme Court. Whereas the plaintiff's arguments were basically the same that they had been in the lower court, the Kansas Board of Review built its appeal on four rationales:

a) Censorship of motion pictures prior to publication or exhibition is not unconstitutional per se.

b) The censorship law, as interpreted by the board, sets forth standards sufficiently clear, definite, and comprehensive as to comply with the constitutional requirements.

c) The right of judicial review granted in Kansas . . . as interpreted by this court, affords appellants due process of law.

d) The presumption of law to which appellants are entitled and evidence submitted conclusively prove the validity of appellant's actions in refusing its certificate of approval.[71]

The Kansas Supreme Court reversed Judge Miller and upheld the constitutionality of the board's authority to decide whether films were fit to be exhibited in the state.

68. *State of New Jersey v. Manfredonia,* Docket no. 65802 (Hudson County Court).
69. *Holmby v. Bessie,* Docket no. 13559 (Cole County Circuit Court).
70. *Holmby Productions, Inc. v. Vaughn,* Docket no. 87943-A (Wyandotte County District Court), Journal Entry of Judgment, p. 2.
71. Supreme Court Docket no. 39699, Appellant's Abstract, pp. 51–52.

The film companies then appealed to the United States Supreme Court and maintained their original arguments. The board asked that the case be dismissed because the alleged deficiencies in their rules had been remedied after the litigation began.[72] The U.S. Supreme Court then reversed the Supreme Court of Kansas. The U.S. Supreme Court gave a per curiam opinion based on the *Miracle* case, the *M* case, and the *La Ronde* case. No oral arguments were heard. The Court held that the terminology of "cruel, obscene, indecent, or immoral, or such as tends to debase or corrupt morals" was too vague and indefinite to support any type of state censorship scheme. Although the Court narrowly allowed the state to continue to censor films, it determined that "a state may not consistently with constitutional guarantees ban a film on the basis of a censor's conclusion that it had a character that came within the scope of those words."[73] The Kansas attorney general asked for a rehearing of the case but was denied by the U.S. Supreme Court on December 5, 1955.[74]

The Kansas Board of Review of Motion Pictures lost its biggest case with *The Moon Is Blue*. Not only did the U.S. Supreme Court decision challenge the wisdom and fairness of the board, but the various legal challenges also contested the right of the board to exist in the first place. From 1954 on, the Kansas Board of Review would find itself on shaky ground with distributors, producers, and Kansas politicians.

A seismic cultural shift was occurring in the United States in the mid-1950s. A free-floating sense of discontent was impacting popular forms of art in many different ways. The emergence of rock and roll was emblematic of this challenge to traditional morality. As the head of the Chicago Crime Prevention Bureau put it, "The obscene material that is flooding the Nation today is another cunning device of our enemies, deliberately calculated to destroy the decency and morality which are the bulwarks of society."[75] The Supreme Court, under the direction of Earl Warren, transformed the American legal system, as an expansion of civil rights and civil liberties occurred under judicial protection. As conservative Americans feared that communists and pornographers were brainwashing the minds of American youth, under the protection of the Supreme Court, the Kansas Board of Review remained as an agency poised to stop this threat.

---

72. Ibid., Motion to Dismiss.
73. *Holmby Productions v. Vaughn*, 350 U.S. 870 (1955).
74. Ibid., 350 U.S. 919, 76 Supreme Court 193, 100 L. Ed. 805.
75. Paul S. Boyer, *Promises to Keep: The United States since World War II*, 139.

Eleven

Jane Russell, Brigitte Bardot, and Ephraim London as the Enemy, 1954–1959

The people of Kansas felt that their state was under attack in 1954. This was the year of the groundbreaking Supreme Court decision of *Brown v. Topeka Board of Education*, which nullified the separate-but-equal doctrine of *Plessy v. Ferguson*. Historian Craig Miner claims, "The *Brown* case marked not only the end of segregation in schools but also be the beginning of a new day in social relations beyond the school, in Kansas."[1] It was also the year in which numerous motion picture companies sued the state, contesting prior censorship. In 1954, the Kansas State Board of Review found itself under legal attack by three separate film distributors. These "new social relations," therefore, included a contested notion that a handful of Kansas bureaucrats had the right to keep the rest of the state population from viewing the films that they wanted to see.

Although most of the controversy and national attention were centered on *The Moon is Blue*, there were two other censorship cases in the court system at the same time. One of these involved the Howard Hughes–produced film *The French Line* (1954) starring Jane Russell. The film was essentially a burlesque musical, designed as an excuse to show off Jane Russell's anatomy.

---

1. Miner, *Kansas*, 345.

Filmed in 3-D, the film's advertising was loaded with sexual innuendo including, "Jane Russell in 3 dimensions—and what dimensions" and "It'll knock both your eyes out." The film suffered from a vacuous and thin plot line with comic numbers that were not really funny and song and dance routines that were remarkably wooden. But the film was one long sexual tease, and male viewers certainly got an eyeful of Jane Russell. Throughout the film, the actress and a number of supporting characters wear low-cut evening gowns and bathing suits. Hughes had his favorite actress in scanty costumes in order to sell his product. In the grand musical finale, Russell belts out a risqué number titled "Lookin' for Trouble" in which she bumps, shakes, and grinds wearing nothing more than a glorified bikini. *Harrison's Reports* claimed, "Her violent wiggling and movements are indeed scandalizing." Apparently, in the publicity campaign surrounding the film, even Russell was offended by the costume, asking Hughes to cut some of the footage.[2]

The French Line was one of the last films handled by Joseph Breen in his role as chairman of the Production Code Administration. At this point, Hughes was Breen's nemesis as a result of *The Outlaw*, and any film produced by the legendary millionaire was bound to be scrutinized. In late 1953, the PCA denied *The French Line* a seal because "it was quite apparent" that the "costumes were intentionally designed to give the bosom peep-show effect beyond even extreme de'colletage and far beyond anything acceptable under the Production Code."[3]

During the script analysis, Breen had warned Hughes's studio, RKO, the producers of *The French Line*, "We direct your attention to the need for the greatest possible care in the selection and photography of the dresses and costumes of your women. The Production Code makes it mandatory that the intimate parts of the body, specifically the breasts of women, be fully covered at all times."[4] Hughes knew that Russell's breasts sold pictures. The primary objection of the PCA to the film was the costuming, with the secondary issue being the dialogue.

As historian Gregory Black has pointed out, Hughes's reaction was "novel." Rather than fight Joseph Breen or ask for a review by the MPAA Board of Directors, Hughes simply scheduled the premiere of the film for the Fox Theater in St. Louis, Missouri, on December 29, 1953. Hughes flooded the large Catholic city with an all-out publicity assault for *The French Line*.[5]

2. Review of *The French Line*, *Harrison's Reports*, January 2, 1954, 2.
3. Memorandum, *The French Line*, January 13, 1954, PCA files for *The French Line*, MPAA, AMPA.
4. Breen to William Feeder, March 25, 1953, in ibid.
5. Black, *Catholic Crusade*, 137.

The Kansas Board of Review demanded that Jane Russell's final production number in *The French Line* (1954), in which she wore this costume, be stricken from screens in Kansas. (Permission granted by Photofest)

Whereas United Artists was not a member of the MPAA when *The Moon Is Blue* was released, RKO was at the time *The French Line* premiered. Hughes had taken control over the financially strapped company the previous year. Technically, according to the PCA, this meant that the RKO could not release the film without a Code seal.

The Legion of Decency and the Catholic hierarchy went into overdrive to condemn the film. Archbishop Joseph E. Ritter claimed that because "no Catholic can with a clear conscience attend such an immoral movie, we feel it is our solemn duty to forbid our Catholic people under penalty of mortal sin to attend." The Catholic magazine *Commonweal* stated, "The picture is a blatant exploitation of sex, exceeded in its vulgarity only by the advertising campaign."[6]

By the time *The French Line* had reached the Kansas State Board of Review, it had become a scandal. On February 3, 1954, the board informed RKO Radio Pictures that the film would be approved if Russell's final dance scene was eliminated. Hughes, never willing to compromise with the censors, refused, and on April 1, 1954, RKO brought suit against the board.[7]

Just after the suit was filed, the film was submitted for reexamination. The board used the revised censorship statute as justification for denying the film entrance into the state. Chairman Frances Vaughn wrote Jim Lewis, the manager of RKO Distributing Corporation, "We wondered if there had been any change in your instruction and would you consider elimination of the dance [Russell's infamous "Lookin' for Trouble" number]? If so we would pass the picture."[8] Even as RKO was threatening the board legally, the members found themselves willing to compromise.

On September 30, 1954, following a second reexamination, Vaughn wrote Jim Lewis, "Please be advised that said film is again disapproved for the reasons that it is sexually immoral, obscene and indecent. The actions of Miss Jane Russell in conjunction with the song she sings in her dance scene in Reel 6-B, together with her too brief and revealing costume portray deliberately and sexually immoral acts between male and female persons." But, once again, the board promised that if the final number was cut, the film would be approved.[9]

RKO delayed the Kansas case pending the outcome of a similar legal challenge in the state of Ohio. The Ohio censorship board had found the

6. Ibid., 138; *"The French Line,"* *Commonweal,* July 17, 1953, 428.

7. *RKO Radio Pictures v. Vaughn,* Docket no. 89313-A (Wyandotte County District Court), 1954, Plaintiff's Petition.

8. Vaughn to Jim Lewis, n.d., Box 58-05-04-13, 1951–1955 File, KSBR Correspondence, KSHS.

9. Ibid., September 30, 1954.

film obscene, and a trial court upheld the board's decision. Hughes's lawyers appealed the case to the Ohio Supreme Court. On December 1, 1954, in a landmark case, the court, in a five-to-two ruling, found that the state censorship statutes and resulting decision making did not meet the implied test of a restrictive and clearly drawn statute that had been called for in the *Burstyn* decision.[10]

The favorable ruling did not mean that Hughes was in the clear. Many major studio chains, including RKO theaters, which were no longer connected to the studio as a result of the *Paramount* decision, refused to book the film. Although Hughes claimed victory in Ohio, he still faced expensive legal challenges in Pennsylvania, Kansas, and New York. Unwilling to lose the lucrative New York City market, Hughes cut some of the more objectionable parts of the film. The "cut" film was acceptable to the Kansas Board of Review, so the case was dropped.[11]

Another RKO picture, *Son of Sinbad* (1955), was contested in court. *Variety* called the film a "fanciful fantasy of the sex and sand variety—no better and no worse than most of the almost countless such films which has preceded it." But *Son of Sinbad* received much more publicity, considering its minimal production costs, due to a number of factors. The Catholic Legion of Decency condemned the film, claiming, "This film in its character and treatment, is a serious affront to Christian and traditional standards of morality and decency because of its blatant and continuing violation of the virtue of purity." What had the Legion of Decency so hot and bothered were the "grossly salacious dances" and "indecent costuming" of the female characters. One of the main attractions of *Son of Sinbad* was Lili St. Cyr. She was one of the most famous strippers in the nation when the film was released. The fact that a stripper could be a film star was perhaps too much for the Legion to take. It asserted, "This picture is a challenge to decent standards of theatrical entertainment and as an incitement to juvenile delinquency, it is especially dangerous to the moral welfare of youth." Of course, the publicity that the Legion gave to *Son of Sinbad* had "the paradoxical effect of turning it into a moneymaker of medium proportions," according to *Variety.*[12]

10. *RKO Radio Pictures v. Department of Education,* 162 Ohio St. 263 (1954), 122 N.E. 2d 769.

11. *RKO Radio Pictures v. Vaughn,* Docket no. 89313-A (Wyandotte County District Court), Order of Dismissal.

12. Review of *Son of Sinbad, Variety,* May 31, 1955; PCA file on *Son of Sinbad,* MPAA, AMPA; review of *Son of Sinbad, Variety,* May 31, 1955.

On March 15, 1954, the Kansas Board of Review demanded the following eliminations from the film: "Eliminate entire dance in reel 1, entire dance at end of reel 2 and two entire dances in reel 4. Dance in Reel 1 where dancers are obscene because of public display of their bodies and their suggestive movements. Dance in reel 2 with dancer, moving muscles of her body in suggestive manner and when she reclines on floor and rolls down steps in a vulgar display. In reel 4 where dancer is nearly nude and the swinging of her callipygian charms as she arises."[13]

RKO once again brought suit against the state. The board, in answer to RKO's petition, changed its reason for disapproval and cited the law as the authority.[14] Like *The French Line, Son of Sinbad* had been released without a PCA Code Seal of Approval. The dance sequences had been contested in several other localities, and Hughes decided to compromise rather than face an extended legal challenge. Some 40 to 60 percent of the dance sequences were eliminated.[15] Again, with the objectionable scenes in the film eliminated, the case against the Kansas Board of Review was dropped.

Prior to 1954–1955, the Kansas Board of Review had completed its work with little public attention. The media storm surrounding *The Moon Is Blue* changed that. The State of Kansas was beginning to incur hefty legal bills due to studio attempts to challenge motion picture censorship in the state. In January 1955, a contingent of Republican lawmakers saw fit to abolish the board. On January 26, Republican Howard Bentley (R–Edwards) and Paul Nitsch (R–La Crosse) introduced House Bill 62, which would require television stations to submit their films to the board. Although this was not an impossible scheme, the goal of the legislation was to focus attention on the inappropriateness of film censorship in the state. The bill was sent to the House Judiciary Committee, where it was killed.[16]

Several months later, the board narrowly missed being axed. The Board of Review was literally saved by a technicality. Disgruntled legislators decided to kill film censorship in a roundabout way. The Senate Judiciary Committee introduced a bill to repeal an obsolete car registration act. When the bill was sent to the House Judiciary Committee, an attachment was added that was

---

13. PCA file on *Son of Sinbad,* censorship report for Kansas, March 31, 1954, MPAA, AMPA.
14. *RKO Radio Pictures v. Vaughn,* Docket no. 89579-A (Wyandotte County District Court), Defendant's Answer.
15. U.S. Congress, Senate, Judiciary Committee, Juvenile Delinquency (Motion Pictures) Hearing Before Subcommittee to Investigate Juvenile Delinquency, 84th Cong., 1st sess., 1954, p. 49.
16. *Kansas House Journal,* 1955, 74.

a repeal of motion picture censorship in the state. After a conference committee of the house and senate, the repeal was passed by both Kansas houses of legislature and sent to Governor Fred Hall for his signature. The governor signed the bill on April 6, 1955, and the Kansas Board of Review was scheduled to permanently close its doors on July 1, 1955.[17]

The bill was passed so quickly through both judiciary committees that one would assume there was near-universal acceptance of the repeal. This was not the case—procensorship forces simply did not have enough time to mount a significant challenge to the bill. Behind the scenes, the women of the Kansas Board of Review were caught off guard. A February 1, 1955, feature on them by the *Kansas City Star* was perhaps a sign of things to come. The author of the piece reported that Frances Vaughn was accustomed to hearing from numerous Kansas citizens that her job was "pretty soft, looking at movies all day."[18]

In the first few days of April, the governor was flooded with telegrams and letters begging him not to sign the censorship-repeal bill. The Johnson County Women's Republican Club asked the governor to please veto Senate Bill 222. Pointing out that "the [Board of Review] is self supporting and a small source of revenue," the women proclaimed, "We want clean pictures for our children." Telegrams from the Archdiocese Council of Catholic Women, Sumner High School PTA, Knights of Columbus, Business and Professional Women's Club of Kansas City, and the Reverend J. Russell Brown of the First AME Church of Kansas City begged the governor not to dissolve the board. Perhaps Claude F. Pack, president of the Home State Bank of Kansas City, Kansas, said it most eloquently:

> Speaking for a wide circle of parents and grandparents located in the area I express the hope that you will see fit to veto Senate Bill 222 repealing the Kansas State Board of Review for Motion Pictures. With all the filth on the magazine racks of the country today there is no assurance that the independent movie producers will not continue to use such filth on the movie screen. It would be a great mistake to eliminate the safety valve and face the consequences of an unrestricted distribution of the stuff that comes out of the independent producers' studios.[19]

17. Ibid., 355.
18. "Women on the Job," *Kansas City Star,* February 1, 1955, Clipping File, KSBR, KSHS.
19. Johnson County Women's Republican Club to Governor Fred Hall, telegram, April 4, 1955; Claude Pack to Hall, April 4, 1955, both in File 9 (Box 27-15-06-02), Records of the Governor's Office, Governor Fred Hall, 1955–1957, KSHS.

The split in the Kansas population regarding motion picture censorship reflected the split in supporters and detractors of Joseph McCarthy, the communist witch-hunter. Historian Richard Kluger describes 1950s Topeka as a town that "viewed with alarm almost anything that smacked of liberalism or foreign infiltration of the Topekan psyche."[20] Cold war fears led many Kansans to believe that traditional morality was under assault. More liberal Kansans, though, were unwilling to have a select group of political appointees determine what was artistically offensive.

One interesting fact is that the Johnson County Women's Republican Club knew that the Kansas Board of Review was self-supporting. How were they privy to that information? The spearhead of the campaign to defeat the repeal of film censorship in Kansas was led by . . . Mrs. Frances Vaughn, chairwoman of the Kansas State Board of Review. Clearly, Vaughn was looking out for her job and those of her colleagues. State controller Ray Shapiro sent a stern warning to Vaughn on April 12, 1955, because she had authorized people to make telephone calls and send telegrams in the interest of her "fight to save censorship." On top of it, Vaughn wanted the state government to pay for these telephone calls and telegrams. Shapiro warned Vaughn that they "cannot be interpreted as having been incurred in accordance with law and regulations under which your agency is authorized to function."[21] Thus, Vaughn was stuck with the bill.

As Vaughn and her fellow censors planned on closing the doors of their office following the governor's signature on the repeal of the motion picture board, a movement was afoot to challenge the constitutionality of the bill. The challenge was not to the substance of the bill but to the manner in which the bill was passed. According to Article 2, Section 16, of the Kansas Constitution, legislative enactments were limited to one issue. Combining car registration with motion picture censorship was deemed to be a violation of this article. On May 18, 1955, Attorney General Fatzer filed a "friendly suit" in Shawnee County District Court, seeking an injunction against Secretary of State Paul R. Shanahan from publishing the act. Publishing the act would have made it official.[22] On May 14, 1955, the attorney general was denied his request. Judge Dean McElemy declared that the secretary of state was obli-

20. Miner, *Kansas*, 345.
21. Roy Shapiro, controller, to Vaughn, April 12, 1955, Box 58-05-04-13, KSBR Correspondence, KSHS.
22. Gaume, "Suppression of Motion Pictures in Kansas," 55.

gated and duty bound to publish the bill. Fatzer then appealed to the Kansas Supreme Court. On June 17, the court issued a memorandum opinion, claiming that the bill was void because it violated the state constitution.[23] The board was less than two weeks from being abolished. Many predicted that it was on its death knell and would soon be abolished either legislatively or judicially by the courts. Surprisingly, it lasted eleven more years.

One of the principal reasons the board was allowed to continue to function was that procensorship supporters began to marshal their forces. The Legion of Decency certainly stepped up its presence in the state this year. On June 3, 1955, the *Eastern Kansas Register,* the Catholic newspaper of the eastern half of the state, published an editorial titled "Where Is the Legion?" The editorial was later reprinted as a broadside and distributed throughout the state. The editorial claimed that within the past six weeks, five pictures that had been condemned by the Legion were playing in local theaters in Kansas City, Topeka, and throughout the archdiocese. These films included *The French Line, The Moon Is Blue, One Summer of Happiness* (1952), *Karamoja* (1954), and *Game of Love* (unknown date). But in this editorial, the Legion leaders not only came after the film distributors and theater owners but the "secular press" as well. The editorial claimed that the *Kansas City Star, Topeka Daily Capital,* and *Topeka Journal* "carry large movie advertisements selling sex and violence under the false guise of entertainment." The author claimed that these newspapers were "some of the "greatest offenders against the forces of decency in the archdiocese." The editorial was a "call to arms" among Kansas Catholics, reminding them to stay local to their Legion pledges, writing in protest to newspapers that advertised films with a C (Condemned) rating, and staying away from such films by "GIV[ING] THEM THE OLD BOX-OFFICE TREATMENT."[24]

As the board fought for survival in 1955, it faced a number of challenges in regard to provocative new films that were submitted for its approval. *Glen or Glenda* (1953), the infamous Ed Wood cult classic, was submitted to the board this year. The film dealt with transgender issues and was an impassioned defense of sexual diversity. The board promptly banned it "because the theme of the picture, which goes into detail on the changing of the sex of either man or woman by surgery, would tend to debase or corrupt morals." *I Want a Baby* (1952) was a latecomer in the live-birth genre and was disapproved because of

---

23. *State of Kansas v. Shanahan,* 178 Kan. 400 (1955), 286 P.2d 742.
24. "Where Is the Legion?" reprint from *Eastern Kansas Register,* June 3, 1955, Box 58-05-04-13, KSBR Correspondence, KSHS.

nudity and live births. *Naked Amazon* (1955) and the aforementioned *Karamoja* belonged to the genre of aboriginal nudity films. Both were clearly exploitation shockers, meant to capitalize on the "primitive" nudity of the local people. But the board took contradictory stances on such films. Whereas *Naked Amazon* was rejected in part "because of extreme nudity," *Karamoja,* which featured scenes of a Ugandan tribe, was allowed.[25]

In May 1955, the board had publicly proclaimed that nudity was forbidden on Kansas movie screens. Possibly, this was because of a rash of nudist pictures making the rounds of exploitation distributors. On May 18, 1955, the board was trapped by its own public proclamation. Mrs. Maria Pack of Newton wrote chairwoman Vaughn to say that she had personally seen *Karamoja* at the 81 Drive-In Theater in Wichita on May 2. She noted that the film was also playing at two other Wichita drive-ins. Pack explained that "the movie contained numerous scenes in which men were entirely nude showing the pubic area just as plainly and matter-of-fact as the rest of the body."[26] The film's distributors capitalized on the full-frontal male and female nudity as part of their exploitation strategy. Pack said there was a full house the night she saw the film.

It is difficult to figure out where the Kansas Board of Review drew the line on screen nudity in 1955. Films like *Striparama* were condemned because of their nudity or because they were "sexually immoral" and appealed to prurient interests.[27] *Karamoja* may have been allowed because it was filmed by an anthropologist, whereas *Naked Amazon* was only masking its seriousness. But clearly, hundreds of Kansans drove out to the 81 Drive-In in Wichita, Kansas, on May 2 to sneak a peak at the forbidden; it was doubtful if many of those in attendance that night were there for educational purposes.

Frances Vaughn's days as board chairman were numbered. Her naïveté in running a state board in a professional, businesslike matter was beginning to be an embarrassment for controversial governor Fred Hall. For one thing, she sent a recommendation to the state legislature asking that the reviewing fee be increased from $1.25 to $3.00 a reel, a 240 percent increase. Film distribution companies, which already considered the censorship scheme a headache, were sure to balk.[28] This recommendation, coupled with her attempt to be reim-

25. Disapproved Features and Shorts, Box 35-6-5-12, KSBR, KSHS.
26. Maria Pack to the KSBR, May 18, 1955, Box 58-05-04-13, 1951–1955 File, KSBR Correspondence, KSHS.
27. Disapproved Features and Shorts, Box 35-6-5-12, KSBR, KSHS.
28. Gaume, "Suppression of Motion Pictures in Kansas," 57.

burscd for communications to save the board in the first half of 1955, eventually led to Hall's decision not to reappoint her. Rather than face such public embarrassment, one of the longest-serving chairwomen of the Board of Review submitted her resignation on January 18, 1956. Her position was assumed by Leawood resident Mary Cook.

Under Cook, the board continued on its slippery slope of problematic decision making. Whereas United Artists's *Sins of the Borgias* (1953) was condemned because it portrayed nudity, *Fruits of Summer* (1955) was disallowed "because the picture was indecent and immoral," with a "low moral theme throughout."[29]

In 1957, the board found itself under attack by the state legislature and the press. Both the *Wichita Eagle* and the *Hays Daily News* ran editorials in February attacking the Board of Review. The editorialist in the *Wichita Eagle* claimed, "Although the Kansas Board has been relatively gentle recently with the censorship hatchet, it still embodies a theory that is not in harmony with democratic principles of freedom." The paper argued that there were other avenues: "Hollywood has its own self-regulating agency, the Breen office. . . . [B]esides there are other watchdog organizations such as the Catholic Legion of Decency which keep zealous watch on the products of the movie industry." The *Hays Daily News* asserted, "There never has been any point to a state board of movie censors. A picture that may appear obscene to one member will not seem objectionable to another member. . . . The Kansas board can do little more than make recommendations. It is about as useful as the vermiform appendix of homo sapiens."[30]

The newspaper editorials critical of censorship were largely a response by newspapermen to growing criticism of the board by members of the Kansas legislature. Members of the legislature and the press were concerned that the board "impose[d] a considerable expense on the state." Its services cost the state more than $30,000 a year yet the board was losing more and more power.[31] On February 14, 1957, Senator Fayette Rowe (R-Columbus) proposed Senate Bill 186, designed to end the Board of Review. The bill was killed in committee, but the anticensorship legislator tried twice more to kill the board. In the house, a bipartisan coalition of representatives proposed

29. Disapproved Features and Shorts, Box 35-6-5-12, KSBR, KSHS.
30. *Wichita Eagle,* February 23, 1957, A6; "Movie Censors Useless," *Hays Daily News,* February 25, 1957, 2.
31. "Movie Censors Useless."

House Bill 334, which would have abolished censorship but prohibited the exhibition of obscene motion pictures. The bill was narrowly defeated on a roll-call vote of sixty-eight to fifty-four. There were extensive hearings on film censorship in the house chambers.[32] Chairwoman Cook testified before the house and gave several examples of provocative pictures that would have been exhibited in the state without the actions of the Board of Review.

In 1957, the United States Supreme Court ruled in one of its most important cases involving First Amendment rights and matters of obscenity. By a narrow five-to-four majority, the Court ruled that "obscene" material had no protection under the First Amendment. Known as the *Roth* decision, the Court argued that guarantees of the freedom of expression were never meant to be absolute protection for every possible utterance. The Court effectively ruled that a work should be considered as a whole, not on the basis of isolated passages, in determining whether it was "obscene." Justice William Brennan, writing for the majority, suggested a standard for determining what would and would not be considered obscene:

> Sex and obscenity are not synonymous. Obscene material is material which deals with sex in a manner appealing to prurient interest. The portrayal of sex, e.g. in art, literature and scientific works, is not itself sufficient reason to deny material the constitutional protection of freedom of speech and press. . . . [I]t is therefore vital that the standards for judging obscenity safeguard the protection of freedom of speech and press for material which does not treat sex in a manner appealing to prurient interest.

The test of obscenity was whether "to the average person, applying contemporary community standards, the dominant theme of the material taken as a whole appeals to prurient interest."[33] Thus, community statutes outlawing obscenity were maintained.

The *Roth* decision, announced on June 24, 1957, should have had a substantial impact on the operations and procedures of the Kansas State Board of Review. The Court was addressing the broad constitutional question of whether obscenity laws were legitimate exercises of governmental police powers. Since "obscenity" was one of the major rationales given for banning or censoring a film, the *Roth* decision was critical.

32. *Kansas Senate Journal,* 1957, 115.
33. *Kansas House Journal,* 1957, 307.

The Kansas Board of Review largely ignored the decision, though, apparently believing that since the case dealt with a purveyor of magazines and books and not motion pictures, it did not pertain to the board. Instead, the board used the *Burstyn* opinion as its standard: "Motion pictures are not necessarily subject to the precise rules which govern other methods of expression."[34] The problem was that this was not a standard or a constitutional guideline but a broad, sweeping statement that basically let the board operate on its own designs.

This series of landmark Supreme Court decisions regarding freedom of speech drew public attention to the Board of Review and to the standards by which it judged films. The question of criteria was pertinent, as Hollywood was loosening its standards of self-censorship in the guise of the Production Code Administration. On December 11, 1956, the MPAA announced a revision of the Production Code. Formerly forbidden subjects such as abortion, childbirth, and drug addiction, all issues heavily censored by the Board of Review in the past, could now be presented, with certain restrictions, in Hollywood movies.[35] This put the Board of Review in a predicament. The board had often used the PCA as a guideline to films that would or would not be allowed in the state. Films without a PCA seal—*The Moon Is Blue, The French Line,* and most exploitation films—were forbidden from the state. Now the Board of Review had to either loosen its own standards to fit the revised PCA Code or come under increased scrutiny as it utilized its plastic set of guidelines.

In December 1957, thirty-one Kansas legislators made a tour of four state agencies in Kansas City in preparation for a budgetary session. The headquarters of the Board of Review was one of their stops. Although the conversation initially began around budgetary matters, it increasingly turned on the administrative and decision-making principles of the board, as reported by the *Kansas City Star*.[36] The visit was an impressionable one for the legislators but not in a positive way; instead, it demonstrated an antisystematic, antimethodical matter of decision making that smacked of Puritanism, simplemindedness, and philosophical naïveté. The legislators were often combative with the censors, testing their philosophy of review.

Earlier in the year, when House Bill 334 was introduced that would have terminated the board, Mary Cook rushed off a letter to Representative Clark

34. *Roth v. United States*, 354 U.S. 476; 77 S. Ct. 1304; L. Ed. 2d (1957).
35. *Burstyn v. Wilson*, 343 U.S. 495, 503; 72 Sup. Ct. 777, 781; 96 L. Ed. 1098, 1106 (1952).
36. Lev, *The Fifties*, 93.

Kuppinger, chairman of the House Affairs Committee. Arguing that there "is more need for a motion picture censor board than ever before," she claimed that "there is quite a little pressure being brought on us to pass pictures of obscene and immoral nature."[37] Examples included *Bedroom Fantasy* (1951) starring stripper Lili St. Cyr and the exploitation feature *Untamed Mistress* (1956). Both films were banned for the nudity they portrayed on the screen but also for the "low moral theme throughout the picture," a difficult statement to prove.[38] Cook acknowledged that some objectionable films, like *Bedroom Fantasy* and *Untamed Mistress*, were American-made. She was much more concerned, however, with foreign-made films that "never see a censor until they run into a State Board."[39] It was this category of foreign films that seemed to worry the censors the most. The immense popularity of Brigitte Bardot films and the realization that European films were more frank with their sexual content were causing hard-pressed distributors and theater owners to acquire "sexy" new foreign pictures for exhibition.

Gina Lollobrigida's *Woman of Rome* (1954) was one such picture forbidden from the state. The Italian feature was more than three years old but an example of distributor and exhibitor demand for foreign product. The overbaked melodrama was condemned by the board, not for nudity or overt sexuality but because of its "immoral theme throughout."[40] Lollobrigida's character is intimate with five men in the film and ends up having an illegitimate child. Since "no punishment is imposed" on the Lollobrigida character or the men, the film was banned.

In 1955, Otto Preminger and United Artists released *The Man with the Golden Arm*, which starred Frank Sinatra as a drug addict. The daring film was released without a PCA seal but demonstrated to the industry how badly its Production Code needed to be revised. *The Man with the Golden Arm* was not an exploitation film but a serious treatment of drug addiction and one of the key films that led to the Production Code's revision in December 1956.

The Board of Review, on the other hand, was unwilling to revise its standards. The André de Toth feature *Monkey on My Back* (1957) involves a prizefighter who becomes a drug addict. The board demanded major cuts

---

37. "Quiz Censor Board," *Kansas City Star*, December 17, 1957, 11, Clipping File, KSHS, KSBR.
38. Mary Cook to Rep. Clark Kuppinger, chairman, House Affairs Committee, March 6, 1957, Box 58-05-04-13, KSBR Correspondence, KSHS; Disapproved Features and Shorts, Box 35-6-5-12, KSBR, KSHS; Cook to Kuppinger, March 6, 1957.
39. Disapproved Features and Shorts, Box 35-6-5-12, KSBR, KSHS.
40. Ibid.

before the film was allowed in the state.[41] While the PCA was willing to change its rules regarding mature themes, the Kansas Board of Review refused to change its standards.

In the period 1955–1960, drive-in theaters were very popular in Kansas. Low real estate rates, the rural nature of the state, and an exploding teenage population made drive-ins a real competition to the standard urban picture house. Film distributors soon realized that teenage audiences did not want to see serious film fare but instead wanted thrillers, action-adventure pictures, and exploitation films. A taste of the forbidden was all too attractive to teenage audiences who were willing to pay money to see on the screen what they could not talk about with their parents. As a result, film distributors pulled exploitation stalwarts like *The Story of Bob and Sally* and *Mom and Dad* out of the mothballs, anxious to show the decade-old films to a generation that had never heard of them. *The Story of Bob and Sally* offended the Kansas censors in numerous ways. Chairwoman Cook claimed, "We refused to pass this picture as it had a low moral theme throughout—too sexy, intimate relations, childbirth also the function of male and female sex organs, also nudity."[42] The board also rejected the picture *Mom and Dad* on December 26, 1957 (again), on the grounds that it violated the board's rule against the portrayal of human birth. This time, though, the distributors decided to file suit against the board, presumably based on a legal climate that was increasingly more circumspect toward prior censorship.

Mom and Dad was originally released in 1945. It had been banned by the Kansas Board of Review (with the various combinations of membership) numerous times. *Mom and Dad* was the most successful pre-1960 exploitation film of any kind; by early 1957, it had grossed eighty million dollars worldwide.[43] Although certainly a forgotten film today, *Mom and Dad* was a phenomenon in the 1950s. The board objected to a number of features in the film, including a pictorial lecture on venereal disease, a description of the menstrual cycle and conception, and a scene of natural childbirth.[44] In a letter to Senator August Lautarbac, chairman of the Senate Ways and Means Committee, chairwoman Cook argued, "*Mom and Dad* [was] disapproved because it showed actual *Child Birth*. It is against our Laws to pass scenes of

---

41. Cook to Kuppinger, March 6, 1957.
42. Schaefer, *Bold! Daring! Shocking! True!* 197.
43. Gaume, "Suppression of Motion Pictures in Kansas," 62.
44. Cook to August Lauterbac, March 9, 1957, Box 58-05-04-13, KSBR, KSHS.

childbirth. Do you honestly think such pictures are proper for theaters where people, young and old, go for entertainment?"[45] Cook, again, demonstrated her lack of knowledge regarding operating procedures. There were no "laws" on the Kansas books not allowing childbirth scenes on film—they were simply self-imposed standards the board had adopted. During the decade of the 1950s, film producers and distributors increasingly recognized that censorship criteria, like those of the Kansas Board of Review, would not necessarily be recognized by the judicial system. They, therefore, began to challenge such standards through the courts.

Mom and Dad did have a long history of attempted censorship throughout the nation. Authorities in Newark, St. Louis, and the state of New York attempted to keep the film out of their localities. In 1956, Capital Enterprises acquired the distribution rights for the film and maintained a willingness to contest prior censorship. Almost simultaneously with the board's rejection of *Mom and Dad* on December 26, 1957, it received a letter from Ephraim London, a New York lawyer representing Capital. London had earned a national reputation for successfully arguing for plaintiffs in obscenity cases, his most famous success being the *Burstyn* decision before the U.S. Supreme Court.[46]

Ephraim London had become the board's *bête noire* in the mid-1950s. The members were apparently well aware that they were playing with a major league hitter with London. At least six different titles were sent by London to the board in the mid-1950s requesting reexamination of films that had been previously censored. In each case, the board rescinded their recommendations, either partially or totally. The board found itself in a difficult position in 1957–1958. If the members chose to fight such contests legally, hefty fees would result. Many members of the Kansas House and Senate were looking for any excuse to eliminate the board, and financial reasons, in the guise of saving taxpayers' money, would be sufficient. So each time the board bent to the prominent lawyer, his successes became its failures.

London began on a conciliatory note with the board regarding *Mom and Dad*. He agreed to eliminate the venereal disease discussion. This would leave the menstrual chart and childbirth scenes, but perhaps London believed this would be a well-intended concession.[47] The board responded by explaining that the film could not be passed with the childbirth scene intact. The film

45. Ephraim London to KSBR, December 23, 1957, in ibid., M File.
46. Hazel Runyan to London, December 26, 1957, in ibid.
47. Fatzer to Runyan, April 28, 1958, in ibid.

was reviewed again on April 28, 1959, and this time Capital agreed to eliminate the menstrual chart scene. Even with this second concession, the board would not budge.[48] The childbirth scene was the drawing card for Capital. Advertising promised "You actually SEE the birth of a baby."[49] The scene showed, just did not talk about, a forbidden subject, and the exhibition of female genitalia, even during childbirth, would be titillating for some audience members. Capital knew that the childbirth scene could not be eliminated without *Mom and Dad* losing much of its "forbidden" credibility, yet the board was unwilling to contemplate childbirth as a form of entertainment.

Capital Enterprises responded by filing suit. London claimed that *Mom and Dad* was primarily "entertainment of the general public and though it contained certain episodes stressing educational matter and moralistic preachments, it was neither cruel, obscene, indecent, immoral or such as would tend to debase or corrupt morals."[50] The case of *Capital Enterprises v. the Kansas State Board of Review* was postponed pending another court decision involving the film in Chicago.

The chief of police in Chicago had forbidden the exhibition of *Mom and Dad* in his city and did not give reasons for his refusal. A federal district decision upheld the decision because the judge found the film "obscene and immoral if exhibited for entertainment."[51] The U.S. Court of Appeals reversed this decision, though, after viewing the film and found: "Our decision rests on narrow but firm grounds for we are satisfied there was absent any sound basis for outlawing the film and the absence of any reasons by the censors for this classification is a forboding guise for arbitrary censoring running afoul of the First and Fourteenth Amendments. . . . A social problem requires defining and that has not been attempted here. Consequently, this 'censorship' results in a curb of free expression."[52]

The Kansas case went to trial on February 9, 1959. The legal team for Capital demonstrated to the court the conciliatory nature of their relationship with the board and their willingness to delete scenes. They also established how extreme precaution had been taken not to expose any parts of the

48. Schaefer, *Bold! Daring! Shocking! True!* 106, 133–34.

49. *Capital Enterprises, Inc. v. Runyan, Stewart, and Frankovich, Members of the KSBR*, Docket no. 99523-A, March 5, 1958 (Wyandotte County District Court), Plantiff's Petition no. 2.

50. Carmen, *Movies, Censorship, and the Law*, 191.

51. *Capital Enterprises, Inc. v. Chicago*, 260 F. 2d 670 (1958).

52. *Capital Enterprises, Inc. v. Runyan*, Docket no. 99523-A (Wyandotte County District Court), Plaintiff's Petition, p. 2.

mother's body during the childbirth scene. Sheets had been strategically placed. Finally, the Capital legal team questioned how *Mom and Dad* could be exhibited in forty-five states without objection from concerned citizens.[53]

Citizens in Kansas were fully aware of the controversy over the film and wrote to the women of the board. A group of Bonner Springs mothers wrote Hazel Runyan, new chairman of the board:

> In view of the fact that J. Edgar Hoover of the FBI has stated salacious magazines and movies [such as *Mom and Dad*] are a contributing factor to the increase of juvenile delinquency, we find it extremely hard to understand how any decent person would put "pressure on the board" for such a movie. All of us who are writing these words of encouragement to you are young mothers, with children ranging from ages 1 to 12 and who are wondering WHAT our children will be viewing in a few years if trash such as *Mom and Dad* is passed now.

Teenager Martha Jo Woods wrote Runyan, "I . . . do not want to be shown this type of movie when I go to a show. I do not regard pictures such as these as entertainment and I do not feel that it would be worth my time to patronize such immoral shows. Therefore, I am in favor of banning these movies from public showing."[54]

One of Capital's arguments in the case was that the standards and mores of the people of Kansas were not apparently different from those of the people of other states in the Union. Was this true? How did most Kansans feel about films such as *Mom and Dad?* Although it is impossible to answer the latter question, several significant trends were impacting Kansas citizens. The baby boom generation was coming of age so that they could go to films by themselves. Parents were increasingly concerned that they would not be able to control what their children saw. Second, as in the early part of the century, many Kansans believed themselves under attack in the 1950s—assaulted by federal judges who were forcing them to change the social fabric of the state; by big-city liberals and intellectuals who were introducing books, films, and works of art that contested acceptable notions of decency; and by the cold war in which many feared that the communists would take over the world. This sentiment is indicated in the letter from the Bonner Springs

53. Various Bonner Springs, Kansas, women to Runyan, June 22, 1958; Martha Jo Woods to Runyan, June 19, 1958, both in Box 58-05-04-13, 1951–1966 File, KSBR Correspondence, KSHS.
54. Gaume, "Suppression of Motion Pictures in Kansas," 67.

mothers to the board. In some Kansans' minds, these threats and standards may have molded into one overarching paranoia. Although Kansas mores and standards may not have been apparently different from citizens of nearby states, they did have an outlet by which they could attempt to control some of these "outside" ideas—the Kansas State Board of Review.

On February 16, 1959, presiding judge O. Q. Claflin reported that he was ready to rule on the board's action. London at this time, though, threw the board and its lawyers for a loop when he asked to submit briefs in the case in which he would contest the constitutionality of the censorship statute. Suddenly, the case was much larger than the simple exhibition of *Mom and Dad*. The judge agreed to defer his decision.[55] Before the decision was announced, a compromise was reached. The board agreed to change its standards of censorship, and Capital withdrew its request that the court rule on the constitutionality of the censorship law.

Joseph H. McDowell, cocounsel for the board, and Attorney General John Anderson sat down with the board to discuss a new set of rules for operation. In this case, as opposed to the previous history of the board, the attorneys presented the new rules and led the discussion. The following guidelines were adopted:

1. Childbirth itself was not a sufficient basis to ban a film.

2. Unless the entire film, taken as a whole, appealed to prurient interest (that is, a shameful or morbid interest in nudity, sex, or excretion), they had no right to censor it.

3. The mere fact that the board did not think a film was proper entertainment, or did not like birth scenes to be in films, was not a basis to censor a film.

4. The only basis they had to censor a film was if it came within the "obscene" definition in the regulation.

5. On the advice of the attorney general the board revised its rule 18-1-22, the rule used to ban *Mom and Dad*, to comply with the *Roth* standards.[56]

The board then determined that within the meaning of General Statute 51-103, a film or reel was deemed obscene when to the average person, applying

55. Joseph McDowell to Runyan, February 23, 1959, Box 58-05-04-13, Rules and Regulations File, KSBR, KSHS.
56. Ibid.

community standards, the dominant theme of the material, taken as a whole, appeals to prurient interest, that is, a shameful or morbid interest in nudity, sex, or excretion, and if it goes substantially beyond contemporary limitations of candor in representation of such matters.[57]

As a result of these new guidelines, Judge Claflin ruled on March 5, 1959, that *Mom and Dad* was not obscene. He also struck down regulation 18-1-22 that had been adopted by the Board of Review on March 15, 1954, that attempted to define both the standard of obscenity and the words *obscene* and *obscenity*. Judge Claflin found this regulation "invalid and contrary" to the law.[58]

The board complied with the court's decision, but Runyan, not fully understanding the limits of her duties, claimed that she would recommend that *Mom and Dad* be shown for adults only. This was, however, beyond her legal capacity as chairman.

The *Mom and Dad* judicial decision had an impact on another film in legal limbo—*The Strange Case of Dr. Laurent* (1957). This French film, distributed by Trans-Lux, caused fits for the PCA, the Legion of Decency, and the Kansas State Board of Review. The semidocumentary film showed a "detailed, prolonged and full length view of an actual childbirth" that climaxed the picture.[59] The problem with *Dr. Laurent* was not the exploitative potential picture—it was quite the opposite. The film blended fictional characters with an earnestness that called for new treatments of pregnancy to reduce the pain of childbirth. The PCA originally would not give the film a seal because it would not allow "sex-hygiene" pictures, but even Geoffrey Shurlock, head of the PCA, admitted after the decision, "The more I think over the *Dr. Laurent* situation, and consider the favorable reviews the picture has received, with specific commendation of the treatment of the birth scene, the more I am convinced that we goofed in rejecting it."[60] The Legion of Decency, usually a much more conservative and heavy-handed arbitrator of screen decency, actually placed *Dr. Laurent* in a special category, believing the film would be instructive for medical students.[61] For the first time, the Legion did not condemn such a film. The Kansas Board of Review did not ban the film in total-

57. Gaume, "Suppression of Motion Pictures in Kansas," 68.

58. Shurlock to Sidney Ginsberg, Trans-Lux Distributing Corporation, June 19, 1958, MPAA file on *The Strange Case of Dr. Laurent*, AMPA.

59. Shurlock to Kenneth Clark, July 3, 1958, in ibid.

60. Richard Brandt, Trans-Lux Distributing Corporation, to Shurlock, July 1, 1958, in ibid.

61. Runyan to Trans-Lux Productions, September 12, 1958, Box 58-05-04-13, 1951–1966 File, KSBR Correspondence, KSHS.

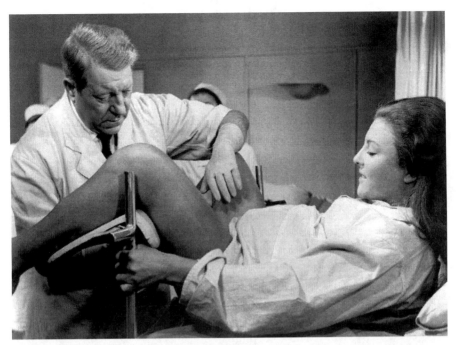

When the Kansas Board of Review was forced to approve *The Strange Case of Dr. Laurent* (1957), Hays residents responded by demanding that the show be closed down in their city. (Permission granted by Photofest)

ity but recommended that the distributor cut a scene "where a man puts his hands on his wife's breasts" and that the entire finale—the childbirth scene—be cut.[62] Following the reversal of the board's prohibition of human births on the screen, they had no choice but to approve *Dr. Laurent.* Trans-Lux had waited to see the outcome of the *Mom and Dad* case, unwilling to spend money on legal fees when the situation might have been resolved by another court decision.

The Strange Case of Dr. Laurent did not play in Kansas without a stir, though. In Hays, the film was canceled due to public pressure. The Reverend E. Loyal Miles, pastor of the First Methodist Church, said the banning of *Dr. Laurent* resulted from "general public reaction." In a threatening tone, he declared that there had not been an organized movement against the film, but there "would have been by nightfall had not the theater manager called off the

62. "Reaction Causes Hays to Ban Film," *Topeka Daily Capital,* May 19, 1960, 28.

show."[63] The minister pointed out that the opposition included both Protestant and Catholic clergymen and the Hays Parents-Teachers Association.

One of the major challenges facing the Board of Review in the period 1958–1959 came in the shapely figure of Brigitte Bardot. Columbia Pictures acquired an art-house distributor, Kingsley Productions, which it used for U.S. distribution of Bardot's films. The breakout year for the sexy, wildly popular French actress was 1958, when she made the list of the top-ten money-making actors and actresses that year.[64]

The women of the Board of Review did not know what to do with the pictures of the infamous sex kitten. Bardot's titillating feature *And God Created Woman* (1957) was originally condemned by the Kansas State Board of Review, then resubmitted and approved in January 1959 after the distributor eliminated a bedroom sequence in which the actress rose from bed, revealing her nude body. *The Night Heaven Fell* (1958) was also banned because of "extreme nudity," then later approved with eliminations. *The Girl in the Bikini* (1959) was approved once "all close up views of nudity of girls in bikini bathing suits" were taken out of reels 1–3. In *Love Is My Profession* (1958), the censors eliminated dialogue, including a scene in which Brigitte asks her boyfriend to come to bed, and he replies, "I'm not in the mood."[65]

Bardot was a symbol (and in some Kansans' minds the cause) of all that was wrong with modern culture. One Dodge City native, Mrs. Bernard Smith, managed to link Bardot's provocative screen fare to juvenile delinquency in the state. She wrote to the board, "I believe a lot of these teenage gangs, barn parties such as Wichita has had, beer parties that have been discovered here in our own town, games of chicken in cars, break-ins and etc. are a result of a lot of the trash put into movies that our children see. Bridgette [*sic*] Bardot is a disgrace even for adult entertainment let alone teenage children." Mrs. Smith verified this statement with little proof: "I don't go to a movie very often. In fact, maybe twice a year," but she stated, "Movies may have to be banned from Kansas altogether—but even that would be better than making our future into juvenile delinquents."[66]

Other European actresses gave the board problems as well. The 1953 French-Italian feature *Flesh and the Woman* was distributed by United Films in

63. "Top Ten Moneymakers Poll, 1958," *International Motion Picture Almanac (2000)*, 15.
64. Disapproved Features and Shorts, Box 35-6-5-12, KSBR, KSHS.
65. Mrs. Bernard Smith to KSBR, November 17, 1959, Box 58-05-04-13, 1951–1966 File, KSBR Correspondence, KSHS.
66. Disapproved Features and Shorts, Box 35-6-5-12, KSBR, KSHS.

Brigitte Bardot caused many headaches for the Kansas Board of Review in the late 1950s. One Kansas citizen blamed her films for juvenile delinquency! (Permission granted by Photofest)

1958 and sent to the board for approval. The film was all Gina Lollobrigida as she played dual roles as a cheating wife and a prostitute. The film was heavily censored by the board. Britain's answer to Marilyn Monroe, Diana Dors, starred in *Room 43* (1958)—a picture that was condemned as "immoral throughout" but allowed to play by the censors "for adults only."[67] Chairman Hazel Runyan was apparently not aware of the limits of her power—she could not classify films specifically for adults. *The Strange Case of Dr. Laurent* got the same tag.

In the period 1955–1960, film distributors began to challenge the board by simply not submitting films to them before they were exhibited. All films were to be reviewed by the board and then stamped with a serial number before they could be exhibited in the state. The board began having problems as early as 1956 when multiple prints of *Lady and the Tramp* (1955) were distributed throughout the state without tags affixed to all of the reels.[68] Certainly, *Lady*

67. Fatzer to Vaughn, October 11, 1955, Box 58-05-04-13, 1951–1966 File, KSBR Correspondence, KSHS.
68. Gaume, "Suppression of Motion Pictures in Kansas," 69.

and the Tramp, a Disney animated classic, was not going to be a film that the Board of Review was going to censor, but the distribution of reels without stamped serial numbers set a dangerous precedent for other film distribution companies. In October 1955, the board had raised its review fee from $1.00 to $1.25 for feature films. Some distributors just stopped submitting films for review, hoping to save the censorship fees.

As the board increasingly came under public attack by members of the legislature and by lawsuits by film distributors, the bypassing of the review process became bolder. The board realized that if they did not crack down on distributors' illegal actions, they would lose all credibility. The board sent a stern warning letter to film distributors in August 1957 reminding them of their legal responsibilities.[69]

In August 1957, Kenneth Beasley, chairman of the Committee on Economy and Efficiency for the Kansas Legislature, reported that in the previous twelve months, approximately thirty-two hundred reels had been distributed in the state without serial numbers. This was costing the state more than $4,000 in lost revenue. As the legislature was preparing the 1958 budget, this revelation put the Board of Review under certain scrutiny. Another warning letter was sent out in September 1958, but the board compounded the problem in December when it raised its reviewing rate from $1.25 to $1.75, a substantial increase. Illegal, uncensored films continued to flow into the state until the attorney general began to take action. First, he threatened to confiscate all films without the Board of Review serial number. Second, he threatened to take distributors and exhibitors who were violating the law to court. Between 1959 and 1961, at least four suits were filed against the guilty parties, including two Dickinson theaters: the Shawnee Drive-In in Shawnee and the Dickinson Theater in Mission. The Junction Theater in Junction City and the Midway Theater in Paola were also prosecuted.[70]

By 1959, the legislative opposition to the board's existence continued. Three successive bills were proposed, but none were successful. Senator Fayette Rowe proposed Senate Bill 80, but it was killed in committee. A bipartisan contingent of representatives proposed House Bill 231, but it went down to

---

69. *State of Kansas v. Dickinson Operating Co.,* Docket no. 7722 (Johnson County Magistrate Court), 1959; *State of Kansas v. Dickinson Operating Co.,* Docket no. 8060 (Johnson County Magistrate Court), 1959; *State of Kansas v. American International Pictures,* Docket no. 6743 (Geary County Court), 1961; *State of Kansas v. Filby,* Docket no. Cr 3812 (Miami County District Court), 1961.

70. *Kansas Senate Journal,* 1959, 86.

defeat. House Bill 333, proposed by Representative Jay Johnson (R-Beloit) found his bill halted by the State Affairs Committee.[71] Despite the growing opposition to state-mandated motion picture censorship in Kansas, supporters still had enough strength to hold on to the system.

The press weighed in on the issue, too. A *Hays Daily News* editorial titled "Movie Censorship Unnecessary" claimed, "Kansas needs a board of movie censors as much as a newspaper needs a public relations director. The movies under the 'czar system' of censoring its own pictures has, on the whole, done a credible job since it was established many years ago. This is one of few states which censors motion pictures. It is useless duplication of record."[72] This "duplication" referred to the work of the Production Code Administration.

One clear-cut example of the "necessity" for film censorship in the minds of many Kansans was the introduction of "nudity" films into the state. Although nudist films had been around for decades, the genre was revived in 1954 when Walter Bibo produced *The Garden of Eden,* the first color feature on the topic. The film was shot at the Lake Como Club, a nudist resort in Florida. The flimsy narrative concerns a young widow who takes her daughter to a nudist camp in order to get away from a troublesome father-in-law. Although *The Garden of Eden* is demure by today's standards, the producers and distributors used exploitation ballyhoo to intrigue thousands of Kansas citizens. The press book for the film included behind-the-scenes information, testimonials from nudists, and full-page color spreads of the film's topless star.[73] Nudist films were guaranteed moneymakers.

The Garden of Eden had been submitted for review in 1957 but had been banned by the board.[74] The distributor of the picture, Excelsior Pictures, believed that the revision of censorship standards following the *Mom and Dad* decision would allow previously banned films the ability to be exhibited in the state. The board considered *The Garden of Eden* an entirely unacceptable film and banned it again.[75] On August 18, 1959, Excelsior brought suit against the board, citing a New York Court of Appeals case. In *Excelsior Pictures Corporation v. Regents of the University,* both the appellate division and

71. *Kansas House Journal,* 1959, 116, 168.

72. "Movie Censorship Unnecessary," *Hays Daily News,* January 30, 1958, Clipping File, KSBR, KSHS.

73. Schaefer, *Bold! Daring! Shocking! True!* 300–301, 109, 130–31.

74. Disapproved Features and Shorts, Box 58-05-04-13, KSBR, KSHS.

75. Runyan to Excelsior Pictures, March 22, 1959, 1951–1966 File, Box 58-5-4-14, KSBR Correspondence, KSHS.

the New York Court of Appeals had declared that *The Garden of Eden* was not obscene and that a license for the exhibition of the film be ordered.[76]

The case in Kansas went to trial on October 14, 1959. O. Q. Claflin, the judge in the *Mom and Dad* case, also presided in this case. He ordered that briefs be submitted in both cases. One intriguing factor is that both the plaintiff and the defendant cited the *Roth* decision but for differing reasons. The board cited the obscenity test in the *Roth* decision: when, "according to the average person, applying our contemporary community standards, the dominant theme of the material taken as a whole appeals to prurient interest," then the film would effectively be considered "obscene."[77] Less than six months prior, the board had adopted the *Roth* standards for its own standards. Members of the board argued that "the contemporary community standards of the average person residing in the Midwest are different from the contemporary standards of an average person living in Massachusetts or New York."[78] This was an old argument that dated back to at least the 1920s, and the board was resurrecting it to save its case. The lawyers for Excelsior claimed, "All ideas having even the slightest redeeming social importance—unorthodox ideas, controversial ideas, even ideas hateful to the prevailing climate of opinion—have the full protection of guarantee unless excludable because they encroach upon the limited areas of more important interests."[79] Although the board claimed that it was an accurate barometer of community standards, Excelsior cited a Massachusetts decision claiming *The Garden of Eden* was not obscene.[80]

The case of *Sunshine Company v. Summerfield* also came up in the arguments of the plaintiff and defendant. In this case, the Supreme Court reversed a lower court decision that had held that the sending of nudist magazines through the mail was unlawful. Producers and distributors of nudist films attempted to have it both ways—they claimed that such pictures were purely educational and not meant to appeal to prurient interests, but they were willing to use exploitation strategies to sell their product. Excelsior claimed that "the only obscenity complained of were pictures of naked men, women and children" and that there was no additional textual or dialogue equivalent to "comment" on the action.[81] The

76. *Excelsior Pictures v. Regents of the State University of New York*, 3 N.Y. 2d 237, 240; 165 N.Y.S. 2d 42, 44; 144 N.E. 2d 31–33 (1960).

77. Ibid., Docket no. 2943-B, Memorandum of Defendant.

78. Ibid., 7.

79. Ibid., Docket no. 2943-B, Memorandum of Plaintiff, p. 6.

80. *Commonwealth of Massachusetts v. Moniz*, 336 Mass. 178; 143 N.E. 2d 196 (1957).

81. *Excelsior Pictures v. Regents of the State University of New York*, Docket no. 2943-B, Memorandum of Plaintiff, p. 2.

board took the strategy of trying to nullify the *Sunshine* decision, arguing that it was rendered per curiam, without explanation.

On November 2, 1959, the Kansas Board of Review finally got a break when it won its case against Excelsior. The court said: "The state of Kansas does have the right to censor and prevent the showing of motion pictures that are obscene; that the statute as presently drawn sets forth the proper test for determining obscenity; and that the statute is drawn with sufficient clarity and definitely to meet the requirements of the law in that respect. The Board of Review did not arbitrarily and capriciously nor did the Board abuse its discretion in refusing to grant approval to said film."[82]

Walter Bibo, the producer, found himself simultaneously engaged in litigation involving *The Garden of Eden* in municipalities and states throughout the country. Surprisingly, he won a number of these cases, but the high legal fees claimed a great deal of the profit he was making from his film. Bibo appealed to the Kansas Supreme Court, but the case kept getting postponed. Excelsior finally ran out of money, and the distributor's attorneys withdrew from the case because they were not getting paid. On May 10, 1963, the case was finally dismissed.[83]

As the 1950s came to a close, the board found itself challenged with an onslaught of adult themes, dialogue, and situations in both Hollywood mainstream and independent exploitation films. Questions of improper sexuality made the board nervous. In *Bonjour Tristesse* (1958), a Columbia feature starring David Niven and Deborah Kerr, a scene in which a young couple are romantically entangled underneath a beach umbrella was eliminated. In the John Saxon film *Cry Tough* (1959), a scene with a young man and woman in bed was eliminated.[84]

Language was increasingly becoming a problem. Eartha Kitt's debut in *Anna Lucasta* (1958) included the words *slut, ass,* and *damn you,* which the censors exorcised. In *God's Little Acre* (1958), Robert Ryan's exclamation "By God!" was not considered acceptable because he took the name of the Lord in vain. In *Room at the Top* (1959), the word *bitch* was eliminated.[85]

Although the board was becoming increasingly hesitant about condemning films outright—it did occur. *The Isle of Levant* (1952), *Back to Nature* (1955), and *Hideout in the Sun* (1960), all films with explicit nudity (but not

82. Ibid., Journal Entry of Judgment, p. 2.
83. Gaume, "Suppression of Motion Pictures in Kansas," 75.
84. Box 35-06-05-13, B File, C File, KSBR, KSHS.
85. Ibid., A File, G File, R File.

overt sexuality), were withheld until the court made the decision on *The Garden of Eden*. Joseph McDowell wrote the board about *The Isle of Levant:*

> [It] is actually a travelogue with no dialogue so that only the part that could be questioned was the scenes in the last few reels showing the nudist camp. The only completely nude bodies were infant children, which were not obscene, and a few adults when in swimming scenes. The balance of the shots showed exposed female breasts. Hence this film gets us down to the simple question of whether showing the human figure, with breasts exposed, is obscene. Every museum in the world displays statutes of the nude human body. The existence of nudist camps are not illegal. We have them in Kansas, Missouri, and in many parts of the world.[86]

McDowell's letter reflects some of the fundamental challenges the Kansas Board of Review faced as the 1950s came to a close. As motion pictures became increasingly more realistic and attempted to deal with modern problems, the board had difficulty in changing its mind-set. The Hollywood confection of happily-ever-after films that dominated studio fare in the 1930s and 1940s was now being challenged by directors and writers who were attempting to reflect the world and by studios who were witnessing their film attendance nose-dive. Filmmakers were using dialogue that reflected how people talked in the real world and depicted sexuality, the carnal aspects of romance, and the pleasures of the nude human body. Although there was always a persistent exploitative element in some of these productions, it was becoming increasingly difficult for the courts and censorship boards to determine what was "adult" and what was "obscene." The 1960s would make that challenge even more severe.

Perhaps the clearest sign that the world was drastically changing was an event that took place on the final day of the 1950s. On December 31, 1959, the film version of D. H. Lawrence's notorious novel *Lady Chatterley's Lover* was ordered by a court decision to be allowed to be exhibited in the state.[87] The novel, which was considered an exemplar of immorality and obscenity, had been filmed and was to play on Kansas film screens. The world had changed.

86. McDowell to KSBR, September 21, 1959, Box 58-5-4-5, 1951–1995 File, KSBR Correspondence, KSHS.

87. *Kingsley International Pictures v. Runyan,* Docket no. 3593-B (Wyandotte County District Court), 1959, Journal Entry of Judgment.

Twelve

The Final Years of Film Censorship, 1960–1966

John Anderson Jr. was governor of Kansas from 1961 to 1965, the waning years of the Kansas State Board of Review. The early 1960s were a time of economic growth and development in the state, and Kansans enjoyed a high standard of living, like most Americans. This era was also one of enormous change that sometimes frightened Kansas citizens. The threat of Soviet expansionism and communism fueled the development of organizations like the John Birch Society in the state. In 1962, in the case of *Engel v. Vitale*, the U.S. Supreme Court handed down a decision making prayer in public schools unconstitutional, and this matter generated a great deal of alarm among the more conservative citizens of Kansas.[1] The Kansas Board of Review also found itself reined in by the Supreme Court, and this frustrated its members.

On Valentine's Day 1961, the women of the Kansas Board of Review wrote Kansas citizen Mrs. Hilma E. Peterson.

> We too are concerned about the type of pictures being produced as we
> realize the majority of the audience in the theaters today is composed of

---

1. State Agency Records, Governor's Office, State Archives Finding Aids, John Anderson, 1961–1965, Administrative Sketch, KSHS.

young people. The Board would certainly like to do more but our power is limited to one word—"Obscenity," A copy of our new ruling (handed down by the Supreme Court) is enclosed and you can see their definition of "Obscenity" is entirely different from the Webster's Dictionary.

We have regarded some pictures in their entirety and made eliminations in others but after reading the ruling you will understand our laws are not very strong. If you and others are interested would you contact your representatives and senators and perhaps something could be done to strengthen them.[2]

By the early 1960s, the Kansas Board of Review was finding its powers increasingly limited by the decisions of the United States Supreme Court. In the period 1953–1961, the Supreme Court heard six licensing cases, and in each case the powers of the censors were further reduced. Many of these were per curiam decisions (usually one-sentence anonymous opinions). The Court continued to strike down the provisions of state and local censorship. In 1961, the basic question of whether it was constitutionally permissible to even have local censorship of motion pictures reached the Supreme Court. This case was *Times Film Corporation v. Chicago.* This was a test case in which the distributor, Times Film Corporation, refused to submit the film *Don Juan* (a film version of Mozart's opera *Don Giovanni*) to the Chicago police commissioner for review as required by municipal law. The City of Chicago responded by not granting *Don Juan* a license for exhibition, and the distributor sued. The film had nothing objectionable about it and was purposefully chosen by the distributor because it was based on a classic and widely respected work of art.

On January 23, 1961, in a five-to-four decision, the Supreme Court upheld the constitutionality of the Chicago censorship ordinance that required distributors to submit their films to the board before they could be publicly exhibited in the city. After a lengthy succession of Supreme Court cases that slowly whittled away the powers of state and local censorship boards, the *Times Film* decision was looked upon as a victory for advocates of censorship. At question in the case was whether film distributors and exhibitors had complete and absolute freedom to screen any motion picture that they wished. The majority of the Court argued that obscenity was clearly not protected by the Constitution. Justice Tom Clark, speaking for the majority, argued that "the capacity for evil may be relevant in determining the permissible scope of

2. KSBR to Mrs. Hilma E. Peterson, Box 58-05-04-13, KSBR Correspondence—General Public, KSHS.

community control." Clark also warned censors that this did not mean that they had the ability to censor something that they found distasteful.[3] The judges in the minority questioned why motion pictures should be treated differently from other mediums of expression when it came to prior restraint. Earl Warren, writing for the minority, contended that the decision "presents a real danger of eventual censorship for every form of communication, be it newspapers, journals, books, magazines, television, radio or public speeches."[4] This created a great deal of alarm among media groups, fearful that local, state, and federal authorities might backpedal when it came to First Amendment freedoms. The present chair of the Kansas board, Mrs. Dorothy Frankovich, believed that the *Times* decision would result in the establishment of censor boards in other states.[5] As Richard Randall points out, though, the number of films rejected by the Kansas board in the period 1961–1963 dropped by two-thirds, demonstrating the limited powers of the board.[6]

Many of the cases coming to the Supreme Court concerned obscenity and motion pictures. They reflected a rapidly changing American culture. Contrary to popular opinion, the sexual revolution did not begin in the mid-1960s. As illustrated by the screen, a loosening up of sexual mores was already present in American society in the 1950s and early 1960s.[7] The Production Code had been amended in the 1950s to allow producers to depict the illegal drug trade, abortion, prostitution, and kidnapping. In late 1961, Geoffrey Shurlock, head of the MPAA, also gave directors the freedom to deal with "sex perversion" (homosexuality) due to a recent number of films that considered this theme.

This loosening of sexual standards had a direct impact on the activities of Kansas censors. In 1960, the Kansas Board of Review most frequently censored displays of female flesh. Perhaps inspired by the enormous popularity of Brigitte Bardot pictures, in which the French sex kitten often romped in the seminude, American independent producers and even some mainstream film companies began pushing the envelope regarding the display of the female body. The British film *Expresso Bongo* (1959), which starred Laurence Harvey and Sylvia Sims, was described as "sleazy" by the *New York Times*.[8] The film was

3. Jowett, "Significant Medium," 269.
4. *Times Film Corporation v. City of Chicago*, 365 U.S. 43; 81 Sup. Ct. 391; 5 L. Ed. 2d 403 (1961).
5. "Sees Rise of Censors," *Kansas City Times*, January 24, 1961, Clipping File, KSBR, KSHS.
6. Randall, *Censorship of the Movies*, 40.
7. Patterson, *Grand Expectations*, 359–60.
8. Review of *Expresso Bongo*, *New York Times*, April 13, 1960.

approved by the board, but only after eliminations in which scenes with dancing girls, some with only pasties over their breasts, were removed from the film.
Love by Appointment (1960) was also edited, because in several scenes dancers
were shown stripped to the waist. *She Walks by Night* (1960), a lurid melodrama
about prostitution, was originally banned by the board but later passed after
extensive editing. The board demanded the following eliminations:

> Reel 3A—In Rosemarie's manager's bedroom where he grabs her breast
> and kisses down the side of the neck to the breast.
>
> Reel 3B—Rosemarie standing by window in her apartment in which
> there is a close-up of her nude picture hanging on the wall.
>
> Reel 4A—Where Rosemarie gets out of bed, goes to bathroom door,
> turns her back to bedroom and her buttocks is exposed.
>
> Reel 5A—Where Rosemarie drops her fur coat and her nude body is
> exposed.

Some films with displays of nudity were considered unsavable. The board
banned *They Wore No Clothes* in 1960 because of "extreme nudity."[9]

The jurisdiction of the board was also at stake as the 1960s began. Universities began exhibiting motion pictures for the purpose of entertaining their
students. These films, along with 16-millimeter educational films, were frequently shipped from New York distributors without the seal of approval of
the board.[10] The members of the board sent several warning letters to these
institutions of higher learning. Little was accomplished in this realm, though,
after the attorney general wrote Kitty McMahon, new chairwoman of the
board, questioning how the board would possibly maintain censorship over
the exhibition of 16-millimeter films in schools and clubs.[11]

Between 1953 and 1961, there had been nine legislative attempts to abolish the Kansas Board of Review. The final attempt took place on January 18,
1961, when Senate Bill 9 went to the Federal and State Affairs Committee.
Less than a week later, the *Times Film* decision was handed down, convinc-

9. Correspondence—E, Correspondence—L, Correspondence—S, Correspondence—T, Box
58-05-04-13, KSBR, KSHS.

10. KSBR Minutes, April 11, 1961, Box 58-05-04-14, KSHS.

11. Attorney General William M. Furguson to Kitty McMahon, May 15, 1961, Attorney General File, Opinion no. 61–185, KSHS. Kitty McMahon, Republican vice chairwoman for Wyandotte County, replaced Dorothy Frankovich, Democratic appointee of former governor George
Docking. The position of censor continued to be a politically motivated appointment through the
1960s; it was part of the patronage system.

ing lawmakers that there was still judicial and popular support for motion picture censorship. The bill later died in committee.[12]

John Anderson's administration prioritized the streamlining of state government in Kansas, though. This plan of bureaucratic modernization put the board in a very precarious position since it appeared to be a governmental organization with little teeth and limited responsibility.[13]

The early 1960s witnessed the strong presence of European art-house cinema. The public accolades, popularity, and influence of films such as *Two Women, The Virgin Spring, The Entertainer, Saturday Night and Sunday Morning*, and *La Dolce Vita*, all released in 1960, were remarkable. As foreign film imports began increasing, the Production Code became increasingly irrelevant since foreign films were not produced and distributed by major Hollywood studios; therefore, they could be freely exhibited without the seal of approval. There was also a strong demonstration that European cinema dealt with adult subject matter in a way that was not necessarily salacious or titillating. All of the above films were sexually daring when compared to contemporary Hollywood releases. British, Swedish, French, and Italian cinema proved that films could be frank and not considered exploitative. As film historian Paul Monaco has argued, "These films sometimes faced censorship problems, but they represented the fictionalized treatment of sex in ways considered more mature, complex and sophisticated than anything permitted by the Hollywood code."[14] The success of these films also demonstrated that there was indeed a market for this type of film. Foreign films competed against Hollywood for both international awards and box-office receipts.[15]

Saturday Night and Sunday Morning was representative of the late-1950s and early-1960s British "kitchen sink" dramas that depicted the lives and hardships of the working class. Albert Finney plays Arthur, a twenty-two-year-old Midlands factory worker who works hard during the week but "drinks, brawls, and plays practical jokes" at the local pub on Saturday night. Arthur has an affair with the wife of a coworker whom he impregnates. When his lover's husband, Jack, learns of the affair, Arthur is beaten senseless. He accepts his punishment and returns to his old girlfriend, Doreen, who has traditional ideas about marriage and sex. The *New York Times*

12. *Kansas Senate Journal*, 1961, 26.
13. State Agency Records, Governor's Office, State Archives Finding Aids, John Anderson, 1961–1965, Administrative Sketch, KSHS.
14. Paul Monaco, *The Sixties: History of the American Cinema*, 69.
15. Hall, *Crossroads*, 50–53.

described *Saturday Night and Sunday Morning* as a "remarkably graphic picture" with a "smoldering of social rebellion as well as sheer lustfulness."[16] In May 1961, the board condemned the film because it was "considered obscene both in theme and dialogue." Laurence Olivier's Academy Award–nominated performance in *The Entertainer* was also hacked by the censors. In the introduction of the film, bare-breasted dancers were shown four times and this section was severely edited.[17]

Ingmar Bergman's masterpiece *The Virgin Spring* was also robbed of critical scenes in its narrative. *The Virgin Spring*, Bergman's first Oscar-winning film, is a medieval allegory of superstition, religious faith, and revenge. The pivotal event of the narrative, which directs the rest of the action in the film, is the rape of a fifteen-year-old virgin girl by two goat herders. When the parents of the young girl discover the crime, they seek revenge upon the rapists. The Kansas censors forbade the use of the word *bastard* in the film and also forced the elimination of the rape scene according to "our rules on obscenity."[18]

Federico Fellini's Academy Award–winning *La Dolce Vita* was a major trend-setting film that chronicled a decadent society imbued with sex and alcohol. Marcello Mastroianni plays a would-be tabloid reporter who spends his time in a series of meaningless relationships, watching a human carnival of excess around him. The constant parties and debauchery make the protagonist world-weary and jaded. Although the Kansas censors may have objected to the overall tone of the film, there was little they could do by 1960–1961 since it would be problematic to object to *La Dolce Vita* in its entirety due to its renown. Instead, they censored the language of the film, including phrases such as "Hi bitch," "I want to amuse myself like a whore," and "That bitch is in love with you."[19]

The internationally respected film that caused the board the most problems was Vittorio De Sica's *Two Women*. Sophia Loren, who won a Best Actress Oscar for this role, among a number of other awards, plays an Italian mother, Cesira, who is trying to survive with her daughter in war-torn Italy. This semi-neorealist film had a romantic triangle between mother; her daughter, Rosetta; and Michele (Jean-Paul Belmondo). The most striking and controversial scene in *Two Women* is one in which mother and daughter are raped by a group

---

16. Review of *Saturday Night and Sunday Morning*, *New York Times*, April 4, 1961, 44:2.
17. Correspondence, File S, Box 58-05-04-13, KSBR, KSHS.
18. KSBR, "Report for August 1961," PCA file for Kansas, MPAA.
19. Ibid.

of Moroccan soldiers. In a number of horrifying close-ups, the anguish and degradation of the rapes are violently apparent on Rosetta's face. The Kansas Board of Review asked for relatively mild cuts in the film. They asked that *Two Women* be cut shortly after the rape when Rosetta "pulls out her breast" and says, "You can have this milk if you want it. I don't need it any more."[20] The producers of the film, Embassy Pictures, refused to cut the scene, arguing that it was vital to the picture and would disrupt the overall impact of the narrative. Embassy filed suit against the board on October 26, 1961. The case was settled out of court when the board rescinded its objection. The cost of defending such decisions was becoming troublesome to the board. The case was dismissed, and the order of dismissal said that the decision was erroneous because *Two Women* showed "an actress exposing a portion of her breast to the camera [that] is not obscene in accordance with the statutory standards."[21]

In the period 1961–1962, the Kansas Board of Review had three major categories of objectionable items that it frequently censored from films. First, the increased use of obscenities in both European and American films was shocking to the censors and, apparently, some Kansas film patrons. The board forbade the use of the words *bitch* (*Blood and Roses,* 1960), *whore* (*Never on Sunday* [1960]), and *slut* (*Angel Baby* [1961], *Divorce—Italian Style* [1961]).[22] Mrs. Leon Stokes of Dodge City reflected the negative reaction to the new frankness in language in film. She wrote the board, "I used to be a fan of Gary Cooper. He has been my idol since I was a child. I took my children to see one of his movies the other evening and I got the thrill of my life. Yes, it sent a chill or something through me because he said 'to Hell with it Damn man what do you think this is.' Since then I haven't been to a movie that hasn't used Hell and Damn in it."[23]

As previously mentioned, nudity continued to be a problem for the board. It tended to deal with this issue in one of two ways. Films in which nudity was the main attraction tended to be banned altogether. One such example was *Not Tonight, Henry* (1960), a "nudie-cutie" film that revolved around a man who could not interest his frigid wife in sex. In this innocuous sexploitation comedy, Henry turns to great historical sexpots like Cleopatra and Lucrezia Borgia to satisfy himself. The film was structured so that half-naked

20. McMahon to George Regan, August 29, 1961, Correspondence, File T, Box 58-05-04-13, KSBR, KSHS.

21. *Embassy Pictures Corporation v. McMahon,* Docket no. 9397-B (Wyandotte County District Court), 1961; ibid., Order of Dismissal, p. 2.

22. Box 58-05-04-13, KSBR, KSHS.

23. Mrs. Leon Stokes to KSBR, November 17, 1959, Box 58-05-04-13, KSBR Correspondence, KSHS.

women would run in and out of the scenes. The censors banned *Not Tonight, Henry* because of its "vulgar theme and extreme nudity throughout."[24] *The Nudist Story* (1959) suffered a similar fate and was rejected in its entirety.

In other features, where nudity may have been a selling point for the film but not the central motif that tied the film together, scenes could be cut and the film could still be exhibited in the state. In *Ritual of Love* (1961), a scene of a woman bathing in the nude beneath a waterfall was exorcised.[25] In *Nude in His Pocket* (1957), a statue comes to life and bounces into the arms of the leading male character, exposing her breasts; the board demanded this scene cut. In *Heat of Summer* (1959), the board ordered the elimination of "all nude scenes where Lena undressed on the beach and wades into the water, comes back and embraces Robert."[26]

The board failed to recognize the overall intention of filmmakers when nudity was projected onto the screen. The value in featuring nudity in anthropological documentaries was lost on the board. In the summer of 1961, the documentary feature *The Sky Above, the Mud Below* was released. The film illustrates "an expedition back to the Stone Age on an unforgettable adventure in the jungles of Guinea." The producers promised "head-hunting cannibals" in a "visually stunning epic of man against nature."[27] The documentarians also promised the primitive New Guineans in their natural state—nude. The board rejected *The Sky Above* in its entirety because "of the extreme male nudity throughout."[28]

Embassy Pictures filed suit against the board on August 22, 1962. The board once again rescinded a previous decision, not wanting to be dragged back into court. The board agreed to approve the film but requested that *The Sky Above* be advertised as a documentary on primitive life. Just as the board did not have the legal ability to determine the classification of films for adults or all audiences, they also did not have the legal right to tell film distributors how to advertise their films. The Academy Award–winning documentary played on Kansas screens.

Depictions of overt sexuality were the third troubling element that the Kansas board frequently censored in the period 1961–1962. *Cold Wind in*

24. Disapproved Features and Shorts, Box 35-6-5-12, KSBR, KSHS.
25. Ibid.
26. PCA file on Kansas censorship, 1961, MPAA, AMPA.
27. *The Sky Above, the Mud Below,* http://www.rottentomatoes.com/m/sky_above_mud_below/about.php.
28. Correspondence—File 2, Box 58-05-04-14, KSBR, KSHS.

August (1961) was rejected in its entirety in the summer of 1962 "because of lustfulness throughout." The film told the story of a tenement boy (Scott Marlowe) having an affair with a stripper (Lola Albright). The lobby card for *Cold Wind in August* advertised it as "strange and sensual . . . a teen-age boy and a mature woman, each searching for a special kind of love in the most exciting yet tender picture in your 'best picture' experience!" Lola Albright was featured on the film poster in what appears to be a cross between a Wonder Woman and a striptease outfit. Kansas's board was not the only censorship apparatus that banned the film—the board received a letter from Sergeant Robert Murphy, commanding officer of the Chicago Censor Section, that his municipality had also banned the film.

The Allied Artists film *Angel Baby* caused real problems for the board. The film was a seedy exposé of the faith-healing racket. Stage actress Salome Jens plays a mute girl whose speech is restored by a crooked traveling evangelist played by George Hamilton. Angel Baby is then exploited on the evangelical circuit by a series of corrupt individuals. In November 1961, the board received a letter of protest from Kansas citizen Beth Elaine Diehm regarding the picture. Included was a petition signed by a number of people of Parker, Kansas, protesting the exhibition of the film. The mixture of religiosity and sexuality was apparently too much for some of the citizens of the fair city of Parker.[29]

The citizens of Kansas were apparently not aware of the legal limbo in which the board found itself in the early 1960s. Although it had the ability to censor some of the more "objectionable" motion pictures and specific scenes in films, it found itself increasingly with its hands tied, as foreign, independent, and major motion picture studios began to produce increasingly adult fare. *The Interns* (1962) was a glossy soap opera, an updated *Dr. Kildare* with a young cast. The film depicts the challenges that would-be doctors face as they compete for internships before they can actually practice their profession. One of the key scenes in the film is a wild New Year's Eve party complete with alcohol, loud music, dancing, and a drunken stripper. The board made minor deletions in the film but allowed the film to be released. Kansas citizen Mrs. Lila Mazanec wrote to the board on September 25, 1962:

> On Sunday evening I took my two children to a local theater to see The Interns. I had read the advertising and there was no stipulation that it was for adults only.

29. Ibid.

I found this movie appalling for a child of twelve years old. The picture showed the birth of a baby, a wild party, the pregnancy of an unmarried woman trying to get an abortion. If the public remains apathetic to the movies showing these kinds of movies without some censorship, I am afraid our children will pay a large price for the revenue which the movies are taking in.

Chairman Kitty McMahon responded: "We are in receipt of your letter of September 25, 1962 regarding the picture 'The Interns' and agree with you that this picture is for adults only. The Board does not classify the films to be shown in Kansas. They are either approved, approved with eliminations or rejected in their entirety. We were able to make an elimination in the dialogue in this particular movie but could do nothing more as our censors powers are limited."[30] By 1962, a disconnect was taking place between what some Kansas citizens believed that the Kansas Board of Review had the power to accomplish and what its actual limited powers were.

Italian cinema had a significant impact on Hollywood filmmaking in the post–World War II era. Neorealist films such as *The Bicycle Thief* (1949) used nonprofessional actors filmed in real locations to give cinema a real sense of authenticity. American films such as *On the Waterfront* (1954) and *Edge of the City* (1957) were influenced by Italian neorealism, using nonactors and New York and New Jersey locations to lend this sense of verisimilitude. In the early 1960s, a second wave of Italian films such as *La Dolce Vita, Divorce—Italian Style, Boccaccio 70* (1962), and *8½* (1963) became enormously popular in the United States, and not just on the art-house circuit. These films dealt with marriage, divorce, carnality, and sexuality in a sophisticated and often hilarious way and Hollywood stood up and took notice.[31]

So did various instruments of film censorship across the nation. All of these Italian films were met with resistance by the Kansas Board of Review. However, in the last few years of the board's existence, it did everything possible to avoid legal entanglements. This strategy was used for several purposes. First, the members of the board realized that their jobs were insecure. There had been numerous legislative attempts in the previous decade to eliminate the Kansas Board of Review in totality. Expensive legal representation

30. Mrs. Lila Mazanec to KSBR, September 25, 1962, Correspondence—File I, Box 58-05-04-13, KSBR, KSHS; McMahon to Mazanec, September 28, 1962, Correspondence—File 1, Box 58-05-04-13, KSBR, KSHS.
31. William H. Phillips, *Film: An Introduction*, 263–66.

was only one more incentive to discontinue the board. Second, the members realized that the judicial stakes were against them as decision after decision at the municipal, district, and federal levels seemed to be decided in favor of the plaintiff.

A significant example of the board's eagerness to reach compromise with the motion picture industry were the Federico Fellini films *La Dolce Vita* and *8½*. The board recommended the following cuts in *La Dolce Vita* when initially screening it:

1. Where the guest says to the girl, "Hi bitch," as a greeting.

2. Where Madeleine says to Marcello, "I want to amuse myself like a whore."

3. Where the blonde says to man, "That bitch is in love with you."

4. Where Emma tells Marcello, "Go back to your whores." Also she says, "I've always been a whore, all my life, and I'm not going to change now."[32]

The distributor of *La Dolce Vita* was Astor Pictures, and it was not willing to succumb to the board's decision. George P. Joseph, vice president of Astor Pictures, sent numerous favorable reviews of the film to the board and claimed that twenty-seven countries and every state and municipality in the United States had approved the film for exhibition.[33] He claimed, "The Kansas State Board of Review is the only group in the entire world which has found it advisable to recommend eliminations in the picture or the subtitles." The board would not back down, and numerous telephone calls went back and forth between New York and Kansas City. Finally, after weeks of negotiation with Mario Devecchi of Astor, the board agreed to give the film its seal of approval if the word *tramp* was substituted for *bitch* and *harlot* or *harlots* was substituted for *whore* or *whores*.[34]

Boccaccio 70 was an anthology of four short adult tales by four leading Italian directors, including Fellini, Vittorio De Sica, Luchino Visconti, and Mario Monicelli. Each playlet deals with sexuality in an intriguing way, and the bodies of Anita Ekberg, Romy Schneider, and Sophia Loren are fully on display. The board asked that the following cuts be made in *Boccaccio 70*:

32. McMahon to Mario Devecchi, September 6, 1961, General Correspondence—File L, Box 58-05-04-13, KSBR, KSHS.

33. Gaume, "Suppression of Motion Pictures in Kansas," 81.

34. George P. Joseph to McMahon, August 14, 1961; KSBR to Devecchi, September 6, 1961, both in General Correspondence—File L, Box 58-05-04-13, KSBR, KSHS.

The Kansas Board of Review's attempts to censor popular Italian films like *Boccaccio 70* in the early 1960s were largely unsuccessful due to the Supreme Court's limitations on the board's powers. (Permission granted by Photofest)

1. Where Dr. Antonio says to the men in the park, "Behave like men not like animals in heat." Eliminate "not like animals in heat."

2. Where Dr. Antonio says to man in office, "Build temples to whores." Eliminate the word "whores."

3. Eliminate scene of the extreme bobbling of nearly bare breasts on billboard girl as she runs.

4. Eliminate scene of the countess standing nude in the background.

5. Eliminate scene of the countess sitting nude by the bathtub.[35]

The legendary Ephraim London represented Embassy Pictures in this case, and the board knew it was in for a fight. London responded to the censors' recommendations on October 31, 1962, by informing them, "The distributor does not agree with your determination and is unwilling to make any

35. McMahon to Joseph, September 6, 1962, in ibid., B File.

cut in the picture that is not dictated by aesthetic considerations. It is our hope that you will agree, after reviewing the sequences in context, that none are obscene and that you will after reconsideration issue a license for the exhibition of the picture."[36]

London then masterfully refuted each of the recommended cuts with a philosophical and aesthetic argument. I quote him in depth to illustrate the strategy that distributors used to counter such censorship in the early 1960s. Regarding the "animals in heat" statement, London antagonistically argued,

> You are aware, of course, that Dr. Antonio was intended as a symbol or representation of the censor. In the statement objected to, Dr. Antonio rebukes a group of men for their inordinate interest in the photograph of a woman. His objection to the men reacting like "animals in heat" is in effect the same as the Review Board's objection to the sequence in question because it "arouses lustful desires." It is error to label Dr. Antonio's statement obscene as it would be to apply that term to the judgment of the Kansas State Board of Review.

Regarding the phrase "they build temples to whores," London pointed out that Ezekiel, chapter 33, used the same terminology and that "the Lord's word cannot be described as obscene, and I do not believe a statement of the same idea in virtually the same words in a film will justify its suppression."[37]

The physical sight of the "extreme bobbling of the nearly bare breasts" were those of Anita Ekberg who London argued was "extremely well endowed." The "bobbling" of her breasts was unavoidable, claimed the lawyer, and furthermore, "the movement of a part of her body cannot properly be the basis of objection." London mischievously argued, "No exception was taken to the views of Miss Eckberg [*sic*] reclining and I believe most normal men would agree that Miss Eckberg running is less likely to arouse lustful desire than Miss Eckberg in repose."[38]

In regard to the countess's nude scenes, London once again quotes the Bible, claiming she was seen standing nude "through a glass darkly." The argument was that she was barely visible and that any normal adult would not be aroused by the scene. The final objection was one in which the countess

---

36. London to KSBR, October 31, 1962, in ibid.
37. Ibid. London specifically used the phrase "arouses lustful desires" because this was the definition of the word *obscene* in the Kansas film censorship regulations.
38. Ibid.

stood nude in the bathroom. London claimed that only part of her body was visible and that this scene could "not be considered more objectionable than any of the others (not disapproved by the board) in which the Countess appears partially undressed."[39]

In summation, London used arguments of hypocrisy, religion, natural physicality, and inconsistency to refute the board's recommended cuts. The board dropped the first four cuts but demanded that the scene in which the countess is sitting on the bathtub, exposing her bare breasts, be eliminated. London countered once again in a letter on November 9, 1962. Using judicial precedent to defend the distributors, he argued that when judging a film obscene, one must consider its theme and "dominant effect." He claimed that the scene was not obscene in this context because it "does not exalt sex but on the contrary disapproves the Count's sensuality and his inability to accept his wife's love until it is offered under a venal arrangement."[40] The board refused to yield over this scene, and Embassy decided not to go to court and spend thousands of dollars over a breast scene.

8½ was Fellini's autobiographical masterpiece about the trials and tribulations of filmmaking. As director Guido Anselmi (played by Marcello Mastroianni) experiences an artistic crisis, his entire life seems to be collapsing around him. *8½* was the third film for which Fellini won an Academy Award. The board demanded minor cuts that revolved around the use of the word *whore*. Ephraim London, once again representing Embassy Pictures, claimed that the use of the word was not for "sensational effect" but that it was "necessary for the proper dramatic effect that the director wished to create."[41] The board reconsidered its decision and rendered that a scene in which one woman calls another a woman "a whore, that cow" would be allowed but one in which Guido tells Carla in the bedroom to "make a face like a whore" was not acceptable.[42] London charged the board with inconsistency, and it later rescinded its recommendations and passed the film.[43]

Pietro Germi's *Divorce—Italian Style* was an enormously successful comedy that won over popular audiences as well as garnered art-house success. Mastroianni stars as Baron Ferdinand "Fefe" Cefalu who falls in love with his sixteen-year-old cousin, Angela. According to the Italian judicial system,

39. Ibid.
40. London to McMahon, November 9, 1962, in ibid., General Correspondence, F File.
41. London to Polly Kirk, July 3, 1963, in ibid.
42. Ibid., July 22, 1963.
43. Kirk to Embassy Pictures, August 2, 1963, in ibid.

there is no way that the baron can divorce his wife to marry this young girl, so the baron envisions a plot in which he will catch his wife committing adultery, giving him license to avenge the crime. The hilarious film won a slew of international awards, including many in the United States. The Kansas State Board of Review recommended eliminations in the dialogue in both the subtitled and English-dubbed versions of the film because it considered the language "obscene." Chairwoman Polly Kirk met with Park McGee of the attorney general's office to determine what legal grounds the board had to dictate these standards. After a lengthy discussion with other board members, "it was with great reluctance that the board decided to rescind their recommendations for eliminations in both versions."[44]

In 1963, the board continued to fight overt sexuality on the screen but was often pressured legally to rescind previous motions. The biblical picture *Adam and Eve* (1962) had been condemned by a previous board, but on August 1, 1963, the board decided to give the film a seal of approval as it believed that the movie would not be considered obscene according to recent rulings on definitions of obscenity.[45]

This is not to say that the board was pressured to accept any film that was submitted to it. It continued to ban films in totality, particularly those of independent or fly-by-night producers and distributors who had few financial resources to contest such a decision. Both *Dangerous Love Affair* (1961) and *The Passionate Demons* (1962) were rejected because the "general theme of the story is lustful throughout." The Russ Meyer exploitation flick *Erotica* (1963) was rejected because of nudity throughout the picture, and *Mischief Makers* (1963) was banned "because the dominant theme of the material taken as a whole would appeal to children as a shameful or morbid interest in sex."[46]

In late 1963, the bulletin of the Governmental Research Center of the University of Kansas, *Your Government*, published a special issue called "Censorship in Kansas." The issue was an interesting snapshot of the Kansas State Board of Review in its past few years of existence. Research assistant K. A. Harris argued that the board was never in a comfortable position: "It has remained the target of its supporters—religious groups and militant defenders of public morals—for its laxity. And from the other side it has endured attacks by liberal thinkers, the press and commercial interests." The

44. KSBR Minutes, February 12, 1963, Box 58-5-4-15, KSHS.
45. Ibid., August 1, 1963.
46. Disapproved Features and Shorts, 1962, 1963, KSBR, KSHS.

author believed that the present board was in a no-win situation. He recommended what would become reality in five years: a system of classification of motion pictures according to the age of the audience. Although the author implied that this classification scheme would be mandated by the state, it was the voluntary rating system by the MPAA that was eventually adopted in 1968. The *Kansas City Times* reported on this study, noting that "the Kansas Board of Review no longer has unlimited authority to censor motion pictures under recent U.S. Supreme Court decisions."[47]

The mid-1960s also witnessed a revitalization of the horror genre but with a twist. Films like *Blood Feast* (1963), *Strait-Jacket* (1964), and *Maniac* (1962) had a level of violence and depravity not evident in previous films. Spurred on by the success of Alfred Hitchcock's *Psycho* (1960) and a subgenre of aging-star shockers such as *What Ever Happened to Baby Jane?* (1962), horror films found new interest with audiences. *Blood Feast* was a milestone in the exploitation genre when it was released in 1963. It was considered shocking and was a bona fide drive-in moneymaker. Director Herschell Gordon Lewis deliberately wanted to horrify his audiences with his tale of a serial killer who murders women and then steals their body parts. The women of the Board of Review did not know what to do with this film and viewed it numerous times to see if it could be saved after eliminations. On September 6, 1963, they recommended the following cuts:

> Reel 1A—before picture—the scene where Ramses holds up fragment and blood on knife and the scene of the severed leg being put in bag and scene of bloody left eye of blonde girl in bath tub.
>
> Reel 1B—the scene of Tony and Marcy on the beach where Ramses holds brain in his hands also the girl lying on the beach with bloody head.
>
> Reel 2A—where Ramses pulls out tongue of blond and holds it up followed by the face of the blond with blood running out of her mouth.
>
> Reel 2B—in ancient Egyptian cult story, the scene where the heart is lifted from the body of the young maiden.[48]

It was not only the female censors who were shocked by this new breed of blood-ladled films—so were Kansas citizens. Governor John Anderson

47. Harris, "Censorship in Kansas"; "Movie Censor Rights Dented," *Kansas City Times*, December 17, 1963, Clipping File, KSBR, KSHS.

48. H. G. Lewis, Box-Office Spectaculars, to McMahon, Correspondence File B, September 6, 1963, Box 58-05-04-13, KSBR, KSHS.

Some Kansas citizens condemned the new breed of horror film like *Strait-Jacket* (1964) that appeared in the 1960s. (Permission granted by Photofest)

received a letter and petition from the citizens of Liberal on January 13, 1964, protesting the pictures *Strait-Jacket* and *Maniac*. The citizens claimed that "during the past week two maniacal pictures have been shown at our local theater." Using the standard argument of "protecting the children," the protesters argued that "it seems that gradually the moving picture industry is serving up more and more movies that degrade the moral fiber of our young people."[49]

The mid-1960s was the height of the civil rights movement, and the board was also more consciously aware of racial slurs and slights on the screen. *Black Like Me* (1964) was based on an actual case in which a white reporter took chemical substances that darkened his skin so he could experience racial prejudice firsthand. The censors reacted to racist language in the film, particularly the use of the word *nigger*.[50]

By 1964, a seismic cultural shift began impacting American popular entertainment. The sexual revolution had begun to blossom, youth culture had taken over America, and directors, artists, and actors were challenging norms of decency in productions such as *Who's Afraid of Virginia Woolf?* (1966).[51] Some Kansans were not prepared for these changes and believed that the Board of Review would save them from this "indecency." On a hot summer night in August 1964, James Hoggard, pastor of the First Baptist Church in Rolla, Kansas, met with his congregation and held a discussion on obscenity and laws attempting to curtail it. Hoggard wrote future governor William H. Avery (elected in 1964) and explained, "The members of the group felt that laws governing decency in movies and literature are very important for the social welfare of our citizens, especially with respect to the effect on the youth and the family structure. It was the consensus of those present that our state compares favorably with others in its legal control of the mass media as it concerns obscenity."[52]

Hoggard and his congregation must not have been aware of the decline of the board's regulatory power. The *Dodge City Globe* reported on this phenomenon almost at the same time. The newspaper's staff was well aware of this cultural shift. They reported that "actors and actresses speak bluntly, embrace unashamedly and sometimes swear like sailors," but the "censors usually must

49. Citizens of Liberal to Anderson, January 13, 1964, File 4, Box 28-01-02-05, Governor John Anderson—General Correspondence, 1961–1965, KSHS.

50. Box 35-06-05-01, KSBR, KSHS.

51. See Arthur Marwick, *The Sixties*.

52. James Hoggard to Avery, Governor William Avery, Correspondence, State Agencies, Review State Board of, 1956–1966, Box 28-02-03-01, KSHS.

sit powerless" because of their limited power due to recent judicial decisions. As Mrs. Polly Kirk, chairwoman of the board in 1964, explained, "We are limited almost entirely to nudity or extreme lustfulness." Kirk illustrated that the board could ban complete nudity but that low-cut gowns went uncensored. She said that the rule of thumb for the board was that a woman had to be covered above and below her waist but that bikinis could "go through." The *Dodge City Globe* also discussed the split reaction among Kansas citizens to this loosening up of standards on the screen. The authors wrote, "To some people the courts' landmark rulings are liberating the country from Puritanism and giving more freedom of expression. To others the rulings mean the way is open for sex, obscenity and immorality on the movie screens."[53]

In the mid-1950s, a series of court decisions had convinced some state legislatures to abolish their censorship boards. The Ohio board was abolished in 1954, the Massachusetts board in 1955, and the Pennsylvania board in 1956. In early 1965, only four state boards of motion picture censorship still existed: in Virginia, New York, Maryland, and Kansas. A test case in the state of Maryland, which resulted in the Supreme Court decision *Freedman v. Maryland*, would cause all state and municipal censorship to come to a crashing halt.

Ronald Freedman was a Baltimore exhibitor who wanted to overturn Maryland's system of film censorship. Freedman often showed exploitation films in his theater with scenes intact that the censors had demanded to be removed. As legal historians Edward de Grazia and Roger Newman claim, Freedman became a "man with a cause," particularly after winning several appellate court decisions that had overturned the Maryland board's initial rulings.[54] As with the *Times Film* case, Freedman decided to use a film that was not exploitative or scandalous in any way, just to demonstrate the apparent ridiculousness of the censorship apparatus. The film was *Revenge at Daybreak* (1965), which concerned the Irish revolution of 1917–1918. Freedman challenged the licensing procedures of the Maryland board, refusing to submit the film. The argument was that he should not be held criminally responsible for a film that was constitutionally protected—there was nothing obscene, vulgar, or scandalous about *Revenge at Daybreak*. The Maryland Court of Appeals upheld the state censorship plan, but the United States Supreme Court overturned this decision on March 1, 1965. The Court did not find the

53. "Power of Kansas State Film Censors Decline," *Dodge City Globe*, August 20, 1964, Clipping File, KSBR, KSHS.
54. De Grazia and Newman, *Banned Films*, 112.

state's licensing scheme unconstitutional but argued that it failed to provide safeguards against undue inhibition of protected expression. The Court was concerned about the procedural safeguards of the licensing process; the justices wanted it speeded up and judicial participation to be built into the process. Justice Brennan, who wrote the unanimous Court's opinion, argued that a censorship scheme had to have three procedural safeguards: "First, the burden of proving that the film is unprotected expression . . . must rest on the censor. . . . Second, while the State may require advance submission of all films, in order to proceed effectively to bar all showings of unprotected films, the requirement cannot be administered in a manner which would lend an effect of finality to the censor's determination whether a film constitutes protected expression. . . . Third, a prompt judicial determination of obscenity must be assured."[55]

The Supreme Court did not say that states and municipalities could not censor films; in fact, they noted that motion pictures "differ from other forms of expression."[56] Nevertheless, the Court had given states much stricter standards in which to censor and license films, and motion picture exhibitors and distributors used the *Freedman* decision to immediately launch an attack on boards in cities and states that continued to censor films. One of the footnotes in the *Freedman* decision stated that Kansas had a censorship law that was similar to that of Maryland's. The Kansas attorney general, Robert Londerholm, knew that it was only a matter of time before his state's censorship apparatus was also embroiled in a life-or-death struggle, and he tried to persuade the state legislature to pass corrective legislation before the recess. Apparently, legislative leaders did not consider the matter important enough or simply ran out of time before the session ended and did not consider new legislation.[57]

Film historian Garth Jowett has argued that the "*Freedman* case was most significant, because it forced censors to adhere to unusually high standards of procedural fairness."[58] Kansas attorney general Londerholm realized that he had to take matters into his own hands if film censorship was going to be maintained in the state. In April 1965, he and Richard Seaton, assistant attorney general, sat down with the board to adopt new rules that would con-

55. *Freeman v. Maryland* 380 U.S. 51 (1965), 59; 85 Sup. Ct. 734, 739; 13 L. Ed. 2d 649, 655.
56. Jowett, "Significant Medium," 271.
57. Richard Seaton, assistant attorney general, to Kirk, March 16, 1965, Box 58-05-04-13, KSBR Correspondence, KSHS.
58. Jowett, *Film: The Democratic Art*, 412.

form to the safeguards in the *Freedman* decision. These rules would have the force of law until the state legislature amended or revoked them.

It appears that Seaton worked with the board most closely yet ignored judicial precedent when revising the standards. From *Roth* through *Freedman*, the United States Supreme Court had deemed that a film had to be taken as a whole when considered censorable; therefore, obscenity was not to be determined by isolated passages. The new rules said that "a film or reel shall be deemed obscene when to the average person, applying contemporary community standards, the dominant theme of the material, taken as a whole, appeals to prurient interest, i.e., a shameful or morbid interest in nudity, sex or excretion, and if it goes substantially beyond contemporary limits of candor in description or representation of such matters."[59] This would significantly change how the Kansas Board of Review had considered films for the past fifty years. Yet Seaton apparently told the board not to worry. In a confidential letter to chairwoman Polly Kirk he explained, "You will notice that I have eliminated all references to orders of eliminations. This won't require any change in the board's practice, since the board can continue to disapprove a film subject to specified eliminations, but it looks better on paper this way."[60] This was an erroneous belief. Perhaps Seaton believed the state legislature would help the board out of its predicament. It certainly put the board in a weakened condition, and the film distributors knew it.

One only had to examine film advertisements in local Kansas newspapers for evidence of the winds of change. In Topeka, it appeared as if the teenagers had taken over. One could see *Help!* (1965) with the Beatles at the Orpheum, *Ride the Wild Surf* (1964) at the Cloverleaf, and *How to Stuff a Wild Bikini* (1965) at the Community Drive-in. In Kansas City, things were a little more adult. Billy Wilder's trashy sex comedy *Kiss Me, Stupid* (1964) was playing at the Park, or one could cross the state line and see the lesbian exploitation flick *Chained Girls* (1965) at the Strand. The film was advertised as "A Film So Daring . . . So Hush Hush—Adults Only" in the *Kansas City Kansan*. Perhaps the film that caused the most controversy was the documentary *Ecco* (1963), which had a successful run at the Shawnee Drive-in in Shawnee. *Ecco* was a follow-up to the highly successful Italian shockumentary *Mondo Cane* (1962), which depicted all types of shocking and disturbing human behavior around the globe. Chairwoman Polly Kirk described *Ecco* as a "so-called documentary

59. Kansas Statutes, 74-2208, 18-1-15.
60. Seaton to Kirk, April 23, 1965, Box 58-05-04-13, KSBR Correspondence, KSHS.

about customs in various parts of the world relating to sex, virginity and teenage promiscuity." The film was given a semblance of taste due to the narration by veteran British actor George Sanders. Apparently, the board viewed and approved the picture on August 20, 1965, without eliminations because it thought that there was nothing that they could legally remove. That did not stop the mothers of Shawnee from protesting, though. Letters poured into the board office, and calls were made to the police department of Shawnee complaining about *Ecco* since it had not been advertised for adults only. Mrs. Vernon Murrow of Topeka wrote directly to Governor William Avery after viewing the film at the Jayhawk Theater with her daughter and son-in-law. She asserted, "We as educated, Christian adults were embarrassed and sickened by what we saw. The scenes depicted were the most sadistic, vulgar things one could imagine. A scene from Sweden showed a young couple on the top of a car giving vent to their sexual desires with a crowd of people about. Another scene showed a man dissecting a live girl. Every other scene was of human torture or sex in a vulgar form." Apparently, Mrs. Murrow had believed she was going to see a documentary about unusual customs around the world. She claimed in the newspaper that *Ecco* was advertised as "recommended for adults over 16," but she obviously did not know what this meant by 1965 standards.[61]

In May 1965, the board began receiving checks from motion picture distributors for review fees paid under protest. This put the board in a precarious situation legally, not knowing whether these checks should be cashed. The attorney general and the board recognized that without cooperation of the major film companies, the entire system of censorship would break down. They called a meeting at the board's office in Kansas City on August 30, 1965, to rectify the situation and to explain the operation of the new rules that had been adopted that spring. Representatives of Warner Brothers, Universal Film, American International Pictures, United Artists, Crest Films, the Exhibitor's Film Delivery and Service and the Motion Picture Association of America were at the meeting.

Former governor John Anderson Jr. represented the MPAA at the meeting. Anderson claimed that rules 18-1-6 and 18-1-7 put the burden of proof

61. Film advertisements, *Topeka Daily Capital,* September 3, 1965; film advertisements, *Kansas City Kansan,* July 2, 1965; Kirk to Seaton, November 2, 1965, Box 58-05-04-13, KSBR Correspondence, KSHS; Mrs. Vernon Murrow to Avery, November 24, 1965, Governor William Avery, Correspondence, State Agencies, Review State Board of, 1965–1966, Box 28-02-03-01, KSHS.

on the film companies, when the *Freedman* decision clearly stated that this should be the responsibility of the board. If a film distributor did not accept board-dictated recommended cuts, then they could be restrained by a court order requested by the board. This also ran counter to the rule that stated that a film should be considered in its totality. Despite Anderson's objections, nothing was changed. The board readopted new rules at the meeting and claimed that they would be officially effective on January 1, 1966 (although they were already the guiding principles of the board).[62]

The film companies stepped up their campaign of paying under protest in the fall of 1965. Columbia Pictures announced in October that it would no longer submit their films to the board for review. Columbia distributed two of its films, *Bunny Lake Is Missing* (1965) and *The Bedford Incident* (1965), without the seal of the board's approval in the state of Kansas. While *Bunny Lake's* child kidnapping plot and homosexual characters may have raised some eyebrows among the board members, *The Bedford Incident* was a cold war story of intrigue that would have easily passed.

Attorney General Londerholm obtained a temporary restraining order against Columbia for showing the films that it had declined to submit to the Review Board.[63] The Shawnee County District Court granted the restraining order pending the outcome of the litigation. Richard Seaton, assistant attorney general, argued, "Obscenity is not involved with either picture.... It is only a test of the requirement which follows an opinion earlier this year by the U.S. Supreme Court which ruled out a Maryland law."[64]

The press noticed the irony of former governor and Olathe lawyer John Anderson Jr. challenging the law—he had been the individual who had appointed the three women currently sitting on the Kansas State Board of Review. After the restraining order was issued, Columbia Pictures, through Anderson, filed a cross-petition contending that the board was illegally constituted under existing U.S. Supreme Court rulings.[65]

The case went to trial, and on January 10, 1966, presiding judge Marion Beatty said that the law was unconstitutional and the new rules did not cure its constitutional problems. Judge Beatty stated, "It is the judgment of this

---

62. KSBR Minutes, August 31, 1965, Box 58-05-04-14, KSHS.
63. "Film Review Test to Court," *Kansas City Times*, November 11, 1965, Clipping File, KSBR, KSHS.
64. "State Moves against Movie Firm," *Topeka Journal*, November 10, 1965, Clipping File, KSBR, KSHS.
65. "Picture Industry Challenges Kansas Board of Review," *Kansas City Times*, November 23, 1965.

court that although the board and its counsel have made a scholarly and dili-
gent effort to update the procedure and make it conform to the latest requirements of the U.S. Supreme Court that statute is invalid."[66]

The attorney general immediately appealed the decision to the state
supreme court and asked the court to stay execution of the decision pending
a final ruling on the appeal. Londerholm claimed that there were two main
points of disagreement between Columbia Pictures and the state. First was
the issue of whether the film exhibitors had immediate judicial review of
administrative decisions by the board. The second issue was whether the state
or the film exhibitors had the burden of proving the acceptability of a film.[67]

As the case made its way through the court system in late 1965 and early
1966, the entire motion picture industry united behind Columbia Pictures. A
formal protest was sent to the governor and the Board of Review claiming
that "the laws of Kansas and the rules adopted thereunder fail to meet the
requirements as set forth by the United States Supreme Court for the protection of rights and freedoms guaranteed by the First Amendment to the
Constitution of the United States."[68] The United Theatre Owners of the
Heart of America, Allied Artists Distributing Corporation, MGM, Paramount Pictures, Twentieth Century Fox, United Artists, the Universal Film
Exchange, and Warner Brothers joined Columbia in this protest. All of the
above companies began paying their review fees under protest in 1966.[69]

On July 27, 1966, the Kansas Supreme Court struck down the fifty-one-
year-old legacy of motion picture censorship in the state. The court said that
the state laws were inconsistent with standards established by the *Freedman*
decision. Justice Harold Fatzer, former attorney general, spoke for the court:
"What the Board of Review had failed to do is to cure constitutional defects
in the Act by the promulgation and filing of rules and regulations adopted by
it for that purpose. The lawmaking power of this state is vested in the legislature and the board cannot breathe constitutional life into a statute by rules
and regulations."[70] After decades of determining its own rules and regulations, without the sanctity of having them enacted by the state legislature, the
board had finally been brought down by its own haphazard decision making.

66. "State Movie Censor Laws Felled in Court," *Topeka Journal,* January 9, 1966.
67. "Londerholm Will Appeal Film Ruling," *Topeka Journal,* January 10, 1966.
68. Formal Petition, "Before the State Board of Review of the State of Kansas," Film Companies File, Box 58-05-04-13, KSBR, KSHS.
69. Film Companies File, Box 58-05-04-13, KSBR, KSHS.
70. *State of Kansas v. Columbia Pictures Corporation,* 197 Kan. 448 (1966), 455; 417 P. 2d 255, 260.

Before the Kansas Supreme Court, Columbia's lawyers questioned how the Board of Review could change its rules and regulations without the approval of the state legislature. They also argued that censors would not have the burden of proof under the new rules because if a film company contested a board decision, it would mean a judicial proceeding in which the company would have to prove a film was not obscene.

What was not decided as a result of this July decision was whether the Kansas State Board of Review was abolished or just stripped of its powers. Charles Henson, assistant attorney general, stated, "If the decision does not actually abolish the board, its three members apparently could continue to collect their salaries, although they would have no official duties to perform."[71]

On July 31, 1966, Governor Avery took matters into his own hands. In a letter, he informed chairwoman Polly Kirk that the board could not continue to operate without remedial legislation. He stated, "After carefully considering all factors, it appears there is no justification that the board continue in operation." The governor requested that the board terminate its operations within the next sixty days. All Board of Review property was to be sold. The board was also to return the $14,285 that had been paid under protest to the film companies. The governor still had a constituency that was very concerned about film content, though. He noted during a press conference that obscenity statutes in the state could still be applied to films. "Discontinuation of the Board of Review does not mean the public will be without protection."[72]

Shortly after the governor's public pronouncement, Edward Cooper, representative of the Motion Picture Association of America, wrote to him. Cooper applauded the governor on his declaration that Kansas could still prosecute motion pictures for obscenity and pornography. But Cooper's letter more accurately reflected the attitude of the industry toward the censorship of motion pictures. Commenting on the erosion of censorship boards across the state, he said, "It is a recognition that people are their own best censors. Parents not only have the right, but the duty, to supervise the activities of their children—what they should read, what they should see, who their companions are, and their social and home activities."[73]

---

71. *Topeka Daily Capital,* July 28, 1966, 11.

72. "Board Has 60 Days to Quit," *Topeka State Journal,* August 1, 1966. Fortunately, many of the records of the KSBR were given to the KSHS.

73. Edward Cooper to Avery, August 4, 1966, Governor William Avery, Correspondence, State Agencies, Review State Board of, 1965–1966, Box 28-02-03-01, KSHS.

In 1968, the MPAA would adopt a motion picture ratings system that did not control the content of motion pictures but at least warned parents about the acceptability of specific motion pictures for their children. The rating system was excellent public relations for the industry since it appeared to be protective of and proactive toward children. But Carrie Simpson and the Reverend Festus Foster would have dropped dead if they had seen the nudity of *Blow-Up* (1966), the raw sexuality of *I Am Curious Yellow* (1967), or the violence of *Bonnie and Clyde* (1967). The times had indeed changed.

Conclusion

Motion pictures were a primary form of entertainment in both rural and urban Kansas for most of the twentieth century. But some early-twentieth-century social reformers saw both dangers and potential for the new medium. This eventually led to more than fifty years of state film censorship. Kansas was one of only a handful of states to ever have official censorship. I firmly believe that the Kansas State Board of Review was founded on the political movement of Progressivism, an earnest attempt to protect children from harmful influences, a long-standing fear of the world outside the state borders, and "Christian" principles. Although Kansans were divided on the issue of film censorship, a majority of citizens passively accepted the system once it was in place, predicated on the fact that the board's decisions were not extreme.

In the first twenty years of the Kansas State Board of Review's existence, the censorship apparatus found itself coming into direct conflict with the changing mores, technology, and fashions of the early twentieth century. The overwhelming popularity of the medium that brought two hours of fun to an entertainment-starved rural population was, in some ways, beyond the control of the board. As the twentieth century progressed, however, the board became part of the state's political machine. Even well into the 1950s, after numerous Supreme Court decisions increasingly stripped the board of its power, it became an entrenched bureaucracy, an entity that seemed impossible to eliminate.

Politics was always an important qualification in the board's actions and existence. Arthur Cole, a contact man for Paramount Pictures, told a Kansas House committee that the board members' standards for acceptability regarding the morality of movies appeared to be based largely on "guessing right in the primary election." Cole explained that this often led to inconsistent decision making. It also contributed to the board's ignorance of the limitation on its powers and the constant fear the censors would anger the governor and lose their positions.[1]

The story of film censorship usually focuses on MPPDA self-censorship in the form of the Production Code Administration or early attempts to censor films in New York City. Very little work has been accomplished on local or state patterns of film censorship. I hope that *Banned in Kansas* will contribute to this discussion. There were definite regional factors that contributed to the origination and maintenance of the Kansas State Board of Review. The fear of the "big city" or looser "East Coast morals" contributed to the development of a procensorship climate in the state. The prohibition of alcohol in Kansas was a definite factor in early control over the screen.

It is also necessary for scholars to examine the relationship between pressure organizations like the Catholic Legion of Decency, the Production Code Administration, and local and state censorship boards. During the height of the studio system, these entities often contributed to the legitimacy of each other, working in tandem to keep certain dialogue, imagery, or ideas off the screen.

I sit in a coffee shop in the summer of 2005 reflecting on Thomas Frank's *What's the Matter with Kansas? How Conservatism Won the Heart of America.* This book has been influential in explaining how Republicans, particularly conservative Republicans, have been successful in gaining control over state and local governments and boards of education in America's heartland. I find myself having a great deal in common with Frank—we both grew up in Kansas City, are approximately the same age, attended the University of Kansas, dallied with the Young Republicans in our youth, left the state, moved to Chicago, and became increasingly liberal as we aged. Also, as Kansas natives, we often find ourselves in the position of having to explain some of the state government's anachronistic practices to our friends, such as how the state can contest the teaching of evolution in the public schools or nominate a woman for state election commissioner who questions female suffrage. I attended graduate school at the University of Kansas when Fred Phelps unleashed his firestorm of hate on good Catholic priests and mothers who had lost their beloved sons. I witnessed western Kansas representatives and senators strip the university system of public funding.

But I will forever be a Kansan. I have always found the vast majority of Kansans hardworking, polite, devout, family-oriented citizens who love their

1. "Censors Said Powerless," *Topeka Daily Capital,* March 15, 1969, 2.

country and respect their ancestors. This book was written with the intention of being a love letter to my state. Although Kansas has always had its fair share of political quackery, most Kansans are the bedrock upon which the nation exists, no matter how much of a cliché Frank believes this has become.

I do not believe that the majority of Kansans are extremists or antigovernment. Perhaps, like their ancestors at the beginning of the twentieth century, they are simply witnessing monumental cultural, scientific, and economic changes and are not quite sure how to react to them. Carl Becker was correct when he stated that Kansas is a "state of mind." But the willingness of Kansans to accept motion picture censorship for more than fifty years along with the teaching of intelligent design rather than scientific principles of evolution are issues that scholars must examine and not merely condemn. Academics must historicize this "mind-set" in order to understand governmental and educational decision making.

The day I completed the final draft of this manuscript, I accidentally discovered that one of the Kansas Board of Review censors was still alive. That day, I had a wonderful telephone conversation with one of the sprightliest individuals I have talked to—eighty-five-year-old Mary Trehey. When I asked her how she had received the position, she explained, "I was a precinct committee woman for over twenty years," confirming my belief that most of the censorship appointments were political. Mrs. Trehey certainly discounted the view that the censors were old maids. She explained that when the female censors discovered a really great film, they invited the firemen upstairs to join them downstairs for a screening. She explained that in the early 1960s they were mostly listening for "nasty words" and were rarely pressured by film company representatives. She did, however, recount one afternoon when a distributor from California tried to convince the Kansas censors that they needed to pass a nudist film. They did not. She also remembered one high-class dinner that the censors attended in Topeka. Kitty McMahon, chairwoman of the Kansas Board of Review, explained to the attendees, "We keep out venereal disease shows," much to the shock of some of the audience members.[2]

One warm June morning I visited the room in the Kansas City, Kansas, fire department at 815 North Sixth Street where the censors made their decisions for more than forty years. Battalion chief Kevin Shirley was kind enough to take me on a tour. I hoped that the spirits of the censors would visit me in some way. In my mind, I could hear the whirring of the motion picture projector

2. Mary Trehey, telephone interview, June 25, 2005.

from the back room, the "tsk-tsk" from a disgruntled female censor, and a sharp buzzer to indicate what frames of the film should be edited.

The members of the Kansas State Board of Review played an influential role in the popular culture of the state for more than fifty years. Not only did they determine what entertainment was appropriate for Kansas motion picture audiences, but their decisions led to weighty questions regarding the First Amendment, freedom of the screen, and governmental interference in popular entertainment.

Appendix

Eliminations Made in *Frankenstein* (Universal)
8 Reels, Star: Colin Clive

Reel 1: Shorten scene in graveyard when Frankenstein and aid are digging up body. This eliminates scene of them hoisting casket from grave and Frankenstein's words: "Here he comes." And following views of casket, of Frankenstein patting side of casket, inside grave, of them lifting casket and dialogue as follows:

Frankenstein: "He is just resting, waiting for a new life to come."

"Here we are—"

Reel 2: Shorten view of body swathed and covered lying on table in laboratory.

Cut 2—Shorten conversation in which it is revealed where parts of body were obtained—from gallows, grave etc. This leaves only spot where Frankenstein shows head to Fritz and speak of "the brain you stole."

Cut 3—Eliminate close-up of scar on wrist showing where hand is sewed on.

Reel 3: (1) Eliminate close-up of body being uncovered.

(2) Eliminate close-up of uncovered body.

(3) Eliminate words by Frankenstein telling Doctor and other two guests how he made body with his own hands and where he got the parts.

(4) Eliminate words by Frankenstein: *"Now I know what it feels like to be God." ("In the name of God")*

Reel 4: Eliminate close-up of creature seated, after his first glimpse of light from sky light. This is spot where camera pans from scars on neck to scars on wrists giving close-up views of both.

(2) Eliminate views of Fritz striking creature with whip and shorten views of Fritz deviling it with torch. This leaves Fritz striking only the floor in front of creature and takes out spots where he jabs at creature with torch.

(3) Eliminate close-up of injection of hypodermic into monster.

(4) Eliminate struggle between creature and Doctor.

(5) Eliminate close-up of creature's face as it falls.

(6) Eliminate horrible sounds made by creature.

Reel 5: (1) Shorten view of partially nude creature being prepared by Doctor for dissection. This leaves Doctor moving from far side of operating table around head and to instrument table; and Doctor bending over creature to listen to its heart.

(2) Eliminate entire scene of Doctor's murder.

Reel 6: (1) Eliminate close-up of creature's face.

(2) "   "   "   "   "   "

(3) "   "   "   "   "   "

(4) Shorten scenes of father carrying drowned child in his arms through streets. (This leaves one shot of him in distant bright light moving through crowd and one scene of him in shadows as he comes through arch. Also shots of him in front of Frankenstein home with crowd and soldiers.)

Reel 7: Eliminate close-up of creature in hills.

(2) Shorten struggle between monster and Frankenstein.

(3) Shorten view of creature dragging Frankenstein up wind mill stairs.

Reel 8: (1) Eliminate close-up of face of creature snarling at Frankenstein.

(2) Shorten struggle between creature and Frankenstein on roof of mill.

(3) Shorten scenes of creature trying to escape flames on roof of mill and his sounds of fear.

(4) Eliminate scene of creature lying on floor of mill pinned down amid flames by falling beam.

Note: A revised version submitted did not include all above xxxx cuts but they were made before the board tagged the picture—including BLASPHEMY uttered by Frankenstein.

NOTE:—

(1) Eliminate from revised version the Biblical quotation tacked on to end of picture.

(2) Change revised version to show original ending instead of putting it in the middle of the picture leaving Frankenstein apparently killed by the creature. While the revised version as submitted with tragic end conforms to the book, the board does not consider it a point that comes under the laws of censorship and does not recommend this change in continuity.

REASON (1) Cruelty

(2) Tends to debase morals.

Note: The second reason is given because of the BLASPHEMY which Webster says is *"Indignity offered to God in words,* writing, or signs, as speaking evil of God; also, *act of claiming the attributes or prerogatives of deity.* Besides being an ecclesiastical offense, blasphemy is a crime at the common law, as well as generally by statute, as *tending to a breach of the peace and being a public nuisance or destruction of the foundations of civil society."*

Kansas City, Kansas

January 5, 1932

Note—The following matter was not in either version of this picture shown to this board and must not be put back in any print shown in Kansas.

Reel 1—(1) All views of hillside at sunset, of funeral procession walking along led by priest carrying banner, of xxxxxxxxxxxxxx four peasants carrying coffin on their shoulders as they move slowly followed by group of peasants, of priest moving to side as camera pans past cross and discloses grave digger near open grave, all other views of funeral procession, of the lowering of casket into grave.

(2) Views of Frankenstein and Fritz moving over near casket on hand cart, of Fritz, holding lantern, moving ahead, of camera panning to crude gibbet, of body hanging from it, partly in scene, of Frankenstein taking lantern from Fritz and moving around the post with knife in hand, starting to climb up post, of Frankenstein telling Fritz to climb up and cut rope and giving Fritz knife, of Frankenstein staring intently to foreground as he holds lantern, close-up views of top of gibbet, views of upper part of beam and rope, of Fritz climbing up with knife in hand, crawling along

beams, putting knife in his mouth, moving to rope, cutting rope, of rope dropping off body falling near Frankenstein, of Frankenstein lowering lantern, of Fritz staring off intently and speaking and of Frankenstein looking off and speaking about the body they have just cut down and accompanying dialogue as follows:

Fritz: "Look, it's still here . . ."
Frankenstein: "Climb up and cut the rope."
Fritz: "Noooo! . . ."
Frankenstein: "Go on . . . it can't hurt you . . . here's the knife . . ."
Frankenstein: "Look out . . ."
Fritz: "Here's the knife. Here I come . . ."
Fritz: "Is it all right."
Frankenstein: "The neck's broken. The brain is useless. We must find another brain . . ."

Reel 6—Eliminate views of monster picking Maria up, of her screaming, of him rising and throwing her into water, of water splashing up as she lights, of Maria sinking, of monster watching water and registering surprise as sinks, and speech by Maria, "No, you're hurting me! Daddy!"

Kansas City, Kansas, January 5, 1932

Bibliography

United States Supreme Court Cases That Directly Affected the Kansas State Board of Review

Joseph Burstyn, Inc. v. Wilson, Commissioner of Education of New York, et al. 343 U.S. 495 (1952).

Freedman v. Maryland. 380 U.S. 51 (1965).

Mutual Film Corporation v. Industrial Commission of Ohio. 236 U.S. 230, 247 (1915).

Mutual Film Corporation v. Hodges, Governor of the State of Kansas. 236 U.S. 248 (1915).

Near v. State of Minnesota. 283 U.S. 697 (1931).

Roth v. United States. 354 U.S. 476 (1957).

Superior Films v. Dept. of Education of Ohio. 346 U.S. 587 (1954).

Times Film Corporation v. Chicago. 365 U.S. 43 (1961).

Records of the Kansas State Board of Review, Kansas State Historical Society Archive, Topeka

Box Contents Inventory

Action on Submitted Films, 1917–1934. Box 58-5-4-5.

Annual and Biennial Reports, 1918, 1920, 1922, 1924, 1936, 1928, 1932, 1944. Box 58-5-4-6.

Board Minutes, 1923–1966. Box 58-5-4-15.

Cartoons and Short Subjects, 1920–1961. Boxes 35-6-5-1 through 35-6-3-4.

Correspondence, 1951–1966. Box 58-5-4-14.

Disapproved Features and Shorts, 1917–1961. Boxes 35-6-6-1 through 35-6-6-3.

Features and Short Subjects, 1920–1961. Boxes 35-6-4-2 through 35-6-5-1.

Fee Registers, 1948–1956. Box 58-5-4-8.

Financial and Misc., 1948–1966. Box 58-5-4-13.

Financial Records, 1948–1956. Box 58-5-4-9.

Financial Records (continued), 1948–1956. Box 58-5-4-10.

Financial Records (continued), 1948–1956. Box 58-5-4-11.

Financial Records (continued), 1948–1956. Box 58-5-4-12.

Financial Records, 1956–1966. Box 58-5-4-16.

Financial Records (continued), 1956–1966. Box 58-5-4-16.

Law Enforcement Officer Reports, 1956–1958. Box 58-5-4-6.

Law Enforcement Officer Reports, 1958–1963, 1966. Box 58-5-4-7.

Lists of Films Reviewed, 1915–1923, 1935–1939. Box 58-5-4-6.

Lists of Films Reviewed, 1956–1958. Box 58-5-4-15.

Monthly and Yearly Review Files, 1952–1966. Boxes 35-6-5-5 through 35-6-5-12.

Review Cards/Copy Cards/Action on Submitted Films. Boxes 35-6-2-1 through 35-6-4-1.

Series and Serials, 1929–1959. Box 35-6-5-12.

Soundies, 1941–1946. Boxes 35-6-6-4 through 35-6-7-6.

List of Kansas Governors

The records of the following Kansas governors are located in the Archives at the Kansas State Historical Society. Both personal correspondence and official records were obtained from the following governors. The dates are their official terms of office.

George Hartshorn Hodges	January 1913–January 1915
Arthur Capper	January 1915–January 1919
Henry Justin Allen	January 1919–January 1923
Jonathan McMillen Davis	January 1923–January 1925
Ben Sanford Paulen	January 1925–January 1929
Clyde Martin Reed	January 1929–January 1931
Harry Hines Woodring	January 1931–January 1933
Alfred Mossman Landon	January 1933–January 1937
Walter Augustus Huxman	January 1937–January 1939
Payne H. Ratner	January 1939–January 1943
Andrew F. Schoeppel	January 1943–January 1947
Frank Carlson	January 1947–November 1950
Frank L. Hagaman	November 1950–January 1951

Edward F. Arn	January 1951–January 1955
Fred Hall	January 1955–January 1957
John McCuish	January 1957–January 1957
George Docking	January 1957–January 1961
John Anderson Jr.	January 1961–January 1965
William H. Avery	January 1965–January 1967

Special Collection

Motion Picture Association of America (MPAA) Production Code Administration Files. Academy of Motion Picture Arts and Sciences, Margaret Herrick Library, Beverly Hills.

Other Sources

Addams, Jane. *The Spirit of Youth and the City Streets.* New York: Macmillan, 1909.

Bader, Robert Smith. *Hayseeds, Moralizers, and Methodists: The Twentieth-Century Image of Kansas.* Lawrence: University Press of Kansas, 1988.

Bailyn, Bernard, et al. *The Great Republic.* Lexington, Mass.: D. C. Heath, 1985.

Balio, Tino. *Grand Design: Hollywood as a Modern Business Enterprise, 1930–1939.* New York: Charles Scribner's Sons, 1993.

Becker, Carl. *Everyman His Own Historian: Essays on History and Politics.* Chicago: Quadrangle Books, 1935.

Berube, Allan. *Coming Out under Fire: The History of Gay Men and Women in World War II.* New York: Plume, 1991.

Black, Gregory D. *The Catholic Crusade against the Movies, 1940–1975.* Cambridge: Cambridge University Press, 1998.

———. *Hollywood Censored: Morality Codes, Catholics, and the Movies.* Cambridge: Cambridge University Press, 1994

Bonnifield, Paul. *The Dust Bowl: Men, Dirt, and Depression.* Albuquerque: University of New Mexico Press, 1979.

Bowser, Eileen. *The Transformation of Cinema, 1907–1915.* New York: Charles Scribner's Sons, 1990.

Bowers, William L. *The Country Life Movement in America, 1900–1925.* Port Washington, N.Y.: Kennikat Press, 1974.

Boyer, Paul S. *Promises to Keep: The United States since World War II.* New York: Houghton Mifflin, 1999.

Brenton, Cranston. "Motion Pictures and Local Responsibility." *American City* 16 (February 1917).

Butters, Gerald R., Jr. "*The Birth of a Nation* and the Kansas Board of Review of Motion Pictures: A Censorship Struggle." *Kansas History: A Journal of the Central Plains* 14, no. 1 (Spring 1991): 2–14.

———. "The Kansas Board of Review of Motion Pictures and Film Censorship, 1913–1923." Master's thesis, University of Missouri, 1989.

Campbell, Craig W. *Reel America and World War I: Film in the United States, 1914–1920.* Jefferson, N.C.: McFarland Press, 1985.

Carmen, Ira. *Movies, Censorship, and the Law.* Ann Arbor: University of Michigan Press, 1966.

Chalmers, David. *Hooded Americanism.* Garden City, N.Y.: Doubleday, 1965.

Chambers, John Whiteclay, II. *The Tyranny of Change: America in the Progressive Era, 1890–1920.* New York: St. Martin's Press, 2000.

Cocks, Orrin G. "Good Movies Go Strong." *New Jersey Municipalities* (May 1916).

———. "A Real Motion Picture Ogre." *American City* 18 (July 1918).

Collier, John. "Censorship and the National Board." *Survey* (October 2, 1915): 9–14.

———. "The Learned Judges and the Films." *Survey* 34 (September 4, 1915): 516.

Crafton, Donald. *The Talkies: American Cinema's Transition to Sound, 1926–1931.* New York: Charles Scribner's Sons, 1996.

Cripps, Thomas. *Slow Fade to Black: The Negro in American Film, 1900–1942.* New York: Oxford University Press, 1977.

Crowley, Byron Monroe. "The Public Career of Arthur Capper prior to His Senatorial Service." Master's thesis, Kansas State Teachers College of Pittsburg, 1938.

De Grazia, Edward, and Roger K. Newman. *Banned Films: Movies, Censors, and the First Amendment.* New York: R. R. Bowker, 1982.

D'Emilio, John, and Estelle B. Freedman. *Intimate Matters: A History of Sexuality in America.* New York: Harper and Row, 1988.

Doherty, Thomas Patrick. *Pre-Code Hollywood: Sex, Immorality, Insurrection, and American Cinema, 1930–1934.* New York: Columbia University Press, 1999.

———. *Projections of War: Hollywood, American Culture, and World War II.* New York: Columbia University Press, 1993.

Dumenil, Lynn. *Modern Temper: American Culture and Society during the 1920s.* New York: Hill and Wang, 1995.

Eastman, Fred. "Our Children and the Movies." *Christian Century* (January 22, 1920): 110–12.

Felder, John Lewis. "Sunday Movies in Kansas." Master's thesis, Kansas State Teacher's College, 1966.

Fisher, Robert. "Film Censorship and Progressive Reform: The National Board of Censorship of Motion Pictures, 1901–1922." *Journal of Popular Culture* 4, no. 2 (1975): 143–56.

Fleener, Nikkie. "Answering Film with Film: The Hampton Epilogue, a Positive Alternative to the Negative Black Stereotypes Presented in *The Birth of a Nation.*" *Journal of Popular Film and Television* 7 (1980): 400–425.

Frank, Thomas. *What's the Matter with Kansas? How Conservatism Won the Heart of America.* New York: Henry Holt, 2004.

Franklin, John Hope. "*Birth of a Nation*—Propaganda as History." *Massachusetts Review* 40 (Autumn 1979): 10–23.

Garesche, Edward F. "Pastors and the Censorship of the Movies." *Ecclesiastical Review* 61 (March 1919).

Gaume, Thomas Michael. "Suppression of Motion Pictures in Kansas, 1952–1975." Master's thesis, University of Kansas, 1976.

Geiger, Joseph Roy. "The Effects of the Motion Picture on the Mind and Morals of the Young." *International Journal of Ethics* 34, no. 1 (1923): 69–83.

General Statutes of Kansas. 1917 (chap. 308); 1931; 1949 (chap. 51, chap. 74, art. 22); 1955 (chap. 74, art. 22). Topeka: State Printer, 1917, 1949, 1955.

Genini, Ronald. *Theda Bara: A Biography of the Silent Screen Vamp.* London: McFarland, 1996.

Golden, Eve. *Vamp: The Rise and Fall of Theda Bara.* Vestal, N.Y.: Emprise Publishing, 1996.

Griffith, Sally Foreman. *Hometown News: William Allen White and the "Emporia Gazette."* New York: Oxford University Press, 1989.

Hall, Mitchell K. *Crossroads: American Popular Culture and the Vietnam Generation.* Latham, Md.: Rowman and Littlefield, 2005.

Hansen, Patricia, ed. *American Film Institute Catalog of Motion Pictures Produced in the United States: Feature Films, 1911–1920.* Berkeley and Los Angeles: University of California Press, 1988.

————. *American Film Institute Catalog of Motion Pictures Produced in the United States: Feature Films, 1931–1940*. Berkeley and Los Angeles: University of California Press, 1993.

————. *American Film Institute Catalog of Motion Pictures Produced in the United States: Feature Films, 1941–1950*. Berkeley and Los Angeles: University of California Press, 1994.

Harris, K. A. "Censorship in Kansas: A Dilemma." *Your Government: Bulletin of the Governmental Research Center* 19, no. 4 (December 15, 1963).

Healey, William. *The Individual Delinquent*. Boston: Little, Brown, 1913.

Hibbard, Darrell O. "Moving Picture—the Good and Bad of It." *Outlook* 101 (July 13, 1912).

Hunnings, Neville March. *Film Censors and the Law*. London: George Allen and Unwin, 1967.

Jacobs, Lea. *The Wages of Sin: Censorship and the Fallen Woman Film, 1928–1942*. Madison: University of Wisconsin Press, 1991.

Jacobs, Lewis. *The Rise of the American Film: A Critical History*. New York: Columbia Teachers College Press, 1968.

Johnson, Walter. *William Allen White's America*. New York: Henry Holt, 1947.

Jowett, Garth. "A Capacity for Evil: The 1915 Supreme Court *Mutual* Decision." *Historical Journal of Film, Radio, and Television* 9, no. 1 (1989).

————. *Film: The Democratic Art*. Boston: Little, Brown, 1976.

————. "A Significant Medium for the Communication of Ideas: The *Miracle* Decision and the Decline of Motion Picture Censorship, 1952–1968." In *Movie Censorship and American Culture*, ed. Francis G. Couvares. Washington, D.C.: Smithsonian Institution Press, 1996.

Kaledin, Eugenia. *Daily Life in the United States, 1940–1959: Shifting Worlds*. Westport, Conn.: Greenwood Press, 2000.

Kansas, State of. Senate Bill 384. In *Session Laws*. Topeka: State Printer, 1931.

Kansas State Board of Review. *A Classified List of Films Approved for Use in Special Programs Selected from Pictures Reviewed between April 1, 1917, and April 1, 1918*. Topeka: State Printer, 1918.

————. *Biennial Reports*. Topeka: State Printer, 1920, 1924, 1926, 1928, 1932, 1944, 1946, 1948, 1950, 1952, 1956, 1958.

————. *Complete List of Motion Pictures Submitted*. Topeka: Kansas State Board of Review, 1915–1966.

————. *Laws and Rules: Motion Pictures*. Topeka: State Printer, 1937, 1948.

Kelly, Andrew. *Cinema and the Great War.* New York: Routledge, 1997.

Koszarski, Richard. *An Evening's Entertainment: The Age of the Silent Feature Picture, 1915–1928.* New York: Charles Scribner's Sons, 1990.

La Forte, Robert Sherman. *Leaders of Reform: Progressive Republicans in Kansas, 1900–1916.* Lawrence: University Press of Kansas, 1974.

Lawson, W. P. "Standards of Censorship." *Harper's Weekly* 60 (January 16, 1915).

Leab, Daniel J. *From Sambo to Superspade: The Black Experience in Motion Pictures.* Boston: Houghton Mifflin, 1975.

Lebsock, Suzanne. "Women and American Politics, 1880–1920." In *Women, Politics, and Change,* ed. Louise A. Tilly and P. Gurin. New York: Russell Sage Foundation, 1990.

Leff, Leonard J., and Jerold L. Simmons. *The Dame in the Kimono: Hollywood, Censorship, and the Production Code from the 1920s to the 1960s.* New York: Grove Weidenfeld, 1990.

Lev, Peter. *The Fifties: Transforming the Screen, 1950–1959.* New York: Charles Scribner's Sons, 2003.

Link, Arthur S., and Richard McCormick. *Progressivism.* Arlington Heights, Ill.: Harlan Davidson, 1983.

Marwick, Arthur. *The Sixties.* New York: Oxford University Press, 1998.

Mast, Gerald. *A Short History of the Movies.* New York: Macmillan, 1992.

May, Elaine Tyler. *Homeward Bound: American Families in the Cold War Era.* New York: Basic Books, 1988.

May, Henry Farnham. *The End of American Innocence.* Chicago: Quadrangle Books, 1964.

McKeown, E. J. "Censoring the Movie Picture." *Common Cause* 4 (July 4, 1913).

McKeever, William A. "The Moving Picture: A Primary School for Criminals." *Good Housekeeping,* August 1910, 184–86.

Miner, Craig. *Kansas: The History of the Sunflower State, 1854–2000.* Lawrence: University Press of Kansas, 2002.

Moley, Raymond. *The Hays Office.* Indianapolis: Bobbs-Merrill, 1945.

Monaco, Paul. *The Sixties: History of the American Cinema.* New York: Charles Scribner's Sons, 2001.

Montague, Gilbert H. "Censorship of Motion Pictures before the Supreme Court." *Survey* 34 (April 24, 1915).

"Morals and Movies." *Harper's Weekly* 60 (December 19, 1914).

"Movies Crimes against Good Taste." *Literary Digest* 51 (September 18, 1915).

"Movie Pictures Morals Attacked and Defended." *Current Opinion* 72 (April 1922).

"Movies Morals and Manners." *Outlook* 113 (July 26, 1916).

"The Moving Picture and the National Character." *American Review of Reviews* (September 1910): 315–320.

Munden, Kenneth, ed. *American Film Institute Catalog of Motion Pictures Produced in the United States: Feature Films, 1921–1930.* New York: R. R. Bowker, 1971.

Musser, Charles. *The Emergence of Cinema: The American Screen to 1907.* New York: Charles Scribner's Sons, 1990.

"The Nationwide Battle over Movie Purification." *Literary Digest* 68 (May 14, 1921).

Neve, Brian. *Film and Politics in America: A Social Tradition.* New York: Routledge, 1992.

"No Censorship." *Independent* 77 (March 30, 1914).

Noggle, Burl. *Into the Twenties: The United States from Armistice to Normalcy.* Urbana: University of Illinois Press, 1974.

North, Joseph H. *The Early Development of the Motion Picture, 1887–1909.* New York: Arno Press, 1973.

O'Brien, Patrick G. "'I Want Everyone to Know the Shame of the State': Henry J. Allen Confronts the Ku Klux Klan, 1921–1923." *Kansas History: A Journal of the Central Plains* 19, no. 2 (Summer 1996): 98–111.

———. "Kansas at War: The Home Front, 1941–1945." *Kansas History: A Journal of the Central Plains* 17 (Spring 1994).

Oliva, Leo E. "Kansas: A Hard Land in the Heartland." In *Heartland: Comparative Histories of the Midwestern States,* ed. James H. Madison. Bloomington: Indiana University Press, 1976.

Patterson, James T. *Grand Expectations: The United States, 1945–1974.* New York: Oxford University Press, 1996.

Perlman, William J., ed. *The Movies on Trial: The Views and Opinions of Outstanding Personalities against Screen Entertainment Past and Present.* New York: Macmillan, 1936.

Phillips, William H. *Film: An Introduction.* Boston: Bedford, St. Martin's, 1999.

Ramsaye, Terry. *A Million and One Nights: A History of the Motion Pictures through 1925.* New York: Simon and Schuster, 1926.

Randall, Richard S. *Censorship of the Movies: The Social and Political Control of a Mass Medium.* Madison: University of Wisconsin Press, 1970.

Records of the Kansas Supreme Court. 1955 (vol. 178, p. 400, *State v. Shanahan*); 1966 (vol. 197, p. 448, *State v. Columbia Pictures Corporation*).

"The Regulation of Films." *Nation* 100 (May 6, 1915): 486–87.

Reports of the Kansas Supreme Court. 1917 (vol. 102, p. 356, *Mid-West Photo Play Corporation v. State*).

Richmond, Robert W. *Kansas: A Land of Contrasts.* St. Charles, Mo.: Forum Press, 1974.

Riney-Kehrberg, Pamela. *Rooted in Dust: Surviving Drought and Depression in Southwestern Kansas.* Lawrence: University Press of Kansas, 1994.

Rodger, Daniel T. "In Search of Progressivism." *Reviews in American History* 10 (1982): 113–32.

Rollins, Peter C., and John O'Connor, eds. *Hollywood's World War I: Motion Picture Images.* Bowling Green, Ohio: Bowling Green State University Press, 1997.

Rosenbloom, Nancy. "Progressive Reform, Censorship, and the Motion Picture Industry, 1909–1917." In *Popular Culture and Political Change in Modern America,* ed. Ronald Edsforth and Larry Bennett. Albany: State University of New York Press, 1991.

Schaefer, Eric. *Bold! Daring! Shocking! True! A History of Exploitation Films, 1919–1959.* Durham: Duke University Press, 1999.

Schatz, Thomas. *Boom and Bust: American Cinema in the 1940s.* Berkeley and Los Angeles: University of California Press, 1999.

Schickel, Richard. *D. W. Griffith: An American Life.* New York: Simon and Schuster, 1984.

Schofield, Ann. "The Women's March: Miners, Family, and Community in Pittsburg, Kansas, 1921–1922." *Kansas History: A Journal of the Central Plains* (Summer 1984): 159–68.

Session Laws of Kansas. 1913 (chap. 294); 1915 (chap. 109, art. 8, sub. 10774–80); 1917 (chap. 308); 1923 (chap. 14); 1955 (chap. 349).

Skinner, James M. *The Cross and the Cinema: The Legion of Decency and the National Catholic Office for Motion Pictures, 1933–1970.* New York: Praeger Publications, 1993.

Sklar, Robert. *Movie-Made America.* New York: Vintage Press, 1975.

Socolofsky, Homer E. *Arthur Capper: Publisher, Politician, and Philanthropist.* Lawrence: University Press of Kansas, 1962.

Sova, Dawn B. *Forbidden Films: Censorship Histories of 125 Motion Pictures.* New York: Facts on File, 2001.

Staiger, Janet. *Bad Women*. Minneapolis: University of Minnesota Press, 1988.

State Laws of Kansas, 1919, chap. 284, sec. 29. *State of Kansas Session Laws, 1919*. Topeka: State Printer, 1919.

Stratemann, Klaus. *Duke Ellington: Day by Day and Film by Film*. Copenhagen: Jazz Media, 1992.

Supreme Court (Kansas) Case Files and Briefs. (1917, *Mid-west Photo Play Corporation v. State*); (1955, *State v. Shanahan*); (1966, *State v. Columbia Pictures Corporation*).

"The Theory and Practice of Censorship." *Drama* 14 (May 5, 1915).

Vasey, Ruth. *The World according to Hollywood, 1918–1939*. Madison: University of Wisconsin Press, 1997.

Vermilye, Jerry. *Films of the Twenties*. Secaucus, N.J.: Citadel Press, 1985.

Walsh, Frank. *Sin and Censorship: The Catholic Church and the Motion Picture Industry*. New Haven: Yale University Press, 1996.

Ward, Larry Wayne. *The Motion Picture Goes to War: The U.S. Government Film Effort during World War I*. Ann Arbor: UMI Research Press, 1985.

Wilson, P. W. "The Crime Wave and the Movies." *Current Opinion* 70 (March 1921).

Wittern-Keller, Laura. "Freedom of the Screen: The Legal Challenges to State Film Censorship, 1915–1981." Ph.D. diss., State University of New York, 2003.

Index

Page numbers in italics indicate illustrations

335

About the Author

Gerald R. Butters, Jr., is a professor of history at Aurora University.
His research and publications examine the intersection of race and gender
in American popular culture.

His books include *From* Sweetback *to* Super Fly*: Race and Film Audiences in
Chicago's Loop* and *Black Manhood on the Silent Screen.*

A Fulbright scholar, Butters has lectured internationally, including an
address to the European Commission in Luxembourg in 2009.